THE FRAGILITY OF POWER

The Fragility of Power

STATIUS, DOMITIAN, AND THE POLITICS OF
THE *THEBAID*

Stefano Rebeggiani

OXFORD
UNIVERSITY PRESS

Oxford University Press is a department of the University of Oxford. It furthers
the University's objective of excellence in research, scholarship, and education
by publishing worldwide. Oxford is a registered trade mark of Oxford University
Press in the UK and certain other countries.

Published in the United States of America by Oxford University Press
198 Madison Avenue, New York, NY 10016, United States of America.

© Oxford University Press 2018

CIP data is on file at the Library of Congress
ISBN 978–0–19–025181–9

9 8 7 6 5 4 3 2 1

Printed by Sheridan Books, Inc., United States of America

Contents

Preface ix
Note on Texts and Translations xi
List of Abbreviations xiii

Introduction 1
    I.1. The tragedy of history 1
    I.2. Literature and ideology 8
    I.3. Critical views of the *Thebaid*'s politics 12
    I.4. Domitian and the elite 18
    I.5. Nero and his world 21
    I.6. Seneca and Lucan 24
    I.7. Caesar's sword 26
    I.8. The pessimism of the *Thebaid* 28
    I.9. Thebes and Rome 32

1. Nero in the Thebaid 38
    1.1. Renaissance 43
    1.2. From *clementia* to *saevitia*: Domitian and the elite 49
    1.3. Nero and Domitian 56
    1.4. Martyrs and survivors: The Annaeans 65
    1.5. The death of Maeon: Reading Nero back into the *Thebaid* 68
    1.6. Myth and reality 72
    1.7. Seneca's *Oedipus* and the *Thebaid* 76
    1.8. Theseus and *clementia* 84

2. *Riding among the stars* 93

    2.1. Solar ideology 94

    2.2. Phaethon 100

    2.3. The solar charioteer 103

    2.4. A race among the stars 106

    2.5. Amphiaraus and the death of the king 110

    2.6. Succession 114

    2.7. Tales of imperial harmony: Amphiaraus and the Dioscuri 116

    2.8. Apollo, Osiris, and Mithras: Domitian and the East 119

3. *Hercules in the* Thebaid 123

    3.1. Hercules' crater 124

        3.1.1. A prize worthy of Hercules 125

        3.1.2. The seven Centaurs 126

        3.1.3. Roman Centaurs 128

    3.2. Heroism in the political arena 130

    3.3. Hercules between epic and tragedy 132

    3.4. The failed Hercules: Polynices 135

    3.5. Between beast and god: Tydeus 138

    3.6. Knocking on heaven's door: Capaneus 142

    3.7. A new Hercules 147

4. *Thebes and Rome* 153

    4.1. Civil war and imperial power 155

    4.2. Imperial power and civil war in the *Silvae* 163

    4.3. Imperial power, civil war, and cosmic upheaval in the *Thebaid* 167

    4.4. Complex chronologies: Being first, being last 176

    4.5. From Aeneas to Vitellius 181

    4.6. Tyranny and civil war 191

5. *The unexpected savior: Coroebus and Flavian ideology* 197

    5.1. Religion and civil war in Rome 198

    5.2. *Ultio deorum* 202

    5.3. The Coroebus episode: A summary 205

    5.4. Perseus and Ganymede 207

    5.5. Callimachus, Virgil, and Statius 214

    5.6. Argos and Alexandria 216

    5.7. Argos and Rome 219

5.8. Coroebus in the *Thebaid* 224

5.9. Coroebus and Flavian Rome 229

6. *The Gauls on the Capitol* 234

　6.1. A Gaul at Thebes 235

　6.2. *Bella Iovis* 237

　6.3. *Magnus Annus* 240

　6.4. The Gallic sack in Flavian culture 244

　6.5. The Gauls on the Capitol under Domitian 246

　6.6. *Corona civica* 250

　6.7. Self-sacrifice and the survival of the city 253

Conclusions 262

　C.1. Beyond the scope of this book 262

　C.2. The *Thebaid*'s political vision 269

　C.3. Statius' *Thebaid* and the survivors of Nero 276

BIBLIOGRAPHY 281

INDEX LOCORUM 295

GENERAL INDEX 315

Preface

THIS BOOK ORIGINATES from my PhD dissertation, written at the Sapienza University of Rome and the University of Cambridge between 2009 and 2012. The book turned out to be quite different: Only three chapters survive from the original dissertation and in a very revised form—which partly explains why it took so long for this book to appear. I incurred many debts of gratitude along the way. First, I wish to thank my two Doktorväter, Alessandro Schiesaro and Philip Hardie. I owe my "conversion" to classics to Alessandro's wonderful lectures on the *Aeneid* in Rome in 2003. Alessandro has guided my every academic step with invaluable support and friendship ever since. Philip offered guidance and encouragement in Cambridge, where I had the opportunity to profit from his friendship, his rare insight and his generosity. Denis Feeney read and improved chapters of this book when it was still the embryo of a dissertation; so did Gianpiero Rosati, who introduced me to the poetry of Statius when I was a student in Pisa and from whose scholarship I have learned a great deal. Stephen Harrison offered precious suggestions on early versions of Chapters 2 and 3. Vicky Rimell commented with great perceptiveness on parts of the thesis and helped me reconsider its theoretical underpinnings. This would have been a very different book without the scholarship of Federica Bessone: It will be clear to readers of this book how much I owe to her work on the *Thebaid*. My revision of Chapter 4 was deeply influenced by conversation with Alessandro Barchiesi; Alessandro's work has been an invaluable source of inspiration throughout the years and I was privileged to have him as a colleague for one semester at New York University. A warm thanks also goes to Andrea Cucchiarelli, who supervised my first thesis as an undergraduate student at the Sapienza University of Rome and introduced me to the study of classical philology. While at the Sapienza I had the privilege of studying Greek literature under the guidance of the late Luigi Enrico Rossi, an irreplaceable teacher and friend. I owe much to his intelligence, learning, and intellectual curiosity, as well as to the lively atmosphere of the Seminari Romani. Beppe Pezzini discussed with me several chapters of this book, helping me see things from a different, more creative angle. I want to thank Beppe for his friendship over the years: My career in classics would not have been such an exciting journey had we not been together on this path. I was fortunate to spend two wonderful years as visiting assistant professor at New York University. For reading and discussing with me chapters of this book, I owe a great thanks to David Levene, Joy Connolly, and David Konstan. The book was completed after my appointment at the University of Southern California. I want to thank all of my colleagues in the Department of Classics for their support and friendship since my arrival, Tony Boyle, Tom Habinek, and Vincent Farenga in particular for sharing their thoughts on parts of this book. Hannah Čulík-Baird helped me revise the English of a substantial portion of the manuscript, improving it in many points. Tommaso Spinelli provided help with the bibliography and notes. None of the aforementioned people should be held accountable for mistakes, inaccuracies, and errors this book may display: These are my entire responsibility. Last but not least, a great thanks to my wife Ester for her patience over many evenings spent working on Statius and the laborious work that it took me to get this manuscript to completion.

Note on Texts and Translations

QUOTATIONS FROM STATIUS' works are from Hill's edition of the *Thebaid* (1996, 2nd ed.) and Courtney's edition of the *Siluae* (1990). Translations of Statius are adapted, with many changes, from Shackleton Bailey's Loeb (2003); I have used Braund (1992) for Lucan and Fitch (2002 and 2004) for Seneca's tragedies and *Octauia*. Translations of shorter passages and occasionally quoted authors are my own, and I make no claim as to their literary merit.

An early version of Chapter 2 was published as an independent article in *ICS* in 2013. Work on this manuscript was completed in January 2016. Inevitably, I was not able to consult important works that appeared as I was finalizing the manuscript for the press (e.g. A. Zissos, ed., *A Companion to the Flavian Age of Imperial Rome*, Chichester, UK/Malden, MA: Wiley Blackwell, 2016; and L. D. Ginsberg, *Staging Memory, Staging Strife: Empire and Civil War in the Octavia*, Oxford/New York: Oxford University Press, 2017).

Abbreviations

Greek authors and works are abbreviated according to the system of the *LSJ*. Latin authors and works follow the system of the *OLD*. Periodicals have been abbreviated on the basis of *L'Année Philologique*.

BMCRE	H. Mattingly and R. A. G. Carson, *Coins of the Roman Empire in the British Museum*, 6 vols., London: Trustees of the British Museum 1923–1962.
CIL	*Corpus Inscriptionum Latinarum*, Berlin: Reimer/De Gruyter 1863–.
D–S	C. Daremberg and E. Saglio, eds., *Dictionnaire des Antiquités Grecques et Romaines,* 5 vols., Paris: Hachette 1877–1919.
FGrH	F. Jacoby, ed., *Die Fragmente der griechischen Historiker,* Berlin: Weidmann/Leiden, The Netherlands: Brill 1927–1958.
IGGR	R. Cagnat, ed., *Inscriptiones Graecae ad Res Romanas Pertinentes*, 4 vols., Paris: Leroux 1906–1927.
IGUR	L. Moretti, ed., *Inscriptiones Graecae Urbis Romae*, 4 vols., Rome: Istituto Italiano per la Storia Antica 1968–1990.
IK Ephesos	H. Wankel, C. Börker, H. Engelmann, R. Merkelbach, et al., eds., *Inschriften griechischer Städte aus Kleinasien.* Vols. 11–17, *Die Inschriften von Ephesos,* Bonn: Habelt 1979–1984.
ILS	H. Dessau, ed., *Inscriptiones Latinae Selectae*, Berlin: Weidmann 1892–1916.

LIMC	*Lexicon Iconographicum Mythologiae Classicae*, Zurich/Munich/Düsseldorf: Artemis 1981–1999.
LSJ	H. G. Liddell, R. Scott, and H. S. Jones, eds., *A Greek-English Lexicon*, 9th ed., Oxford: Oxford University Press 1940.
LTUR	E. M. Steinby, ed., *Lexicon Topographicum Urbis Romae*, Rome: Quasar 1993–2000.
OLD	P. G. W. Glare, ed., *Oxford Latin Dictionary*, Oxford: Clarendon 1968–1982.
PIR²	E. Groag, A. Stein, et al., eds., *Prosopographia Imperii Romani. Saec. I, II, III*, 2nd ed., Berlin: De Gruyter 1933–.
RE	G. Wissowa, ed., *Paulys Real-Encyclopädie der classischen Altertumswissenschaft*, Stuttgart: Metzler/Munich: Druckenmüller 1894–1980.
RIC² II	A. I. Carradice and T. V. Buttrey, *The Roman Imperial Coinage. Vol. II Part I. Second fully revised edition. From AD 69 to AD 96, Vespasian to Domitian*, London: Spink 2007.
Roscher	W. H. Roscher, ed., *Ausführliches Lexikon der griechischen und römischen Mythologie*, Leipzig: Teubner 1884–1937.
RPC I	A. Burnett, M. Amandry, and P. P. Ripollès, *Roman Provincial Coinage. Vol. I. From the death of Caesar to the death of Vitellius (44 BC–AD 69)*, London: British Museum Press/Paris: Bibliothèque Nationale 1992.
RPC II	A. Burnett, M. Amandry, and I. Carradice, *Roman Provincial Coinage. Vol. II. From Vespasian to Domitian (AD 69–96)*, London: British Museum Press/Paris: Bibliothèque Nationale 1999.
TrGFr	*Tragicorum Graecorum Fragmenta*, 5 vols., I. *Poetae minores*, B. Snell, ed. (1971; rev. R. Kannicht, 1986); II. *Adespota*, R. Kannicht and B. Snell, eds. (1981); III. *Aeschylus*, S. Radt, ed. (1985); IV. *Sophocles*, S. Radt, ed. (1977, 1992); V. *Euripides*, R. Kannicht, ed. (2004); Göttingen: Vandenhoeck & Ruprecht.

Introduction

1.1 THE TRAGEDY OF HISTORY

haec finis Priami fatorum, hic exitus illum
sorte tulit Troiam incensam et prolapsa uidentem
Pergama, tot quondam populis terrisque superbum
regnatorem Asiae. iacet ingens litore truncus,
auulsumque umeris caput et sine nomine corpus.
A. 2.554–8

Such was the end of Priam's fate; such death was he allotted, to see Troy in
flames and Pergamon in ruins, he who had once ruled proudly over so many
lands and peoples of Asia. He lies, a huge trunk upon the shore, a head severed
from the neck, a corpse without a name.

This is a famous scene from Virgil's *Aeneid*. King Priam is dead, his headless body
washed up onto the shore. The power of the picture is heightened by what was al-
ready recognized in antiquity as an allusion to Roman history. The headless body on
the shore reminded readers of Pompey's death along the shores of Egypt.[1] This type
of historical allusion—based on re-creating a sequence of events or a picture that

---

[1] Serv. *A.* 2.557; Horsfall (2008) 417–18.

I

has equivalents in historical incidents—is by no means the only way in which epic narratives, let alone the *Aeneid*, interact with the here and now of their audiences. What interests me in this passage is the nature of the allusion. It affects the narrative concerning one point, but the connection it establishes with the present is not meant to create a system of correspondences in an allegorical fashion. The association between Pompey and Priam does not turn Pyrrhus into an equivalent of Caesar, or the sack of Troy into an allegory of the last phase of the civil war between Pompey and Caesar. Again with reference to book 2 of the *Aeneid*, ancient scholars warn us that there may be an allusion to Marius in Virgil's description of Sinon's hiding place in the swamps outside the Greek camp.[2] Virgil is clearly interested in evoking civil-war contexts in his narrative of the destruction of Troy, but the fact that he blends allusions to different historical episodes within the same narrative sequence speaks against the possibility of reading *Aeneid* 2 as straightforward allegory.

This type of "punctual" historical allusion is frequent in the *Thebaid*. Indeed, it is somewhat more frequent in Statius than in the *Aeneid*, and one can see why: Virgil can avail himself of more direct avenues to connect his narrative with Roman actualities (for instance, prophecies) that are not available to Statius. As an example, in Chapter 3 I argue that Polynices' momentous fall from his chariot (*Theb.* 6.504–12), in the very first version of the Nemean games, is meant to evoke Nero's fall from a chariot at Olympia. However, it would be wrong to assume Polynices' identification with Nero in every scene of the poem. Other passages featuring Polynices are clearly unhelpful to this identification. In the *Thebaid*, historical and political allusions take this punctual form. They tend to be confined to the episodes in which they occur. Most important, they are constantly kept below the level of systematic and consistent correspondence that is necessary for allegorical interpretation. As with the *Aeneid*, often the same episode is connected to multiple historical experiences, or multiple characters are used to reflect on the same historical figure. It is important to keep this in mind if we are to avoid the risk of forcing a somewhat allegorical reading onto a text that, as we shall see, seems designed precisely to resist this type of hermeneutic approach.

Statius' primary goal in writing the *Thebaid* is not to produce a political pamphlet. First and foremost, the *Thebaid* aims to be a literary masterpiece, engaging the audience through powerful narrative, impressive command of language and meter, and complex character construction. The poem's political dimension is developed in such a way as not to spoil its literary aims. Allegorical or nearly allegorical one-to-one correspondences tend to weaken the audience's empathic connection,

---

[2] See Serv. *A.* 2.135; cf. Plu. *Mar.* 38.2; Luc. 2.70; see Horsfall (2008) 143.

which is Statius' primary goal. Allegory is completely inconsistent with the most significant strategy Statius enacts to establish a bond between the audience and his characters, which consists in keeping his poem in the tragic mode. By "tragic mode," I mean a construction of character and plot that strives for empathy, and to this end complicates moral and emotional responses to characters and their actions, so that readers can neither distance themselves entirely nor completely endorse the action of a certain character.[3]

This effect can be achieved in many ways. One way consists in constructing characters who partake of good and evil in equal measure and so leave the audience incapable of formulating a unilateral moral judgment. Another way of engendering this "split" reaction is to multiply levels of motivation. There can be little sympathy for a character who suffers purely on account of his or her own mistakes, moral shortcomings, or both. Stronger empathy is achieved when characters are driven by forces over which they have no control. The gods are an excellent resource for an author aiming for a tragic effect, but divine machinery is by no means the only tool to achieve tragic empathy. An author can also complicate motivation at the human level. Book 16 of the *Iliad* provides a classic example. Patroclos has his armor stripped by Apollo, is wounded by Euphorbos, and is slain by Hektor. His death is, however, his own responsibility, for he exceeds Achilles' orders, failing to fall back once he has driven the Trojans away from the ships. It is also Achilles' fault: He failed to accept Agamemnon's apology and allowed Patroclos to enter battle wearing his armor—a plan initially devised by Nestor, who also shares in the blame. The youth's death is ultimately also Zeus' responsibility: The king of the gods predicts the whole sequence and casts blindness on Patroclos, yet he too might be simply obeying the dictates of Fate. Homer keeps the different levels of motivation active at the same time without clearly establishing which has priority over the others and without bringing them into direct confrontation. Thus, he can look at the story of Patroclos through various tragic prisms.[4]

That the *Thebaid* is firmly in the tragic mode hardly needs to be demonstrated. Statius is fully conversant with the range of strategies just described. Complex character construction is an example: From Senecan tragedy, Statius inherits a way of fashioning characters as inextricable combinations of good and bad. Action, diction, and imagery contribute to complicating moral responses, so that readers can neither completely embrace nor completely reject the characters' actions. Complex motivation is also present. The civil war that destroys Thebes and Argos is Oedipus'

---

[3] Although I use the term "tragic," this phenomenon is by no means exclusive to tragedy. It is fair to say that the *Iliad* is firmly in the tragic mode: See Janko (1994) 4.

[4] Janko (1994) 3–7.

responsibility, for he curses his children. But Eteocles and Polynices are also to blame: They abuse their father, fail to observe the pacts they themselves have laid out, and subsequently resist any attempt at stopping the war. The war is at the same time Jupiter's responsibility. The king of gods has decided that both Thebes and Argos should be punished for their impiety.[5] This complex motivation is reflected in the *Thebaid*'s twofold beginning. The action is set in motion both by Oedipus' summoning of the Fury and by Jupiter's summoning of Laius from the underworld.[6] Later, Statius even triples the level of responsibility through his treatment of underworld powers. The Furies, once summoned by Oedipus, act independently of both him and the Olympians, and although their plan coincides to an extent with Jupiter's design, in the climactic narrative of book 11 Jupiter withdraws from the action—and indeed from the poem—so that the final fratricide is staged under the direction of the Furies alone.[7] Statius emphasizes the tragic nature of his narrative by keeping all levels of motivation active throughout the narrative. Characters are fully responsible for their doom, and at the same time they are not: They are led astray by higher forces that they cannot oppose—and are part of grand events for which responsibility is shared by many individuals—but are also morally flawed and accountable for their own ruin.

In Polynices we see a combination of some of the techniques just described. Polynices is a complex character, a partaker of both good and evil, and his actions are both humanly and divinely motivated in a way that complicates audience responses. He is endowed, like his brother, with a thirst for power, and he is responsible for abusing Oedipus together with Eteocles. He is the polluted son of Oedipus who will never manage to break free from his family curse.[8] Unlike Eteocles, however, he is also capable of compassion: compassion for his mother and sister, compassion for his wife and child, and love and compassion for his friend. Unlike his brother, he is seriously tempted to stop the conflict on several occasions.[9] As far as motivation is concerned, Polynices is led by his own thirst for power and glory. However, several characters, both human and divine, share responsibility with him: He would have agreed to parley with his brother in book 7 had Tydeus not intervened and had the

---

[5] Oedipus' curse: *Theb.* 1.56–87; abuse of Oedipus by his children: *Theb.* 1.74–80; failure to preserve the pacts: *Theb.* 2.410–51; refuse of compromise: *Theb.* 7.528–63, 11.329–53, 387–92; Jupiter's decision to destroy Thebes: *Theb.* 1.214–47.

[6] Oedipus' summoning of Tisiphone: *Theb.* 1.56–87; Jupiter's council and his summoning of Laius: *Theb.* 1.197–302.

[7] *Theb.* 11.119–35.

[8] Adrastus' reassurances to Polynices that he may break free from his impious family background carry a special irony (*Theb.* 1.688–92): The rest of the poem will prove that the opposite is true.

[9] Polynices' compassion: *Theb.* 2.353–5 (for his wife); 9.46–81 (for Tydeus); Polynices tempted to stop the conflict: *Theb.* 7.528–63, 11.136–54, 193–204, 382–9.

Furies not driven the Theban tigers mad.[10] In book 11, his participation in the duel is prompted by repeated intervention on the part of the Furies.[11]

The complex character, partaker of both good and evil, nobility and baseness, is expedient to the tragic effect. But tragedy also feeds on a simpler and more direct type of characterization, one that reduces complexity and obscures nuances. Statius exploits this typology when he investigates the figure of the tyrant, a character who is not meant to attract sympathy and whose profile is less complex than that of other characters. This type of character is instrumental to a tragic narrative in another way. The tyrant's excesses allow the author to focus on the suffering of those who oppose the tyrant, the innocents who are the victims of his folly. Eteocles and Creon are closer to this tragic type. They both have motives for their actions: Polynices' attack on his fatherland is a monstrosity that adds legitimacy to Eteocles' defensive war, and even Creon's law against burying the Argives is tied to his personal grief at the death of his son Menoeceus.[12] And yet both attract very little sympathy: They are just too wicked, too blind, too corrupt. Unlike other Statian characters, such as Capaneus, there is no grandiosity in their evil: They are not cast from the same mold in which Seneca's Atreus is cast. However, Creon's monstrosity is necessary to bring into focus the sufferings of Antigone, Argia, and the Argive women (and to an extent also of the Theban subjects forced into war once again). Eteocles' cruelty highlights the heroic sufferings of Maeon, Aletes, and the citizens of Thebes.

This is not a book on tragedy in the *Thebaid*, however. I am interested in drawing attention to the presence of tragic strategies in the poem because they bear on our understanding of the political dimension of Statius' work. The question of how exactly the tragic and the political interact and influence one another is perhaps *the* question of critical approaches to Roman epic. For present purposes, I limit myself to stating that Statius' tragic vision marks the space within which his political discourse unfolds. One could say, in other words, that political allusion is subordinate to the poem's tragic vision, in that Statius avoids strategies that would spoil the tragic effect. In this context, the punctual, or episodic, nature of Statius' historical allusions is key, for it facilitates the coexistence of the poem's political and literary agendas.

One example clarifies my point. In the first part of the poem, Oedipus is presented as the frightening figure who conjures up the war and cynically rejoices when the conflict between his two children is under way.[13] This cruel character, however, undergoes a sudden change toward the end of the *Thebaid*. In book 11,

---

[10] *Theb.* 7.528–63.
[11] Intervention of the Furies in book 11: *Theb.* 11.136–54, 196–204, 382–404, 482–96.
[12] *Theb.* 12.60–104.
[13] *Theb.* 1.56–87, 8.240–54.

he rediscovers his humanity: Natura and Pietas come back to him and return fatherly feelings to his heart. The poem ends with Oedipus' despair at the death of his children: The grief he expresses in book 11 is sincere, and the audience is expected to feel compassion for him. His initial anger is revealed at the end as yet another instance of tragic blindness: Through his curse, Oedipus has destroyed himself yet again.[14] This sudden transformation is for tragic effect. It turns Oedipus into an object of compassion. However, this tragic patterning of Oedipus' story works against using the character of Oedipus for political allegory: If Oedipus is an image of Nero *throughout* the poem, then what is the audience to make of the scene in book 11? In Chapter 1, I argue that allusions to Nero are among the ways in which the audience experiences the character of Oedipus, but they are kept below the level of allegory and are subordinated to the tragic texture and patterning of this character's life. The complement to this episodic nature of historical allusions is the fact that allusions to the same historical figure are attached to more than one character. In the course of this book, I argue that the figure of Nero is evoked in connection with Eteocles, Polynices, and Oedipus. The three different characters provide different tragic lenses through which to look at the historical figure of Nero: the inexperienced reckless youth (Polynices), the cruel, ever-suspicious tyrant (Eteocles), and the polluted ancestor who brings ruin to his descendants (Oedipus). None of these characters is an equivalent or an allegory for Nero throughout the poem, but all of them participate in the poem's reflection on the historical experience of Nero's reign.

Although the *Thebaid*'s construction of a political and ideological discourse is subordinated to the poem's literary agenda, the two dimensions should not be seen as opposing one another. On the contrary, they enhance one another. Historical allusion makes what is distant close, increasing the power of narrative art for pathos and empathy. In Chapter 1, I argue that Statius' description of the death of Maeon may evoke the tragic deaths of Nero's victims. Picture Statius reciting portions of the *Thebaid* in the house of Argentaria Polla, one of his patrons, whose husband Lucan had been executed by Nero. Recognizing allusions to Nero's executions in Statius' poem may have provoked on her the same effect that Virgil's Marcellus had on Augustus' sister Octavia.[15]

At times, however, the poem's political and literary agendas interact in a more complex way. An interesting example is discussed in Chapter 6. In this chapter, I argue that the siege of Thebes in book 10 evokes Roman traditions pertaining to the sack of Rome. These traditions focused on the terror of the city's annihilation. They were particularly present to readers of the *Thebaid* because of the

[14] *Theb.* 11.605–26.
[15] The anecdote is in Donatus' *Vita Vergili* 32 and is discussed by Horsfall (2013) 595.

recent experience of war in Rome, including the episode of fire on the Capitoline in 69 CE. In spite of this, Statius self-consciously styles his account of Capaneus' assault as an artistic climax to his narrative, destined to arouse the admiration of his readers.[16] Statius is acutely aware of the paradox whereby something that is morally despicable and deserving of neglect can at the same time constitute the subject of great poetry that is worthy of memory. To an extent, the greater the *nefas* [crime], the greater the poetry that narrates it. In the *Thebaid*, the language of crime plotting has metaliterary resonances; a poem concluding with the author's wish for eternal memory asks his readers (with the exception of kings) to forget its narrative climax, the duel of the Theban brothers.[17] This understanding of the relationship between crime and poetry is central to the poetics of Senecan tragedy, by which Statius is strongly influenced. This poetics generates a mismatch between aesthetic and moral agendas.[18] The issue is far too complicated to be treated here.[19] For the purpose of this book, suffice it to say that although the *Thebaid* is interested in exploring these paradoxical interactions of ethics and poetics, the poem's reflection on the poetics of crime is not carried out to the extent of completely undermining the poem's ability to convey a recognizable ethical and political discourse.

A few words on the scope of this book. Statius' interaction with earlier authors (Seneca, Lucan, Virgil) is central to my investigation of the poem's ideological texture, but I do not provide a comprehensive study of Statius' allusions to earlier authors. Rather, in this book I wish to provide intellectual frameworks within which the *Thebaid*'s extensive intertextual relationships can be evaluated. Likewise, I offer no comprehensive analysis of how themes of Statius are anticipated or echoed by the other Flavian epicists, nor do I follow their ramifications into Statius' second epic poem, the *Achilleid*. Even with reference to the *Thebaid*, my analysis is selective. I concentrate in particular on the poem's narrative prior to the close of book 12, and within the first 11 books I select episodes that best exemplify the defining features of my approach. In the conclusion to this book, I suggest some directions in which the type of analysis I propose in this book could be expanded, with reference to passages in the *Thebaid* not covered in this book and those of other Flavian authors.

---

[16] *Theb.* 10.827–31. On the metaliterary aspects of Capaneus' *aristeia* see Leigh (2006).

[17] For the metaliterary resonances of the language of crime plotting, besides the Capaneus episode, see also *Theb.* 11.97–101. Statius wishes that the *Thebaid* be remembered in the poem's envoy (12.810–19), but cf. his introduction to the final duel of Polynices and Eteocles (*Theb.* 11.574–9).

[18] Schiesaro (2003), especially chapters 2 and 3, pp. 26–138.

[19] The whole question is addressed brilliantly by Bessone (2011) 75–101, to whom I defer.

1.2 LITERATURE AND IDEOLOGY

At some point during the reign of Vespasian, a group of citizens approached the emperor with a theory. They sought to prove that Vespasian's family was descended from one of Hercules' comrades. Vespasian laughed at them and sent them away.[20] The attempt, however, was far from absurd. There had been precedents. Everyone knew Hercules had visited Italy on his return from the West and had left children behind. Supporters of Antony made the claim that from one such child of Hercules (the otherwise unknown Anton), the gens Antonia had sprung. This explained why Antony looked so much like the hero and added dynastic legitimacy to Antony's attempt at styling himself as a new Hercules.[21] It is not impossible to imagine why Vespasian turned down the compliment, but I am interested in another conclusion that can be drawn from this story. It was not entirely clear to subjects of Vespasian what elements were acceptable as praise of this emperor. Would he be amenable to bombastic claims of divine ancestry? Or did he rather like to resort to more modest, traditional terms? The individuals who approached Vespasian with the outcome of their research on his ancestors clearly did not have an answer to these questions. This episode captures well the peculiar dynamics of imperial ideology. Imperial ideology was not imparted from above as a unified discourse or as part of a consistently organized communication strategy. (Hence, it is misleading to use the term "propaganda.") There was no office laying out clear outlines, and no memos were circulated. Practitioners had to rely on precedent, hearsay, and the (relatively rare) occasions on which the emperor directly suggested a certain comparison or seemed to appreciate a text or monument in which he had been portrayed in a certain way.

Another example is offered by Statius in *Siluae* 1.6:

Tollunt innumeras ad astra uoces
Saturnalia principis sonantes
Et dulci dominum fauore clamant:
Hoc solum uetuit licere Caesar.
Silv. 1.6.81–4

They raise countless voices to the stars, resounding the Saturnalia of the emperor, and they acclaim him as lord with sweet favor: this was the only license not allowed by Caesar.

---

[20] Suet. *Ves.* 12.1. I discuss this anecdote again in Chapter 1, Section 1.3 and Chapter 3, Section 3.2.
[21] Zanker (1988) 45–6.

Statius lets us know that Domitian did not allow the crowds to call him *dominus* [lord]. A similar *recusatio* of monarchical titles, in the spirit of "democratic kingship," is attributed to Augustus.[22] Statius' claim is, however, contradicted by other sources. In Suetonius, Domitian does not object to the crowds addressing him this way, and goes so far as to dictate a letter beginning with the words "our lord and god orders," which gave rise to the habit of addressing him thus in official correspondence— a story supported by Dio.[23] This is indirectly confirmed by Martial, who, after Domitian's death, implies that *dominus et deus* [lord and god] was a popular way of addressing the last Flavian emperor, one that is no longer appropriate under the new dynasty.[24] Obviously, later sources might be misrepresenting the evidence to emphasize Domitian's tyrannical nature. Alternatively, Statius may be trying to make Domitian look more respectable than he actually was.[25] But even on the basis of the Statius passage alone, it seems clear that two opposite things could be said of Domitian at the same time. Statius took the safe course of sticking to Augustan precedent; the crowds were bolder and went for the much more compromising praise. There was little risk either way: The emperor might allow the flattery or turn it down under pretense of modesty, as Statius says he did—which did not necessarily prevent the crowds from attempting the same kind of praise on a later occasion, upon which Domitian might have been more indulgent. What made it possible for Statius

---

[22] Suet. *Aug.* 73.

[23] Suet. *Dom.* 13.1–2; D.C. 67.4.7. Cf. also D.C. 67.13.3–4 and D.Chr. 45.1. Later writers repeat the story and add that Domitian ordered the use of the formula: Aurelius Victor *De Caes.* 11.2; *Epit. de Caes.* 11.6; Eutropius 7.23; Orosius 7.10.

[24] Mart. 10.72.3. On Martial's use of *dominus et deus* see Henriksén (2012) 280–1.

[25] The question is complex and has attracted much scholarly work. Griffin (2000, 81) lays it out clearly: There was nothing scandalous about using the title *dominus* to refer to the emperor in the third person (this was done before Domitian and continued after his death); what was problematic was *addressing* the emperor by the title *dominus* (*et deus*)—that is, in the second person or vocative, whether in person or in official documents. There is little doubt that the compliment was attempted; what is unclear is whether Domitian took the lead in encouraging this type of address and whether he went so far as to use it to refer to himself in official contexts. For this last aspect we are entirely dependent on Suetonius and Dio, as there is no epigraphic or documentary evidence of the title used of Domitian in official contexts. The *Siluae* passage evidently contradicts Suetonius and Dio on this point: Domitian was almost certainly not using *dominus et deus* as an official title when Statius composed *Siluae* 1.6—or else Statius would be embarrassing himself. With Jones (1992) 108–9, I find it unlikely that the matter can be solved by assuming that Domitian made use of this official title later in his reign, so that the passage in Statius can be reconciled with Suetonius' remarks (*contra* Scott 1936: 102–12). Miriam Griffin (2000, 80–3) endorses the idea of a strong lead by the emperor in using the title and dismisses the *Siluae* passage in light of its context: During the Saturnalia social practices and hierarchy could be reversed; hence Domitian did the contrary of what he usually did by refusing the compliment—an explanation I do not find entirely convincing. *Siluae* 1.6.84 seems to imply the opposite. Domitian was so modest that he did not allow the compliment even in a context in which everything was permitted (the Saturnalia). With Jones (1992) 109, I am inclined to think that there was no explicit indication by Domitian that he appreciated the title been used, which in turn explains passages such as *Silv.* 1.6 (see Section I.2).

to write, in the same few lines, that the crowds hailed Domitian as lord and that Domitian did not accept the compliment is the fact that it was not entirely clear what exactly Domitian would allow people to say about him. The emperor's attitude toward politically loaded titles such as *dominus* was the object of speculation.

These two examples bring into focus a number of important elements that inform my reading of political content in Statius' poetry. A first notable point pertains to method. A distinction between the literary foreground and the historical background is not always possible. Much of what we profess to know about imperial ideology in the Flavian period is based on literary sources such as Statius and Martial. The scholar seeking to assess Statius' "response" to imperial ideology soon finds himself reading Statius' poetry against an ideological background that is by and large reconstructed on the basis of Statius' own poetry. The second aspect that I would like to emphasize is the lack of coherent lines from the court and the importance of individual initiatives. Imperial ideology is shaped by a constant process of feedback between the court and the initiatives by individual practitioners. Let us imagine that Vespasian had accepted the Herculean genealogy proposed to him by his panegyrists. This may have inspired local magistrates to dedicate statues or mint coins of Vespasian in the guise of Hercules; the comparison would soon have found its way into panegyric poetry, and so on. The new element is suggested by an individual, and the emperor's approval contributes to giving it currency, which in turn stimulates the reproduction of the same imagery in yet more contexts. There is constant two-way traffic between forms of artistic representation and the emperor's own construction of his public image and public persona.

In many cases, the direction of the process cannot be reconstructed. I find it difficult to discern whether the initiative in resuming the comparison of Domitian to Hercules, which I discuss in Chapter 3, lies with the court or was suggested to the emperor by panegyrists, artists, and poets. At times, a strong imperial impulse can be postulated with some degree of confidence, but even then we cannot assume that the process actually started with the court. Early in his reign, Domitian restored Augustus' sundial in the Campus Martius and proposed to rename a month after himself. The erection of an obelisk followed at some point during his reign.[26] These acts certainly provided strong grounds for those who, like Statius, compared Domitian to the Sun god. However, the court's interest in solar ideology might have been triggered by the earlier work of imperial panegyrists, who devised a way of transferring to Domitian a series of solar symbols that Nero and

---

[26] Domitian's renaming of a month after himself: Suet. *Dom.* 13.3; Plin. *Pan.* 54; Coleman (1988) 80. Restoration of Augustus' sundial: Heslin (2007) 7–8. On Domitian's obelisk see Grenier (2009). On Domitian's use of solar symbols and his building program in the Campus Martius see Chapter 2, Section 2.1.

earlier emperors had utilized extensively. In this book, I generally avoid formulating hypotheses as to the direction of the process. When I talk about Statius' response to elements of imperial ideology, I do not imply that those elements originate with the court and that Statius is responding to dictates from above. I merely mean that Statius is engaging with aspects of the emperor's representation that, one way or another, have acquired some currency in his specific historical and cultural context. By "Domitianic ideology," I mean the different constructions of Domitian's imperial persona that become available at a certain moment within the dialogue between the court and individual practitioners.

The difficulty in drawing a line between imperial ideology and panegyric poetry (the historical background and the literary foreground), and the peculiar ways in which these boundaries are constantly blurred by the reality of political communication in Rome, recommend abandoning vertical models of understanding political communication—models, that is, based on reconstructing the court's message and then assessing the individual poet's response to that message. Imperial ideology is better understood horizontally, as a dialogue within a language that is fluid, constantly created and re-created, and with gray areas and points of uncertainty.

It is precisely this fluidity that allows imperial panegyric to perform a function on which I insist repeatedly in this book. Scholars have recently drawn attention to the marked protreptic element in Roman panegyric.[27] Panegyric is not just slavish repetition of motives from imperial "propaganda." The language of praise constrains as much as it praises, directing the dedicatee toward a certain line of action or the fulfillment of a certain political ideal. Pliny's *Panegyricus* performs this function, styling a portrait of Trajan as merciful king at the same time as it invites Trajan to remain faithful to this ideal.[28] Before that, Seneca's *De Clementia* offers an example of political theory and political advice framed as panegyric.[29] In this work, Seneca claims to present Nero with his own image, as if reflected in a mirror: The ideal sovereign sketched by the treaty is but a reflection of Nero.[30] However, the portrait of Nero emerging from Seneca's treatise becomes a standard that Nero is implicitly asked to

---

[27] Braund (1998); Whitby (1998) 1; for the relevance of this critical landscape for approaching the *Siluae* see Newlands (2002) 20–1.

[28] Cf. Pliny's own explanation of his rationale for composing the *Panegyricus* in *Ep.* 3.18.2–3, and see *Pan.* 4.1. On the *Panegyricus* as an expression of Pliny's own political agenda see Molin (1989) 792–7; Braund (1998) 58–68, esp. 62, 66; Flower (2005) 264. A survey of scholarly approaches to the *Panegyricus* is provided by Fedeli (1989) 492–7.

[29] On the didactic stance of *De Clementia* see Griffin (1976) 136–41 (a helpful discussion of the motivations and different audiences for the treatise); Braund (1998) 71–4; Braund (2009) 53–6. Important precedents before Augustus are offered by Cicero's "Caesarian" speeches, especially his *Pro Marcello*; on the programmatic aspects of this speech see Braund (1998) 68–70.

[30] Sen. *Cl.* 1.1.1–5, with Braund (2009) 154.

live by. Likewise, when Statius praises Domitian for being a clement king in *Siluae* 1.1, he is not simply echoing a motive from imperial "propaganda": He is inviting the princeps to adjust himself to the ideal described by Seneca's *De Clementia*. To go back to my former example from *Siluae* 1.6, the fact that Statius wishes for Domitian to embody the "constitutional" princeps who refuses to be called *dominus* is more important than Domitian's actual attitude toward those who called him thus.[31]

1.3 CRITICAL VIEWS OF THE *THEBAID*'S POLITICS

A good starting point for approaching modern scholarly assessments of the *Thebaid*'s politics is David Vessey's 1973 book.[32] According to Vessey, the political view that emerges from the *Thebaid* is that of a committed supporter of Domitian's regime. This positive view of power is reflected in the poet's conception of the world and of human history. In Vessey's view, the *Thebaid*'s world is governed by a stoic Jupiter, executor of fate and fulfiller of a providential design that entails the punishment of sinners and reestablishment of justice.[33] The poem is characterized by a strong polarization between wicked and good characters, the former being figures of *ira* the latter incarnations of *pietas* and stoic virtue.[34] Among positive heroes, the most important is Theseus. Vessey sees Theseus as an embodiment of the just king; Theseus' final arrival at Thebes provides a positive resolution to the poem's tensions.[35] Theseus is also implicitly viewed as an image of Vespasian and of Domitian, with the poem's finale read as a celebration of the Flavian dynasty's victory in 69 CE.[36] According to Vessey, the *Thebaid* was an epic "not of sin, but of redemption, a chronicle not of evil but of triumphant good," and "Statius was an overt and committed supporter of Domitian, of the *diuina domus* and of its courtiers."[37]

---

[31] Marks (2005a) reads panegyric of Domitian in Silius' *Punica* within this didactic framework. Silius' construction of kingship in the poem provides an ideal that the emperor is invited to follow: Marks (2005a) 244, 285–88. A comparable approach to political content in the *Thebaid* is fruitfully adopted by Bessone (2011) 29–33, 147–50.

[32] For useful overviews of recent scholarship on the *Thebaid* see Dominik (1996); Coleman (2003) 9–24, 29–37. A survey of political readings of Statius' *Thebaid*, with particular reference to the poem's finale and the character of Theseus, can be found in Bessone (2011) 128–32. The following survey does not claim to be comprehensive. I limit myself to highlighting a few scholarly tendencies in order to clarify my own work's position within the scholarly panorama on the *Thebaid*.

[33] Vessey's Jupiter is thus very similar to his Virgilian counterpart. See in particular the last section of chapter II: Vessey (1973) 82–91.

[34] Vessey's "figures of pietas" include Coroebus (101–6); Maeon (107–15); Hopleus, Dymas, and Menoeceus (116–30); Argia and Antigone (131–3). In particular Maeon is read as an embodiment of the stoic hero.

[35] Vessey (1973) 307–16.

[36] Vessey (1973) 315 n. 11.

[37] Vessey (1973) 6–7, 316.

Vessey, like other scholars after him, responded to negative prejudices against the *Thebaid*'s literary merits. Vessey aimed to demonstrate that the *Thebaid*, though not as great as the *Aeneid*, shared some of its model's literary merits. Vessey's optimistic and stoicizing reading of the *Thebaid* sought to transfer to Statius' poem a certain understanding of the *Aeneid*, implicitly considering Statius' relationship to Domitian's court comparable to Virgil's role within the Augustan establishment. Yet Vessey's Domitian was nothing like Augustus. For all his rehabilitation of Statius, Vessey's view of Domitian was essentially the negative portrait we find in post-Domitianic authors. Vessey's depiction of Statius as a supporter of such a problematic ruler hardly made the poet sympathetic to modern readers.[38] However, a reading of the *Thebaid* as supportive of the Flavian regime allowed Vessey a coherent view of Statius' production, one that could reconcile the *Thebaid* with the many panegyric passages of the *Siluae*.

A response to Vessey came some 10 years later. In Frederick Ahl's essay on the *Thebaid*, the attempt to rehabilitate Statius as a poet was coupled with a different interpretation of his relationship with the princeps.[39] Ahl reacted to the widespread scholarly depiction of Statius as a mannerist and to scholarly views of the *Thebaid* as little more than a rhetorical exercise with nothing to say about the world. Ahl read the *Thebaid* as a reflection on the recent trauma of civil war through the lens of Greek myth: Thebes could be seen as an image of Rome, and the subject of civil war was instrumental to an epic that, like Lucan's *Bellum Ciuile*, was not devoted to the celebration of absolute power but to its indictment.[40] Ahl viewed the *Thebaid*'s engagement with civil war as a condemnation of the Flavian dynasty's success in the 69 CE conflict and saw Statius' portrait of the *Thebaid*'s tyrants as influenced by the oppressive atmosphere of Domitianic Rome.[41] Whereas Vessey's Statius looked very much like (Vessey's) Virgil, Ahl's Statius resembled his Lucan, as the author of a coherently anti-imperial text.

Ahl read Statius' praise of Domitian through the lens of the ancient rhetorical technique of "safe criticism." In a previous article, Ahl had argued that Statius mocks imperial pretenses by means of "figured speech," a rhetorical trope whereby a seemingly panegyric statement ends up conveying, through allusion and ambiguity, a negative view of the addressee.[42] This type of expression consists in creating statements that can be interpreted in more than one way: A superficial panegyric reading

---

[38] This aspect of Vessey's argument has been criticized by Ahl (1986) 2811–12.

[39] Ahl (1986).

[40] Ahl (1986) 2812–16.

[41] Ahl (1986) 2832–4. Ahl retains this position in a recent contribution (2015).

[42] Ahl (1984a) 78–91; (1984b). For a reading of *Siluae* 1.1 along these lines see Ahl (1984a) 91–102.

allows the author to be safe from retaliation, while the space left open to double entendres permits the author to channel his opposition to the sovereign. This position influenced later approaches to the *Thebaid*, in particular the idea that criticism of power in the *Thebaid* is implicit and takes the form of ambiguities and double meanings that undermine the superficial panegyric dimension of the text. Ahl read the praise of Domitian at the beginning of the *Thebaid* within this framework.[43]

The major obstacle to a coherent anti-imperial reading of Lucan's *Bellum Ciuile* is the praise of Nero at the beginning of the poem.[44] The *Thebaid*, however, couples a panegyric beginning with a somewhat happy ending involving Theseus. Ahl's reading of the poem's politics demanded a critical reevaluation of Theseus. This was delivered by highlighting elements of continuity between Theseus and the poem's tyrants. In addition, in Ahl's view, a number of problematic elements in Statius' depiction of the Athenian king effectively deconstructed Statius' seemingly positive evaluation of this hero. In particular, Ahl emphasized Statius' mention of incidents from Theseus' past that cast a dubious light on the Athenian sovereign.[45]

The influence of Ahl's work contributed to a strong polarization of the debate on the interpretation of the *Thebaid*. Readings of Statius' main poem tended to reproduce the opposition between European scholars and the so-called "Harvard School," which had long dominated criticism of the *Aeneid*.[46] Ahl's "pessimistic" reading of the *Thebaid* was particularly influential on the works of Dominik (1994) and McGuire (1997). In his 1994 book, Dominik followed up on Ahl's approach by arguing that all manifestations of power in the poem, both human and supernatural, are given negative features.[47] Dominik suggested that the *Thebaid*'s controlling ideas, such as the inherently negative nature of monarchical power, reflected Statius' perception of the political situation in Flavian Rome; that Statius was critical of Flavian emperors and of Domitian, whose portrait was hinted at in the depiction of Theban tyrants; and that Statius' praise of Domitian in the *Siluae* was not sincere, used "figured speech," and was meant to guarantee an insurance against retaliation.[48]

---

[43] Ahl (1986) 2819–21.

[44] On the praise of Nero in Lucan's *Bellum Ciuile* see Chapter 4, Section 4.1.

[45] The adventures with Proserpina and Ariadne and the story of Hippolytus, whom Theseus cursed. Ahl also argued that Statius' comparing of both Theseus and the Theban brothers to bulls established a connection between the Athenian king and Oedipus' children. He also read in Statius' words an allusion to an attempt by Theseus to deceive his father Aegeus into committing suicide; Ahl (1986) 2894–8.

[46] See Braund (1996a) 16–19; Bessone (2009) 179; (2011) 128–9. A similar opposition between optimistic and pessimistic readers is reflected in the scholarship on Silius' *Punica*. See Marks (2005a) 245–52.

[47] Dominik (1994) 1–75 on supernatural power, 76–98 on human power.

[48] Dominik (1994) 130–80. In particular, for the *Thebaid*'s tyrants and Domitian see Dominik (1994) 148–9 (Eteocles), 157 (Creon). On Maeon and Aletes, Dominik (1994) 154–6. On figurate speech and lack of sincerity in Domitian's praise: 133, 139, 167–76.

He too saw Theseus as a dubious character, a sovereign too eager for war whose depiction is constantly undermined by unfavorable comparisons, a flawed hero destined to convey criticism of Domitian.[49] A similar approach is visible in McGuire's study of suicide and silence in Flavian epic, in which the figure of Domitian is seen as looming large behind Statius' depiction of tyranny.[50] Ahl, Dominik, and McGuire did not challenge the portrait of Domitian we get from post-Domitianic sources. The rehabilitation of Statius proposed by these scholars was achieved by detaching the poet from the prince, rather than by challenging views of Domitian as a tyrant.

The scholarship produced in the wake of Ahl's seminal essay has benefited the *Thebaid* in multiple ways. An important effect of this approach was to stimulate closer attention to the poem's relationship with the historical reality of Flavian Rome, with special reference to the recent experience of civil war (69 CE). Another beneficial effect was to overcome Vessey's somewhat simplistic reading of the *Thebaid* as a sort of morality play, with the action split between heroes and villains. Statius' characters are complex, endowed with many nuances, and carefully drawn so as to discourage one-sided appraisals. This approach also drew attention to the distortions inherent in molding the *Thebaid* in the cast of the *Aeneid*. In particular, Vessey's stoicizing view of the poem and its gods was abandoned. Also positive was the relevance given to post-Virgilian authors, especially Lucan and Seneca, as important sources for both the diction and the political views of the *Thebaid*.

The investigation of the ambiguities in the character of Theseus has been continued in more recent studies. In his book on Statius and Virgil, Ganiban questions Statius' presentation of Theseus on the basis of stoic theories of passions. In his view, the Athenian sovereign acts out of *misericordia* [compassion], an irrational impulse toward indiscriminate forgiveness that, according to Seneca, should be banished from the sage's mind.[51] As a sovereign, Theseus is the best the *Thebaid* has to offer, and yet he "is one of the most disturbingly transgressive characters in the *Thebaid*."[52] Along the same lines, in her work on madness in Greek and Roman epic, Hershkowitz draws attention to the continuity between Theseus and other heroes in the poem: "Theseus is himself inscribed, along with the rationality he purports to represent, within the overwhelming madness of the *Thebaid*."[53] In his monograph on the *Thebaid* and the traditions of Callimachean poetry, Charles McNelis touches on the political implications of the *Thebaid*'s finale. He sees Theseus' triumph as

---

[49] On Theseus see Dominik (1994) 93–6, 156–8.
[50] McGuire (1997) 147–54, 177.
[51] Ganiban (2007) 217–24. Cf. Bessone (2011) 186–8.
[52] Ganiban (2007) 229–30; quote from p. 229.
[53] Hershkowitz (1998) 301; for her analysis of Theseus see 296–301.

connected to Roman triumphs but highlights the Athenian hero's problematic intertextual pedigree, especially in light of Theseus' role in Catullus 64. He sees *clementia* [mercy] as a positive value, but one that is effective at the individual level, independent of the activities of sovereigns and states, and one from which Theseus is somewhat removed.[54] In a recent article, Neil Coffee draws attention to Statius' assimilation of Theseus to Mars, arguing that the association with a god who, in Statius' view, delights in excessive slaughter casts a dubious light on the Athenian sovereign and undercuts his connection with the values embodied by the altar of Clementia.[55]

In the years following Ahl's essay, a number of studies were published that sought to mediate between the two positions, arguing that the *Thebaid* resists unilateral interpretations. Philip Hardie raised important doubts as to the status of the *Thebaid*'s last book, drawing attention to the ambivalences and uncertainties of the close.[56] Similarly, Denis Feeney saw the poem's finale as not offering a final resolution to the tensions engendered by the narrative: The idea of a "purification" of the preceding "miasma" was undermined by the perfunctory air of Theseus' intervention, as well as by the absence of the gods from the finale.[57]

A reaction to the prevalence of pessimistic readings of the poem came in 1996. Susanna Braund's article on the *Thebaid*'s finale highlighted Statius' ability to provide an effective closure to his narrative.[58] Earlier approaches had emphasized the ambiguity in Statius' finale, to an extent reading it as a deeply problematic coda along the lines of the *Aeneid*'s ending. Braund shows that, while alluding to Virgil, Statius intentionally excised a number of elements that rendered the end of the *Aeneid* problematic.[59] In addition, Braund underlines Statius' styling of *clementia* as a quintessentially imperial virtue; she sees Theseus as an embodiment of this ideal

---

[54] McNelis (2007) 172–7.

[55] Coffee (2009).

[56] Hardie (1993) 46: "Does it [i.e. the finale of the *Thebaid*] represent a satisfactory dismantling of the engines of civil war, or is it merely a perfunctory and unpersuasive cap?" A similar position is taken by Hershkowitz (1995) 63.

[57] Feeney (1991) 361–3.

[58] This is accomplished through the addition of three supplements to the close of the *Aeneid*: the truce (12.782–96), and the laments at the funerals (12.797–809), and the coda (12.810–19); Braund (1996a) 5–8. Braund aptly notes that allusions to the prosecution of hatred, even after the end of war (such as the flame on Eteocles' and Polynices' pyre) are matched by hints at a durable ceasing of hostilities and a breaking of boundaries between the two sides. Cf. in particular the simile describing the Argive women as Bacchants at the end of the poem (12.791–3). Bacchants are typically associated with Thebes; the simile dissolves the boundaries between Argives and Thebans; Braund (1996a) 5.

[59] The duel between Creon and Theseus alludes to the final duel between Aeneas and Turnus in the *Aeneid*, but Creon does not ask for mercy: Braund (1996a) 3–4.

and as an idealized figure of the Roman emperor (possibly with hints of panegyric of Domitian).[60]

New impetus for optimistic readings of the *Thebaid* was provided by the work of French scholars. Ripoll drew attention to Statius' emphasis on *clementia* as a central moral value throughout the poem.[61] More decidedly political is Delarue's vision of the interconnection between Theseus' presentation as a merciful sovereign and Domitian's portrait in the *Siluae*. In Delarue's view, Theseus is an idealized sovereign, part of a somewhat exceedingly positive happy ending.[62]

An important attempt at synthesis was recently proposed by Federica Bessone.[63] Bessone rejects the notion of the *Thebaid* as an "epic of triumphant good." The poem's hope in the ability of power to provide a solution to human catastrophes is embedded in a pessimistic framework that emphasizes the fragility of human achievements in the absence of a divine sanction. The poem ends with tragic mourning and endless lamentation; war, violence, and power are so deeply compromised by Statius' account of books 1–11 that even Theseus' resolution is somewhat contaminated by the negative energies expressed in the former books.[64] Within this pessimistic framework, Bessone argues forcefully for a constructive view of Statius' relationship with imperial power by analyzing Statius' treatment of *clementia* in depth. Bessone shows that underlying Statius' description of the altar of Clementia is a complex intellectual operation. Statius creates a myth of origin for the Roman imperial virtue of *clementia* and does so by appropriating the rhetorical tradition of the praise of Athens, in which the Athenian democracy is presented as a champion of justice and a defendant of human rights and freedom. Key to this appropriation is Statius' engagement with Euripides' *Supplices*, in which Theseus is explored as an embodiment of the values of the Athenian democracy.[65] In the process, *clementia* is redefined. No longer narrowly conceived as restraint in inflicting punishment, *clementia* is understood as a broader concern for the rights of humans that builds on Greek and Roman notions of *humanitas*.[66] This enrichment of the concept of *clementia* has an

---

[60] Theseus: Braund (1996a) 9–12. Theseus and Domitian: Braund (1996a) 13; see also p. 18, where Braund notes that the poet uses the epithet *magnanimus* twice in the closing lines of the poem, once with reference to Theseus (12.795) and once with reference to the emperor (12.814).

[61] Ripoll (1998) 441–6.

[62] Delarue (2000) 368–74. On the poem's optimistic ending: Delarue (2000) 86, 372; (2006) 120.

[63] Bessone has dedicated a number of contributions to the *Thebaid*'s last book and the political dimension of Statius' poem: Bessone (2006, 2008a, 2008b, 2009). These are now fully reworked in her monograph, Bessone (2011), to which I subsequently refer in my summary of her position.

[64] Bessone (2011) 177–83.

[65] Bessone (2011) 102–27.

[66] For this aspect, Bessone builds and improves on Burgess (1972), an important contribution on *clementia* in Statius.

important precedent in Seneca's *De Clementia*, whose significance for the cultural world of the *Thebaid* Bessone convincingly underscores.

This reconstruction of the ideological and cultural background underpinning Statius' definition of *clementia* allows her to argue against attempts at severing Theseus from *clementia*. The Athenian sovereign effectively sets out to defend the rights of oppressed humans and the laws of nature. Theseus' encounter with the Argive women at the altar of Clementia, his action in battle, the duel with Creon, and Theseus' final entry into Thebes show him as a credible embodiment of this renewed ideal.[67] In the process, Bessone responds to arguments based on Theseus' mythical background by providing a fuller account of the traditions and texts on the Athenian sovereign engaged by Statius.[68] Bessone also resists the idea that Statius' problematic depiction of the gods reflects a negative view of imperial power. She shows that Statius draws on a tradition in which imperial power is seen as complementing and even surpassing divine models, so that Theseus' power does not merely parallel but improves on Jupiter's control over human affairs. Statius' dysfunctional gods leave a void open that human action is summoned to fill.[69]

1.4 DOMITIAN AND THE ELITE

Assessments of the *Thebaid* have tended to take for granted the negative picture of Domitian projected by historians and intellectuals active under the following dynasty. My reading of the *Thebaid* is based on a more nuanced appraisal of this emperor, one that, I argue, was available to the early audiences of the *Thebaid*. I contend that the stereotypical image of Domitian that we find in post-Domitianic literature could have consolidated only after the emperor's death. During Domitian's life, perceptions were more complex and fluid. I do not aim to provide a full critical reassessment of Domitian's principate, but I hope to show that at the time in which the project of the *Thebaid* consolidated, views of Domitian were diverse enough that efforts at projecting Domitian as an enlightened sovereign could be seen as credible attempts at directing the emperor toward a certain position rather than desperate flattery. I also argue that with the gradual worsening of Domitian's relationship with the elite, different readings of the *Thebaid* became available and pressed themselves onto Statius' text.

In Chapter 1, I lay the groundwork for my analysis by exploring Domitian's relationship with the senatorial elite. The beginning of Domitian's reign is marked by a

---

[67] Bessone (2011) 150–99.

[68] Bessone (2011) 136–50.

[69] Bessone (2011) 45–74.

remarkably lenient attitude toward the senate. In particular, Domitian granted pres-
tigious offices to members of the senatorial elite whose families had suffered under
previous emperors.[70] Domitian's marriage to Domitia, the daughter of Domitius
Corbulo, granted him a connection with powerful families persecuted by Nero.[71] In
this respect, Domitian's attitude deviated not only from Nero's policy but also from
his own father's. The new emperor was trying to pass the message to the senatorial
class that a new era had started.

These initiatives cast a new light on the enthusiastic tone found in panegyric of
Domitian, in which this emperor's principate is presented as the return of *libertas*
[freedom], and in which Domitian is depicted as an embodiment of the enlightened
king inspired by *clementia*.[72] This type of praise is no invention of the Domitianic
period. It draws on experiments with panegyric modes for earlier emperors, with
a marked influence of the rhetoric and the political reflection of the early reign of
Nero. What matters is that this language was, to an extent, matched by certain con-
crete initiatives by the princeps. Domitian's policy raised the expectations of the
elite, providing grounds to those who sought to project him as an embodiment of
the merciful princeps described by Seneca in his *De Clementia*. This initial phase
marked by a friendly relationship is gradually suppressed by the bias of later sources.
Suetonius still distinguishes between a promising start and a gradual descent into
autocracy. In Pliny the Younger, the "time of terror" under Domitian has no tem-
poral qualifications, and Tacitus openly speaks of a terror that lasted 15 years, that
is, all of Domitian's tenure.[73] Recovering this initial alignment between elite expec-
tations and Domitian's policy is central to the type of work I do on the *Thebaid*. It
will allow us to retrieve a number of responses to Statius' poem that the following
generation's demonization of Domitian has obscured.

Attention to this initial alignment between imperial policy and elite expectations
allows me to explore connections between the *Thebaid* and other products of the
cultural life of Flavian Rome. In particular, I speculate on the *Thebaid*'s connection
with the cultural activities sponsored by survivors of Nero. Survivors of Nero formed
an influential group within Flavian society. Statius was close to aristocrats gathering
at the house of Argentaria Polla, Lucan's widow.[74] Polla commissioned poems to
keep up the memory of Lucan more than 20 years after his death. *Siluae* 2.7, the

---

[70] I discuss the evidence in Chapter 1, Section 1.2. Jones (1992) 180–92 is essential on this subject.
[71] D.C. 66.3.4; Suet. *Dom.* 1.3. On Domitia Longina see Jones (1992) 33–8. Corbulo was executed by Nero. On
the political implications of Domitian's marriage to Corbulo's daughter see Jones (1992) 168; (1973) 86–8;
Levick (1999) 191.
[72] I discuss the evidence in Chapter 1, Section 1.1.
[73] Suet. *Dom.* 10.1; Tac. *Ag.* 3.2; Plin. *Ep.* 9.13.3; cf. also 5.1.7, 7.19.6. See Chapter 1, Section 1.2.
[74] More on Polla in Section I.6.

poem composed by Statius at Polla's request, features a violent attack on Nero and an apologetic view of Lucan's relationship with the emperor. A similar position is reflected in another, most likely Flavian, text, *Octauia*.[75] Biographies of survivors of Nero abound under the Flavians, and the rehabilitation of the Annaeans is reflected in other (lost) works of the Flavian period.[76]

In this book, I suggest that the political vision that emerges from the *Thebaid* is compatible with the interests of senatorial groups, especially survivors of Nero. On the one hand, there is an emperor who seeks to present himself as an embodiment of *clementia*, a friend of the Senate, and the polar opposite of Nero. On the other hand, we find members of the elite who have everything to gain from this new policy and whose influence in Roman society depends on Domitian's fulfillment of his promises of *libertas*. The *Thebaid*'s political project originates at this temporary alignment of elite and imperial expectations. In this context, I argue that the *Thebaid* reflects an attempt at constraining Domitian to live up to his initial promises and abide by a policy that would be expedient to members of the senatorial elite.

This alignment was, however, temporary. Domitian continued his tolerant policy until very late in his reign; Statius' production keeps emphasizing the emperor's *clementia* until the very end.[77] Yet Suetonius' idea of a gradual deterioration cannot be dismissed out of hand. If nothing else, in 93 CE Domitian ordered the execution of members of the same families he had benefited, the connections and relatives of Nero's and Vespasian's victims. This string of executions must have dealt a serious blow to the relationship among Domitian, these families, and the senatorial class in general.

In this context, chronology is relevant. Not only is the *Thebaid* one of the few complete epic poems handed down to us, it is also one of the few poems whose date of composition can be recovered with a good degree of certainty. The *Thebaid* was begun around 80 CE, close to the time of Domitian's accession to the throne, and was completed before 93 CE.[78] Statius is likely to have offered preliminary readings of parts of his poem in the intervening years. The intellectual project of the *Thebaid* is shaped by the atmosphere of the early years of Domitian's reign; the executions of

---

[75] On *Octauia* and its date see Ferri (2003) 5–30; Boyle (2008) xiv–xvi. On the politics of *Octauia*, its view of Seneca, and its relationship to the Annaeans see Ferri (2003) 70–5, 71–5 (on the presentation of Seneca); 26 (on *Octauia* and the *Annaeans*); Chapter 1, Sections 1.4 and 1.6; Chapter 4, Section 4.1.

[76] I discuss the evidence in Chapter 1, Section 1.4; see Champlin (2003a) 39–40.

[77] Chapter 1, Sections 1.1 and 1.2.

[78] On the date of the *Thebaid* see Coleman (1988) xvi–xvii; Newlands (2012) 2. The catalogue of Domitian's victories at the beginning of the poem (*Theb.* 1.16–21) does not feature the emperor's triumph over the Sarmatae (93 CE). If we are to trust poetic statements such as that of *Theb.* 12.811–12, it took Statius 12 years to complete his poem.

93 CE postdate the publication of Statius' poem. An oppressive vision of Domitian's regime may have represented the perception of a gradually increasing number of members of the poem's audience, but to think that it represented the general perception of this emperor, especially at the time in which the *Thebaid* was composed and first made public, is anachronistic.

Although I emphasize the importance of Domitian's early years for the intellectual project of the *Thebaid*, I also demonstrate that, to an extent, the picture of Domitian created by the following dynasty and the growing dissent against Domitian among members of the aristocracy created the conditions for a different appraisal of the *Thebaid*. As an uncompromisingly negative picture of Domitian consolidated, it became possible and to an extent difficult not to read the *Thebaid* as an indictment of Domitian. Crucial to this phenomenon, as we will see, was the transformation of Domitian into a second Nero. I do not attempt to dismiss anti-Domitianic readings of the *Thebaid*, which I think hold a legitimate place in the reception of Statius' text. My goal is to enrich our approach to Statius' epic by making room, alongside them, for readings of the poem against a more benign vision of Domitian that is plausible down to 93 CE.

I.5 NERO AND HIS WORLD

A pivotal aspect of my inquiry into the political vision of the *Thebaid* stems from an attention to the ambiguities of Domitianic Rome's relationship with the literary and political culture of Nero's Rome. In particular, I draw attention to the construction of a tyrannical portrait of Nero and to the heroization of Nero's victims. I also focus my attention on the consequences of a remarkable paradox of Domitianic ideology: Although Nero is officially demonized, elements of continuity and overlap between the political culture and imperial ideology of Nero and Domitian are perceivable.

In Flavian literature and culture, the image of Nero crystallizes into a somewhat stereotyped portrait of a tyrant. Views of Nero were much more nuanced during his life, and indeed Nero remained popular and influential long after his death.[79] Unlike what is sometimes assumed, there is no official reevaluation of Nero under Domitian. On the contrary, Nero is largely exploited as the paradigm of the worst possible emperor, whose faults make Domitian's virtue shine in comparison. Parallel to this, the Flavian period sees the development of a literary tradition centering on the words and deeds of Nero's victims, a tradition that I call martyrology. Opponents of Nero

---

[79] Chapter 1, Section 1.3 and introduction to Chapter 1.

are celebrated and idealized, their works and deeds made popular. This tradition contributes to the official demonization of Nero promoted under Flavian emperors.

Appreciating the relevance and currency of anti-Neronian ideology within Domitianic Rome opens up new frameworks for approaching the *Thebaid*'s representation of tyranny. Scenes containing criticism of tyranny in the *Thebaid*, such as the dialogue between Maeon and Eteocles in book 3, can be read within this anti-Neronian framework. Statius' representation of tyranny is influenced by the Flavian vulgate on Nero the monster; the *Thebaid* also interacts with portraits of idealized resistance to the tyrant such as those that we find in the traditions on Nero's martyrs. The conspicuous presence of Nero in Statius' poem allows for a different appreciation of the political import of Statius' indictment of tyranny. Because criticism of Nero was part of official ideology, Statius' discourse on tyranny is compatible with a positive view of Domitian's regime. The *Thebaid*'s tyrants are not necessarily aliases of Domitian, and, as we will see, because the idea that Domitian is a second Nero becomes prevalent only after Domitian's death, allusions to Neronian Rome do not immediately translate into criticism of Domitian. In addition, reevaluating the influence of the Flavian vulgate on Nero allows us to underscore the similarities between Statius' vision and the intellectual positions reflected in texts produced by survivors of Nero.

Alongside the persistent effects of this demonization of the figure of Nero, I draw attention to the profound influence of Neronian Rome on the culture, literature, and political thinking of the Domitianic period. A central aspect within this cultural process is the transferal to Domitian of a conceptualization of imperial power that was consolidated during Nero's tenure and most extensively formulated in Seneca's *De Clementia*. The *Thebaid* is also influenced by the idea of political and cultural renaissance, a conspicuous trait of Nero's reign, especially at its beginning. In Neronian texts such as Calpurnius' *Eclogues* or Seneca's *Apocolocyntosis*, Nero's accession is celebrated as a return to the Golden Age. After the abuses of Claudius, the principate of Nero brings about the return of *libertas*, the restoration of the prerogatives of the senate, and a revival of the rule of law. Although Nero's principate is presented as a return to the splendor of the Augustan principate, Neronian panegyrists also make the point that Nero outdoes all of his predecessors, including Augustus. This new era is made possible by the emperor's merciful attitude, his *clementia*, the imperial virtue discussed at length in Seneca's *De Clementia*. [80]

This presentation of Nero and the whole idea of cultural and political renaissance exercise a strong influence on the political culture of Domitianic Rome. Statius and

---

[80] I discuss the evidence in Chapter 1, Section 1.1.

Martial borrow images and themes from Seneca's *Apocolocyntosis* and Calpurnius' *Eclogues*. In the *Siluae*, Domitian appears as an embodiment of the merciful sovereign described by Seneca in his *De Clementia*; his accession marks a new era characterized by peace and the return of justice.[81] Most important, Domitianic panegyric appropriates from Neronian poets the idea that Domitian surpasses all of his predecessors. In the aftermath of Nero's death, this notion allowed poets to recuperate elements of Nero's praise without implying Domitian's equation with Nero. After Augustus' and Nero's failures, Domitian would finally materialize the new age of peace promised in vain by his predecessors.

The influence of Neronian culture and ideology is visible in a more profound and subtle way. Although Domitian is officially presented as Nero's opposite, elements of continuity between the cultural policies and self-representation of the two emperors are perceivable. As a matter of fact, the principate of Domitian testifies to the fact that it was impossible to renounce Nero's innovations entirely. In Chapter 1 (Section 1.3), I examine some of these elements of continuity. I make a case in particular for the renewed emphasis on solar symbols and for the use of certain mythological figures as counterparts of the emperor. There are also other aspects of continuity that I do not address in this book. My aim is not so much to provide a comprehensive picture of ideological overlap between the age of Domitian and that of Nero as it is to highlight some of the consequences of this peculiar cultural milieu for our understanding of the *Thebaid*.

The *Thebaid* employs complex strategies to navigate the ambiguities of Domitian's relationship to Nero. In particular, the poet strives to address certain aspects of Neronian ideology revived under Domitian without implying that Domitian is a new Nero. In Chapter 2, I show that Statius constructs an intricate discourse on solar symbols to demonstrate that although Domitian harnesses Nero's solar ideology, he is no second Nero. In Chapter 3, I show that Statius' use of Herculean imagery is mindful of Domitian's renewed interest in Hercules, a divine figure closely associated with Nero. Among other things, as we will see, Statius' depiction of a new kind of Herculean heroism aims to recuperate for Domitian the Hercules comparison exploited by Nero without implying identification with Nero. This attention to the ambiguities in the relationship with Neronian Rome will allow us to appreciate the *Thebaid*'s interaction with some complex aspects of Domitian's cultural policy. In Chapter 2, I show that Domitian's renewed interest in solar symbols may be related to his self-presentation in the East and his interest in retaining the favor of legions influenced by cults akin to Mithraism.

---

[81] *Siluae* 1.1 is key in this context; cf. also *Silv.* 1.4.38–49; full discussion in Chapter 1, Section 1.1.

The *Thebaid*, the earliest literary evidence for Mithras and its cult, is singularly mindful of this context.[82]

The relationship with Nero is also important in light of the impact it subsequently had on perceptions of Domitian's principate. The reputation of Domitian followed the same trajectory as that of Nero. Under the next dynasty, an uncompromisingly negative portrait of Domitian was styled. Post-Domitianic intellectuals borrowed from the Flavian vulgate on Nero to create their tyrannical picture of Domitian. In hindsight, the two started to look like one another; elements of continuity between Nero and Domitian could now be construed as evidence for Domitian's interchangeability with the great Julio-Claudian tyrant. Domitian's executions of 93 CE contributed to the image of Domitian as a second Nero by making him an enemy not just of the senatorial elite, but of the families victimized by Nero. The consequences of this progressive transformation of Domitian into a second Nero for readings of the *Thebaid* are remarkable. Once Domitian has been turned into a new Nero, it becomes natural to read the antityrannical aspects of Statius' poem in an anti-imperial, and even anti-Domitianic, fashion.

1.6 SENECA AND LUCAN

Nero was passionate about acting, and Oedipus was one of his favorite characters. This histrionic emperor invited audiences to relate the story of the king of Thebes to the events of his life: While playing the role of Oedipus, he wore a mask bearing his own features. For Nero, the theater was not just a favorite pastime. Nero promoted tragedy as a tool to manipulate perceptions of his actions and made the theater central to the construction of his own public image. The story of Oedipus, for instance, dramatized rumors about Nero's incest with his mother. Identification with Oedipus allowed Nero to cloud his life in the aura of myth. Under the mask of Oedipus, he appeared as the unfortunate and unaware accomplice of divinely sanctioned crimes. This programmatic confusion of myth and reality had important consequences for the literary production and culture of Domitianic Rome. Nero became progressively indistinguishable from his theatrical aliases. At the end of Nero's life, the people recalled that the last line sung by Nero in public was from a piece on Oedipus in exile: "My father and co-husband drives me to a pitiable death."[83] In hindsight, the line was revealed as prophetic, for soon after Nero followed in his favorite character's footsteps, leaving the city to commit suicide in a suburban villa.

---

[82] Mithras is named by Statius as an oriental equivalent of Apollo at *Theb.* 1.720; I discuss this passage and its implications in Chapter 2, Section 2.8.

[83] D.C. 63.28.5; cf. also Suet. *Nero* 46.3. I discuss this passage again in Chapter 1, Section 1.6.

Nero's direct and aggressive harnessing of myth for political communication influenced the reception of Neronian literature under Domitian. Looking back at the time of Nero, Flavian readers found a body of tragic texts (Seneca's tragedies) concerned with exploring the realities of Imperial Rome through the lens of Greek myth. Some of these plays centered on tyrannical figures and involved characters whom Nero had repeatedly impersonated and whom he associated with his imperial persona (e.g. Oedipus and the mad Hercules). The author of those tragedies, a close collaborator of Nero and a major political figure of Neronian Rome, had also left a treatise on kingship in which he advertised the figure of the merciful king (*De Clementia*). In retrospect, the possibility of a somewhat oversimplified reading of Seneca's production emerged, whereby the tyrants portrayed in the tragedies were regarded as the direct opposites of the ideal figure introduced by *De Clementia*. The two strands of Seneca's production thus came together to form a coherent unit: Seneca wrote his tragedies as implicit attacks on Nero, turning on Nero's mythical aliases to portray him as the opposite of the ideal sovereign he had hoped for in *De Clementia*. This tendentious reading was convenient in many ways: The materials from Seneca's tragic world could be harnessed to construct the tyrannical figure of Nero. This reading also projected an apologetic view of Seneca that would have been particularly appealing to supporters and connections of the Annaeans: The philosopher was revealed as a critic of the regime with which he had been so problematically involved.

Such a reception of Seneca's works is implicit in *Octauia*, which was likely a product of the Flavian period. In this play, allusions to Senecan tragedy are used to shape the portrait of a tyrannical Nero, and the author of *Octauia* selects Senecan materials according to Nero's own favorite mythical characters. He also represents Nero as falling short of the principles outlined by Seneca in his *De Clementia*.[84] To a lesser extent, this politicized reception of Senecan tragedy is influential on Statius' *Thebaid*. In Chapter 1, I show that Statius' interaction with Seneca's *Oedipus* is shaped by this ideological approach to Seneca's production. I also capitalize on the idea that Nero's mythical aliases provide a particularly fertile terrain for alluding to Nero.

The other key author to my investigation is Lucan. In this book, I explore some of the ways in which the reception of Lucan contributes to the *Thebaid*'s political and ideological vision. Allusions to Lucan are instrumental to Statius' engagement with the historical and political reality of Rome. By reworking the text of Lucan, Statius conjures up the reality of Roman civil wars within his mythological poem.[85]

---

[84] Chapter 1, Section 1.6.
[85] Chapter 4, Sections 4.4 and 4.5.

This is not, however, the only way in which Lucan is relevant to the political vision of the *Thebaid*. In Chapter 4, I explore Statius' reaction to the *Bellum Ciuile* and its vision of imperial power. From this point of view, the *Bellum Ciuile* appeared to Flavian readers as a problematic and ambiguous text. The poem starts with praise of Nero, implicitly connecting Nero's principate to the absence of civil war in Rome. However, other passages of Lucan's text are endowed with a clearly anti-imperial stance, whereby Lucan seems to perceive no difference between Nero and his imperial predecessors and in which the end of the Republic coincides with the death of Rome.[86] Statius takes advantage of these contradictions. He harnesses Lucan's praise of Nero and his presentation of imperial power as the force that restrains the world from falling into civil war again. But at the same time he uses the anti-imperial aspects of Lucan's text by projecting the antityrannical passages of the *Bellum Ciuile* as an indictment of one specific type of emperor, one similar to Nero and one whom Domitian can surpass.

Statius' reception of Seneca and Lucan is also relevant to the subject of this book for another reason. Statius uses his engagement with both Seneca and Lucan to frame his own position as a politically engaged poet and intellectual. Through his reading of their works, Statius turns both Seneca and Lucan into exemplary characters.[87] They are powerful intellectual figures who sought to direct Nero and who made their poetry an instrument of resistance once Nero proved to be unable to follow their advice. Engaging these great authors allows Statius to claim their intellectual prestige and influential role. Statius too sees himself as an adviser of kings. Like Lucan and Seneca, he seeks to direct Domitian toward an illuminated kingship. Like Lucan and Seneca, he is ready to turn his back on the emperor should he fail to live up to the poet's ideals. The reception of Lucan and Seneca is key to Statius' own claim of intellectual independence.

1.7 CAESAR'S SWORD

Vitellius' campaign against Otho in 69 CE began with a symbolic gesture. His legionaries awarded him the sword of Caesar, which was kept in a nearby temple.[88] This was meant as an auspicious gift, expressing the hope that Vitellius' descent into Italy would be as successful as Caesar's. Perhaps it also implied an attempt at legitimating Vitellius' coup by styling him as a latter-day Caesar, the glorious general

---

[86] Praise of Nero: Luc. 1.46–52; different views of principate: e.g. Luc. 1.669–72, 7.638–41; more passages reflecting a negative view of the principate are listed by Roche (2009) 4–5; see introduction to Chapter 4.

[87] See Chapter 1, Sections 1.4 and 1.8; on Seneca's transformation into a model for the elite see Habinek (2000).

[88] Suet. *Vit.* 8.1. See Chapter 4, Section 4.5.

forced into war by the schemes of a corrupt, Rome-based oligarchy. Other passages of Suetonius and Tacitus align the civil war of 69 CE with the conflict between Caesar and Pompey in 49–48 BCE.

In this book, I give particular attention to the ways in which the *Thebaid* evokes the most recent Roman civil conflict, the civil war of 69 CE. In this context, I look for punctual allusions to facts and events of the 69 CE civil war within the body of Statius' narrative. I also consider the presence of the 69 CE context in a more general way. In Chapter 5, for instance, I reflect on the religious feelings associated with civil war, with particular attention to the 69 CE war. I then examine the impact of these religious feelings on both Domitian's religious policy and Statius' view of the gods in the *Thebaid*. In the same chapter, I make the point that certain elements of Statius' narrative, such as his references to the practice of *deuotio*, should be read in connection with the centrality of *deuotio* to narratives of the 69 CE civil war.

More frequently, however, I seek to show that Statius evokes the recent civil conflict in a less direct way. He engages certain narratives that in the Flavian period had been associated with the war among Otho, Vitellius, and Vespasian. The war between Caesar and Pompey is one of these narratives. In Chapter 4, I show that the text of Lucan becomes a particularly salient source of historical allusion because the war between Pompey and Caesar was constantly present to Statius' contemporaries as they looked back at the war of Vitellius and Otho. Other narratives play the same role. In Chapter 6, I seek to show that Vitellius' descent into Italy and the burning of the Capitol by Vitellius' soldiers in 69 CE are associated by Statius and other authors with the destruction of Rome by the Senones Gauls in 390 BCE. I then show that Statius' allusions to Gauls and Gallic battles in the *Thebaid* are instrumental to interactions with ideological representations of the 69 CE civil war.

Intertextuality is also relevant to the question of how the *Thebaid* engages the events of 69 CE in another way. Statius uses allusion to link his mythical narrative to several historical moments in Rome's past. Allusions to the *Aeneid* allow Statius to forge a connection between the war at Thebes and the ancestral battles fought by Trojans and Latins. References to Lucan bring the *Thebaid* into dialogue with the history of the late Republic and the civil war fought by Caesar and Pompey.[89] Allusions to these two texts are often combined to achieve what I call the telescopic effect of Statian intertextuality. Through different intertexts, the reader is transported increasingly further back in time. Combining allusions to Virgil and Lucan allows Statius to bring to mind the whole spectrum of Roman civil wars, from

---

[89] See Chapter 4, especially Section 4.5.

the early, quasi-fraternal conflict narrated by Virgil in the second half of the *Aeneid* to the wars of Caesar and Pompey narrated by Lucan.

1.8 THE PESSIMISM OF THE *THEBAID*

In this book, I try to show that although the *Thebaid* lends itself to being read as criticism of Domitian, there are nearly equal grounds in the text for benign readings of the poem's political implications, even within the dark narrative of the first 11 books. In the following chapters, I examine some of these constructive moments. But it is imperative to keep in mind that there are important limitations to the poem's constructive vision. Indeed, constructive action in the *Thebaid* is possible only within a generally pessimistic and disillusioned outlook on human and divine matters. Losing sight of these limitations might produce a somewhat unbalanced and incomplete picture of Statius' poem.

Let us start with Statius' view of human nature. In the *Thebaid*, humans are by nature prone to evil. The Theban brothers are a clear example of this. Tisiphone's intervention, in response to Oedipus' curse, triggers the conflict between them. Yet Eteocles and Polynices have already revealed their true colors by disrespecting Oedipus, who tells the Fury that she will find his children well disposed to her evil influence.[90] In particular, human beings are attracted to power. In Chapter 4, I show that Statius subscribes to a view in which love of riches is *not* the main reason why humans strive for power.[91] In the world of the *Thebaid*, the human desire for dominion over others is more concerning precisely because it is not instrumental to the acquisition of wealth. One could argue that Eteocles and Polynices' wickedness is, to an extent, a family curse, the hereditary madness that runs in Oedipus' bloodline.[92] However, Statius makes it clear that he regards the Theban brothers as an example to instruct kings of any time and place, and he speculates on what the strife of Polynices and Eteocles would have been had greater riches and greater power been at stake, a sign that he regards the dynamics at Thebes as applicable to other contexts.[93] If indeed this disposition is not limited to members of particular families and does not stem from some sort of divine curse—if, in other words, this is the natural condition of human beings—what hope is there that they will ever live in peace?

---

[90] *Theb.* 1.86–7. Fantham (1997) 202–3; Venini (1971) 30–1.

[91] See especially *Theb.* 1.150–1; Chapter 4, Section 4.4.

[92] "Genetic determinism" in the poem has been thoroughly explored by Bernstein (2008) 64–85. See also Davis (1994).

[93] *Theb.* 1.155–64.

In Statius' view, human nature inclines to sin. Wrongdoings will be more serious and have greater consequence when performed by those in power, but humans fare no better in their capacity as subjects. Statius' pessimistic view of the nobles, reflected in his portrait of Eteocles and Polynices, is compounded by a somewhat disillusioned view of the commoners. A key passage in this connection is the speech by the anonymous Theban in book 1. This speaker is an innocent victim of the powerful who complains about the consequences of Eteocles and Polynices' strife. This scene is part of an epic tradition that goes back to Homer, but it is Lucan's version of this topos that is particularly influential on Statius. However, unlike his literary predecessors, Statius presents his anonymous citizen as malicious and unruly at heart, always eager for change no matter who is in power.[94] Statius seems to imply elsewhere that this disposition is not peculiar to Theban citizens.[95] In general, the *Thebaid* emphasizes the self-destructive tendencies of the masses and the necessity of a strong, centralized power for the preservation of order.[96] This view of the unruliness of the commoners helps us put into perspective the particularly disillusioned view of supreme monarchical power that Statius develops in his poem.

Statius' view of mankind's inclination to evil is made more dramatic by his acute awareness of the fragility of the human condition. Both humans and gods can destroy life with incredible ease. The bond of affection among the living, once destroyed by death, cannot be restored, and there is no compensation for human pain. A remarkable example of this grim reality is found in book 5. A monstrous snake that dwells in the woods of Nemea—a monster sacred to Jupiter—kills the child Opheltes without even realizing his presence. At the same time, the monster crushes the life of his parents, who are overwhelmed by grief, and of the child's nurse (Hypsipyle), who risks being put to death.[97] The snake is nearly symbolic of the war: a monstrous creature belonging to Jupiter, so lethal and so much greater than humans that it destroys life without even realizing its presence. At the end of the poem, Theseus' victory against Creon eliminates tyranny from Thebes and grants burial to the Argives. But this resolution does not cancel the suffering of the peoples involved: The poem in fact concludes not on a note of triumph for Theseus' victory but by remarking how impossible it is for the poet to represent such pain appropriately.[98] And Statius

---

[94] The speech of the anonymous Theban: *Theb.* 1.158–96. Cf. in particular 1.171–2. I discuss this passage in Chapter 4, Section 4.3.

[95] Cf. *Silv.* 1.4.40, discussed in Chapter 4, Section 4.3.

[96] The innate evil will of subjects against those who control them seems to even have its counterpart in the natural order: See my discussion of storm imagery and cosmic upheaval in Chapter 4, Section 4.3.

[97] *Theb.* 5.499–709.

[98] *Theb.* 12.797–809.

emphasizes this dramatic view with his many portraits of familial bonds shattered by war.[99]

Another source of the *Thebaid*'s pessimism is Statius' presentation of the gods. If humans are flawed, fickle, and prone to evil, the gods are hardly better. Divinities such as Apollo, Bacchus, and Diana seem concerned with the welfare of only their protégés. They are particularly good at punishing their enemies and singularly ineffective at protecting their favorites.[100] Unlike the other gods, Jupiter does not act purely out of concern for his human connections: He acts according to a certain notion of retributive justice and legitimizes his action with reference to the laws of nature.[101] As is typical of tragic deities, however, he fails to preserve the distinction between the innocent and the guilty. Innocent Argives and Thebans are punished because of their rulers' wickedness. In the *Thebaid*, the solidarity of family and city bonds is such that guilt as well as punishment extends vertically from generation to generation and horizontally among members of the same social groups. More important, Statius' Jupiter knows only how to punish. We hear a lot about the chastisement of the guilty yet little about the rewards for the pious. Jupiter has no plan for what happens after his vengeance is carried out. Unlike his counterpart in the *Aeneid*, he has no long-term providential vision for the peoples involved in the action of the poem.

The solidarity of family and city bonds, the mainly punitive and retributive nature of divinity, the capricious gods who produce unjust sufferings: These are all traditional ideas, familiar to us from the world of Greek literature and religion. What makes the *Thebaid* striking in this respect is its distance from the religious world of the *Aeneid*. Hereditary guilt calling for divine retribution is not absent from the *Aeneid*, but it is certainly not emphasized. Jupiter's role in the *Aeneid* is not purely punitive. The king of the gods has a vision for the future of Aeneas' people and of humanity, involving the establishment of Roman power and eventually the providential kingship of Augustus. The *Thebaid* turns the clock back to more primitive versions of the pantheon.

The reasons for this choice are complex. First, the poem's religious outlook is conducive to the tragic effects Statius aims to achieve.[102] Second, these primitive ideas, always present in Roman religious thought, are particularly prone to emerge at

---

[99] Argia and Polynices are obvious examples (see *Theb.* 12.105–348); cf. also Ide (3.133–68); Atys and Ismene (8.607–54), etc.

[100] As an example, Apollo is successful at exterminating the population of Argos in book 1 but can do nothing to save a single individual, Amphiaraus, from death (*Theb.* 7.772–7). On this aspect of Statius' portrayal of the gods see Feeney (1991) 371–6.

[101] Cf. in particular *Theb.* 7.215–18.

[102] See Section I.1 of this chapter.

times of great stress, and there is some evidence that their currency increased during Domitian's principate. In Chapter 5, I show that Statius' vision of a harsh, punitive Jupiter was consonant with the gloomy religious climate in the aftermath of the 69 CE civil war and of the great natural catastrophes of 79 and 80 CE. Another example pertains to the notion of familial and social solidarity, according to which the gods punish children for the sins of their parents and subjects for their rulers' impiety. In the empire, the government not just of a city, but of the world, depends on one man. The idea that catastrophe can strike the commonwealth and loom large because of the misbehavior of the one individual in power was a harsh reality of Imperial Rome in Statius' time, even when the gods are not part of the equation. The idea that Nero's impiety attracted divine punishment is a sentiment often found in reactions to the reign of Nero. The civil war of 69 CE, which many traced back to Nero's irresponsible running of the state, made more vivid the perception of the worldwide consequences of flawed governance.

Another distinctive feature of Statius' view of the gods comes from the fact that the powers of the underworld act independently of divine forces. In the *Aeneid*, the Furies (Allecto) and the Dirae (whether they are one and the same matters little for my argument) are crucial to the development of the plot in the second part of the poem. But they act under instigation from the Olympian gods and can only go so far as the gods allow.[103] In Statius, the Furies respond to the prayers of a human and are not summoned by the gods. Jupiter's plan seems to align temporarily with that of the Furies, but the Furies remain in play even after Jupiter has withdrawn from the scene. And from book 8 on, the powers of the underworld become more directly involved, when Dis decides to unleash his own forces against the Olympians, so that the topic of fraternal war is extended even to the divine plan. This too is a traditional concept. The independence of the Furies from the Olympians is at home in Greek archaic culture and Greek tragedy. In Roman literature, the closest parallel for this type of interference by underworld powers comes from Senecan tragedy. Statius' Tisiphone has her nearest relative in the Fury who sets in motion events at the beginning of Seneca's *Thyestes*.[104] Statius' choice is, again, striking when set against the highly hierarchical religious world of Virgil. It is not so much the fact that the Olympians have recourse to underworld powers as it is the lack of a hierarchy between Olympians and nether powers that differentiates the *Thebaid*'s pantheon from the religious world of the *Aeneid*.

Jupiter's inability to engage in constructive action is linked to an aspect of the poem's finale that scholars have rightly found disturbing: the absence of the gods.[105]

---

[103] See *A.* 7.310–571, 12.843–952.
[104] Sen. *Thy.* 1–121.
[105] Feeney (1991) 361–3.

There is no divine sanction of the new order established by Theseus, no promise of divine benevolence, no certainty that Jupiter, or the forces of the underworld, will finally release the city from their grip. True, the Furies' action is particularly motivated by the behavior of Oedipus' male descendants, and we may hope that their extinction, together with the death of Creon, will appease the gods. Yet the only glimpse of the future of Thebes that we get in Jupiter's words in book 7 is of a time when the children of the Argives will avenge their fathers by defeating Thebes.[106] Theseus' restoration brings with itself no *imperium sine fine* [empire without end], and the death of the city seems only postponed. In the absence of the gods, constructive action is up to humans. It takes Theseus to restore order to the city of Thebes. Yet he achieves a fragile and possibly temporary triumph.

1.9 THEBES AND ROME

The myth of Thebes has a long history of literary and nonliterary adaptations in both Greece and Rome. For the purpose of this book, it is necessary to consider briefly the ways in which Theban myth, and particularly the story of Eteocles and Polynices, was adapted in Roman literature and culture prior to the *Thebaid*.[107] I am particularly interested in the ideological implications that underlie Roman appropriations of the myth of Oedipus' children. Imperial literature might give the impression that Thebes is relevant to Roman authors primarily as a prompt for reflecting on civil war. But the *Thebaid* responds to a longer tradition, one that encompasses other ways of using the myth of the Seven against Thebes in politically loaded contexts.[108] It is important for us to keep these earlier adaptations in mind if we want to grasp the full spectrum of political and historical implications in the story of the Seven in the *Thebaid*.

    Civil strife and civil war are something of an obsession for the Romans, especially in the first century BCE. The first explicit reference to the Theban brothers as a match for warring Romans dates to this period. In one of his letters, commenting on the civil war of Caesar and Pompey, Cicero describes Caesar's intentions through a famous statement by Eteocles in Euripides' *Phoenissae*—the quote implicitly compares Caesar to Eteocles, and entails for Pompey, forced out of Rome, the role

---

[106] *Theb.* 7.218–21.

[107] On this topic see Braund (2006); Barchiesi (1988) is also useful. Braund concentrates on the importance of Thebes as a tool for meditating on Rome's origins, marked by fraternal strife, and on the topic of civil war; she takes only literary sources into account.

[108] For the ideological valence of Thebes as a mirror-opposite of Athens in Athenian drama see Zeitlin's (1986) seminal essay.

of the exile Polynices.[109] The notion of citizens as brothers, and therefore of civil war as fraternal war, makes it easy to translate the Theban fratricide to Roman reflections on civil war.[110] The idea of regarding Caesar and Pompey as the Theban warring brothers finds its continuation in Lucan, but there is indirect evidence that Romans kept turning to Eteocles and Polynices to meditate on civil war in the decades after Caesar's death. The poetry of Propertius provides evidence for Augustan adaptations of the myth of Eteocles and Polynices in the aftermath of Actium.[111]

The story of the two Theban brothers is present in Virgil's imagination in creating the *Aeneid*.[112] Philip Hardie drew attention to Juno's words to Allecto in book 7, where she mentions Allecto's ability to arm "unanimous brothers" against one another (*A.* 7.335); the epithet "unanimous brothers" is more appropriate for Eteocles and Polynices than Romulus and Remus or Aeneas and Turnus.[113] Hardie also highlighted a possible allusion to the myth of the Theban Spartoi (the warriors sprung from the teeth of the dragon killed by Cadmus) in Virgil's reference to a "crop of swords" in his account of the beginning of hostilities between Trojans and Latins.[114] In addition, echoes of Aeschylus' *Septem contra Thebas* are perceptible in Virgil's catalogue of the Latin forces in *Aeneid* 7, especially in the description of Turnus' armor.[115]

Ovid harnesses the idea of using Rome as a foil for Thebes in a more explicit fashion, even though he does not deal at length with Eteocles and Polynices. Ovid's Theban stories in *Metamorphoses* 3 and 4 repeatedly highlight points of contact and similarities between Thebes and Rome. This effect is typically achieved through allusions to Virgil's *Aeneid*. Similarities are particularly strong in the story of the origins of the two cities. Cadmus, an exile and an easterner like Aeneas, founds a city after killing a monster and witnesses the first ominous civil war fought by "Theban brothers" (the fight of the Spartoi). The association with the two stages of Rome's foundation (Aeneas' arrival in

---

[109] Cic. *Att.* 7.11.1; the quote is from E. *Ph.* 506. In *Off.* 3.82 Cicero records Caesar's habit of quoting other lines from Euripides' *Phoenissae* (*Ph.* 524–5); Braund (2006) 266.

[110] The war of Eteocles and Polynices is the subject of republican tragedies, but the fragmentary status of the evidence does not allow us to speculate on the political and ideological relevance of these Roman adaptations. It may or may not be relevant that the first Roman version of a play on the subject of the Seven against Thebes, Accius' *Phoenissae*, broadly coincides with a time of great social and political unrest in Rome.

[111] Braund (2006) 264–5; Prop. 1.7.1–5 (Propertius seeks to dissuade his friend Ponticus from writing on Thebes: see especially Prop. 1.7.1–6), 2.34.37–46 (while commending love poetry, Propertius seems to imply that his friend Lynceus is intent on composing poetry on the subject of Thebes). The first book of Propertius is usually considered to postdate the battle of Actium (31 BCE); a pre-Actium date has been recently advocated by Heslin (2010). For Caesar and Pompey as Eteocles and Polynices in Lucan see subsequently in this section.

[112] I explore this subject at length in a forthcoming article. See Rebeggiani *forthcoming* (2).

[113] Hardie (1990) 230.

[114] *A.* 7.526; Hardie (1990) 230.

[115] *A.* 7.783–8 with Horsfall (2000) 509.

Latium; Romulus and Remus' fight) is difficult to resist.[116] The idea of an initial act of
fraternal strife (Romulus and Remus) repeated several generations later by Roman civil
wars is well established in the Roman imagination: the sequence formed by the Spartoi
and Oedipus' children matches it on the mythical level.[117] The interchangeability of
Rome and Thebes is also suggested by the cup that Anius gives to Aeneas on his way to
Latium, an object that represents an episode from Theban myth.[118] A second influen-
tial aspect implied by Ovid's use of Thebes is the idea that other incidents in the history
of Thebes (such as the stories of Pentheus, Niobe, etc.) can be used to reflect on Rome
and its destiny. This is once again suggested through engagement with the *Aeneid*.[119]
In Ovid, Thebes is not only a meditation on the beginning but also on the possible
end of Rome. A city similar to Rome in many ways, Ovid's Thebes is also famously not
eternal, a divine foundation never emancipated from divine anger and never ceasing
to repeat its past. Thebes' story forms a powerful warning, detailing the fragility and
precariousness of achievement.[120]

Theban stories are also important for Lucan. Lucan advises his readers not
to look for mythical *exempla* of civil war. Rome has its own warring brothers at
home, at the beginning of its history: Eteocles and Polynices look like a distant and
weak paradigm set against Romulus and Remus.[121] Yet Lucan evokes the Theban
brothers in connection with the war of Caesar and Pompey. At the Feriae Latinae,
the bonfire splits into two tongues of fire, in imitation of the pyre of the Theban
brothers:[122]

> Vestali raptus ab ara
> ignis, et ostendens confectas flamma Latinas
> scinditur in partes geminoque cacumine surgit
> Thebanos imitata rogos.
> Luc. 1.549–52

From Vesta's altar fire was stolen.
The flame which marks the Latin Festival's completion

---

[116] Hardie (1990) 226–7; Braund (2006) 267–9.
[117] Hor. *Epod.* 7.13–20; Luc. 1.93–5; Hardie (1990) 230; Micozzi (1999) 359–61.
[118] *Met.* 13.681–99; Hardie (1990) 225 n.12.
[119] Hardie (1990) 231–5.
[120] A parallel to Carthage, another city the Romans think about while considering their possible final destruc-
tion; Hardie (1990) 228–9. On Thebes as an emblem of the inescapability of one's past see Braund (2006)
262 *et passim*.
[121] Luc. 1.93–5.
[122] On this passage and its models see Narducci (2002) 55–6. Cf. in particular Ov. *Trist.* 5.5.135–6 and the parallel
scene in Sen. *Oed.* 321–2 (discussed in Chapter 1, Section 1.7).

is split in two and rises with twin tongues,
resembling the Theban funeral-pyre.

Later, the suicide of Vulteius and his comrades repeats the fratricidal war of the Spartoi.[123] The description of Pharsalus, with its mention of *semina Martis* [seeds of Mars], brings to mind the fields of Mars, the place in Thebes where the teeth of the dragon slain by Cadmus were sown.[124] The references to Thebes highlight the pessimistic aspects of Lucan's poem. After the battle of Pharsalus, Rome will be just a name, precisely like Thebes in Ovid.[125]

The Roman dimension of Theban conflicts is equally present in Seneca's tragedies on the house of Oedipus (*Oedipus* and *Phoenissae*). Seneca too builds on the idea of Rome as a new Thebes, but he takes a further step by adding a distinctive imperial dimension to his narrative. Seneca's *Oedipus* and *Phoenissae* offer a study of the connections between ineffective kingship and civil war that becomes particularly relevant for Statius in the aftermath of Nero's death.[126] Statius' Theban narrative is indebted to this rich tradition. From Ovid, he inherits the study of similarities between the history of Rome and that of Thebes, from Seneca the reflection on the interconnection of civil war and kingship in a Roman context, and from Virgil and Lucan the general idea of Eteocles and Polynices as aliases of Roman generals at war. From Ovid, Statius also takes the idea that the similarities of Rome and Thebes can be brought to the fore by engaging Virgil's *Aeneid*. Statius is also influenced by the idea of aligning the origins of Thebes with Rome's origins and draws a parallel between Rome and Thebes in light of these cities' inability to escape civil war.[127]

Civil war is, however, not the only point in Roman receptions of Theban stories. There is a parallel tradition, less visible in imperial texts but nonetheless influential on Statius' poem. This tradition consists of receptions of Theban stories in which the primary emphasis is not on civil war but on the threat posed to the city by a barbarian force. This tradition goes back to Aeschylus' *Septem contra Thebas*. In this play, the center of interest is not so much the enmity between the two brothers as it is the threat posed to the city by what is presented as a terrifying foreign invasion. The first part of the play consists of the dialogues between Eteocles and the

---

[123] Luc. 4.549–51. Micozzi (1999) 361.

[124] Luc. 6.395; cf. Luc. 4.549–51; Micozzi (1999) 362–3; even the *Bellum Ciuile*'s proem, with its mention of *bella plus quam ciuilia* [wars more than civil, Luc. 1.1], might adapt a sentence applied to the Theban conflict in Seneca's *Phoenissae*: Cf. Sen. *Phoen.* 354–5, with Narducci (2002) 19.

[125] Luc. 7.391–6; with Narducci (2002) 167–9. Cf. Ov. *Met.* 15.429; Hardie (1990) 225.

[126] Chapter 1, Section 1.7.

[127] See Chapter 4, Section 4.4.

chorus: The latter voices its fear and desperation at the approach of the assailants, while Eteocles, a champion of civic virtues, advises calm, organizes the defense, and relies on the help of the gods for the salvation of the city. This atmosphere of terror is heightened by the way in which the Seven Argives are presented. The Seven are depicted as monstrous figures, tied to the forces of the underworld.[128] Most important, the Seven are presented as culturally incompatible with the Thebans: They are foreign and barbarians. Aeschylus goes so far as to say that they speak a "foreign language"; their horses whistle in a "barbarian manner."[129] This specific interest in the "city under attack" theme and the characterization of the Argives are hardly surprising in light of the historical context in which the play was written, just a few years after the Persian invasion. The atmosphere of a city threatened by terrifying barbarian forces is still something Aeschylus' audience can easily connect with.[130] Euripides' *Phoenissae* retains this "monstrous" characterization of the Argives, yet it combines it with a closer focus on the topic of fraternal strife.

In Roman Republican culture, there are traces of this simplified adaptation of Theban myth to historical contexts. One example is provided by the statuary group displayed by Lutatius Catulus in the Temple of Fortuna Huiusce Diei in the Campus Martius. This temple was built to celebrate Catulus' victory over the Cimbri, a barbarian tribe that invaded Italy and threatened the destruction of Rome. Catulus added to the temple a statuary group by the famous sculptor Pythagoras representing the Seven against Thebes.[131] As I demonstrate in a forthcoming contribution, Catulus' choice of the fight of the Seven against Thebes was connected to the idea of using the Argive assault as a symbol of a barbarian invasion that the city survived thanks to divine help.[132] The story of Thebes thus accompanies Roman adaptations of fifth-century Athenian paradigms of the Greek versus barbarian conflict.

This second tradition is important for the *Thebaid* as well. In Chapter 6, I show that Statius' poem interacts with Flavian attempts at presenting Vitellius' invasion of Italy as a foreign and barbaric invasion. To this end, Statius capitalizes on the monstrous characterization of the Seven Argives going back to Aeschylus' play and hints at the barbaric nature of the assailants in his account of the Argive assault on Thebes in book 10. There is an element of paradox in Statius' relying on both strands

---

[128] This characterization emerges clearly during the messenger's speech, in which the Seven are seen as arrogant and blasphemous and are compared to the impious Giants: A. *Th.* 375–652.

[129] A. *Th.* 170, 463–4; Snell (1928) 78.

[130] Snell (1928) 78–80; Rosenbloom (1993) 188–90.

[131] The statuary group is lost; the evidence for its subject and location is provided by Pliny *Nat.* 34.60. On this temple see *LTUR* II s.v. *Fortuna Huiusce Diei, aedes* 269–70 (P. Gros).

[132] See Rebeggiani *forthcoming* (1); for a different interpretation of the presence of the Seven within the collection of the Temple of Fortuna Huiusce Diei see Bravi (2012) 57–8.

of Roman adaptations of the story of Eteocles and Polynices. In the tradition that regarded Eteocles and Polynices as a symbol of Roman civil wars, the emphasis is on the similarity and closeness of the two warring sides: The closest possible relationship, kinship, is subverted into war. In the second tradition, the focus is not on similarity but on difference: The Seven Argives are a monstrous army, culturally incompatible with Thebes.

Statius' combination of both traditions in the same text is facilitated by the peculiar way in which the topic of civil war is approached in official contexts in Rome. In Roman reflections on civil war, the similarities between the two forces and the monstrosity of perverting familial and ethnic bonds are underscored. Alongside this approach, however, we find attempts at reducing the scandal of civil war by representing civil conflicts as wars against foreign enemies. A classic example is provided by the *Aeneid*. The *Aeneid* depicts at length a war between peoples that will one day become one, the Trojans and the Latins. In hindsight, this is a civil war of sorts, one that Virgil brings into connection with actual Roman civil wars and one that is endowed with the most disturbing attributes of civil conflicts.[133] In another section of the poem, in book 8, the civil war of Antony and Octavian is, however, transformed into a clash between East and West, barbarians and Romans.[134] These two approaches to civil war are equally represented in the *Thebaid*. The perversion of kinship in the brothers' war is central to Statius' allusions to Roman civil wars, and especially to the 69 CE conflict. At the same time, Statius' poem is influenced by ideological attempts at presenting the civil war of 69 CE as a war against a foreign enemy, at styling Vitellius as a barbarian and presenting the Flavian victory as a triumph of reason against madness, order against chaos. This is one of the great advantages of Theban myth. It allows Statius to look at civil war through different ideological lenses within the same mythological context.

[133] For references to Roman civil wars, cf. e.g. Juno's reference to *socer* [father-in-law] and *gener* [son-in-law] at *A.* 7.317, with Horsfall (2000) 220. On these aspects see Hardie (1993) 22–6.
[134] *A.* 8.671–728.

1

Nero in the *Thebaid*

<hr>

IN THE SUMMER of 68 CE, abandoned by everyone, Nero fled the imperial palace and took refuge in the villa of one of his freedmen. Here, with the help of his secretary, Epaphroditus, he drove a sword through his throat.[1] The news of his death spread quickly. Reactions were not uniform. Senators and equestrians rejoiced, and the people ran through the streets of Rome wearing the *pilleus*, the cap of freedmen. But the lowest-status Romans were appalled by the loss of their beloved emperor and eager to believe any rumor. For some time after his death, the people kept bringing fresh flowers to Nero's tomb. Statues of him were raised in the Forum at night, and edicts written in his own name were produced, attesting that he would soon return. Stories circulated that he was still alive and hiding, ready to come back to defeat his enemies.[2]

And come back he did. The first of the "false Neros" appeared in Asia around 69 CE. He was a slave from Pontus (or a freedman from Italy) who resembled Nero and could sing like him, accompanied by the lyre. After persuading a few deserters and some legionaries from the Syrian army to declare for him, the impostor was eventually killed by an imperial delegation at the command of L. Nonius Calpurnius Asprenas. The second aspirant was a certain Terentius Maximus, a native of Asia. He claimed that he was the Emperor Nero, adding that he had survived the soldiers

<hr>

[1] Suet. *Nero* 48.3–49.4.
[2] Suet. *Nero* 57.1; Tac. *Hist.* 1.4. Champlin (2003a) 6–9.

sent to kill him in 68 CE and had been living in concealment ever since. Terentius Maximus gained the support of a few adherents, managed to cross into Parthia, and was received by Artabanus III, a rival for the crown of Parthia, who made preparations for restoring him to power in Rome. The last recorded aspirant appeared under Domitian, some 20 years after Nero's demise. We do not know his name, but we know that, pretending to be Nero, he too managed to enter Parthia, where he gained the support of the Parthian king. He was probably hunted down by the Syrian garrisons under P. Valerius Patruinus.[3]

The stories of the false Neros are particularly instructive, as they capture the ambivalent and contested nature of Nero's legacy. The Flavian dynasty sees the consolidation of a negative portrait of Nero, yet the false Neros demonstrate the Roman world's unending fascination with this *enfant prodige* and the long-lasting power of his memory. This ambivalence is of great importance for the cultural world of the *Thebaid*. In Domitianic ideology, the last Julio-Claudian is a negative model, the dreaded tyrant whose ghost makes Domitian shine in comparison. Yet he is also a powerful source of inspiration. In many ways, Domitian's cultural politics is a witness to the impossibility of renouncing Nero's innovations. In particular, Flavian negotiations of Neronian ideology, especially Domitian's own marking of continuity and discontinuity with Nero, are central to the *Thebaid*'s construction of its own political vision. More generally, both Domitian's self-representation and elite responses to this emperor's policy are influenced by the revival of political thinking and panegyric from the time of Nero. Reintroducing Nero into the ideological, poetical, and imaginative world of the *Thebaid* is therefore crucial.

In this chapter, I lay the foundations for my approach to the *Thebaid* by considering two interconnected phenomena. The first concerns Domitian's relationship with the elite, its gradual deterioration, and the consequences for both the historiography on this emperor and readings of Statius' *Thebaid*. The second pertains to two different aspects of the influence of Neronian culture on Flavian Rome: (a) the reception of panegyric modes and constructions of kingship from the time of Nero and (b) Domitian's ambiguous relationship with Nero's fashioning of his own imperial persona. These two phenomena are interconnected in various ways and cannot be dealt with separately. The reception of panegyric of Nero and of Neronian constructions of kingship in Domitianic Rome arises in connection with, and is, to an extent, stimulated by, Domitian's attitude toward the senatorial

---

[3] On the false Neros see Champlin (2003a) 10–12; Jones (1992) 157–9; Tuplin (1989). First false Nero: Tac. *Hist.* 2.8–9; Zonar. 11.15, cf. D.C. 64.9.3; Terentius Maximus: D.C. 66.19.3; Zonar. 11.18; John of Antioch fr. 104M; see Tuplin (1989) 372–7; third pretender: Suet. *Nero* 57.2; see Jones (1983); Tuplin (1989) 377–82; Jones (1992) 158–9.

elite. The demonization of Nero—what I will call anti-Neronian ideology—links Domitianic ideology with the cultural activities of certain aristocratic groups whom Domitian benefits at the beginning of his reign and with whom Statius is in contact. Domitian's demonization under the following imperial dynasty turns this emperor into a second Nero, thus engendering a new appraisal of the criticism of Nero encoded in Statius' narrative.

But let us proceed in order. I begin, in Section 1.1, by providing evidence for the reception of Neronian panegyric and Neronian constructions of kingship under Domitian. By surveying the panegyric poetry of Statius' time, I show that the Flavian world adapts certain ideals formulated by panegyrists and political thinkers active under Nero to praise of Domitian. Next, in Section 1.2, I look at Domitian's relationship with the elite. I start by discussing a neglected phase in Domitian's rapport with the senatorial class, showing that this emperor, who had family connections with victims of Nero, enacted a policy of leniency and trust toward families victimized by earlier emperors. I then suggest that it is possible to link the currency given to Senecan constructions of kingship—and to elements of Neronian panegyric—to elite responses to Domitian's attempt at inaugurating a new era in his relationship with the senate marked by *clementia*. Finally, I show that this initial alignment between the expectations of the senatorial class and the emperor's policy has been erased by the bias of later sources. Although it is possible to observe a gradual deterioration of Domitian's relationship with Rome's political elite, I argue that aristocratic responses to this princeps must have remained diverse until his assassination. Under the next imperial dynasty, however, Domitian was demonized, so that not only was his initial policy forgotten, but the sense of a gradual loss of popularity among Rome's upper classes was lost.

Recovering a sense of Domitian's shifting relationship with the elite and combining it with an awareness of Domitianic Rome's indebtedness to the political culture of Nero's Rome is central to the type of work I do on the *Thebaid*. It allows us to retrieve a number of responses to Statius' poem that the following dynasty's demonization of Domitian has obscured. Among other things, I aim to show that many of the ideals that we tend to associate with the opposition to Domitian were in fact part of the official ideology. This provides a different vantage point from which to look at Statius' depiction of the clash of tyranny and *libertas* [freedom] in his poem. I also aim to show that the ghost of Nero looms large within Statius' portrait of tyranny.

Finally, I argue that the best way to approach the political message of the *Thebaid* is to look at it from a didactic perspective. Statius' poem sketches a political ideal that is offered to Domitian as a model and a demanding standard by which to live. Most crucially, I aim to show that this didactic project consolidates at a specific moment within the trajectory of Domitian's relationship with the elite, at a time, that is, when perceptions of Domitian were diverse enough so that efforts at projecting Domitian as an enlightened sovereign could be seen as credible attempts at directing the emperor toward a certain policy rather than desperate flattery.

My reconstruction of this cultural and historical framework allows me to consider Statius' place within Domitianic culture from a new angle, exploring the overlap between the *Thebaid*'s political vision and the position and activity of certain aristocratic groups, such as the clan of the Annaeans, with whom Statius was in contact (Section 1.4). In addition, this reconstructed background allows me to tie the surfacing in the *Thebaid* of notions of kingship that become prominent under Nero, especially the Senecan ideal of the merciful king, to a specific cultural and political context. In particular, in the last section of this chapter (Section 1.8), I investigate the influence of Senecan constructions of kingship on the poem's finale and measure the *Thebaid*'s construction of Theseus as a ruler figure against the portrait of Domitian as an idealized king found in panegyric of Domitian.

The second thread of inquiry pertains more specifically to Domitian's relationship with Nero's policy and with Nero's construction of his imperial persona. In Section 1.3, I investigate the place of anti-Neronian ideology within Flavian culture. I show that the Flavian period contributed to consolidating a negative portrait of Nero as the quintessential imperial monster and that Domitianic ideology retained and propagated this view. Domitian's demonization of the last member of the Julio-Claudian dynasty paralleled Nero's own denigration of Claudius and the demonization of Domitian under Nerva and Trajan. Along the way, I also hope to clear up the somewhat common misconception that Domitianic Rome promoted an official rehabilitation of Nero and that Domitian showed himself sympathetic to the memory of this emperor. I then complicate this picture by drawing attention to what is, in my view, one of the most peculiar aspects of Domitianic culture. Under Domitian, official denigration of Nero is accompanied by the reception of some of the most peculiar aspects of Nero's self-representation, such as the preference for certain mythical characters and the use of solar symbolism.

This reconstruction of Domitian's ambiguous relationship with the legacy of the last Julio-Claudian affects my reading of the poem in several ways. In Chapters 2 and 3, I highlight a number of strategies deployed by Statius in order to navigate Domitian's dangerous recuperation of Neronian traits. But we do not have to wait for Chapter 2 to reap the fruits of my reconstruction. In Section 1.5 of this chapter, I read a crucial episode, the death of Maeon in book 3, against the background reconstructed in Sections 1.1–1.4 of this chapter. My aim is to show that a number of responses to this passage can be recovered by projecting the *Thebaid* against a context in which Domitian could credibly be characterized as an embodiment of the ideals of *libertas* and *clementia*. In this context, allusions to Nero contributed to styling the *Thebaid*'s treatment of tyranny as an indictment of the former tyrant(s) (Nero and his cronies). However, I also use this passage to point out that, in light of Domitian's progressive alienation of the favor of the upper classes and of this emperor's damnation under the following imperial dynasty, the text of the *Thebaid* soon became amenable to different readings.

Next, in Section 1.6, I lay the foundation for my second experiment in reading Nero back into the *Thebaid* by examining another cultural phenomenon that characterizes Flavian Rome's attitude to its Neronian past. I consider Nero's use of myth for the fashioning of his imperial self, and I document the role of Neronian literature in the creation of the Flavian vulgate on Nero. Through his intensive use of the theater as a means to project a certain version of his own imperial persona, Nero engendered a constant confusion between myth (as the subject matter of literature and drama) and reality. This in turn created the conditions for a certain ideological appropriation of Seneca's tragic production in the aftermath of Nero's death. This analysis allows me to uncover an important allusive dimension whereby Statius uses Neronian literature as a prism through which to look back to the time of Nero. In Section 1.7, I read Statius' engagement with Seneca's *Oedipus* in light of Nero's use of myth and in light of Flavian ideological appropriations of Senecan tragedy as a reflection on Nero's tyranny.

Considering these two threads of inquiry together (Domitian's rapport with the elite and the influence of Neronian culture on Domitianic Rome) has further important advantages. The demonization of Nero, which I document in Section 1.3, complements the portrait of the merciful king (itself by and large a creation of Neronian culture) that was applied to Domitian (see Section 1.1). Neronian culture also supplied conceptual models for articulating the transference of certain panegyric notions from one emperor to the other. In addition, the idea that Nero embodies the opposite of panegyric constructions of Domitian as a merciful king is paralleled by a certain ideological use of Senecan tragedy by Flavian authors, whereby Seneca's tragic heroes (Atreus, Oedipus, and Hercules) are regarded in some significant way as mirror opposites of the portrait of the enlightened king sketched in *De Clementia* and are exploited as stand-ins for Nero. This understanding of the two parts of Seneca's production (the tragedies and *De Clementia*) as two sides of the same coin is influential on the *Thebaid*.

This chapter, especially in the first sections, is heavy in historical materials, with the focus on Domitian and his culture rather than on Statius' poetry. I hope the reader will bear with me. This discussion paves the way for the following chapters, in which we shall look at the *Thebaid* more closely.

I.I   RENAISSANCE

The principate of Nero was marked by great hopes of a new beginning. His accession was accompanied by an emphasis on soteriological themes, the idea of a turning point in world history and of a principate marked by a return to orderliness and peace—a new Golden Age under the sign of an emperor who is identified with Apollo.[4] This atmosphere is reflected in the *Eclogues* of Calpurnius Siculus (especially 1 and 4). In the first poem, two herdsmen come upon a mysterious piece of writing inscribed on the trunk of a tree—a prophecy by the rustic deity Faunus. The text announces the dawning of a second Golden Age, marked by peace and the return of justice (personified as the goddess Themis). This new age is concomitant with the kingdom of a young man who, thanks to his *clementia*, will bring about the end of civil war and of all wars.[5] Similar notes are struck in the *Bucolica Einsidlensia* and are reflected in the praise of Nero at the beginning of Lucan's *Bellum Ciuile*.[6] Seneca's *Apocolyntosis* is another important document. This polemical pamphlet on the topic of Claudius' "pumpkinification" features a 32-line hexametric passage of prophetic tone. In this passage, the Fates spin the thread of Nero's life, assisted by Apollo; the thread turns spontaneously to gold and there is no end to it, indicating that Nero's life will be longer than that of any other mortal (4.3–19). Apollo admits that Nero resembles him in his looks and voice (4.20–2). The rule of Nero will break the silence of the laws, marking a return to regular procedure after Claudius' abuses and his reign of terror (4.23–4). Apollo goes on to compare Nero to the Morning Star, the Evening Star, and the Sun in his radiance and beauty (4.25–32).

These panegyric statements are complemented, and to an extent triggered, by a number of initiatives implemented by Nero himself. His initial discourse to the Senate, where he proposed to model his principate on that of Augustus, as well as his initial resolutions, raised high hopes for the beginning of a new season in the relationship with the Senate, marked by a return to *libertas* and a policy inspired by *clementia*.[7] Importantly, the recuperation of the messianic tone found in panegyric of Augustus is accompanied by the idea that Nero will surpass Augustus. For

---

[4] Convenient survey in Braund (2009) 11–16; see also Wiseman (1982). I discuss this topic again, from a different perspective, in Chapter 4, Section 4.1. After Augustus, ideas of renaissance and of the emperor as a providential figure are not exclusively found with reference to Nero's accession (cf. e.g. Seneca's praise of Claudius as savior in *Dial.* 11.13.1, 11.16.6). Nonetheless, praise of Nero in this early phase distinguishes itself for the amplification of traditional motifs from Augustan propaganda and for the introduction of some new and distinctive elements.

[5] *Eclogue* 4 of Calpurnius also celebrates the new Golden Age and the return of justice.

[6] For my view on the debated question of whether the praise is sincere see Chapter 4, Section 4.1 n. 20.

[7] Nero's accession speech: Tac. *Ann.* 13.4–5; early acts of *clementia*: Suet. *Nero* 10; Griffin (1984) 50–66, esp. 64–6 with reference to a policy inspired by *clementia*.

instance, Calpurnius Siculus implies that Nero will outdo even his most noble predecessor and will secure a time of peace that Augustus failed to fully realize.[8]

The other distinctive element of this initial phase of Nero's reign is the elaboration and advertisement of an imperial ideology centering on *clementia*. Nero delivered a speech on this topic to the Senate in 54 CE. The speech was written by Seneca, who also penned *De Clementia*, the most thorough attempt at making *clementia* the cardinal virtue for an emperor.[9] Seneca's treatise too sees the principate of Nero as the great turning point in imperial history. Nero outdoes his predecessors, especially in light of his ability to display *clementia*. Because of this virtue, he surpasses not only controversial figures such as Alexander, but even Augustus, who learned late how to use *clementia*.[10] *Clementia* consists in the ability to curtail punitive action:

> clementia est temperantia animi in potestate ulciscendi uel lenitas superioris aduersus inferiorem in constituendis poenis.
> *Cl.* 2.3.1

> Mercy consists in restraining one's mind when it has the power to exact revenge, or the leniency of a superior toward an inferior in establishing punishments.

Seneca's ideal ruler owes the stability of his kingdom to his merciful nature. Being reluctant to inflict punishment and ready to forgive, the new emperor bases his power on the love of his subjects rather than on their fear.[11] The emperor's new attitude means a return to *libertas*, which consists in a greater degree of freedom by the Senate and in the removal of the atmosphere of repression that characterized the principate of Claudius.[12]

Domitian's principate is accompanied by a recuperation of this enthusiastic atmosphere and an emphasis on the soteriological aspects of the new principate

---

[8] Calp. *Ecl.* 1.46–51, discussed in Chapter 4, Section 4.1.

[9] Nero's speech of 54 CE: Tac. *Ann.* 13.4–5. On Seneca's authorship see Tac. *Ann.* 13.11; Griffin (1984) 76. The importance of *clementia* as a political virtue is no invention of the Neronian principate; one barely needs to recall the famous (or infamous, according to Lucan) *clementia Caesaris* or the four virtues emblazoned on the shield awarded to Augustus by the Senate *uirtus, clementia, iustitia,* and *pietas*); there are also important precedents during the Republic. See the survey by Braund (2009) 30–44, esp. 33–8 for precedents in Roman history.

[10] Alexander: *Cl.* 1.25.1–1.26.4 with Braund (2009) 367–8. Outdoing of Augustus through *clementia*: *Cl.* 1.9.1, 1.6.1, and 1.11.1–3; Braund (2009) 61–4, 174, 260. Cf. passages from Calpurnius and the *Bucolica Einsidlensia* discussed in Chapter 4, Section 4.1.

[11] *Cl.* 1.1.3–4 (Nero's merciful behavior), 2.3.1–2.7.5 (definition of *clementia*), 1.3.3–4, and 1.11.4–1.13.5 (*clementia* grants security).

[12] Cf. passages from Calpurnius and the *Bucolica Einsidlensia* discussed in Chapter 4, Section 4.1. For *libertas* under Nero and its definition see Sen. *Cl.* 1.1.8, with Braund (2009) 181; *Apoc.* 1.1, 12.2. On post-Augustan notions of *libertas* under the emperor see Wirszubski (1968) 124–67.

that connects directly and in manifold ways to the early years of Nero.[13] The so-
teriological themes of Virgil's and Calpurnius' *Eclogues* are resurrected by Martial
and Statius, who keep insisting on the topic long after Domitian's accession. The
anticipated birth of an heir to Domitian gives Martial the opportunity to predict a
new Golden Age:

> nascere Dardanio promissum nomen Iulo,
> uera deum suboles; nascere, magne puer:
> cui pater aeternas post saecula tradat habenas,
> quique regas orbem cum seniore senex.
> ipsa tibi niueo trahet aurea pollice fila
> et totam Phrixi Iulia nebit ouem.
> Mart. 6.3

Be born, name promised to Dardanian Iulus, true offspring of the gods; be
born, great boy, so that after centuries your father may entrust to you the
eternal reins, and you may rule the world as an old man with your older father.
Julia herself will draw for you golden threads with her white finger and spin the
whole ram of Phrixus.

The image of Julia (Domitian's deceased niece) spinning the golden thread of the
new child's life adapts the picture of Seneca's *Apocolocyntosis*. This poem is also in-
debted to Calpurnius' *Eclogues* and their Virgilian models.[14] Statius too brings back
the tone and imagery of Seneca's *Apocolocyntosis* and applies it to Domitian:

> sed mihi non epulas Indisque innixa columnis
> robora Maurorum famulasque ex ordine turmas,
> ipsum, ipsum cupido tantum spectare uacauit
> tranquillum uultu sed maiestate serena
> mulcentem radios submittentemque modeste
> fortunae uexilla suae;
> *Silv.* 4.2.38–43

Not on the banquets, not on the Moorish wood resting on Indian columns,
not on the ordered troops of servants; on him, on him only had I leisure to fix

---

[13] On the reception of panegyric themes from the time of Nero cf. Nauta (2010) 253–65, who downplays the
presence of shared motifs.

[14] Grewing (1997) 84–92; Nauta (2010) 257; Sen. *Apoc.* 4.1.7–11; Calp. *Ecl.* 4.137–40.

my eager gaze, calm in his countenance, softening his radiance with serene maj-
esty, modestly lowering the banner of his fortune;

The image of Domitian who softens his radiant splendor reworks a compliment
made by Seneca to Nero in the *Apocolocyntosis*.[15] The *Thebaid*'s proem recalls di-
rectly the praise of Nero at the beginning of Lucan's *Bellum Ciuile*.[16] The idea that
Domitian will outdo all of his predecessors is well represented in the *Siluae*. In *Siluae*
4.3, for instance, the Sybil proclaims that no earlier recipient of imperial power was
worthier than Domitian.[17] In *Siluae* 4.1, Domitian is celebrated as a solar sovereign.
He is the initiator of a new era of peace, marked by the return of law. And he is su-
perior to Augustus.[18]

Domitian's advantage over former rulers is often articulated in the terms proposed
by Neronian intellectuals, with a visible influence of Seneca's *De Clementia*. An ex-
traordinary document of this revival of Neronian ideology is *Siluae* 1.1. Statius'
poem celebrates the erection of Domitian's equestrian statue on the occasion of the
emperor's return from his campaigns to the Rhine and Danube.[19] In spite of the
military subject of the statue, Statius emphasizes the visible kindness in Domitian's
facial expression. He is *mitis* [gentle], a keyword in Seneca's portrait of the ideal
sovereign:[20]

... hunc mitis commendat eques: iuuat ora tueri
mixta notis, bellum placidamque gerentia pacem.
Silv. 1.1.15–16

... this horse is commended by his gentle rider: it is pleasing to contemplate his
face, where marks are mingled; war it bears and gentle peace.

---

[15] Sen. *Apoc.* 4.1.31–2; Nauta (2010) 258–9.

[16] On the relationship between the two proems see Chapter 4, Section 4.3; Chapter 2, Section 2.2.

[17] *Silv.* 4.3.127–32. The Sybil's speech in this passage looks back at Anchises' prophecy that Augustus will be the culmination of the Julian *gens* in *Aeneid* 6. In that episode the Sybil accompanied Aeneas to meet his father in the underworld: *A.* 6.791–805; see Coleman (1988) 131. When the prophetess announces in Statius' poem that, from the time of Aeneas, no one is worthier than Domitian to hold the reins of empire, she implicitly states that Domitian is superior to Augustus and that his principate will be the final fulfillment of a long series of frustrated promises. Cf. Mart. 5.19.1–2.

[18] Solar sovereign: *Silv.* 4.1.1–4; see Chapter 2, Sections 2.1–3. Return of peace and the rule of law: *Silv.* 4.1.13–5; outdoing of Augustus: *Silv.* 4.1.28–33.

[19] Domitian was back in Rome by the end of year 89 CE (D.C. 67.7.1–3). The statue must have been dedicated in 90 or 91 CE. On Domitian's equestrian statue see Coarelli (2009b) 81–3; Hannestad (1986) 139–42.

[20] Cf. Sen. *Cl.* 1.9.1; Sen. *Dial.* 11.16.6, 11.6.5, 11.17.4.

Statius also highlights Domitian's difference from Caesar. The occasion for the comparison is offered by the statue's proximity to the Temple of Divus Iulius:[21]

> ... discit et e uultu quantum tu mitior armis,
> qui nec in externos facilis saeuire furores
> das Cattis Dacisque fidem ...
> *Silv.* 1.1.25–7

> ... from your countenance he learns how much gentler in arms you are: slow at raging even against the madness of foreigners, you give quarter to Cattians and Dacians ...

Caesar stained his hands with his countrymen's blood.[22] Domitian, on the contrary, is merciful even to external enemies.[23] His main characteristic is, again, that of being slow to anger (*nec ... facilis saeuire, Silv.* 1.1.26). This type of praise echoes themes of Seneca's *De Clementia*. Here, Nero is commended for his clement nature, according to which he is not inclined to shed blood:[24]

> praestitisti, Caesar, ciuitatem incruentam, et hoc, quod magno animo gloriatus es nullam te toto orbe stillam cruoris humani misisse, eo maius est mirabiliusque, quod nulli umquam citius gladius conmissus est.
> *Cl.* 1.11.3

> You provided, Caesar, a state unstained by blood. Your proud boast, that you did not spill a single drop of human blood in all the world, is greater and more admirable because the sword was never entrusted to anyone at an earlier age.

In *De Clementia*, a ruler such as Alexander is unlikely to remain in power for long or entrust his kingdom safely to a successor.[25] Statius notes that Alexander's equestrian statue has been turned into a portrait of Caesar (*Silv.* 1.1.85–91), a powerful

---

[21] Cf. also *Silv.* 1.1.85–91.

[22] Criticism of Caesar is found repeatedly in Seneca's prose works and was a well-established theme of the traditional Roman *declamatio* of imperial times. See Morford (1967) 13–19.

[23] Statius' remark on the emperor's mildness is read as implicit mockery, alluding to Domitian's limited military ability, by Ahl (1984) 93.

[24] Cf. also *Cl.* 1.21.3.

[25] Criticism of Alexander: *Cl.* 1.25.1. Instability of such a ruler: Sen. *Cl.* 1.25.3, 1.11.4; cf. Lucan's hostile presentation of Caesar's fascination with Alexander and how he shows Caesar rushing to go and gaze at the body of Alexander (Luc. 10.14–19), whom Lucan describes as *proles uesana Philippi* [mad offspring of Philip], and *felix praedo* [lucky bandit] (Luc. 10.20–1; cf. also 10.42).

symbol of the ephemerality of power.[26] Domitian's horse, on the contrary, will remain his eternally and never change its rider (*Silv.* 1.1.52–5).[27]

The influence of *De Clementia* is visible in another poem of the *Siluae*. In *Siluae* 1.4, a thanksgiving for the recovery of Rutilius Gallicus (the prefect of the city), the dedicatee is seen as replicating the virtues of Domitian at a lower institutional level.[28] A passage in praise of Gallicus has been aptly described by Federica Bessone as a summary of *De Clementia*:[29]

> quae tibi sollicitus persoluit praemia morum
> urbis amor! quae tum patrumque equitumque notaui
> lumina et ignarae plebis lugere potentes!
> non labente Numa timuit sic curia felix
> Pompeio nec celsus eques nec femina Bruto.
> hoc illud, tristes inuitum audire catenas,
> parcere uerberibus nec qua iubet alta potestas
> ire, sed armatas multum sibi demere uires
> dignarique manus humiles et uerba precantum,
> reddere iura foro nec proturbare curules
> et ferrum mulcere toga. sic itur in alta
> pectora, sic mixto reuerentia fidit amori.
> *Silv.* 1.4.38–49

What reward of virtue did Rome's anxious affection pay you! How sad the eyes of Senate and Knights I then noted, and those of the common folk unable to mourn the powerful! Not so afraid was the flourishing Senate House when Numa was failing, nor the noble Knights for Pompey, nor the women for Brutus. And here is why: to hear unwilling the clank of chains, to spare the lash and to refuse to go where the height of power commands, but rather to renounce much of one's own armed might and pay heed to humble pleas and the words of petitioners, to give justice to the Forum and yet not push aside the civil authorities, and to temper violence with the gown—that is the way to go deep into hearts. Thus does reverence rely on the love with which it is combined.

---

[26] Newlands (2002) 66. She rightly remarks on the admonitory function of the comparison.

[27] More on this passage in Chapter 2, Section 2.4.

[28] See Rühl (2006) 347–51; Nauta (2008) 151–3.

[29] Bessone (2011) 42. On Rutilius Gallicus' career see Nauta (2002) 206–10.

The modern reader might wonder about this paraded reception of Neronian motifs, especially in light of Nero's patent inability to live up to these standards. Yet Neronian ideology itself offered a way to accommodate these ideas and praise the new princeps in a way that did not imply Domitian's equation with Nero. Neronian reception of Augustan panegyric is constantly accompanied by the idea that Nero will finally fulfill the promises frustrated by Augustus' principate. This assumption underlies the Flavian reception of Neronian praise. The implication is that Domitian will finally introduce the Golden Age that Nero and Augustus failed to bring about. As we will see more clearly in Chapters 2–4, this understanding of Domitian's relationship to his imperial predecessors is key to Statius' framing of his own responses to Domitian's continuity with Nero. In addition, as we will see more clearly in Section 1.3, the praise of Domitian as the one who fulfills the soteriological expectations of peace and the political expectations for a return of *libertas* is supported through a stigmatization of Nero as the epitome of the tyrannical emperor, precisely as the praise of Nero in Neronian texts is accompanied by the transformation of Claudius into an imperial monster.

1.2 FROM *CLEMENTIA* TO *SAEVITIA*: DOMITIAN AND THE ELITE

This reception of Neronian panegyric and Neronian constructions of kingship can be tied to a certain political direction that Domitian applied to his relationship with the Senate. Domitian implemented a policy that recalled Nero's early overtures to the Senate in 54 CE. By means of this policy, he distanced himself from his father and brother and sought to start a new phase in the relationship with the senatorial class.[30]

Vespasian's relationship with the senatorial elite was marred by the capital punishment of Helvidius Priscus, a blunt supporter of the old prerogatives of the Senate, whose execution may have been carried out at the instigation of Titus.[31] Domitian

---

[30] On Domitian and the elite, Jones (1992) remains fundamental. Jones (1992) is the most thorough attempt at reaching a balanced view of this emperor that moves beyond the biased portrait provided by post-Domitianic writers. Southern (1997), on the contrary, does not question the traditional portrait of Domitian as a tyrant. Much of interest is to be found in Waters (1964), a revisionist appraisal of the last Flavian emperor; see also Waters (1969) for continuity between Domitian and Trajan. For Domitian and the senate, Pleket (1961) is still of value, despite some limitations. Sablayrolles (1994) reevaluates Domitian by highlighting similarities between Domitian and Augustus, with evidence drawn especially from Domitian's building program. Domitian's ability as an administrator, especially with regard to the provinces, is the only aspect of this emperor's governance to have found some degree of scholarly appreciation, yet even in this area there is no consensus: see Syme (1930); Pleket (1961); for a more skeptical view see Levick (1982).

[31] On Vespasian and his opponents, including Helvidius Priscus (*PIR*² H 59), see Levick (1999) 79–94, with relevant sources. Titus' initiative: Levick (1999) 192.

began his reign with emphatic attempts at reconciliation, directed especially toward senatorial families who had suffered under previous emperors. Early in his reign, Domitian promoted Helvidius Priscus' son to the consulship, a remarkable choice in light of his father's fate as well as the family connections of his stepmother Fannia, daughter of Thrasea Paetus.[32] In 85 CE, the younger Helvidius' son-in-law, M. Annius Herennius Pollio, was made consul. Salvidienus Orfitus, whose father had been a victim of Nero, was awarded a suffect consulship at about the same time.[33] In 87 and 88 CE, two descendants of a prestigious republican family decimated by Claudius, Nero, and Mucianus (the Licinii Crassi–Calpurnii Pisones) were elevated to the consulship.[34] Domitian retained this attitude even after the revolt of Saturninus in 89 CE, wrongly assumed to herald the beginning of a "reign of terror."[35] In 92 CE, he granted a consulship to Arulenus Rusticus, the author of a book in praise of Thrasea Paetus, and he may have also awarded a consulship to Arulenus' brother, Junius Mauricus.[36] Domitian had personal connections with the victims of Nero: Domitian's wife, Domitia Longina, was the daughter of Domitius Corbulo, who had been executed by Nero.[37] His marriage to her secured him the friendship and loyalty of Corbulo's personal friends and relatives.[38] As late as 93 CE, yet another friend of Thrasea, T. Avidius Quietus, became consul.[39] Until 93 CE, the closest connections of the "martyrs of Nero" and the most virulently anti-Neronian intellectuals of the time were actively supported by Domitian.

As Jones rightly points out, before 93 CE, Domitian's attitude to the connections of former antagonists was not only opposite to that of Nero's late years, it was more

---

[32] The younger Helvidius: *PIR²* H 60; Jones (1992) 187. Pliny the Younger (*Ep.* 9.13.2–3) talks of the younger Helvidius as living in retirement out of fear under Domitian. Jones (1992) 168 notes that this is a strange way of referring to a man who had been made consul by Domitian, perhaps an attempt at excusing the senator's early collaboration with the regime. Helvidius' "retirement" can refer to only the late years of Domitian, for Pliny is well aware of Helvidius' consular rank, attained under Domitian (*Ep.* 9.13.2).

[33] M. Annius Herennius Pollio: *PIR²* H 119; Jones (1992) 168, 234 n. 30. Ser. Cornelius Scipio Salvidienus Orfitus: *PIR²* C 1445; Jones (1992) 168; Salvidienus' father: *PIR²* C 1444.

[34] C. Calpurnius Piso Frugi Licinianus (*PIR²* C 259) was consul in 87 CE, his brother Libo Frugi in 88 CE (*PIR²* L 166).

[35] Jones (1992) 168–9.

[36] Q. Junius Arulenus Rusticus: *PIR²* I 730; as tribune in 66 CE, he had intended to veto the senate's condemnation of Thrasea, but the latter forbade him to do so (Tac. *Ann.* 16.26.4–5); Junius Mauricus: *PIR²* I 771; Jones (1992) 169, 31; (1973) 89–90. On the names, families, and geographic provenance of these two brothers see Syme (1991) 580–4.

[37] D.C. 66.3.4; Suet. *Dom.* 1.3. Corbulo: *PIR²* D 142. On Domitia Longina see Jones (1992) 33–8.

[38] Jones (1992) 168; (1973) 86–8; Levick (1999) 191.

[39] T. Avidius Quietus (*PIR²* A 1410) was a friend of Thrasea Paetus, Arria, and Fannia (Plin. *Ep.* 6.29.1, 9.13.15–6). See Jones (1992) 169, 234 n. 32 (Jones notes that the date of Quietus' consulship was not known to the author of the *PIR²* entry, who wrongly assumed it to be in 97 CE).

lenient than that of his father.[40] Domitian was clearly seeking to pass the message to the senatorial elite that a new season was beginning. The impression of Domitian's early reign must have been remarkable, and it has been obscured by the bad press he received after his death. What was Domitian's intent? First, the new emperor was trying to present himself as a restorer of *libertas* (conceived not as a return to the Republic, but rather as freedom of speech, security from oppression, and respect for the senatorial tradition).[41] The other key word is *clementia*.

In *De Clementia*, Seneca praises Augustus for pardoning and granting offices to those who had previously plotted against him. This attitude, the true hallmark of a merciful sovereign, is what the philosopher recommends to gain and retain the favor of the upper classes.[42] The evidence collected in this section shows Domitian actively pursuing this policy until late in his reign. As we saw in Section 1.1, that Domitian could be portrayed as an embodiment of Seneca's idealized sovereign did not escape the attention of panegyric poets of the time. These panegyric statements were, at least partly, triggered by the emperor's own initiatives.

The picture of Domitian as the terror of the aristocracy that we receive from later historians is certainly exaggerated. Suetonius has left us a list of 10 consular victims, among "numerous senators."[43] Emphatic statements such as the one found in one of Pliny the Younger's letters, in which a senator protests "let us, the survivors [of Domitian], be safe," can hardly be taken to support the notion of a vast number of senatorial victims: The context in which they emerge is simply too biased.[44] It is perhaps worth remembering that in his shorter tenure, Claudius executed about 35 senators and more than 200 equestrians, and the Senate voted for his deification anyway. Chronology is important. Although not all executions of consulars can be dated, the majority of them, and certainly the most spectacular, fell in the last part of Domitian's reign.[45] Dio mentions executions and banishments of members of the

---

[40] Miriam Griffin plays down the impact of Domitian's granting of consulships to survivors of Nero [Griffin (2000) 66–7]: The early appointment of the younger Helvidius she explains as "part of the customary moves by a new emperor to gain support." However, nothing similar is attested for Vespasian or Titus: See Jones (1992) 169. As for the appointment of friends of Thrasea in the 90s, she connects it to Domitian's reaction to Saturninus' revolt. In her view, the latter had made Domitian fear that the events of 68–69 CE would repeat themselves. By appointing enemies of Nero, Domitian was trying to emphasize his difference from Nero and retain favor. Yet it is difficult to see how the favor of prestigious Rome-based senators would have shielded Domitian from threats such as those posed by Saturninus, a low-born legate who capitalized on the restlessness of the army and whose interests had very little in common with those of Domitian's senatorial appointees.

[41] On this notion of *libertas*, which emerges especially in post-Augustan reflections on the role of the senatorial elite under the emperor, see Wirszubski (1968) 158–71.

[42] Cf. Sen. *Cl.* 1.9.2–12.

[43] Suet. *Dom.* 10.2; two more consulars can be added to Suetonius' list; see Jones (1992) 182–8.

[44] Plin. *Ep.* 9.13.8. *Contra* Griffin (2000) 68.

[45] On Domitian's senatorial executions and their chronology see Jones (1992) 182–8.

Roman elite not long after Domitian's accession, but he is not able to provide any names (D.C. 67.3.3).[46] Tacitus' generic comment that Domitian's cruelty lasted for 15 years serves the purposes of his *Agricola* but is backed by no internal evidence; when Tacitus turns to his emphatic recollection of Domitian's senatorial victims, he focuses on the executions of 93 CE and admits that Domitian's cruelty before this final season was sporadic.[47] Suetonius has no sympathy for Domitian, and yet he is prepared to acknowledge that the beginning of Domitian's reign was marked by *clementia*. He turned to *saeuitia* [cruelty] only of late, after Saturninus' revolt (89 CE).[48]

Domitian's lenient attitude toward the senatorial elite—especially the connections of victims of earlier emperors—was abandoned in 93 CE, under circumstances that are far from clear.[49] This year sees the execution of the younger Helvidius, Arulenus Rusticus, and Herennius Senecio; the exile of Arulenus' brother (Junius Mauricus) and wife (Gratilla) together with Arria and Fannia (mother and daughter, wives of Thrasea Paetus and Helvidius Priscus, respectively).[50] Arulenus Rusticus was executed for "publishing eulogies of Thrasea Paetus and Helvidius Priscus" and for calling them "the most upright of men" (Suet. *Dom.* 10.3) and for engaging in philosophy (D.C. 67.13; see also Plin. *Ep.* 1.5.2, 3.11). Suetonius is probably wrong: Tacitus (*Ag.* 2.1), Pliny (*Ep.* 7.19.5), and Dio (67.13.2) attribute the composition of eulogies for Helvidius Priscus to Herennius Senecio. The younger Helvidius was charged with having attacked Domitian's divorce from his wife in a theatrical piece on Paris and Oenone.[51] The eulogy of Thrasea alone was hardly sufficient motivation for execution. Praise of Thrasea was acceptable under an emperor who presented himself as a friend of the aristocracy and a restorer of *libertas*: Otherwise Martial's praise of Decianus for being a follower of Thrasea and Cato would be tantamount to a public accusation of treason.[52] Even the memory of Helvidius Priscus, an opponent

---

[46] For similar generic statements without names see also D.C. 67.3.3–4 (83 CE), 67.4.5 (85 CE), 12.2–3 (91/2 CE), 13.3 (93 CE), 14.2 (95 CE); for similar vague charges cf. also Orosius 7.10.2; Eutropius 7.23.2, with Jones' (1992) 182 skeptical remarks.

[47] Fifteen years of cruelty: Tac. *Ag.* 3.2. Sporadic cruelty before 93 CE: *Ag.* 44.5. Recollection of Domitian's consular victims of 93 CE: Tac. *Ag.* 45.1–2.

[48] Suet. *Dom.* 10.1, 10.5; cf. also *Dom.* 3.2. The same trajectory is attested by Eutropius, who sees Domitian as moderate at the beginning of his reign but turning to *saeuitia* later on, on his assumption of the title *dominus et deus* (see Eutropius 7.23). See Jones (1992) 119–20.

[49] On this important turning point and on the last 3 years of Domitian's rule Syme (1988) is of great value. For a revisionist approach to Domitian's terror see Waters (1964) 68–77.

[50] Consular victims of Domitian: Jones (1992) 182–8. Exiles: Plin. *Ep.* 7.19.6; Jones (1992) 188–92. See also Waters (1964) 71–7.

[51] Suet. *Dom.* 10.4; cf. also Plin. *Ep.* 3.11 and Tac. *Ag.* 45.1. The younger Helvidius: *PIR²* H 60 (his *cognomen* is not attested).

[52] Mart. 1.8. In this poem, Martial implies that it is possible to follow the precepts of these great stoic heroes (as Decianus does) without necessarily risking one's life. Stoicism and even the admiration of stoic martyrs are not

of Vespasian, may not have been compromising, given Domitian's rehabilitation of
the family through appointment of his son. In addition, the biographies (of Thrasea
and Helvidius Priscus) and the theatrical piece might have been published years be-
fore the condemnation. This seems like the kind of element a prosecutor would pro-
duce to support his case rather than the actual motivation for the indictment. The
situation is probably far more complex than depicted in our sources.[53]

This series of executions is sometimes referred to as Domitian's repression of the
"stoic opposition," a label that is deceptive in more than one way. An interest in
stoic philosophy is attested only for Arulenus Rusticus, and only in his case are we
told that practicing philosophy was one of the motivations for his indictment.[54]
Writing to eulogize the victim of a former emperor (e.g. Herennius Senecio's eu-
logy of Helvidius Priscus) does not necessarily imply a profession of philosophical
ideals. More confusing is the use of the term "opposition," insofar as it posits a group
that is at first "tolerated" and then finally annihilated by Domitian as his autocratic
tendencies emerge.[55] This scenario fails to appreciate Domitian's revolutionary

---

problematic per se. They can, however, become an element of risk in connection with other factors (such as
conspiracy activities).

[53] See Jones (1992) 122–3. Syme rightly dismisses the alleged accusations as pretexts and sees the downfall of this
clan as brought about by rivalries and old feuds with other senatorial groups. He suggests that the imperial
favor received by the younger Helvidius, Herennius Senecio, and Arulenus Rusticus (and their associates)
might have made them too arrogant, exacerbating rivals: In 93 CE, Herennius Senecio had successfully
brought down another senator, Baebius Massa, who demanded that Senecio be indicted for high treason in
return; Plin. *Ep.* 7.33.7; Syme (1991) 575–7, (1988) 254–6. According to Pleket (1961) 298, endorsed by Waters
(1964) 73, the real motivation was the existence of a conspiracy against Domitian; both scholars, however, rely
on Rogers (1960) and are influenced by the idea that Helvidius and the other victims belonged to the "stoic
opposition," conceived of as a subversive party active from the inception of Domitian's reign.

[54] D.C. 67.13; Plin. *Ep.* 1.5.2.

[55] Such a view is represented in MacMullen's influential book [MacMullen (1966) 46–94] and is retained in
some modern contributions [e.g. Haaland (2005) 302–5; a more balanced view can be found in Sherwin-
White (1966) 95, 242–3, and Penwill (2003) especially 360 n. 51]. MacMullen stresses the continuity between
the earlier generation of victims of Nero (Thrasea Paetus especially) and Domitian's victims of 93 CE and links
their demise to their profession of philosophical ideals and allegiance to anti-imperial ideology [see especially
MacMullen (1966) 54–6, 67]. MacMullen (1966, 46–94) discusses our three senators (the younger Helvidius,
Herennius Senecio, and Arulenus Rusticus) in a chapter titled "Philosophers," alongside Greek philosophers
such as Epictetus and the Roman Thrasea Paetus, whose devotion to philosophical ideals is much better
documented than that of our three senators. Syme's reconstruction seems more convincing: Although phil-
osophical interests might have been a defining character for some of these individuals, this group of senators
was not unlike other Roman clans, a faction held together by family and possibly geographic ties intent on
advancing the interests and position of its own associates: Syme (1991). The senatorial executions of 93 CE
occurred in the same year as Domitian's expulsion of philosophers, to which the senatorial executions are
variously connected in our sources (cf. D.C. 67.13; Plin. *Ep.* 3.11; Suet. *Dom.* 10.3). This has contributed to the
ranking of the three senators with the philosophers in a scenario in which the executions and the expulsion
are seen as two sides of the same coin. The link between the two provisions might be an invention of post-
Domitianic sources; alternatively, the expulsion of philosophers might have been proposed to corroborate the

attitude toward these individuals in his first decade or so of reign and the impression this must have made on contemporary viewers. People such as the younger Helvidius and Arulenus Rusticus had not been opponents of Domitian; Domitian had actively supported them until that point. Such a reconstruction also fails to see that Domitian had made the pro-*libertas* ideas of some of these individuals, and their anti-Neronian positions, a crucial tenet of his own imperial ideology (see Section 1.3).

The executions of 93 CE must have had an impact on Domitian's relationship with the elite. It is reasonable to assume growing dissent in a scenario in which perceptions of Domitian are still fluid. Toward the end, Domitian's imperial career ended up resembling that of Nero more closely.[56] His repression of the friends and relatives of victims of Nero aligned him with the emperor who put Seneca and Lucan to death.[57] Domitian thus compromised his relationship with the elite, and specifically with those senators who linked themselves to martyrs of earlier emperors, by doing something that made him literally step into the role of their archenemy Nero.

After Domitian's murder, the history of his kingdom was substantially rewritten. Domitian is subject to memory sanctions of an unprecedented kind and extent: His physical presence through monuments and inscriptions is erased from the cityscape of Rome under compulsion of an official edict.[58] The new regime sought legitimation by denigrating the former emperor. Courtiers, poets, and intellectuals active under Nerva and Trajan resorted to the same denigratory strategies employed by the Flavians with reference to the memory of Nero. The traits of the tyrannical portrait of Nero created by the Flavians are transferred to Domitian, who grows into a second Nero. In parallel, the ideals of *libertas* and *clementia*, which both Nero and Domitian had made integral to their self-advertisement, are transferred to Nerva and Trajan. This time, they are validated by presenting the old emperor (Domitian) as the polar opposite of the ideals announced by the new regime.[59]

"official" motivation for the indictment (Syme 1991, 576). I hope to be able to return to this intricate question in a future publication.

[56] Syme (1991) 577: "Two years passed after Thrasea's end and Nero joined the sequence of his victims which had extended to take in army commanders. Domitian in the comparable epoch was far from having alienated the whole body of educated opinion in the upper order . . . Nevertheless, the resemblance to Nero grew even more sharp and visible, in the process to multiply its manifestations."

[57] The parallel between Domitian and Nero on account of the executions in the last part of Domitian's reign is noted by Tacitus, according to whom Domitian was even worse than Nero: Tac. *Ag.* 45.1–2.

[58] Official sanctions by the Senate targeting Domitian's memory are recorded by Suet. *Dom.* 23.1 (cf. also D.C. 68.1). For the extent of Domitian's *damnatio* and its trace on the material and epigraphic record see Flower (2005) 234–62.

[59] On the appropriation of denigration strategies by the new establishment, especially as reflected in Pliny's *Panegyricus*, see Flower (2005) 262–5.

In this context, intellectuals such as Pliny the Younger sought to link themselves to the renovation by rewriting the past—their own past, among other things. Pliny the Younger had been a close collaborator of Domitian, to whom he owed his speedy career as imperial administrator.[60] In the *Panegyricus* and in the letters, Pliny passes his own official appointments under Domitian in silence and presents himself as a close ally and advocate of Domitian's victims.[61] His thanksgiving speech to Trajan (*Panegyricus*) should not be understood as pure praise or flattery: While strengthening his own position within the Trajanic establishment, Pliny also seeks to constrain Trajan to remain faithful to his beginnings and his commitment to *libertas*.[62] In the process, the sense of a gradual deterioration of Domitian's relationship with the elite is lost. The memories of an initial phase of collaboration between Domitian and the elite are obscured: As we have seen, in the emphatic statements of the reigns of Nerva and Trajan, Domitian's tenure has turned into 15 years of terror, and close collaborators of Domitian such as Pliny the Younger can style themselves as having lived under a cloud while the tyrant was alive.[63]

This context is of critical importance for the reception of the *Thebaid*. Statius' major poem was completed and published before the senatorial executions of 93 CE.[64] This means that there were no "stoic martyrs" of Domitian until after the *Thebaid* was published. The *Thebaid*'s ideation, composition, and first recitations coincided with a period of relative peace between Domitian and the elite, at a time when Domitian sought to be perceived as a restorer of *libertas* and an embodiment of *clementia*. In this phase, praise of *libertas* is part of the official ideology, not a label of the opposition. We have to make the effort of reading the *Thebaid* against a context in which what some educated Romans said of Domitian was not terribly different from what Pliny says of Trajan in his *Panegyricus*. Or, better, we should place the *Thebaid* at a time when, in light of the emperor's conciliatory policy, it seemed reasonable to try and direct Domitian toward the same libertarian ideals toward which Pliny the Younger seeks to direct Trajan in his *Panegyricus*.

---

[60] On Pliny's career see Syme (1958) 75–85; Sherwin-White (1966) 72–82.

[61] Pliny's silence on his career under Domitian: Flower (2005) 264–8. On Pliny's self-styling as a friend of Domitian's victims (Arria, Fannia, Helvidius the Younger, Arulenus Rusticus, Herennius Senecio) see Plin. *Ep.* 1.5, 3.11, 3.16, 7.19, 7.33, 9.13; Sherwin-White (1966) 303–4; Flower (2005) 267.

[62] Flower (2005) 264; Molin (1989) 792–7; Braund (1998) 58–68, esp. 62, 66.

[63] Pliny's supposed dangers under Domitian: Plin. *Ep.* 1.5, 3.11, 7.14, 7.27.14, 4.24 (cf. also 7.33.7–8); *Pan.* 90.5, 95.3–5.

[64] On the date of the *Thebaid* see Coleman (1988) xvi–xvii; Introduction, Section I.4.

1.3 NERO AND DOMITIAN

In Section 1.1 I looked at the importance of Neronian panegyric and political thinking as a source for Flavian constructions of Domitian as an ideal princeps. I now turn to the second crucial aspect of the influence of Neronian culture on Domitianic Rome. This pertains to the official view of Nero under Flavian rule and to Domitian's ambiguous relationship with the language of Neronian ideology.

In reviewing the role of Nero under Domitian, it is necessary to clear up a somewhat common misconception: the idea that Domitian intentionally styled himself as a second Nero. This notion originates in the remarks of post-Domitianic writers, who compare Domitian to Nero in order to censure Domitian. Juvenal famously made Domitian a *caluus Nero* [a bald Nero], and Pliny the Younger refers to him as *simillimus* [most similar] to Nero.[65] Similarities between the two are visible in post-Domitianic literature even when the comparison between the two emperors is not explicitly made.[66] These statements have sometimes been taken as evidence of Domitian's sympathy for the memory of the last Julio-Claudian.[67] An investigation of Flavian attitudes toward Nero will prove that this was not the case. At the same time, we will encounter one of the most complicated aspects of Domitianic culture: its reception of elements of Neronian ideology alongside a formal rejection of Nero.[68]

Attitudes toward Nero shifted considerably after his death. Galba presented himself as the anti-Nero; he put an end to Nero's extravagant public largesses and executed several of his collaborators.[69] But Otho and Vitellius sought to profit from the enduring popularity of the last Julio-Claudian. Otho, the former husband of Nero's second wife, Poppaea Sabina, had been a partner in the dissolute life of the emperor and an accomplice in the murder of Agrippina. He was believed to physically resemble Nero. The soldiers and people hailed him as Nero Otho, a title he also adopted to sign official dispatches and letters. He restored statues of Poppaea and

---

[65] Juv. 4.37–8; Plin. *Pan.* 53.3–4; Nauta (2010) 242–3. Another passage often quoted in this context is Mart. 11.33. Whether this poem refers to Domitian through the name Nero is, however, debated: See Nauta (2010) 243–4; Schubert (1998) 302–3; Kay (1985) 144–5.

[66] See, for instance, Suetonius' description of both Nero's and Domitian's physical appearances: Suet. *Nero* 51; *Dom.* 18.1.

[67] Thus, for instance, Courtney (1980) 208: "Domitian . . . was sympathetic to Nero's memory"; Braund (1996b) 244: "He [Domitian] associated his imperial identity with Nero's."

[68] On views of Nero under the Flavians see Schubert (1998) 254–337; Degl'Innocenti Pierini (2007); I am particularly indebted to Nauta (2010). For a comparative approach to the two emperors see the papers in Bönisch-Meyer et al. (2014).

[69] Plu. *Galb.* 16–17; Suet. *Gal.* 10.1. See also Galba's exploitation of tyrannicide rhetoric in his uprising in 68 CE and his self-styling as restorer of freedom after Nero's tyranny: Gallia (2012) 12–28.

allowed private citizens to display busts and statues of Nero. He also reinstated the Neronian collaborators who had lost their offices under Galba and channeled substantial funds to the completion of Nero's Golden House. Otho contemplated marrying Nero's last wife, Statilia Messalina, and took Sporus, the slave youth Nero had castrated and "married" after the death of Poppaea, into his house.[70] Vitellius too had been a close connection of Nero, with whom he shared a passion for gambling and chariot racing. After the victory of Cremona I, Vitellius' march on Rome saw him grow more and more into the likeness of his former friend, surrounded by Nero's favorite company: actors and eunuchs.[71] Vitellius made public sacrifices to the shade of Nero and praised Nero's poetical compositions. Under Vitellius, Sporus was asked to star in a theatrical performance in the role of Proserpina.[72]

The reign of Vespasian marked a major turning point. Vespasian honored the memory of Galba and regarded Claudius as the last lawful member of the Julio-Claudian dynasty, restoring his dignity as deified emperor. The Colossus of Nero was dedicated as a statue of the Sun god.[73] Titus proved groundless the fears of those who dreaded he would become a second Nero, and erected statues of Britannicus, with whom he had been educated.[74] This negative view of Nero is reflected in the historiography of the period. The lost histories of Pliny the Elder, the most influential historical work of Vespasianic Rome, were fiercely anti-Neronian; the same is true for Fabius Rusticus.[75] Josephus too has a negative view of Nero.[76] Flavian poetry contributes to this negative portrait. In *Octauia*, wrongly attributed to Seneca, Nero is a monster and a tyrant, the murderer of his mother, and the arsonist of Rome.[77]

---

[70] Otho and Nero: Tac. *Hist.* 1.78; Plu. *Oth.* 3.1–2; Suet. *Otho* 7; Champlin (2003a) 7–9. Otho and Statilia Messalina: Suet. *Otho* 10.2. Otho and Sporus: Plu. *Galb.* 9.3; D.C. 64.8.3. On Sporus see Champlin (2003a) 145–50.

[71] Tac. *Hist.* 2.71; cf. Suet. *Vit.* 10. I use "Cremona I" and "Cremona II" to refer to the two decisive engagements of the civil war of 69 CE, the first opposing Otho and Vitellius, and the second Vitellius and Antonius Primus (on behalf of Vespasian).

[72] Tac. *Hist.* 2.71. For Vitellius' summoning of Sporus to recite the part of Persephone at the games see D.C. 65.10.1.

[73] On the Colossus see *LTUR* I 295–98 *s.v.* Colossus Nero (C. Lega); Lega (1989–1990); Bergmann (1993). The traditional view is that the Colossus, a massive statue of the Sun god, was originally designed to bear Nero's features. The resemblance to Nero was then removed by Vespasian. This assumption has been challenged by R. R. R. Smith (2000), followed by Champlin (2003a) 129–31, who maintains that the view that the Colossus initially resembled Nero is unsubstantiated.

[74] Titus as second Nero: Suet. *Tit.* 7.1; statue of Britannicus: Suet. *Tit.* 2.1.

[75] Pliny's attitude to Nero is evident from his *Naturalis Historia*, in which Nero is presented as the enemy of mankind; see e.g. *Nat.* 7.46; cf. 34.45, 35.51, 22.96, 37.50; Champlin (2003a) 40–1; Schubert (1998) 312–24; Degl'Innocenti Pierini (2007) 148–55. On Fabius Rusticus see Champlin (2003a) 42.

[76] On Josephus and Nero see Schubert (1998) 325–37.

[77] Our literary documentation is better for the time of Domitian (see subsequent discussion in this section). The pseudo-Senecan *Octauia* is likely of Flavian date but might belong to the reign of Titus or Domitian. For discussion of this play's date see Ferri (2003) 5–30; Boyle (2008) xiv–xvi. For more on Nero in *Octauia* see Section

The reign of Vespasian saw the consolidation of an uncompromisingly negative por-
trait of Nero that would prove influential on later views of the last Julio-Claudian.

This anti-Neronian position was retained under Domitian. Coeval poetry offers
important indications. The portrait of Nero that emerges from the poetry of Statius
and Martial is consistently negative.[78] In *Siluae* 2.7, Nero is the incendiary of Rome,
persecuted in Tartarus by the ghost of his mother. In Martial he is the beastly king
whose house has swallowed the entire city.[79] Notably, criticism of Nero is included
in poems addressed to the emperor or to members of his entourage and is meant to
style Domitian as the polar opposite of Nero. An example is *Siluae* 4.3. Written in
95 CE, one year before Domitian's death, the poem celebrates Domitian's building of
the Via Domitiana.[80] The opening contrasts Domitian and Nero:

> quis duri silicis grauisque ferri
> immanis sonus aequori propinquum
> saxosae latus Appiae repleuit? ...
> ... nec frangit uada montibusque caesis
> inducit Nero sordidas paludes,
> sed qui limina bellicosa Iani
> iustis legibus et foro coronat,
> quis castae Cereri diu negata
> reddit iugera sobriasque terras,
> quis fortem uetat interire sexum
> et censor prohibet mares adultos
> pulchrae supplicium timere formae ...
> *Silv.* 4.3.1–3, 7–15

What monstrous sound of hard flint and heavy iron has filled paved Appia on
the side that is close to the sea? ... Nero is not breaking the lagoons and cleaving
the mountains as he brings in filthy marshes. No, it is he who surrounds Janus'
warlike temple with just laws and a Forum. By these laws he restores to chaste
Ceres acres long denied her and sober fields, and he forbids virility to perish

---

1.6 of this chapter and Chapter 4, Section 4.1. On allusions to Nero in Valerius Flaccus see Schubert (1998)
304–6; Taylor (1994) 228–31; Heerink (2014) 89–92; Chapter 2, Section 2.2 n. 42; Conclusions, Section C.1.

[78] Nero in Domitianic literature: Schubert (1998) 290–311; Nauta (2010); Degl'Innocenti Pierini (2007).

[79] Stat. *Silv.* 2.7.61–2, 118–19 with Newlands (2011) 250–1; Degl'Innocenti Pierini (2007) 138–42; Mart. *Sp.* 2.1;
cf. also Mart. 7.34.4 *quid Nerone peius?* [what is worse than Nero?].

[80] On the date of this poem see Coleman (1988) xix–xxi. Cf. also *Silv.* 5.2.31–4, with its mention of *ferus Nero*
[beastly Nero].

and, as Censor, stops adult males from fearing the punishment of handsome appearance . . .

Domitian's public works had nothing to do with Nero's hubristic attempts to connect Rome and Baiae by a channel, and Domitian prohibited the castration of youths, a perverse practice indulged by Nero.[81] My second example comes from the fragments of another Domitianic poet, the satirist Turnus:

> ex quo Caesareas suboles Lucusta cecidit,
> horrida cura sui tutelaque nota Neronis.[82]
> Frg. 1 Blänsdorf

Since Caesar's progeny was murdered by Lucusta, frightening darling and well-known guardian of her Nero.

Evidently Nero was a target of Turnus' satirical invective.[83] By calling Britannicus *suboles Caesareas* [Caesar's progeny], the poet suggests that Nero, who did not really belong in the imperial family, murdered the last legitimate scion of the Julio-Claudians, Britannicus.[84] Turnus is one of the few figures for whom the title of court poet is not controversial: The scholia to Juvenal describe him as *potens in aula* [powerful at court].[85] Lines such as these could hardly have found sympathy from an emperor who admired Nero. Turnus' activity is usually placed in the last years of Domitian (92 to 97 CE).[86] Both *Siluae* 4.3 and the fragment by Turnus suggest that Nero found little sympathy at Domitian's court until the very end.

A look at Domitian's legislation corroborates this view. Certain measures implemented by Domitian seem aimed at correcting tendencies stimulated by Nero. Among these corrective measures, a good example is Domitian's legislation

---

[81] Nero sought to build a canal to improve connections between Rome and Baiae (Tac. *Ann.* 15.42; Suet. *Nero* 31. 3). Water parties in artificial basins were a symbol of Nero's debauchery, and Baiae was one of the favorite locations of the emperor's excesses (Statius' *sordidas paludes* [filthy marshes] are very charged). The need to keep Domitian and Nero apart in this poem is particularly pressing. In improving connections between Rome and Campania, Domitian was finalizing, although in a different manner, a project Nero had long tried to realize; Champlin (2003a) 156–60; Coleman (1988) 102. On the emasculation of youths see the subsequent discussion in this section.

[82] I print, *exempli gratia*, the conjecture by Tandoi (1979) 813 (*tutelaque*) for the corrupt *uerna*.

[83] Fragments of Turnus: Blänsdorf (2011) 133. On Turnus: Tandoi (1979); Schubert (1998) 309–11; Courtney (1993) 362–3.

[84] The accusation of not really belonging to the Julio-Claudians in light of his real father Domitius is commonly leveled at Nero: cf. Suet. *Nero* 7; *Oct.* 249 with Ferri (2003) 195; Tandoi (1979) 816–18.

[85] Schol. Iuv. *Sat.* 1.20. Cf. also Mart. 11.9 on Scaevus Memor, Turnus' brother who triumphed in Domitian's Capitolia. Quint. *Inst.* 10.1.94 probably alludes to Turnus as a distinguished contemporary author of satire.

[86] Tandoi (1979) 821 n. 51.

against the castration of youths. Nero, who castrated Sporus and publicly married him (perhaps setting an example to others), was the obvious target.[87] Nero loved actors and acting, especially pantomime, and involved senators and equestrians in his performances. Domitian forbade the staging of pantomimes and the staging of public shows by private individuals and went so far as to banish from the Senate a former quaestor because of his excessive love for dancing and acting.[88] His enforcing of the *lex Iulia de adulteriis coercendis* (a law against adultery) and of the *lex Scantinia* (which prohibited homosexual intercourse with freeborn males) can also be seen as a reaction to the excessive licentiousness of the Neronian period.[89] Nero's impiety was notorious: He neglected cults, angered the gods, contaminated sacred places, and went so far as to rape a Vestal virgin.[90] Domitian's ostentatious piety, his obsession with ritual purity, and his observance of religious minutiae contributed to setting him up as an opposite of Nero.[91]

On the surface, the time of Domitian does not harbor significant changes as far as official attitudes to Nero are concerned. If there were similarities between him and Domitian, they were certainly not the consequence of a rehabilitation of Nero or of an explicit intention to harness his memory, as in the case of Otho and Vitellius. In fact, the demonization of Nero by the Flavian regime made it impossible for anyone to use the comparison, except to openly censure the emperor. Detractors may have equated Domitian with Nero during his life, but only privately; in writing it could appear only after his death. Pliny's and Juvenal's notion of Domitian as a second Nero was also fostered by the negative portrait of Domitian proposed by the new dynasty. Domitian's transformation into a tyrant and a monster, a process analogous to the vilification of Nero under the Flavians, contributed to the apparent similarities between the two emperors in post-Domitianic accounts. Furthermore,

---

[87] Domitian's law against castration (82 CE): Suet. *Dom.* 7.1; Amm. Marc. 18.4.5; D.C. 67.2.3; Philostr. *VA* 6.42; mentions of the provision in Martial and Statius: *Silv.* 4.3.13–15 with Coleman (1988) 107; *Silv.* 3.4.73–7; Mart. 2.60, 6.2, 9.7; Statius touches on it in passages in which he attacks Nero (*Silv.* 4.3). On Sporus see Champlin (2003a) 145–50.

[88] Nero's love for dancing and pantomime: D.C. 63.18.1; Suet. *Nero* 54; Champlin (2003a) 78–9. Senators and equestrians involved in performances: Champlin (2003a) 68–77 with full references; Domitian's ban of pantomime: Plin. *Pan.* 46.1–2; Suet. *Dom.* 8.3.

[89] Plin. *Pan.* 42.1; on the *lex Julia* cf. Mart. 6.2 and 6.4; Jones (1992) 107. Domitian's enforcing of the *lex Scantinia*: Suet. *Dom.* 8.3; D.C. 67.12.1; Stat. *Silv.* 5.2.102; Mart. 6.7, 22, 45; Jones (1992) 107; Griffin (2000) 79. On the *lex Scantinia* see Mommsen (1887–1888) 703–4.

[90] Rape of Vestal virgin: Suet. *Nero* 28.1; impiety (bathing in the Aqua Marcia): Tac. *Ann.* 14.22. Nero's impiety is heightened in anti-Neronian accounts under the Flavians: cf. *Oct.* 89, 240–1, 449. Reality was more complex: Champlin (2003a) 132–5, 395–6 n. 65.

[91] Cf. Jones (1992) 101–2; Suet. *Dom.* 8.3–5; see Chapter 5, Section 5.2.

once Nero had been turned into a paragon of the "bad emperor," every subsequent disgraced emperor was likely to borrow some of his traits.

Behind the official proclamations of the court and its anti-Neronian facade, however, we do find elements of continuity. This is perhaps the most intriguing aspect of Domitianic culture: Appropriation of elements of Nero's ideology coexists with a condemnation of Nero. This problem has different facets and can be approached from multiple points of view. In what follows, I review some aspects of continuity that pertain to the emperor's self-representation and some of his rulings. I highlight a process whereby the historical figure of Nero is separated from his message: The latter is rescued, though not without corrections and cautions, whereas the former is condemned.

Solar ideology is an area in which Domitian distances himself from Vespasian and Titus and moves gradually in the direction of Nero.[92] Nero's exploitation of solar imagery had its roots in Augustus' ideology centering on Apollo, but Nero surpassed his predecessor by a great deal. A more direct emphasis on the syncretism of Apollo and Sol allowed Nero to bring together, under the sign of one god, his love for singing at the lyre and his passion for chariot racing.[93] Nero was acclaimed as Apollo after his performances as *citharoedus* as early as 59 CE and was assimilated to Sol in iconography. His Golden House was designed as the abode of a solar sovereign, a mansion meant to be as radiant as the Sun, with gardens reproducing the world that the Sun illuminates and a massive statue of the Sun god (perhaps with features of Nero) raised in its vestibule.[94] A set of solar events was at the center of Nero's settlement of the Parthian question, culminating in the Golden Day of 66 CE, when he was addressed as Sun Mithras by Tiridates, king of Armenia. In his "triumph" of 67 CE, through which he celebrated his successes at games in Greece, Nero dedicated the crowns received for his victories around the obelisk in the Circus. He also visited the temple of Palatine Apollo and dedicated statues of

---

[92] I deal with this topic extensively in Chapter 2, Section 2.1, but a summary is in order here.

[93] See extensively Champlin (2003a) 112–44. In Champlin's view, Nero harnessed Apollo and Sol substantially only after 59 CE. This is contradicted by the literary evidence offered by Calpurnius Siculus' *Eclogues* and Seneca's *Apocolocyntosis*, but Champlin supports a third-century date for Calpurnius and considers the lines on Nero as Sol in the *Apocolocyntosis* a later addition, perhaps by Seneca himself: See Champlin (2003b).

[94] Acclaimed as Apollo after performances: Tac. *Ann.* 14.14–15; D.C. 61.19–20. Iconography: Champlin (2003a) 119, 301 nn. 16 and 17; D.C. 63.6.2 (Nero as the Sun depicted on the curtains of the theater of Pompey); wearing radiate crown: Bergmann (1998) 167–9; for coinage and inscriptions see the evidence collected by Champlin (2003a) 116–17; legends about Nero's solar birth: Suet. *Nero* 6.1; D.C. 61.2.1. Golden House: Champlin (2003a) 127–32, 200–9; the following entries in *LTUR* are all relevant for the Domus Aurea: Domus Aurea, Vestibulum, Area dello Stagnum, Porticus Triplices Miliariae, Palazzo sull'Esquilino, Complesso del Palatino, Domus Transitoria, Domus Tiberiana, and Aedes Fortunae Seiani. Gardens as a miniature of the world: Suet. *Nero* 31. For the Colossus see n. 73 in this section.

himself in the guise of a lyre player in his palace.[95] Solar imagery naturally permeates texts in praise of Nero.[96]

After Nero's excesses, Vespasian and Titus turned to a more moderate use of solar imagery, limited to the by-now-conventional portrait with radiate crown.[97] With Domitian, things were significantly different. First, there was Domitian's building program in the Campus Martius. This involved restoration of Augustus' sundial and erection of Domitian's own obelisk, after which Domitian claimed the same honor as Augustus, that of naming a month after himself.[98] Domitian's obelisk was inscribed with hieroglyphs advertising his succession to Vespasian in the solar terms typical of pharaonic ideology.[99] The panegyric poetry of Statius and Martial is rich in solar imagery; Statius goes so far as to resurrect the lines dedicated by Seneca to Nero the Sun in the *Apocolocyntosis* and the proem to Lucan's *Bellum Ciuile,* in which Nero is invited to replace Sol as the new Sun god.[100] The syncretism of Apollo and Sol is affirmed in texts in praise of the emperor. A problematic association with Nero emerges especially when Apollo/Sol is summoned to praise Domitian's poetic ability.[101] Domitian was passionate about chariot racing, just as Nero was, even though he never personally took part in a race.[102] Another delicate area was the syncretism with eastern religions. Solar ideology allowed Nero to forge a connection with the imperial theology of Parthia and its solar god Mithras. Imperial ideology assumes more distinct solar traits in Egypt under Domitian, and the identification of Mithras with Apollo/Sol, witnessed by Statius' *Thebaid,* might resonate with the imperial cult.[103]

Another aspect of proximity is visible in the use of divine comparisons. Hercules is a case in point. It is quite standard for the emperor to be likened to the greatest of heroes.[104] Yet, in this as in other areas, Nero went further than others. Legends circulated that he, like Hercules, strangled snakes as an infant.[105] Hercules was one of Nero's favorite tragic roles. During his tour of Greece, he expressed a desire to

---

[95] The Golden Day: Champlin (2003a) 221–9; the triumph of 67 CE: Suet. *Nero* 25.1–2; D.C. 63.20.1–21.1; Champlin (2003a) 229–34.

[96] Cf. e.g. Sen. *Apoc.* 4.1.20–32; Calp. *Ecl.* 4.159, 7.83–4; *Buc. Eins.* 1.37, 2.38, etc.

[97] Bergmann (1998) 231–3.

[98] See Chapter 2, Section 2.1.

[99] On the obelisk, its inscription, and its location see Grenier (2009); Chapter 2, Section 2.3 and n. 26.

[100] See Section 1.1 and Chapter 2, Sections 2.1, 2.2, and 2.3.

[101] *Silv.* 5.1.14–15; Mart. 5.6.18–19; perhaps also Mart 9.34.5.

[102] Domitian added two factions to the races: *Dom.* 7.1; cf. also Mart. 5.25.9–10, 10.50, 10.53, 11.1.16 (on the exploits of the famous charioteers Scorpus and Incitatus); Jones (1992) 105, 219 n. 34.

[103] More on this in Chapter 2, Section 2.1 n. 27, 2.8.

[104] On Hercules as a model for Roman emperors see Chapter 3, Section 3.2.

[105] Tac. *Ann.* 11.11; Suet. *Nero* 6.

imitate the hero by killing a lion in the arena. He was praised as a new Hercules on his return from Greece.[106] His project of cutting the Isthmus of Corinth too was styled as one of Hercules' toils.[107] Nero's Herculean impersonations were foreign to the spirit of post-Actium Augustan ideology, with its focus on *pietas* and religious renewal.[108] Vespasian famously laughed at those who sought to prove that the Flavian family descended from a comrade of Hercules.[109] Domitian followed in Nero's footsteps. He is constantly compared to Hercules in poetry, but he also let himself be represented as Hercules. A massive statue of the god stood in Domitian's throne room in the Palatine palace, perhaps bearing the features of the emperor. There is evidence of a portrait type of Domitian as the young Hercules. And in the Hercules Temple on the Appian Way, the cult statue was given Domitian's features.[110]

Under Augustus, quinquennial games were established at Actium and Naples. Augustus promoted games in Rome as well, but these did not include competitions in poetry and music.[111] He was surpassed by the philhellene Nero, the first to give his city a full program of Greek games, including poetical and musical contests, with the institution of the Neronia. Vespasian and Titus discontinued the practice. Domitian's Capitolia restored the full program of Nero's games.[112] Of course, there were differences: Domitian was careful not to name the games after himself, and, unlike Nero, he did not personally take part in the competitions; it is possible that the distinction between Nero and Domitian was made clear by the choice of subject for the poetical contests and other aspects of the games.[113] But it was precisely the necessity of these cautionary measures that proved the risk of an assimilation with Nero. The games were reduced but not suppressed by Trajan. The disdain with which they are regarded by Pliny the Younger, who praises Trajan's decision to terminate similar games in Vindobona (modern Vienna), is telling.[114]

---

[106] Killing a lion in the arena: Suet. *Nero* 53. Nero acting the role of the mad Hercules: D.C. 63.9.4–5, 63.10.2, 63.22.6; Suet. *Nero* 21.3; Philostr. *VA* 5.7; Champlin (2003a) 103–7. Acclaimed as Nero Hercules on his return from Greece: D.C. 63.20.5. Nero as Hercules on coins: *RPC* I 1278, cf. 1275–81. See Chapter 3, Section 3.2.

[107] Philostr. *Nero* 5. Cf. also *Her. O.* 82–4, with Champlin (2003a) 137–8, 307 nn. 83–5.

[108] On this important turning point see Zanker (1988) 85–9, 101–66.

[109] Suet. *Ves.* 12.1.

[110] The evidence for Domitian's identification with Hercules in iconography and coinage is discussed in Chapter 3, Section 3.2.

[111] Caldelli (1993) 21–37, 38 n. 165.

[112] Neronia: Suet. *Nero* 12.3; Domitian's Capitolia: Suet. *Dom.* 4.4; Caldelli (1993); Nauta (2002) 328–35; Hardie (2003) 125–34, 142–7.

[113] Cf. Nauta (2010) 252. Nero's participation in the games: Tac. *Ann.* 16.4; Suet. *Nero* 21. On the possible anti-Neronian implications of the choice of Phaethon as a subject for one of the poetry competitions see Chapter 2, Section 2.2 and n. 49.

[114] Plin. *Ep.* 4.22.7 with Nauta (2010) 252; on the Capitolia under Trajan: Caldelli (1993) 59–67, 113.

Philhellenism is another common trait. Nero is the immediate precedent for Domitian's passion for all things Greek, Vespasian and Titus being no match for him in this area.[115]

In the adoption of certain traits of Nero's imperial persona, as with the rhetoric of anti-Neronian ideology, it is reasonable to imagine the customary process of exchange and feedback between the emperor (the court, really) and individual actors or donors that typically marks political communication and the construction of imperial ideologies in Rome. Certain initiatives arose outside of the court itself (Domitian, for instance, may have reacted more kindly than his father to those who suggested his proximity to Hercules), whereas others were instigated by the emperor. Solar imagery in poetry was matched by monumental adaptations (such as Domitian's obelisk) that were directly promoted by the court. In the case of games, imperial agency is certain; dedicators of the Hercules' statue on the Via Appia and local mints who paired Domitian with Hercules were encouraged by the Hercules on the Palatine. However, Domitian may have found reassurance in projecting a certain image of himself in the poets' and courtiers' willingness to praise him in certain terms. In turn, the emperor's acceptance of certain forms of praise stimulated the production and promotion of such imagery in literature and the arts.

Be that as it may, Domitian's ideology rested on a seeming contradiction: It retained on the surface the anti-Neronian bias of Vespasian and Titus while at the same time reviving elements of Nero's self-representation. The motivations for this partial reception of Neronian ideology are complex; it exceeds the scope of this book to investigate them. One basic explanation was the popularity of Nero with certain strata of Rome's population. The figure of Nero was an important mediator in relationships with Parthia. In addition, certain aspects of Nero's self-presentation (such as the solar cult) were beneficial to the emperor's relationship with his troops.[116] More generally, Nero had left such a profound mark on the construction of imperial identities that, in many respects, it just seemed impossible to move backward. However, continuity with Nero in imperial presentation created special problems for poets, namely the constant need to keep Domitian separate from Nero while engaging certain aspects of Domitian's public persona. But Neronian culture itself, as we have seen in Section 1.1, offered an important ideological tool to accommodate Domitian's continuity in a constructive way, allowing Statius to present Domitian

---

[115] It is impossible to enter into detail on such a vast and complex subject. For the historical evidence on Domitian's philhellenism, Jones (1992) 112 is a starting point; on Nero's philhellenism: Champlin (2003a) 173–4, cf. also 136–7; Griffin (1984) 208–20.

[116] See Chapter 2, Section 2.8.

as someone who fulfills the soteriological expectations raised by Nero's principate without repeating Nero's mistakes.

1.4 MARTYRS AND SURVIVORS: THE ANNAEANS

In this section, I continue my investigation into the fortune of Nero under the Flavians. I do so by extending my analysis to other documents and by examining the position of elite groups within Rome's society. As we will see in this section, teasing out Domitianic Rome's ambivalent relationship with Nero and putting it in dialogue with the trajectory of Domitian's attitude toward the elite is helpful for understanding the *Thebaid* for a further reason: It allows us to better understand the cultural activities and the place within Domitianic culture of certain groups with whom Statius is in contact. In addition, connecting the ideology of the *Thebaid* with other cultural centers in Flavian Rome allows us to make some hypotheses as to which groups in Flavian Rome had a political agenda and views that might have been particularly influential on the political outlook of Statius' *Thebaid*.

The anti-Nero rhetoric that I discussed in Section 1.3 is not limited to the panegyric poetry of Domitian's time. It is also visible in a different class of texts—a bulk of literature we might call martyrology—in which the lives and works of Nero's victims are celebrated. For example, Gaius Fannius wrote a text titled *Exitus occisorum aut relegatorum a Nerone* [*The Deaths of Those Slain or Exiled by Nero*]. Another example is Arulenus Rusticus' biography of Thrasea Paetus, the famously defiant senator executed by Nero. The practice is extended to victims of other emperors: Herennius Senecio wrote a laudatory biography of Helvidius Priscus, a victim of Vespasian; Atedius Melior commissioned poems in honor of his mentor Blaesus, murdered by Vitellius.[117]

In the same category fall the activities fostered by survivors of the Annaeans. Poems by Martial and Statius provide evidence for patronage activities devoted to promoting the memory of members of the Annaean family. Argentaria Polla is our best witness, but other survivors of the clan may have fostered similar undertakings. Polla, herself the daughter (or granddaughter) of a poet (Marcus Argentarius), commissioned poems from Statius and Martial—and possibly other professional poets—to celebrate the memory of her former husband, Lucan, more than 25 years

---

[117] Martyrology: Champlin (2003a) 39–40. Arulenus Rusticus: Suet. *Dom.* 10.3; Tac. *Ag.* 2.1; *PIR*² I 730. Gaius Fannius: Plin. *Ep.* 5.5. Herennius Senecio: *PIR*² H 128; on Atedius Melior, the dedicatee of Statius' book 2 and of three individual poems (2.1, 2.3, 2.4), see Hardie (1983) 66–7; Melior's reverence for the memory of Blaesus is mentioned by Statius (*Silv.* 2.1.189–207; cf. also 2.3.77); Martial 8.38 reveals that Melior paid the *Collegium Poetarum* to commemorate Blaesus annually.

after his death. Statius attended meetings at her house.[118] If she was, as it seems likely, the wife of Pollius Felix, she and her husband were among Statius' most significant patrons.[119] Statius spent much time at their estate in Campania, where he composed and recited poetry, relying on the judgment and literary taste of Pollius, himself a poet.[120]

Statius' poem in praise of Lucan gives us an idea of this group's cultural agenda and political outlook. In *Siluae* 2.7, Lucan is a champion of freedom who moves from support for Nero to hatred and rebellion—a rebellion reflected in his literary works, especially the *Bellum Ciuile*. Nero, in contrast, is a monstrous tyrant, responsible for the fire of Rome.[121] A similar position, defense of the Annaeans coupled with criticism of Nero, is found in the work of Fabius Rusticus, a disciple of Seneca who may have operated under the patronage of members of the Annaean clan.[122] Patronage by associates of the Annaeans has also been suggested for the pseudo-Senecan *Octauia*.[123] This work too combines hatred of Nero with a revisionist take on Seneca's involvement with the former dynasty.[124] The evidence collected so far shows that there were in Flavian Rome other centers from which anti-Neronian feelings radiated, with individuals seeking legitimation and prestige by advertising their connection to the martyrs of the former regime. These groups, like Domitian, had a stake in the creation of the vulgate of Nero the monster. They were also interested in sanctifying the memory of Neronian poets and writers, especially Lucan and Seneca, and in clearing their reputation and upholding their literary fame. Statius was very close to at least one of these groups.

It is sometimes suggested in scholarship that the Annaeans too formed part of the opposition to Domitian, partly because survivors of Nero would naturally be ill disposed toward the "second" Nero, and partly because, like some of the victims of Domitian's later reign, they had connections to victims of Nero.[125]

---

[118] Cf. *Silv.* 2 *praef.* 23–6.

[119] Pollius Felix is the dedicatee of book 3 of the *Siluae*; Pollius' villa in Surrentum is the subject of 2.2; Pollius' son-in-law, Julius Menecrates, is the recipient of 4.8; Pollius' Hercules shrine in Campania is celebrated in *Silv.* 3.1; on Pollius see Hardie (1983) 67–8; Newlands (2011) 21; Nauta (2002) 223–5; on Argentaria Polla: Newlands (2011) 21–2; Nisbet (1978). The identification of Argentaria Polla with Polla, wife of Pollius Felix, was proposed by Nisbet (1978) and accepted by Hardie (1983) 4. Nauta (2002) 223–5 and Newlands (2011) 21 are more cautious.

[120] *Silv.* 3 *praef.* 4–8. On Pollius' literary activity: *Silv.* 2.2.137 [if we read *plectri*, with Hardie (1983) 67 n. 76; the text is problematic: Newlands (2011) 154]; on his familiarity with Greek culture: *Silv.* 2.2.95–6.

[121] *Silv.* 2.7.58–61, 100–4. More on *Siluae* 2.7 later in this chapter, Sections 1.4, 1.5, and 1.6.

[122] Champlin (2003a) 42.

[123] Ferri (2003) 26.

[124] On *Octauia* and its politics see Ferri (2003) 70–5; esp. 71–5 (on the presentation of Seneca); 26 (on *Octauia* and the *Annaeans*).

[125] Ferri (2003) 27; at p. 26 he suggests a connection with the Annaeans for the play's author. See Section 1.2 for the notion of a "stoic opposition" stretching from the time of Nero to that of Domitian.

Yet, direct evidence for Domitianic hostility to the Annaeans is lacking. Statius' close connection with the house of Polla, at a time when he also enjoyed imperial favor, seems to suggest otherwise: The poet would hardly have advertised his ties to survivors of the Annaeans had they been regarded with suspicion by the emperor. On the contrary, the anti-Neronian attitude of the group was consistent with the tenets of Domitian's ideology. People gathering at the house of Polla would have reacted positively to Domitian's policy of trusting relatives and fans of the victims of the older regime with prestigious offices. More important, survivors of earlier emperors would personally have benefited from Domitian's policy of *clementia* and his promises of restoring *libertas*. They were interested in Domitian's continuation of this program.

Reconstructing this web of relationships and paying attention to convergences between Statius and the political views of some of his patrons have important consequences. They allow us to get a sense of the agency, or, more generally, the political and cultural milieu by which the ideological framework of the *Thebaid* is strongly influenced. In the course of this book I insist on the didactic stance behind Statius' political discourse. I see the *Thebaid* as a text that is presented to the emperor as a standard to follow, an attempt to direct the ruler toward an ideal that would be expedient to the interest of certain groups within Roman society. It is my contention that this project consolidated at a time when, in light of Domitian's extraordinary overtures toward the senatorial class, it seemed reasonable to try and direct Domitian toward a policy dominated by *clementia* and *libertas*.

This position was in line with the interests of the senatorial class in general. However, we can try and narrow our focus to more restricted groups within Rome's society. Groups of survivors of Nero—whose activity we reviewed in this section— would have been particularly receptive to some elements of the *Thebaid*'s political outlook. One common aspect would be the demonization of Nero, which, as we will see in Sections 1.5–1.7 of this chapter and in Chapters 2 and 3, influenced important passages of the *Thebaid*. The importance of Seneca's political thought and an apologetic view of both Seneca and Lucan, which we encountered in *Siluae* 2.7 and in *Octauia*, is also present in the *Thebaid*. Finally, the Annaeans and other survivors of earlier regimes would have been particularly impressed by Domitian's early policy of entrusting families victimized by Nero with important offices and had a stake in his retention of this policy. It is possible that the ideology of the *Thebaid* was shaped in a special way by Statius' collaboration and interaction with groups of survivors such as the one operating under Polla's auspices.

Exploring the influence on Statius of groups of survivors of earlier regimes allows us to complicate views of the politics of Statius' poem, forcing us to abandon vertical models whereby Statius is seen as accepting or subverting the message from the court. The relationship is rather triangular, involving the court, Statius, and his patrons. In my reconstruction we see groups of intellectuals who contribute to the political discussion of the time and seek to direct the emperor toward a certain ideal. This convergence between elite expectations and imperial policy was momentary and gradually disintegrated, but its imprint is still visible in Statius' text.

That the *Thebaid*'s political dimension is shaped by Statius' interaction with survivors of Nero is a hypothesis, not a certainty. But the advantage of formulating this hypothesis is that it makes us receptive to certain aspects of Statius' poetry. In the remainder of this book, it will be expedient to keep in mind that Statius' reception of Lucan and Seneca may have been shaped in a special way by the needs and agendas of survivors of the Annaeans, who, to an extent, administered the cultural legacy of the Annaean family. As we will see in the next section, reading the *Thebaid* from the perspective of survivors makes us alert to historical allusions encoded in some of the *Thebaid*'s most famous scenes.

1.5 THE DEATH OF MAEON: READING NERO BACK INTO THE *THEBAID*

The *Thebaid*'s response to continuity between Nero and Domitian will concern us in Chapters 2, 3, and, to an extent, 4. In what follows, I would like to introduce my first experiment in reading Nero back into the *Thebaid*. I am interested in highlighting a number of responses to Statius' text that can be recovered by assessing the role of anti-Neronian ideology within Domitianic culture, and by taking into account Domitian's appropriation of *libertas* and *clementia*, as well as Statius' relationship with survivors of Nero.

My first experiment involves the story of Maeon. In book 2, Tydeus goes as an envoy to Thebes to request that Eteocles yield the kingdom to his brother, now that the appointed year has passed.[126] Eteocles scorns his brother's requests. He even sends 50 warriors to ambush Tydeus on his way back to Argos. But Tydeus kills all of his opponents except one, Maeon, who returns to deliver the news of the massacre and openly accuses Eteocles. The tyrant instantly orders the hero's death, but Maeon anticipates him by killing himself.[127] The prominence and space Maeon receives in the *Thebaid* is somewhat surprising. He is granted a long speech before the tyrant (*Theb.* 3.59–77) and is the recipient of a pathetic apostrophe by the poet:

---

[126] I look at the episode of Tydeus' embassy and its aftermath from a different but complementary point of view later, in Chapter 4, Section 4.6.

[127] *Theb.* 2.482–3.98.

tu tamen egregius fati mentisque nec umquam
(sic dignum est) passure situm, qui comminus ausus
uadere contemptum reges, quaque ampla ueniret
libertas, sancire uiam: quo carmine dignam,
quo satis ore tuis famam uirtutibus addam,
augur amate deis? . . .
. . . nunc quoque Tartareo multum diuisus Auerno
Elysias, i, carpe plagas, ubi manibus axis
inuius Ogygiis nec sontis iniqua tyranni
iussa ualent;
Theb. 3.99–104, 108–11

But you, splendid of fate and soul, will never suffer oblivion (as is fitting); you
dared to scorn kings face-to-face and open a path for the coming of ample
freedom—what song, what words of mine shall suffice to add due fame to your
merit, augur beloved of the gods? . . . Now too go, take the Elysian fields, far away
from Tartarean Avernus, where the sky is closed to Theban shades and the guilty
tyrant's unjust orders have no power;

The poet feels inadequate to speak of Maeon's glory. Maeon's fame will be eternal.
Apollo mourns the death of his favorite by suspending his prophetic activity. Even
more striking is the specific Roman coloring of the apostrophe. Maeon dared to de-
spise kings and is said to have opened a way for the coming of *libertas* (3.101). As has
been recognized, the reference to *libertas* places the conflict of Maeon and Eteocles in
the world of Roman politics, touching on a particularly controversial topic of imperial
discussions.[128]

Scholars have tended to tease out the anti-Domitianic connections of this ep-
isode, seeing in Eteocles a version of Domitian and assuming a context in which
the readership of the *Thebaid,* or at least its elite members, are already in their vast
majority alienated from the emperor.[129] And yet a different reading of this passage

---

[128] On the political resonances of the scene see Dominik (1994) 153–6; Ahl (1986) 2830–2.

[129] In Ahl's view, the story of Maeon highlights the impossibility of free speech under a tyrant—Eteocles—whose
portrait in other sections of the poem Ahl sees as reminiscent of Domitian; Ahl (1986) 2830–4. McGuire
(1997) does not press the analogy of Domitian and Eteocles in his treatment of Maeon (197–205); yet he
considers Eteocles an image of Domitian (148–54, 177). Dominik connects Maeon with Thrasea Paetus, a
victim of Nero (154–5), but he sees Eteocles' tyrannical rule as an allusion to Domitian's regime (148–9) and
lists both Thrasea and victims of Domitian as possible historical counterparts for victims of Eteocles (153).
He states (156) that "there is no evidence to show that the scene involving Eteocles is intended to evoke a
specific comparison with Domitian," yet he concludes his analysis of Maeon by asking (156), "could the gen-
eral significance of the foregoing parallels between the Theban court and Principate really have escaped the

becomes possible if we project it against the context reconstructed in the previous sections: taking into account Domitian's early policy marked by *clementia* and his demonization of Nero, as well as Statius' own connection with survivors of Nero, and regarding the *Thebaid* as an attempt to direct Domitian toward a line of action from which members of the elite would profit.

The death of Maeon can be read with reference to Nero and his repression of Roman aristocrats. There is a telling web of correspondences between this passage and *Siluae* 2.7. The description of Eteocles in *Thebaid* 3 matches Statius' portrait of Nero in *Siluae* 2.7: Both are said to be *rabidi tyranni* [savage tyrants].[130] There is a further correspondence with *Siluae* 2.7 in the description of the fate of Maeon's soul. In Statius' poem the soul of Lucan goes to the Elysian fields, where he joins the heroes of the *Bellum Ciuile*, at a far remove from Tartarus, where Nero is detained (*Silv.* 2.7.116–19). The same is said of Maeon in *Thebaid* 3: He goes to the Elysian Fields, a place that will be inaccessible to the soul of the tyrant who has caused his death (*Theb.* 3.108–10). A further connection comes from the use of *libertas*, the word Statius applies to Lucan's Cato in *Siluae* 2.7, the same Cato with whom Lucan is united after death.[131] The way in which Maeon's death occurs resembles an imperial execution: The seer commits suicide after his death has already been decreed, very much like Lucan, Seneca, and the other victims of Nero.

Statius does not necessarily direct his readers toward a specific historical figure from the Neronian period. Yet the possibility that Statius has Lucan in mind is attractive. Statius' use of the word *uates* [seer] and the double role of Apollo as protector of both seers and poets might encourage this reading. Lucan is called *uates* in *Siluae* 2.7, and the same word is applied to Maeon here (*Theb.* 3.82). The possibility of an allusion to Lucan would also explain a detail of the scene. After his suicide, Maeon's body is said to be taken by his wife and parents.[132] If this text alludes to the death of Lucan, then the *coniunx* [wife] of the hero is Argentaria Polla, for whom Statius wrote *Siluae* 2.7. There is no decisive evidence to support this identification, but it is tempting to see here an homage by Statius to his powerful patrons.

One could argue that the similarities between *Siluae* 2.7 and *Thebaid* 3 are motivated by the fact that both texts draw from stereotypical imperial representations of tyranny, but we should remember that in the 80s, readers of Statius were accustomed

---

understanding of an audience with the same culture, traditions and education as its poet?" As he states in the preface, Dominik proposes a reading of how the *Thebaid* may have been understood from a senatorial, anti-Domitianic point of view: Dominik (1994) xiii–xiv.

[130] Stat. *Theb.* 3.96; *Silv.* 2.7.100.

[131] *Silv.* 2.7.68 (*libertas*); Cato and Lucan together in Elysium: *Silv.* 2.7.111–15.

[132] *Theb.* 3.93–5.

to seeing this stereotypical portrait associated with Nero in particular. It is true that Maeon is in some ways an epic version of Thrasea Paetus, but we should remember that there was no credible equivalent of Thrasea Paetus under Domitian until after the *Thebaid* was published.[133] Statius describes Maeon as someone who paved the way for the coming of *libertas* (3.101–2). Read in response to the policy of an emperor who made eloquent gestures in favor of Nero's victims, Statius' text can be read as expressing the hope that Domitian's principate would materialize the return of *libertas* for which Nero's martyrs had suffered. The relatives of Nero's victims, the people who could recognize the fate of their families and friends in the story of Maeon, were the recipients of imperial favor. As suggested by the correspondences with *Siluae* 2.7, placed in the cultural context of Rome in the 80s and early 90s, this passage could be read with reference to Nero and his martyrs. This dimension was accessible to every reader and formed a first, predictable response to the text. Of course, some readers would not have stopped there. Opponents of Domitian could press the similarities between him and Nero so as to read *prima facie* criticism of Nero as also directed at Domitian. But it seems to me that in the 80s elite responses to the principate of Domitian were complex enough that this reading would not have been as immediate and widespread as is often assumed.

However, it is not surprising that this passage has become central to modern anti-Domitianic readings of the *Thebaid*. Pro-Domitianic approaches to Statius' text were obscured by the transformation of Domitian's image in the last years of his reign and under the following dynasty. An important factor was the deterioration of Domitian's relationship with survivors of Nero. This process made the emperor transition from an anti-Nero and a champion of the martyrs into a close resemblance of the great Julio-Claudian tyrant. The other key factor was Domitian's *damnatio* by the following generation. Traits of the stereotypical portrait of Nero could now be transferred to Domitian, increasing, in retrospect, the similarities between the two. Scenes created as indictments of Nero became readable as criticism of Domitian. It became difficult for scholars approaching the *Thebaid* from the perspective of post-Domitianic historiography not to read the *Thebaid*'s depiction of tyranny as reflecting perceptions of Domitian's reign. After reading chapter 10 of Suetonius' life of Domitian, one is tempted to see the younger Helvidius as the historical counterpart to Statius' Maeon—except that Statius' text may already have been in circulation several years before Helvidius' execution.

---

[133] On Maeon and Thrasea Paetus see Dominik (1994) 154–5; cf. also 153, where Dominik lists Thrasea Paetus together with Herennius Senecio, the younger Helvidius, and other victims of Domitian as narrative counterparts for victims of Eteocles.

It is possible that scenes such as the Maeon episode started to become open to anti-Domitianic readings already in the last years of Domitian, especially after the executions of 93 CE. Was Statius aware of this potential fluctuation in the understanding of his poem toward the end of Domitian's reign? It is hard to provide a definitive answer. It is possible, but by no means provable, that the *Siluae*, composed and published mainly in the last part of Domitian's reign, reflected a growing preoccupation with the ways in which Statius' poem was being perceived.[134] As will become clear in the course of this book, the *Siluae* interact substantially with Statius' major poem, and they often seem to impose a pro-Domitianic appraisal of the text. It is not impossible that the way in which the *Siluae* provide a more explicitly pro-Domitianic commentary on certain scenes of the *Thebaid* reflects a growing preoccupation by Statius with the ways in which his poem was being interpreted.

1.6 MYTH AND REALITY

In my earlier analysis of Flavian responses to Nero in Section 1.3, I noted that the Flavian age saw the formation and growth of the vulgate of Nero the monster. A closer look at this creation will provide the starting point for my second attempt at reading Nero back into the *Thebaid*. For this exploration, I focus on the role of Seneca's tragedies in shaping post-Neronian receptions of Nero and on the *Thebaid*'s exploitation of the potential for political allusion inherent in the reception of Seneca's texts.

Rome was a city deeply accustomed to the interactions of myth and politics and to the theater as a mirror for the political scene.[135] Nero left an indelible mark on both political adaptations of myth and politicized uses of the theater. Nero acted the role of certain mythical characters on stage and explicitly invited audiences to read the events of his life through those mythical stories. The identification of the emperor with the play's protagonists was explicitly suggested when Nero wore a mask bearing his features or, in the case of female characters, those of Poppaea.[136] Nero's favorite roles in tragedy were Oedipus, Thyestes, the mad Hercules, Alcmaeon, Orestes, and Canace giving birth.[137] As has been recently suggested by Champlin, Nero's preference for these characters was aimed at manipulating popular perception of his actions. For instance, Nero's use of the Orestes myth dramatized his involvement

---

[134] Note that in *Siluae* 1 *praef.* 5–9 Statius' concerns about the *Thebaid* do not seem to be related to the poem's political views.

[135] Champlin (2003a) 92–6.

[136] D.C. 63.9.4–5; Suet. *Nero* 21.3.

[137] Nero's favorite roles in tragedy: D.C. 63.9.4–5, 63.10.2, 63.22.6; Suet. *Nero* 21.3, 46.3; Philostr. *VA* 5.7; Juv. 8.228.

in the murder of Agrippina. The story was not meant to deny Nero's responsibility; like Orestes, Nero had killed his mother. Yet the mythological context placed the action in a different light: Nero appeared as the pious son of Agamemnon, guilty but legitimated by his mother's wickedness and the injunction of Apollo. In a similar way, the story of the mad Hercules dramatized the emperor's murder of Poppaea Sabina, casting him in the role of the mighty hero blinded by a god-sent frenzy. Nero's interest in the Oedipus myth—Oedipus was probably his favorite role— reflected the emperor's personal life, providing a mythological framework for his incest with Agrippina. In the guise of Oedipus, Nero appeared as the wretched hero who becomes king through crimes he is not aware of committing and suffers because of them.[138]

Nero's appropriation of mythical characters was so powerful and pervasive that it set in motion a constant confusion of myth and reality, fact and fiction, which went beyond previous Roman experiments in mythical role play. It became difficult— both during Nero's life and even more after his death—to think of certain mythical figures without thinking of Nero, and vice versa. Jokes centering on Nero's mythical counterparts were already popular during his lifetime.[139] Several years after his decease, there were still those who questioned Nero's appropriation of certain mythical figures.[140] At the time of Nero's demise, people remembered the last line the emperor had sung from a piece on Oedipus in exile: "my father and co-husband drives me to a pitiable death." The events had turned the play into reality, as Nero left Rome to find his death in a suburban villa.[141] An interesting case study is provided by accounts of Agrippina's death. Both Tacitus and the author of *Octauia* give the same version of Agrippina's last moments, recounting how she enjoined her assassins to strike the womb "which bore such a monster." The same actions and words are attributed to Jocasta in Seneca's *Oedipus*.[142] Because Seneca's *Oedipus* most likely predates Nero's murder of Agrippina, it seems that the identification of Nero and Oedipus was strong enough to prompt Tacitus and the author of *Octauia*, or their source, to embroider their account with a detail taken from Seneca's tragedy.[143] Nero's mythical doubles became part and parcel of the negative vision of Nero formulated by Flavian

---

[138] Champlin (2003a) 96–101 (Orestes), 101–3 (Oedipus), 103–7 (Hercules). On theatricality and the interchange between reality and myth in the Neronian period see the important study by Bartsch (1994), esp. 36–62.

[139] Cf. the lines quoted by Suetonius at *Nero* 39.2, poking fun at Nero's identification with Orestes.

[140] Cf. later discussions questioning Nero's appropriation of Orestes and remarking on the differences between the two: Juv. 8.215–21; Philostr. *VA* 4.38; Philostr. *Nero* 10; Suet. *Nero* 39.2.

[141] D.C. 63.28.5, cf. also Suet. *Nero* 46.3 (whose slightly different text is probably corrupt).

[142] Tac. *Ann.* 14.8 (Tacitus does not explain the reason for striking the womb); cf. D.C. 61.13; *Oct.* 368–76; Sen. *Oed.* 1038–9.

[143] Boyle (2011) lxxxi–ii; Champlin (2003a) 197 n. 42. See also Hind (1972).

authors. For instance, *Siluae* 2.7 turns Nero's identification with Orestes against him when it portrays Nero in Tartarus with the greatest sinners of humanity persecuted by his mother in the role of a Fury.[144]

That Seneca's tragedies were soon involved in this process is no surprise. They featured Nero's mythical aliases, provided powerful images of tyrants, and were rich in allusions to imperial politics. *Oedipus*, in particular, provided fertile material for this type of operation. The play on Nero's most famous alias is an investigation of power with an eye to the realities of the Roman Empire, written by a man directly involved in the politics of Nero's court. And historical events conspired to heighten, in retrospect, the play's potential for political allusion. Rome was swept by a plague during Nero's time; Nero too, like the hero of Seneca's play, was said to have performed necromancies. It was also held that he attracted catastrophe through his impious behavior, a topic well represented in Seneca's play.[145] Nero's "exile" and death were followed by the civil war of Otho and Vitellius, just as Oedipus' exile in myth was followed by the war of Eteocles and Polynices. Both Otho and Vitellius stressed their continuity with Nero and were considered very similar to him: They could indeed be regarded as his "children." Whereas the catastrophe of 69 CE could be imputed to divine anger at Nero's impiety, salvation had come through a family unconnected with the former dynasty. In the story of Thebes too, the civil war of Eteocles and Polynices—a consequence of Oedipus' curse—led to the eradication of both branches of the Theban royal house—the Labdacids and the descendants of the Spartoi (Menoeceus, Haemon, and Creon).

The pseudo-Senecan *Octauia* provides an example of how to capitalize on the potential for political allusion inherent in Seneca's *Oedipus*. The author of *Octauia* harnesses Seneca's production in a way that envisions the tragedies and Seneca's political theory as two complementary parts of the same political discourse. Nero speaks the words of Seneca's tyrants, while Seneca gives advice to Nero based in the sentiment of *De Clementia*.[146] In other words, Seneca's tyrants, of which Nero is a historical counterpart, provide the reader with a version of what a sovereign should not be like—of what a sovereign turns out to be when he falls short of the directions provided by Seneca's treatise. It is worth considering this text in some in detail.

---

[144] *Silv.* 2.7.118–19; Newlands (2011) 251.

[145] Plague: Suet. *Nero* 39; necromancies: Suet. *Nero* 34.4; Plin. *Nat.* 30.14–17; impious behavior attracting catastrophe: Tac. *Ann.* 14.22; *Oct.* 235–7.

[146] Cf. *Octauia*'s refashioning of a typical scene from Seneca's plays, that of the dialogue between tyrant and attendant, in which the latter seeks to restrain the tragedy's protagonist from an evil plan. In *Octauia*, the attendant is the philosopher Seneca, who tries to dissuade Nero from ordering the death of Sulla and Plautus. Cf. in part *Octauia* 437–61, with Ferri's (2003) notes *ad loc.* 253ff. and 72–3.

In *Octauia*, Nero has merged with his mythical aliases, especially Oedipus; *Octauia* establishes a constant dialogue with Seneca's play. This operation projects backward an allegorical reading of Seneca's tragedy as an indictment of Nero. Take the exchange between Nero and Seneca, in which Nero repeats the words uttered by Seneca's Oedipus in one of his most tyrannical moments, when he commands Creon's imprisonment in accordance with his theory of terror-based rule.[147] Another distinct echo of Seneca's *Oedipus* is audible in Octavia's words regarding her husband later in the play:

> utinam nefandi principis dirum caput
> obruere flammis caelitum rector paret,
> qui saepe terras fulmine infesto quatit
> mentesque nostras ignibus terret sacris
> nouisque monstris; uidimus caelo iubar
> ardens cometen pandere infaustam facem, . . .
> . . . en ipse diro spiritu saeui ducis
> polluitur aether, gentibus clades nouas
> minantur astra, quas regit dux impius.
> non tam ferum Typhona neglecto Ioue
> irata Tellus edidit quondam parens:
> haec grauior illo pestis, hic hostis deum
> hominumque templis expulit superos suis
> ciuesque patria, spiritum fratri abstulit,
> hausit cruorem matris—et lucem uidet
> fruiturque uita noxiam atque animam trahit!
> *Oct.* 227–32, 235–44

If only heaven's ruler, who often shakes the earth with storming thunderbolts and frightens our minds with supernatural fires and strange portents, would plan to heap fire on the monstrous head of this evil emperor! We have seen a comet's menacing flames spread their blazing radiance through the heavens, . . . Look, how the very sky is tainted with the menace breathed by this savage leader: the stars threaten new disasters for the nations ruled by this impious sovereign. Not such a savage was Typhon, born once in anger by mother Earth in Jove's despite; this scourge is graver than that, this foe of gods and men has expelled divinities from their temples and citizens from their fatherland,

---

[147] *Oct.* 439–71; Sen. *Oed.* 669–708; cf. in particular *Oct.* 471; alluding to Sen. *Oed.* 702.

robbed his brother of life, drained his mother's blood—and he still sees the
light of day, is blessed with life and draws his pestilential breath!

Nero's pollution of the sky (*Oct.* 236) recalls Oedipus' admission of his own polluting
influence in Seneca (*Oed.* 36), but the influence of *Oedipus* is not limited to this echo.
In Seneca, Oedipus' admission of his own nefarious influence is part of his reaction
to the plague: The king of Thebes suspects that he might be the cause of the pesti-
lence, even though at this stage he has not received any indication that this might be
the case. The plague in Seneca is accompanied by a number of divine portents, whose
description is indebted, as we subsequently see, to lists of *omina* [omens] traditionally
accompanying Roman civil wars. The analogy between the divine signs announcing
Oedipus' guilt and Roman traditions about civil war *omina* is tied to an important
thematic nucleus within Seneca's play to which I will return in Section 1.7: the causal
connection between Oedipus' crimes and civil war. In the *Octauia* we find a similar sit-
uation. The guilty Nero, who is literally called a plague [*pestis, Oct.* 240], brings about
the contamination of the *aether* that is traditionally associated with pestilences. The di-
vine anger his impious behavior attracts is also manifested by portents, some of which
have counterparts in lists of civil war omens. Lauren Ginsberg has demonstrated the
influence on this passage of Virgil's and Horace's accounts of the prodigies following
the death of Caesar and of Lucan's own retrojecting of those prodigies back to the
time of Caesar's war with Pompey.[148] She also argues persuasively that *Octauia*'s in-
teraction with civil war accounts has the function of anticipating Nero's death and
alluding to the ensuing civil war.[149] By incorporating civil war imagery in its descrip-
tion of Nero's impiety, *Octauia* reproduces the strategy enacted by Seneca in *Oedipus*.
Thus *Octauia* uses Seneca's *Oedipus* to construct its view of Nero's responsibility in the
ensuing civil war.

1.7 SENECA'S *OEDIPUS* AND THE *THEBAID*

My second experiment in reintroducing Nero into the imaginative world of the
Thebaid consists in reading the *Thebaid*'s engagement with Seneca's *Oedipus* against
the cultural and ideological background sketched in Section 1.6. I read the *Thebaid*'s
intertextual relationship with Seneca's *Oedipus* in light of Nero's own exploitation
of this theatrical character and in light of Flavian uses of Seneca's tragedies as a lens

---

[148] Ginsberg (2013) 656–63.
[149] Ginsberg (2013) 666–9.

through which to look back at the time of Nero.[150] Reading the *Thebaid*'s use of Senecan tragedy according to this perspective provides a new way of interpreting the political import of Senecan intertextuality, one in which the *Thebaid*'s reflection on tyranny is projected against the historical context of the kingdom of Nero and of the difficult transition of 69 CE rather than Domitian's principate.

Statius' indebtedness to Seneca's play has long been acknowledged by scholars.[151] I am particularly interested in the ways in which *Oedipus* works as a structural model for Statius' poem, contributing to configuring the *Thebaid* as both a sequel to and a reenactment of Seneca's drama.[152] Before I move on to demonstrate how Statius' text turns Senecan intertextuality to this use, let me consider two aspects of Seneca's play that are particularly important for the *Thebaid*. The first is the centrality of the father figure. This aspect is most visible in Seneca through the replacement of the revelation of Oedipus' guilt by Tiresias (in Sophocles) with a scene of necromancy in which Oedipus' guilt is revealed by the ghost of Laius.[153] The second aspect is the connection between Oedipus' crimes and civil war. Seneca's play begins with Oedipus' own description of the plague affecting Thebes. Oedipus feels that the plague might be divine retaliation for an act he has committed.[154] His sin costs the lives of citizens who are given distinctly Roman traits.[155] The plague is accompanied by monstrous *omina* that have equivalents in literary accounts of prodigies portending civil war: the howling of dogs at night, fountains stained with blood, ghosts coming back from the underworld, and earthquakes.[156]

The plague is not the only consequence of Oedipus' sin for the city of Thebes. Seneca's play makes it clear that ruin will extend to the next generation through the ultimate result of Oedipus' violations: civil war. This causal nexus between Oedipus' guilt and civil war is highlighted several times. The first attempt by Tiresias and Manto at divining Laius' murderer involves an inspection of sacrificial fire. Manto sees the flame change color a few times and finally turn black. Then the flame splits

---

[150] My experiment concerns the *Thebaid*'s interaction with Seneca's *Oedipus*, a play that, as we have seen, was central to constructions of Nero's image under the Flavians, but other plays could benefit from being explored from this angle; see Conclusions, Section C.1.

[151] On Statius and Senecan tragedy see Legras (1905) 56–7, 96–8, 174–6; Venini (1971) 55–80; Ganiban (2007) 159–65; and most recently Augoustakis (2015). On Seneca's *Oedipus* and the *Thebaid* in particular: Boyle (2011) xc–xciii, and see the bibliography quoted subsequently in this section about the *Thebaid*'s necromancy scene.

[152] On the *Thebaid* as a sequel to Seneca's *Oedipus* see Augoustakis (2015) 384.

[153] Sen. *Oed.* 530–658; Boyle (2011) lxiii.

[154] *Oed.* 1–109; on Oedipus' sense of guilt at the beginning see Boyle (2011) lvii–iii, cvii–cix, 117; Paduano (1988).

[155] The Roman characterization of the Thebans appears especially in the first choral ode: Sen. *Oed.* 110–25, 114–16, 117–19 with Boyle (2011) 146–8.

[156] Sen. *Oed.* 171–9; Boyle (2011) 155–7.

into two tongues, predicting the future war of Eteocles and Polynices.[157] In the ensuing inspection of entrails, the liver displays two bulging heads, one of which—the hostile one—is endowed with seven veins—an allusion to the civil war of Eteocles and Polynices and the seven Argive chiefs.[158] In the following necromancy, the climax of Laius' speech is a prophecy of the impending civil war that will erase the house of Oedipus:

te, te cruenta sceptra qui dextra geris,
te pater inultus urbe cum tota petam
et mecum Erinyn pronubam thalami traham,
traham sonantis uerbera, incestam domum
uertam et penates impio Marte obteram.
Oed. 642–6

You who hold the scepter in your bloodied hand, I shall seek you out, your unavenged father, along with the whole city; with me I shall bring the Erinys who attended your bride chamber, bring those whose whips resound; I shall overthrow this incestuous house, and wipe out its lineage in unnatural warfare.

This topic is echoed in the following choral ode, which references the civil war at the beginning of Thebes' history, the fratricidal war of the Spartoi, a war that prefigures the conflict of Eteocles and Polynices in many ways.[159]

The *Thebaid*'s subject is the aftermath of Seneca's play, and Statius emphasizes the continuity between the two works by having the *Thebaid* literally begin from the end of *Oedipus*. At the beginning of the *Thebaid*, the author's description of Oedipus' self-inflicted punishment evokes the conclusion of Seneca's play:[160]

impia iam merita scrutatus lumina dextra
merserat aeterna damnatum nocte pudorem
Oedipodes longaque animam sub morte trahebat.
Theb. 1.46–8

---

[157] Sen. *Oed.* 314–28 with Boyle (2011) 193; the war of Eteocles and Polynices is already alluded to by the Delphic Oracle at *Oed.* 237.

[158] *Oed.* 359–64 with Boyle (2011) 199 *ad loc.*

[159] Sen. *Oed.* 730–50. The Spartoi's connection with Eteocles and Polynices is already in Euripides; cf. *Ph.* 638–89 with Mastronarde (1994) 330; on the Spartoi as anticipation of Eteocles and Polynices in Seneca see Boyle (2011) 276, 285.

[160] Cf. Sen. *Oed.* 965, 977, 949; Boyle (2011) xc–xci.

Oedipus had already searched his impious eyes with his guilty hand and, condemning his shame, had plunged it into an eternal night; he was dragging out his life in a long-drawn-out death.

At the same time, Statius presents the *Thebaid* as a repetition of *Oedipus*. Jupiter's speech, a second programmatic scene at the beginning of the poem, combines allusions to both the beginning *and* the end of Seneca's play. In his portrayal of Oedipus as enduring a long death, Jupiter echoes the end of Seneca's play.[161] But his description of Oedipus' incest and parricide repeats the prophecy by the Delphic Oracle at the beginning of Seneca's tragedy.[162] The Delphic response sets in motion events in *Oedipus*, very much like Jupiter's programmatic speech in the *Thebaid*, contributing to the impression that the *Thebaid* will reenact the action of Seneca's *Oedipus*.

Jupiter's project in his initial speech is not unlike that of Laius in Seneca, for the supreme god plans to erase Thebes by way of civil war and goes on to summon Laius to accomplish his plan. In Seneca, Laius replaces Tiresias as the one who reveals Oedipus' guilt (the revelation takes place within a necromancy). Statius reduplicates Seneca's idea. In the *Thebaid*, the old king is summoned to the upper world twice. Laius is first tasked with enticing Eteocles into breaking his truce with Polynices; in this scene of the *Thebaid* Laius aptly appears disguised as Tiresias.[163] Then Laius appears again during the necromancy to underscore Oedipus' guilt.

Statius' transformation of the *Thebaid* into a repetition of or sequel to Seneca's *Oedipus* culminates in the necromancy scene of book 4. In Seneca's *Oedipus*, the necromancy is introduced after the failed rituals of act 2 with the purpose of discovering the culprit of Laius' death, the ultimate cause of the plague sweeping the city. As we have already seen, the description of the plague in Seneca's *Oedipus*, especially in the chorus (154–79), has much in common with Roman accounts of portents announcing civil war. In Statius' *Thebaid*, the necromancy comes as a response to a version of the by-now-conventional list of civil war portents, with distinct echoes of Seneca's chorus.[164] Statius' narrative elicits a sense of fulfillment, as

---

[161] *Theb.* 1.236–8; *Oed.* 948–51 with Boyle (2011) 328.

[162] *Theb.* 1.235 and *Oed.* 238; Boyle (2011) xci.

[163] *Theb.* 2.94–124. The scene of Laius' appearance to Eteocles is heavily indebted to another play by Seneca, *Thyestes*, as well as to other epic models: see Conclusions, Section C.1. Yet the idea of bringing back Laius builds on Seneca's *Oedipus* and its obsession with Laius: see Boyle (2011) xci.

[164] The detail of revenants, ghosts, or underworld creatures wandering outside the kingdom of death (Sen. *Oed.* 171–5) is found in Virgil [*G.* 1.476–7; Boyle (2011) 155], Statius, and Lucan, but the detail of the spring of Dirce stained with blood (Sen. *Oed.* 178) is distinctively echoed by Statius (*Theb.* 4.375–6); Parkes (2012) 204.

the reader sees Eteocles responding to the same portents that motivated his father's investigation of the dead. As a follow-up on the analogy between plague and civil war established by Seneca, Statius has his civil war omens replace Seneca's plague. We have seen how in *Octauia* the topic of divine portents connects Nero's actions with the future civil war: The portents marking Nero's rule are short-circuited with those announcing civil war after Caesar's death. The combination of the *Thebaid* and *Oedipus* produces the same sense of symmetry observed in *Octauia*. In the *Thebaid*, the omens accompanying Oedipus' rule in Seneca are recast as the portents marking the civil war that follows after Oedipus' self-punishment.

As is well known, Statius adapts the central scene of Seneca's play, the necromancy in which the guilt of Oedipus is revealed. The influence of Seneca is evident in the *Thebaid* passage, in terms of both structure and diction.[165] In both texts, the necromancy is carried out by Tiresias with the help of Manto. The arrival of souls from the underworld is marked by nearly identical words.[166] In both texts, the reader is then led through a parade of figures from Thebes' past. In both *Oedipus* and the *Thebaid*, Laius is eventually summoned to provide the climactic revelation. The overlapping of the dramatic time of the *Thebaid* and *Oedipus* is visible when Laius notes that Tiresias should have summoned Oedipus, not him, to divine the future of his children, exactly as Oedipus summoned Laius in Seneca's play.[167] The fact that Eteocles is now in his father's position combines the sense that the *Thebaid* repeats Seneca's *Oedipus* with the notion that Eteocles is, in some relevant sense, a "double" of his father. Importantly, the *Thebaid*'s necromancy brings Oedipus to the center. Laius' speech underscores the centrality of Oedipus' crime in producing civil war; Eteocles' and Polynices' misdeeds are not even mentioned.[168]

Other allusions to Seneca's *Oedipus* emerge in book 7.[169] In the *Thebaid*'s *teichoscopia* (the traditional epic scene in which the heroes in the battlefield are described by characters watching from the city walls), Phorbas is the servant who guides Antigone to the tower and discloses the identity of the heroes she sees from above. In Seneca's *Oedipus*, Phorbas is the servant of Laius who handed over the baby Oedipus to the old man from Corinth. He is the messenger of the play's climactic

---

[165] This passage's interaction with Seneca's *Oedipus* has been studied extensively: see Narducci (2002) 466–70; Boyle (2011) xci–ii; Parkes' (2012) notes on the episode at pp. 214ff.; Taisne (1991); and most recently Augoustakis (2015) 377–85. On the necromancy scene in the *Thebaid* in general: Vessey (1973) 235–58; Ganiban (2007) 65–9; Keith (2002) 397–402.

[166] Cf. Sen. *Oed.* 558 and *Theb.* 4.519; Sen. *Oed.* 572 and *Theb.* 4.520.

[167] *Theb.* 4.626–32. The *Thebaid* passage is marked by a conspicuous allusion to Seneca's *Oedipus* (638–40): Oedipus is identified by Laius through the same words Laius had used to describe Oedipus in Seneca; Augoustakis (2015) 84–5.

[168] *Theb.* 4.633–44.

[169] Boyle (2011) xciii.

revelation, as he uncovers that the same baby (whom Oedipus has already recognized as none other than himself) was a son of Jocasta and Laius. Statius' Phorbas too is a faithful servant of Laius, and he is the one who witnessed the king's death at the hands of Oedipus (*Theb.* 7.354–8). Statius' intertextual play conjoins Seneca and Sophocles brilliantly here. In Sophocles, the same slave who handed over Oedipus to the Corinthian is also the only witness of Laius' death. Phorbas, who handed over baby Oedipus in Seneca, is in Statius made a witness of Laius' death, so that the combination of Seneca and Statius re-creates the identity of person introduced by Sophocles. Evoking the murder of Laius, a very kind king [*mitissime, Theb.* 7.355], at this stage—the very beginning of war—emphasizes once again Oedipus' responsibility for the ruin of Thebes, the inextricable connection between his crime and the ensuing civil war.

Act 2 of Seneca's *Oedipus,* with the ritual inspection of fire and entrails, is echoed by Statius in two different episodes. The first is in book 10. Once again the city is at great risk and Tiresias is summoned. He too, like his Senecan counterpart, seeks to divine the future by observing the shape of the sacrificial flame. The scene is designed to be read as a continuation of Seneca's divination. In Seneca, the fire's splitting into two tongues forms the last stage of the ritual. In Statius, the fire splits into two tongues but then goes on to announce the next episode in the Theban saga (the self-sacrifice of Menoeceus), taking the form of a snake.[170] The following sacrifice scene we see in the *Thebaid* may also have been inspired by Seneca's divination through fire. When Eteocles offers a sacrifice of thanksgiving to Jupiter for routing Capaneus, a black flame arises from the fire onto Eteocles' face and burns his crown. In Seneca, something similar happens to Oedipus at the end of the fire inspection. A black cloud of smoke encircles his head, foreshadowing Oedipus' blinding.[171] In the *Thebaid*, the prodigy signifies Eteocles' impending loss of power, stressing once again the continuity between father and son.

In the *Thebaid*, the duel of the brothers is followed by Oedipus' appearance on stage. The scene has manifold connections with the *Thebaid*'s beginning, also inspired by *Oedipus*, and *Oedipus* itself. Once again, the Senecan topic of Oedipus' *longa mors* [long-drawn-out death] is evoked: The narrator speaks of Oedipus' *mortem imperfectam* [incomplete death] and goes on to compare him with Charon.[172] Oedipus' appeal to *natura* and *pietas* recalls Oedipus' own words at the beginning of Seneca's play.[173] The desire Oedipus expressed in the prologue is now

[170] *Theb.* 10.598–603.
[171] Sen. *Oed.* 325–7; *Theb.* 11.226–7.
[172] Cf. *Oed.* 948–51 and *Theb.* 11.580–82. Cf. also *Theb.* 11.753, 4.614 for the idea of Oedipus' blinding as *longa mors.*
[173] Boyle (2011) xciii; *Theb.* 11.605–7; *Oed.* 19, 25.

fulfilled, his children have reiterated his crimes, but Oedipus now regrets his curse, and he complains that his children have proved too similar to him.[174] A crime as monstrous as his own incest and patricide has been committed, which prompts Oedipus to repeat the act that concluded his tragedy in Seneca: He wishes he had eyes so he could make himself blind again.[175] Oedipus' last words appropriately echo the final line spoken by Oedipus in Seneca.[176]

The sense that the *Thebaid* is a repetition of *Oedipus* is intensified by the fact that not only is Jocasta still alive throughout this second phase of Oedipus' story (as in Euripides' *Phoenissae*), but her actions are closely patterned on Jocasta's actions in Seneca's *Oedipus*. In book 11, her attempt to discourage Eteocles from the duel with his brother is reminiscent of Seneca: Note in particular the simile comparing her with Agave and her mention of death through the womb.[177] She kills herself at the end of the poem, in concomitance with her husband's "second" self-blinding. As noted by Boyle, her incestuous suicide—on the bed couch with the sword of Laius—is inspired by the parallel scene of Jocasta's suicide in Seneca's *Oedipus*.[178] In spite of having lived his own tragedy twice, Oedipus has not learned the lesson yet. A few lines later, he utters another curse, a close parallel to the curse he pronounced at the beginning of the poem (*Theb.* 11.673–707). Creon will inherit the Theban throne under the same star as that of Laius and Oedipus. A tragedy has just ended, and a new one is about to begin, with a new tyrant, Creon. The curse of Oedipus extends to the other branch of the Theban royal house, as Creon is caught in the paradigm of Seneca's *Oedipus*.[179] It appears clearly that salvation in Thebes must come from a king unconnected to both the Labdacids and the descendants of Echion.

Statius' presentation of the *Thebaid* as both a sequel and a reenactment of Seneca's *Oedipus* goes hand in hand with Statius' tendency to transfer to the children some of the most notorious sins of the father, including incest, effectively turning them into "doubles" of Oedipus. Eteocles shares many traits with Oedipus' character.[180]

---

[174] *Theb.* 11.611: *crudeles nimiumque mei* [Cruel ones, too truly mine].

[175] *Theb.* 11.614–15: *o si fodienda redirent | lumina et in uultus saeuire ex more potestas* [Ah, if only I could have my eyes back, to gouge them and rage against my face as is my custom.] *Ex more*, as he is accustomed from earlier performances, such as the one in Seneca's text; see Feeney (1991) 341.

[176] *Theb.* 11.707; *Oed.* 1061; Boyle (2011) xciii.

[177] *Theb.* 11.318–20, 342; *Oed.* 1005–6, 1038–9; Boyle (2011) xciii.

[178] *Theb.* 11.634–41; *Oed.* 1032–9; Boyle (2011) xciii.

[179] Creon has much in common with Eteocles. Statius calls him a *rex cruentus* [bloody king; cf. *Theb.* 12.184, 680] several times, matching Laius' remarks on Oedipus in Seneca's play (*Oed.* 634). Cf. also the parallel scenes of Tydeus' embassy at Thebes and Phegeus' encounter with Creon: McGuire (1997) 177–9.

[180] Like his father in Seneca, he is dominated by fear, is prone to anger and always suspicious of rivals, and knows no diplomacy; his immediate reaction to any form of opposition is to resort to violence. Cf. e.g. *Theb.* 2.410–51, 3.1–32, 11.298–308; Sen. *Oed.* 518–19, 659–708.

Polynices' characterization is more complex, yet he too has inherited some of his father's characteristics. Once in Argos, Adrastus reassures the young hero by saying he can show that he is not like his father (*Theb.* 1.688–92). But the narrative proves him wrong: Statius has already portrayed him wandering the desert land of Thebes as an exile, very much like his father before his arrival in Thebes.[181] In his play, Seneca compares Oedipus to the Sphinx, both monsters of a confused nature (Sen. *Oed.* 640–1). Polynices has a Sphinx on his sword (*Theb.* 4.87): Like the Sphinx, he will provoke the death of many Thebans. But this is also a reminder that he resembles his father in his confused nature. He too is many things at the same time: son and brother of Oedipus, son and grandson of Jocasta. Oedipus problematically defines his union with his mother as *dulces furias* [a sweet madness, *Theb.* 1.68]. The phrase is echoed in the description of Polynices' longing for Thebes (*Theb.* 4.92).[182] Returning to Thebes would imply not only a return to power: Polynices also sees it as a return to his mother's bosom, a dangerous reminder of his father's "return" to the womb that bore him (*Theb.* 1.235). The incestuous nature of Polynices' longing for Thebes emerges clearly in an interconnected series of bull similes, within which Polynices and Eteocles are constructed as rivals for the love of Jocasta.[183]

What is the effect of this insistent intertextual summoning of Seneca's text? If we build on the identification of Nero with his mythical alias—which, as we have seen, had some currency in Statius' time—and if we apply to the *Thebaid* Flavian readings of Seneca's tragedy as an indictment of Nero, we are left with a set of correspondences whereby the historical relevance of the *Thebaid* is mapped onto the period of Nero's tenure and the 69 CE civil war. The causal connection between Oedipus' sin and civil war—which the *Thebaid* emphasizes through its reception of *Oedipus*—resonates more fully in this context, matching current perceptions of Nero's responsibility in bringing about the chaos of 69 CE. This type of perception, as we have seen, is the same encouraged by *Octauia* through its reception of Seneca' *Oedipus*. Statius protracts the narrative sequence of Seneca's *Oedipus* so as to involve his children and uses Seneca's text to highlight Eteocles' and Polynices' interchangeability with their father. This aspect too heightens the narrative's legibility with reference to the time of Nero. Statius' construction of Eteocles' and Polynices' similarities to Oedipus is paralleled in Flavian perceptions of Otho's and Vitellius' resemblances to Nero. Through Statius' reprise of Seneca, the atmosphere of the court of Nero, marked by divine displeasure at an impious tyrant, is extended to the civil war context of 69 CE,

---

[181] Polynices' journey away from Thebes is modeled on his father's journey as an exile from Corinth: see *Theb.* 1.312–14; Vessey (1973) 92–4; Hill (1990) 107; Henderson (1991) 42–6.

[182] Hershkowitz (1998) 277–82.

[183] Similes: *Theb.* 2.323–32; Hershkowitz (1998) 271–7.

with two of Nero's cronies reaping the final fruits of their father's sins. This accursed line of successors must be eradicated; as in the *Thebaid*, salvation can come only through the arrival of a conqueror with no connection with the Theban line.

This "Neronian" reading of Senecan intertextuality, as we will see in the following chapters, is further recommended by a number of elements. For the time being, I would like to emphasize that the cultural conditions under which the *Thebaid* was published were such that it would have been hard for Statius to prevent anti-Neronian readings of his own use of Seneca, even if he meant his political bias to lie elsewhere. The Flavian vulgate on Nero had substantially appropriated both Nero's mythical aliases and Seneca's texts. Nothing, of course, prevented readers from seeing criticism of the Flavian dynasty encoded in the Theban story, applying the Oedipus paradigm to Vespasian and his children.[184] But then some important elements would be lost. One of these is the sequence featuring crimes of an imperial tyrant and civil war, an element on which Statius insists throughout his reprisal of Seneca. Never is such an uncompromisingly negative view of all of the three members of the Flavian dynasty attested that it would justify Statius' contention that Eteocles and Polynices are substantially like their father. The opportunity of capitalizing on Nero's own mythical aliases and of conjuring up a popular and well-attested network of connections and allegorical readings would also be lost. No other emperor had enmeshed his own image with that of his mythical aliases to such a degree and with such influence on later accounts. The life of no other emperor had so closely resembled that of his mythical aliases.

1.8 THESEUS AND *CLEMENTIA*

The action of the *Thebaid*, like the action of the *Aeneid*, climaxes with a duel. The two sons of Oedipus kill one another; the last word of the *Aeneid* (*umbras*) is also the last word of *Thebaid* 11 (*umbra*). But the *Thebaid* is not finished yet: A whole new book brings about new developments. Argia and Antigone manage to bury the body of Polynices in defiance of Creon's orders. The Argive women successfully entreat Theseus to defend their right to bury their loved ones. An embassy is sent to Creon, who rejects it. War follows, with Theseus quickly dispatching Creon in an individual duel. The dead can finally be buried, while the Thebans welcome Theseus to their city like a victorious commander and a god.

In this monograph I concentrate on the *Thebaid*'s action prior to the resolution of book 12. It is, however, necessary to jump ahead to the end of the poem and deal

---

[184] Dominik (1994) 148–50 sees Vespasian as an image of Oedipus and identifies Domitian with Eteocles.

with the *Thebaid*'s close and with the figure of Theseus. The poem's finale, as we saw in the Introduction, is central to political approaches to Statius' poem. From the point of view of the analysis proposed in this book Theseus is particularly relevant, for his depiction allows Statius to engage many of the political ideas surveyed in Section 1.1 of this chapter, especially the Flavian reception of Neronian panegyric and of a construction of imperial ideology centering on *clementia*. My intention is to establish to what extent Theseus embodies the idealized portrait emerging from Flavian panegyric poetry, a construction of kingship that I link to elite's responses to Domitian's lenient policy at the beginning of his reign and that I interpret as an attempt at constraining Domitian to abide by certain standards.[185]

At the beginning of this chapter, I considered the enthusiastic tone found in panegyric poetry under Domitian. Neronian panegyrists emphatically announced the coming of a new age marked by a return of justice, granted by an illuminated sovereign endowed with *clementia*. Domitianic poetry recovers this set of images and concepts: Domitian's portrait in the *Siluae* is influenced by the ideal of the merciful sovereign, and his tenure is celebrated as a new Golden Age, superior to every other period in Roman history.[186]

The tone at the end of the *Thebaid* is remarkably different. Theseus comes in to finally grant peace to Thebes, yet the atmosphere is hardly one of triumph. Although it is true that the Thebans rejoice in their enemy's victory (!), the poem ends with a note on Statius' inability to adequately represent the bereavement of the Argive women.[187] There is a sense of overwhelming grief, only partly balanced by the possibility of finally mourning one's loved ones. Theseus brings no compensation for the suffering represented in the poem, nor is Statius naïve enough to think that a political solution, or a change in power, can entirely compensate for the tragedies of tyranny and civil war.[188] The *Aeneid* ends problematically and abruptly with Turnus' death, yet the future of Rome has already been written in book 1 with the prophecy of Augustus' rule and the return of a Golden Age.[189] The *Thebaid* adds a book to the *Aeneid*, and its final duel is emphatically less controversial than the one between Aeneas and Turnus.[190] But the Golden Age promised in the *Aeneid*

---

[185] For views of Theseus in scholarship see Introduction, Section I.3, and the subsequent discussion in this section. Convenient surveys of scholarly views of the poem's finale, with full references, can be found in Bessone (2011) 102–3; Ganiban (2007) 212–14.

[186] See Section 1.1.

[187] *Theb.* 12.797–809.

[188] This aspect can be suggestively read from the point of view of survivors of Nero, with whom Statius had connections: The dead of civil war will not come back, nor will the victims of Nero. Under the new regime, however, it will be possible to mourn them—for instance by composing *Siluae* 2.7.

[189] *A.* 1.257–96.

[190] Braund (1996a) 3–4.

finds no counterpart in the *Thebaid*.[191] In the *Thebaid* one does not find the notion of a new era, secured by the divine support granted to an extraordinary ruler, with which Domitian is associated in the *Siluae*. No god is there to ratify Theseus' victory. This is a purely human conquest: It remains a precarious and possibly momentary achievement.[192] More than this, as we see in Chapters 4 and 5, the close of Statius' *Thebaid* conveys a problematic sense of the necessity of violence and of the inescapable need for a somewhat oversized monarchical power to prevent the world from drifting into chaos.[193] The frame for this close is, in short, the pessimistic view of humanity and the gods that I outlined in the Introduction.[194]

In this context, the value of *clementia* is given a central position. This is a concept that, as we saw, is given great emphasis in Neronian ideology, and one that is extensively resurrected by panegyrists of Domitian. Statius introduces the "altar of *Clementia*" as the location for the encounter between Theseus and the Argive women. The altar itself is no invention of Statius; Greek writers know of a βωμὸς Ἐλέου [an altar of Compassion] in the Athenian agora.[195] But the Latin word used by Statius denotes a value that is distinct from compassion (the Latin equivalent of Greek ἔλεος is *misericordia*) and is central to Roman discussions of political action, particularly in the imperial period. This operation is exceptionally important, and not only because it foregrounds *clementia* as a key value in the close of the poem and as a response to the crisis opened by the first 11 books.[196] The transformation also allows a complex ideological operation: By finding a space for Roman *clementia* in the prehistory of Athens, Statius is able to forge a connection between this imperial value and a Greek tradition focusing on Athens as a champion of the oppressed. This is the tradition of the "praise of Athens," reflected in Euripides' *Supplices* and later works such as Isocrates' *Panegyricus*, a set of notions with which Statius interacts substantially in his description of the altar of *clementia*. The quintessentially Roman value of *clementia* is given a Greek myth of origin and is broadened and redefined in the process.[197]

Before we look more closely into Statius' redefinition of *clementia*, let me consider the initial lines in Statius' description of the altar of Clementia. Statius insists that

---

[191] Contrast, for instance, Silius 3.571–629, especially lines 607–29, in which Domitian's future triumphs and his apotheosis are already sanctioned by fate and warranted by Jupiter's authority.

[192] This victory is, however, achieved by a king who, in some ways, is more than human, as we see more clearly in Chapter 4, and in a context in which the goddess Clementia is presented as a divine virtue that abides in the chests of mortals (*Theb.* 12.93–4); see Chapter 4, Section 4.3.

[193] See Chapter 4, Section 4.3; Chapter 5, Section 5.4.

[194] Introduction, Section I.8.

[195] The key passage is Paus. 1.17.1; see Stafford (2000) 199–225; Bessone (2011) 105 n. 2.

[196] *Inclementia* [lack of mercy] is a feature of Creon at *Theb.* 11.684.

[197] Bessone (2011) 102–27.

the goddess Clementia does not have an image and receives no bloody sacrifices. Her cult is aniconic; she does not abide in statues of metal, but in the hearts of men. Federica Bessone has proposed a suggestive reading of these lines as an attempt at rejecting previous, opportunistic appropriations of *clementia* in political contexts.[198] No emperor can claim to possess *clementia* just because he performs sacrifices to an image of this goddess in a temple; true *clementia* does not live in temples but abides in the hearts of men and is displayed by their actions. From my point of view, this reading is in line with a process I discuss several times in this book: the attempt at detaching certain concepts from previous, especially Neronian, appropriations and redefining them in a positive way. As far as *clementia* is concerned, I previously observed that the reprise of themes of imperial panegyric implies the idea that the current emperor will be the first to truly embody the new style of government based on *clementia*, which had falsely been advertised by his predecessors.[199]

A text that is substantially connected to the praise of Athens as a guide for humanity and defendant of justice, Euripides' *Supplices*, covers the same ground as Statius' book 12 and is substantially engaged by the *Thebaid*.[200] In the *Supplices*, Theseus is a constitutional sovereign, a stand-in for the values of Athenian democracy. His exchange with the Theban herald contrasts Athens' rule of the people with Thebes' tyrannical regime.[201] In the *Thebaid*, this democratic dimension of the Athenian sovereign is absent; for instance, there is no hint at any codivision of power in Statius' narrative.[202] Statius is not interested in presenting the advantages of one constitution over the other. Athens does not bring a system of government that is superior to the one in Thebes: Athens brings a different kind of absolute monarch. What makes the difference in the *Thebaid* is the intrinsic nature of the sovereign. As is typical of Roman imperial reflections, the discussion centers on the qualities of a good ruler, not on the intrinsic values of constitutions. The constitutional background is similar to that of *Siluae* 1.1 and of the poetry for Trajan, in which panegyrists make the point that even Cato would want to live under a sovereign such as Domitian or Trajan, not because they would restore the Republic but because the sovereign's value surpasses even the Republic (or perhaps brings back the Republic and its values in a surrogate way).[203]

---

[198] *Theb.* 12.93–4; Bessone (2011) 109–10.

[199] See Section 1.1, and Chapter 4, Section 4.1.

[200] Bessone (2011) 20–2, 132–5, 105–6; Criado (2015) 294–300; Pollmann (2004) *passim* (see index s.v. Euripides at p. 311).

[201] E. *Supp.* 399–462, esp. 406.

[202] Criado (2015) 298–300; see also Pollmann (2004) 139–40.

[203] Mart. 11.5.9–12; *Silv.* 1.1.27–8; discussed in Chapter 4, Section 4.2.

Neronian propaganda advertised a return of justice in connection with the rule of law. This topic finds no direct equivalent in the *Thebaid*, except in a broader form: The kind of laws Theseus sets out to restore are the laws of nature.[204] Theseus feels compassion for his fellow human beings. He perceives that the Argive women's request for justice is legitimate and that natural laws binding all human beings are being violated.[205] As Federica Bessone has shown, the ideal of *clementia* is broadened through reference to the system of notions surrounding the concept of *humanitas*.[206] What Theseus allegedly displays in the close of the poem is not just *clementia* narrowly conceived—readiness to forgive and the ability to curtail punitive action—but a broader commitment to defend certain naturally sanctioned rights of human beings.[207] In book 3, Maeon is greeted as the one who prepared the way for the coming of *libertas*. Statius does not provide enough details to help us verify whether Theseus fulfills this statement. Theseus obviously does not bring any sharing of power, but if by *libertas* we mean the limited notion of *libertas*, common to imperial authors, as freedom of speech (the type of *libertas* that Maeon seems concerned with), the best we can do is to integrate Statius' portrait based on the idea, observed in *De Clementia* and Neronian panegyric, that *libertas* is a corollary of any kingdom endowed with *clementia*. But the text does not go so far as to make this connection for us.

It remains for us to see to what extent Theseus is a credible embodiment of the complex values evoked by Statius' description of the altar of Clementia. This is a point on which there has been much discussion among scholars.[208] Let me just mention a few points that seem to suggest that Theseus and *clementia* can hardly be separated.[209] Statius has effectively redefined *clementia* as concern for fellow human beings who are wronged in disrespect of universal laws that should bind all humans. Theseus' intervention brings these values into effect as he intervenes in defense of the Argive

---

[204] *Theb.* 12.642–4.

[205] *Theb.* 12.555–8; cf. also 12.165–6.

[206] Bessone (2011) 116–22.

[207] This broadening of the concept of *clementia* in connection with *humanitas* is already anticipated by Seneca's *De Clementia*: Bessone (2011) 121–2.

[208] Several scholars question Theseus' credibility as an embodiment of *clementia* and/or see the Athenian sovereign at a certain remove from the values embodied by the altar: Ahl (1986) 2898; Dominik (1994) 3 n. 11, 54, 92–8, 125, 152–3; McNelis (2007) 172–3; Ganiban (2007) 220–2; Coffee (2009) 224–8; constructive views of Theseus' relationship with *clementia* are expressed by Ripoll (1998) 432–50; Delarue (2000) 109–11; I am particularly influenced by Bessone (2011) 128–99; see also Introduction, Section I.3.

[209] I am not convinced that Statius uses Theseus' mythical past to undermine this character (Ahl 1986, 95–6); I find Bessone's arguments against this type of reading convincing: Bessone (2011) 136–50. This reading of Statius' allusions to Theseus' past is not consistent with the didactic approach I take in this monograph: If Theseus is an image of what Statius would want Domitian to be like, why should he direct Domitian toward an intrinsically flawed model, which the poet himself subtly undermines?

women and forces Creon to behave as a human.[210] The traditional Roman notion of *clementia*, as the ability to curtail punitive action and readiness to forgive, also appears in Statius' account of Theseus' campaign against Creon. Theseus' encounter with the Argive women is staged at the altar of Clementia, and here the Athenian sovereign decides to heed their request.[211] He brings war to Creon, but only after his offer of peace is turned down.[212] Even in war his *clementia* is visible: The animal simile of the mild lion, a *topos* of exhortations to sovereigns (found in Seneca's *De Clementia*, in Martial, and in the *Siluae*), provides an image of Theseus' moderation in battle.[213] Theseus is quick to forgive, just as the enlightened sovereign of *De Clementia* is: Only the caricature tyrant Creon finds his deserved punishment.[214] The Thebans are not willing to fight for Creon, and they abandon him. As soon as Creon is dead, peace is made in the midst of battle: The citizens of Thebes rush to embrace their enemies and welcome Theseus to their city. Theseus' final victory is a joy for the defeated.[215] We have observed some of Theseus' traits in connection with Domitian in *Siluae* 1.1. In general, the influence of the ideal of the merciful sovereign is the closest link between the portrait of Theseus and panegyric constructions of Domitian encountered in the *Siluae*.[216]

The central role attributed to *clementia* in the poem's finale is relevant to my argument also for another reason. In this chapter, I have suggested that the *Thebaid* may be influenced by a certain ideological way of reading the two parts of Seneca's production, the tragedies and his philosophical works, as complementary. I have proposed that both the encounter between Maeon and Eteocles and Statius' use of Seneca's *Oedipus* conspire to connect the Theban tyrants to Nero and his cronies. In *Octauia*, Seneca's political philosophy provides the counterpart to the tyrannical

---

[210] Cf. *Theb.* 12.165–6.

[211] Argive women at the altar of *clementia*: *Theb.* 12.512.3; encounter with Theseus: *Theb.* 12.540–98; Braund (1996a) 12.

[212] *Theb.* 12.677–92.

[213] *Theb.* 12.736–40; Bessone (2009) 202, (2011) 190–8; cf. Sen. *Cl.* 1.5.5; Stat. *Silv.* 2.5; Mart. 1.6, 14, 22, 48, 51, 60, 104. See Weinreich (1928) 90–103; Citroni (1975) intr. to 1–6 and comm. to single epigrams; Lorenz (2002) 126–34; Nauta (2002) 402–12; Rosati (2006) 41–52, 45–8; Coleman (2006), *passim* (Intr., lxxix ff.; comm. to Mart. *Sp.* 12 [10], 20 [17], 21 [18]).

[214] Braund (1996) 4, 14. Coffee (2009) 227 argues that Theseus' killing of Creon shows that the Athenian king is very far from the values embodied by the altar of *clementia*, pointing out that "Clementia shelters suppliants precisely in Creon's situation, namely those who, 'deprived of the rule of kingdoms and guilty of erring by committing crimes, have come to seek reconciliation'"; yet he overlooks the fact that, unlike Turnus, Creon does not ask for mercy and is seeking no reconciliation. *Parcere subiectis* [spare the vanquished] does not apply here: Creon is intent on killing Theseus when he receives the final blow.

[215] *Theb.* 12.782–8.

[216] For instance, the idea that Theseus is able both to inspire fear and to command the love of his subjects is paralleled in *Siluae* 1.1; see Section 1.1.

Nero, whose character is fashioned through the words and attitudes of Seneca's tragic tyrants. The centrality of *clementia* to the poem's close creates a similar pattern in the *Thebaid*: Tyrannical figures inspired by Seneca's tragedies and influenced by the vulgate of Nero are set against a character who is brought into close connection with the ideals of Seneca's *De Clementia*.[217]

In Theseus' portrait there are elements that can be read with reference to Flavian ideology. The Flavians came to bring peace after the civil war between Otho and Vitellius; like Theseus, they were unrelated by blood to the ruling dynasty.[218] In the years in which the *Thebaid* is concluded Domitian comes back to Rome from a campaign in the Northeast, like Theseus, who is seen returning from a campaign against the Amazons. Even the Bacchic imagery that accompanies Theseus' triumph, although common to Roman triumphs, has parallels in monuments erected to celebrate Domitian's victories in the Danube.[219] Divine models conspire to set Domitian and Theseus one beside the other: Both are supported by Minerva, and both have close connections with Jupiter.[220] And the creation of a Greek myth for the birth of *clementia* is in line with the philhellenic tendencies of the emperor who resumed the tradition of Greek games in Rome.

But the point of this Flavian resonance is not to make Theseus into a panegyric portrait of Domitian. Rather, the Athenian sovereign is an image of the kind of ruler Statius would like Domitian to embody. It is a disillusioned ideal from many points of view, more realistic and far less idyllic than the portrait introduced by the *Siluae*. As we see more clearly in Chapter 4, Statius' depiction of Theseus shows that kingship cannot prescind from violence and fear and that the world cannot do without a somewhat hypertrophic and fragile absolute power. It is a picture that draws attention to the fragility of political achievement and emphasizes human responsibility. In the absence of the gods, it is up to the individual to make the difference between tyranny and good government, without any support or guarantee of success from divine powers.

---

[217] To this type of reading of Senecan tragedies I return in Chapter 3, Sections 3.3 and 3.6.

[218] On Theseus and Flavian emperors: Vessey (1973) 315 n. 1; Ripoll (1998) 495–502.

[219] See Martial's colorful description of the Temple of Fortuna Redux at 8.65, with his reference to the elephants towing the emperor's chariot on the monument's frieze; see *LTUR* II 275–6 s.v. Fortuna Redux (F. Coarelli). The temple was erected after Domitian's return from the Pannonian War of 92 CE against the Suebi and Sarmatians. Statius may have seen the temple iconography only after the *Thebaid* was completed, but the *Thebaid* may be reacting to the circulation of Bacchic imagery in connection with Domitian's Danube triumphs around the time of the poem's completion (or on the occasion of earlier triumphs by Domitian), for which the temple is evidence. On Domitian's campaign of 92 CE see Suet. *Dom.* 6.1; Tac. *Ag.* 41; *ILS* 1017.

[220] Domitian and Minerva: *Silv.* 1.1.37–40; Suet. *Dom.* 15.3; Philostr. *VA* 7.24; Mart. 4.1.5, 5.2.6–8 etc. See Sauter (1934) 90–6; Scott (1936) 166–88; Fears (1981) 77–8; Bessone (2011) 45 n. 3; on Theseus and Jupiter see Chapter 4, Section 4.3.

The *Thebaid* expresses the hope that Domitian will embody this ideal. This is, to an extent, a familiar portrait: the benign sovereign who, though mighty at war, is ready to forgive and has *clementia* as its guiding virtue. It has much in common with the ideal sketched by Neronian panegyrists and is similar to the kind of portrait that emerges as an elite ideal in the initial phases of the following dynasty; a few years later, Pliny the Younger would swear to see a remarkably similar imperial prototype realized by Trajan. At the beginning of Domitian's reign, the hope that Domitian would fulfill this ideal was no less reasonable than it was at the beginning of Trajan's reign. Statius' attempt at directing Domitian toward this ideal of illuminated kingship would not have seemed desperate flattery to all of his readers, although some may have thought that Statius' hopes were going to remain as ineffective as those of Nero's panegyrists.

It is time to draw some conclusions. In this chapter, I documented the reception of Neronian panegyric in texts in praise of Domitian. I connected this reception to the fact that Domitian's principate, like Nero's, began with gestures in favor of the senatorial elite and with attempts to present him as a restorer of *libertas*. I sought to explain how this reception of Neronian modes of praise could be coupled with the construction of Nero as the imperial monster and the polar opposite of Domitian. I then discussed Domitian's ambiguous relationship with Nero and his negotiation of Neronian ideology and drew attention to Statius' connection with groups of survivors of Nero. Finally, I experimented with reintroducing anti-Neronian ideology into readings of the *Thebaid*. I showed that a constructive reading of the Maeon episode is possible and that an ideological reception of Seneca's tragedies, such as that documented by the pseudo-Senecan *Octauia*, provides a suggestive scenario for the understanding of Statius' adaptation of Seneca's *Oedipus*.

Through this reconstruction, we can see the *Thebaid* responding to an initial coinciding of the elites' interests with Domitian's agenda. Individuals gathering at the house of Polla had a stake in Domitian's support of the martyrs of former emperors. They had everything to gain from Domitian's adoption of Seneca's *De Clementia* as a rulebook. Domitian, in turn, courted their approval. The political project of the *Thebaid* originates in this short-lived and precarious intersection of cultural and political projects. This analysis allowed us to appreciate some aspects of the political thought of the *Thebaid*, such as the influence of Seneca's *De Clementia*, to which we will return in other chapters. I also suggested that, to an extent, the *Thebaid*'s construction of its own ideology relies on hermeneutic operations centering on Neronian literature. Statius co-opts the works of Seneca and, as we will see in Chapter 4, Lucan, to its own political agenda by providing an ideologically loaded reading of these texts.

The recasting of Seneca's plays as two complementary sides of one discourse on power has the effect of bridging the gap between the tragic poet and the philosopher–statesman, casting Seneca's poetical activity as a means to propagate the same standards encoded in his political thinking. In Statius' view, Seneca and Lucan were courageous enough to make their work an instrument of criticism. In hindsight, the Neronian poet emerges as someone who praised the emperor as long as he was good, but who turned his literary production into a weapon for criticism as soon as the emperor started to fall short of the standards set for him by poets. Through his ideological reception of Seneca and Lucan, Statius claims for himself the autonomy and intellectual independence of the hero–poets from the earlier generation.

2

Riding among the stars

IT WAS STILL night when the Flavian troops took their positions in front of Vitellius' army on the day of the second battle of Cremona, the crucial engagement of the 69 CE civil war. Antonius Primus gave a speech to the ranks, which combined encouragement and threats. Then something uncanny happened: The Sun appeared over the horizon, and the soldiers of Legio III Gallica turned toward it and hailed it, raising a great cry of war.[1] The Vitellians were thrown into confusion, suspecting that the troops were saluting the arrival of Mucianus' legions. I will return to this scene at the end of this chapter. My purpose is to show that this episode has relevance for our understanding of Domitian's ideology and its relationship with Nero, and that it is part of a cultural process that is singularly reflected in Statius' epic.

This chapter builds on the discussion of Chapter 1, concentrating on a specific element of continuity between Nero and Domitian, namely the harnessing of solar symbols. I begin with a brief survey of imperial uses of solar symbolism, with particular attention to Augustus and Nero—the two emperors whose cultural policy had the strongest influence on Domitian. For this analysis, I take literary evidence into account, but I also pay attention to the three emperors' building programs. I then consider the myth of Phaethon and its use in political contexts, both under Nero and in the aftermath of his death.

---

[1] Tac. *Hist.* 3.24.

Next, I analyze the presence of solar imagery in the *Thebaid*. My starting point is the chariot race narrative in book 6. As I try to show, not only does the race feature allusions to Rome's recent history, especially to Nero, but it also functions as the starting point of a complex strategy by which the poet interacts with Domitian's reception of solar symbols and touches on some of the most pressing problems of the contemporary political debate. Statius' strategy makes use of the two protagonists of the chariot race, Polynices and Amphiaraus. The race foreshadows the destiny of the two heroes and prefigures the scenes of both Polynices' and Amphiaraus' deaths. More important, the race introduces Amphiaraus and Polynices as embodiments of two different patterns of solar kingship.

The opposition between Polynices and Amphiaraus is also important for understanding the episode of Amphiaraus' succession in book 8. This scene allows Statius to provide his own reflection on the topic of succession and to interact with pro-Flavian accounts of the relationship between Domitian and Titus. At the end of the chapter, I speculate on the reasons for Domitian's interest in solar symbols. To this end, I consider a final passage from Statius' *Thebaid*, namely the hymn to Apollo in book 1.

2.1 SOLAR IDEOLOGY

Apollo and Helios were initially two distinct divinities. The process leading to their conflation, which began in Greece, proceeded gradually. In Rome, Sol was a local god venerated in the Circus, whose cult had been instituted, according to tradition, by Titus Tatius. Sol was imagined as racing the heavens in his orbit across the zodiac on a fiery chariot; he was thus connected to chariot racing. Sol's temple stood in the middle of the Circus so that the races literally took place before his eyes.[2] The association of Sol, chariot racing, and the Circus eventually grew into a complex astronomical allegory, according to which the Circus represented the cosmos: The arena was the Earth, its *euripus* [water course] the sea, the obelisk in the center the Sun, the 24 races the 24 hours, the 7 laps the days of the week, the 12 gates from which the chariots started the race the 12 months or the 12 signs of the zodiac, and the 4 racing teams the 4 seasons.[3]

Solar imagery as an attribute of power arrived in Rome toward the end of the Republic, under the influence of Hellenistic culture. It received great emphasis under Augustus. Expectations of a new Golden Age under the sign of Apollo/Sol

---

[2] Tertullian *De Spectaculis* 8. On the temple and its appearance see *LTUR* IV, 333–4, "Sol (et Luna), Aedes, Templum" (P. Ciancio Rossetto).

[3] Wuilleumier (1927).

were alive in late republican culture, connected to the hope for redemption and a new beginning after the crisis of civil war: Virgil's fourth eclogue is a key witness to this tradition. Octavian made the most of these expectations. Legends circulated that he had been marked out at birth as an embodiment of the providential solar king. He also made Apollo his tutelary deity, an assimilation that favored reception of solar imagery in certain contexts.[4] The summit of the temple of Palatine Apollo was surmounted by a quadriga depicting the Sun god, but within the temple, Apollo appeared without his solar attributes.[5] The syncretism of the two divinities was encouraged by this ideological climate, but under Augustus the two maintained a certain religious and iconographic autonomy.[6]

Identification of Augustus and Sol is frequent in the literary record, as is solar imagery.[7] In iconography, we see Augustus wearing the radiate crown, a solar symbol already used by Hellenistic kings, and in the guise of Sol/Helios.[8] This identification appears in two splendid cornelians. In the first, Augustus is depicted as the Sun god ascending to heaven on a quadriga; in the second, Augustus' head is given the attributes of Sol/Helios, the handsome unshorn god.[9] The latter is believed to be modeled on a statue of Augustus with the attributes of Sol in the Palatine library.[10] Important in these depictions of Augustus is the connection among Sol, chariot racing, and ideas of apotheosis (ascending to heaven). The same connection weaves together a cluster of monuments erected in the Campus Martius and the Circus Maximus.

Several years after the building of the Palatine temple, a season of renewed emphasis on solar ideology was inaugurated in Rome. Around 10 BCE, Augustus erected two obelisks, originally from Heliopolis in Egypt, in Rome. The first was placed in the center of the Circus Maximus. It emphasized the cosmic allegory inherent in the Circus and visually responded to the quadriga of the Sun god on top of the temple of Palatine Apollo, visible from the Circus.[11] The second was erected in the Campus

---

[4] Legends of Octavian's birth as a new Apollo: Suet. *Aug.* 94.4–6, 95.1; Apollo and Augustus: Zanker (1988) 47–65; Miller (2009) 15–53.

[5] The quadriga of the Sun god on the roof of the Palatine temple: Prop. 2.31.11; Kienast (1999) 223; La Rocca (2014) 142. The temple of Palatine Apollo: Sauron (1981) 286–94; Zanker (1983); Simon (1986) 20–4; Kellum (1985) 172–5; Galinsky (1996) 213–24; Gurval (1995) 111–31; Miller (2009) 185–252.

[6] La Rocca (2014) 142; Matern (2002) offers a comprehensive study of Helios/Sol in iconography and cult.

[7] Cf. e.g. Hor. *Carm.* 4.5.5–8, 4.2.45–8.

[8] Hellenistic kings: Bergmann (1998) 58–84 pls. 9, 10.3, 11.2, 11.4, 12.1–4; Augustus and Sol: Bergmann (1998) 99–126, esp. 103–7.

[9] Bergmann (1998) 104, pl. 20.6; Dacos–Giuliano–Pannuti (1973) 59–60 no. 29 fig. 22; Giuliano (1989) 228 no. 152.

[10] On the statue of Augustus in the Palatine library: Schol. Hor. *Ep.* 1.3.17; Serv. *Ecl.* 4.10; La Rocca (2014) 142.

[11] On the influence of this visual relationship on the imagination of imperial poets such as Ovid see Barchiesi (2009).

Martius as the gnomon of a large sundial.[12] The shadow cast by the obelisk on the marble pavement made visible the constant yearly trajectory of the Sun across the zodiac. The monument was part of a complex including the Ara Pacis, completed nearly at the same time (9 BCE), and two monuments of earlier construction, the Mausoleum of Augustus and the Pantheon. The latter had strong connections with the topic of the apotheosis of the princeps, and the sundial complex was linked to Augustus' implementation of Caesar's calendrical reform.[13]

Before Julius Caesar, the civil calendar based on a cycle of 365 days had lost its synchronization with the sidereal year (since it takes the Earth 365 days and 6 hours to complete a full lap around the Sun). Caesar's solution consisted of adding a day every fourth year, but the reform was wrongly implemented by Lepidus, the pontifex maximus in charge after Caesar's death, because of an error of inclusive counting (the extra day was added every 3 years).[14] Augustus finally rectified the situation in 9/8 BCE, and his massive sundial proved his reform right: The Sun's shadow could now be seen returning to its appointed place on the marble pavement on the same day every 4 years. To celebrate his successful correction of the calendar, Augustus gave his name to a month, as Caesar had done after his reform.[15] Augustus' building program in the Campus Martius around 10/9 BCE linked solar identity to the emperor's apotheosis and centered on the role of the emperor as dispenser of order and well-being: The Sun guarantees order and welfare to the Earth through his recurring trajectory; so does the emperor through his earthly rule. The accurate sundial proved that order had been returned to the cosmos.

Nero's exploitation of solar imagery was rooted in Augustus' practice. Yet the pervasiveness of the imagery, its connection with the emperor's performances, and certain specific ideological implications have no parallel under Augustus.[16] Legends about Nero's solar predestination, comparable to those attested for Augustus, are recorded: It was rumored that he was born at the break of dawn and touched by the Sun's rays before he even touched the ground (that is, before his father picked him up from the ground, where he had been laid, to acknowledge him); or that at birth

---

[12] The two obelisks and their positions are referenced by Pliny the Elder: *Nat.* 36.71–2. The inscriptions on their socles: *CIL* VI 701 (= *ILS* 91); *CIL* VI 702 (= *ILS* 91). On the Solarium Augusti (Augustus' monumental sundial) there is a vast debate. The papers in Haselberger (2014) provide the most up-to-date discussions of this complex monument.

[13] For a holistic view of Augustan monuments in the Campus Martius, their mutual relationship, and ideological implications see La Rocca (2014).

[14] Macrob. *Sat.* 1.14.13–15 and Solinus 1.45–7, with Samuel (1972) 156–8.

[15] Censorinus 22.16; Suet. *Aug.* 31.2; Schütz (1990) 447–8; on the Julian calendar see Feeney (2007) 196–201.

[16] On Nero and Apollo/Sol see Champlin (2003a) 112–77.

a mysterious sunlight surrounded him while it was still dark.[17] A more direct emphasis on the syncretism of Apollo and Sol allowed Nero to bring together, under the sign of one god, his love for singing at the lyre and his passion for chariot racing.

Nero is acclaimed as Apollo after his singing performances in 59 CE. The emperor's solar ideology is reflected in his iconography. After the fire of 64 CE, Nero began construction of the Golden House, whose project capitalized on solar symbolism: The house, covered in gold and pearls, was as radiant as the Sun, its garden a miniature version of the world that the Sun illuminates in his course; the Colossus, a massive statue of the Sun god (perhaps with features of Nero), was designed to be raised in its vestibule.[18] A set of solar events was at the center of Nero's settlement of the Parthian question, culminating in the Golden Day of 66 CE, when he was addressed as Sun Mithras by Tiridates, king of Armenia. According to Dio, Nero's "triumph" of 67, a celebration of the emperor's successes at games in Greece, culminated in Nero's dedication of his victory crowns around the obelisk in the Circus. In Suetonius' account, the parade climaxed with Nero's visit to the Temple of Palatine Apollo, after which Nero dedicated statues of himself in the guise of a lyre player in his palace.[19] In literature, a reflection of the emperor's preference for solar symbols is found in Seneca's *Apocolocyntosis*, Calpurnius' *Eclogues*, and Lucan's *Bellum Ciuile*.[20]

Under Vespasian and Titus solar symbols are used much more sparingly.[21] The emperor who laughed at those who sought to make him a descendant of one of Hercules' comrades did not conceal his humble origins: No legends of solar descent are attested for the Flavii from Reate.[22] As far as we can tell, the same applies to the very short reign of Titus. With Domitian, things are significantly different. First, there is the evidence for Domitian's building program in the Campus Martius, where reconstruction was made necessary by the fire of 80 CE. Augustus' sundial was no longer accurate during Pliny the Elder's time: Perhaps the ground had settled, or perhaps, as Pliny suggests, the laws of the universe had been altered and the Sun was straying from his regular

---

[17] Legends about Nero's solar birth: Suet. *Nero* 6.1; D.C. 61.2.1.

[18] Acclaimed as Apollo after performances: Tac. *Ann.* 14.14–5; D.C. 61.19–20; Nero claimed that he could equal Sol as charioteer and Apollo as singer: Suet. *Nero* 53. For Nero as Sol in iconography, coinage and inscriptions, see n. 94 in Chapter 1. On the Golden House and the Colossus see nn. 73 and 94 in Chapter 1.

[19] On the Golden Day and the "triumph" of 67 CE see Chapter 1, Section 1.3 and n. 95.

[20] Sen. *Apoc.* 4.1.20–32. Another key text is the praise of Nero at the beginning of Lucan's *Bellum Ciuile*, to which we return in a moment.

[21] Use of solar imagery under Vespasian and Titus seems limited to the conventional representation of the emperor wearing a radiate crown. See Bergmann (1998) 231–3.

[22] Miracles (not involving the Sun) are, however, attested, marking Vespasian's predestination for imperial power: Levick (1999) 67–8.

course.[23] The pavement uncovered by Buchner in his excavations in search of the pavement of Augustus' sundial has been proved to date from the time of Domitian, who must have undertaken restoration of the sundial.[24] Caesar gave his name to a month after his reform of the calendar, Augustus after his correction of the same. Domitian claimed the same honor after restoring Augustus' monumental sundial.[25] By seeking to rename a month after himself, he wished to be inserted as third in the list of great leaders who had "returned order to the universe." This was not enough. The obelisk placed in the Campus Martius by Augustus was inscribed with hieroglyphs. Their subject was the succession of Ramses II to his father Sethos, described in solar terms, as is customary of pharaonic succession. Domitian erected his own obelisk and inscribed it with hieroglyphs advertising his succession to Vespasian as the new pharaoh. In this inscription too, and in the accompanying images, the succession is described in the solar terms typical of pharaonic ideology.[26] In Egypt, the cult of Sarapis, a key divinity for the imperial cult, was given solar traits under Domitian.[27] Domitian's association with Helios is recorded in provincial coinage.[28] Significantly, Trajan replaced the pavement of Augustus' sundial with a pool, erasing part of the solar connection of the monument and destroying continuity with an emperor who had by now been turned into a *caluus Nero*.

The currency given to solar imagery in official discourse under Domitian is reflected in coeval poetry. The emperor who restored Augustus' solar monuments in the Campus Martius rises like the Sun in *Siluae* 4.1:

laeta bis octonis accedit purpura fastis
Caesaris insignemque aperit Germanicus annum
atque oritur cum sole nouo, cum grandibus astris,
clarius ipse nitens et primo maior Eoo.
Silv. 4.1.1–4

Joyfully the purple is added to the twice eight consulships of Caesar, and Germanicus opens an extraordinary year. He rises with the new Sun and the

---

[23] Plin. *Nat.* 36.71–3.

[24] Buchner (1982) 66; Heslin (2007) 7–8.

[25] Suet. *Dom.* 13.3; Plin. *Pan.* 54; Heslin (2007) 16–17; Coleman (1988) 80.

[26] On the obelisk and its inscription see Grenier (2009). The obelisk was moved from the Circus of Maxentius to its present location (Piazza Navona in Rome) in the 17th century. Its original location is unknown. Grenier (2009) 237–8 rightly dismisses the widespread scholarly view that Domitian's obelisk was originally placed within, or in close proximity to, the temples to Egyptian divinities (the Isaeum and Serapeum) in the Campus Martius.

[27] The evidence comes from the coinage: Under Domitian the Egyptian god Sarapis is associated with Helios and his solar traits are emphasized; see *RPC* II no. 2519.

[28] *RPC* II nos. 170–2: laureate head of Domitian on the obverse, Helios galloping in quadriga on reverse.

great stars, shining more brightly than they, greater than the morning star when it rises.

This praise recalls Horace's *Carm.* 4.5.5–8, a poem whose publication is close in time to Augustus' solar operations in the Campus Martius.[29] In *Siluae* 1.1, Domitian's statue is said to be radiant like the Sun, and that is no surprise: It was aligned, as demonstrated by Coarelli, with the Colossus, a statue of the Sun god.[30] Statius resurrects the lines dedicated by Seneca to Nero the Sun in the *Apocolocyntosis* and the proem to Lucan's *Bellum Ciuile*.[31]

Domitian's solar and pharaonic ideology does not necessarily imply a return to Nero. Domitian's restoration of the *solarium Augusti*, it has been convincingly suggested, conveyed the opposite message: He had returned the Sun to its regular course after Nero the impostor.[32] Lucan, building on a rich tradition, compared the chaos of civil war to the disruption of the cosmic order.[33] Domitian, after the civil conflict was quelled—not without his contribution—was now returning the cosmos to normality. Domitian's idea of giving his name to a month forged a direct link with Augustus, the emperor who had rescued the world from civil war and then restored the Sun to its proper course.

Yet the issue was delicate: Critics of power were ready to cast the accusation of being a new Nero at every sign of misconduct.[34] The use of Neronian literature may have been misinterpreted; certain aspects of Domitian's use of solar imagery had no precedent under Augustus and highlighted continuity with Nero.[35] Another delicate area was the syncretism with eastern religions. Solar ideology allowed Nero to forge a connection with the imperial theology of Parthia and its solar god Mithras. As we have seen, in Egypt, the solar traits of Sarapis were emphasized under Domitian. The *Thebaid* promotes the equation of Apollo/Sol with Osiris, Mithras, and Titan (*Theb.* 1.717–20). Domitian's choice to abandon the restraint shown by his father and to retain this aspect of Nero's ideology, at the risk of being misinterpreted, is particularly important. At the end of this chapter, I discuss what was at stake in this decision

---

[29] Cf. also Hor. *Carm.* 4.2.45–8; Mart. 8.21; Nauta (2010) 258; Coleman (1988) 66. For the publication date of Horace's fourth book of odes see Thomas (2011) 5–7.

[30] *Silv.* 1.1.33, 1.1.71, 1.1.77; cf. also 1.1.55. Domitian's statue is compared with the Colossus of Rhodes, a statue of the Sun god: *Silv.* 1.1.103–4. On the statue's alignment with the (once) Colossus of Nero see Coarelli (2009b) 83.

[31] See Section 2.2; Chapter 1, Section 1.1; Chapter 4, Section 4.3.

[32] Heslin (2007) 18.

[33] See Chapter 4, Section 4.3.

[34] Cf. the fear that Titus might turn out to be a new Nero mentioned by Suetonius (*Tit.* 7.1) and later dissipated by Titus' behavior as princeps.

[35] As we have seen, a problematic connection with Nero emerges, for instance, when Apollo is summoned to praise the poetic ability of the emperor: See Section 2.1.

and Statius' peculiar awareness of the emperor's concerns. For the time being, let us concentrate on the consequences of this choice: the necessity of accompanying solar imagery with the qualification that Domitian was not a new Nero. This was a challenge for Flavian authors. To this end, as we will see, a mythological figure came to the help of poets.

2.2 PHAETHON

Nero is celebrated as a new Sol in the proem to Lucan's *Bellum Ciuile*:

> te, cum statione peracta
> astra petes serus, praelati regia caeli
> excipiet gaudente polo: seu sceptra tenere
> seu te flammigeros Phoebi conscendere currus
> telluremque nihil mutato sole timentem
> igne uago lustrare iuuet, tibi numine ab omni
> cedetur, iurisque tui natura relinquet
> quis deus esse uelis, ubi regnum ponere mundi.
> Luc. 1.45–52

You, when your duty is fulfilled
and finally you seek the stars, will be received in your chosen palace
of heaven, with the sky rejoicing. Whether you choose to wield
the sceptre or to mount the flaming chariot of Phoebus
and to circle with wandering fire the earth entirely unperturbed
by the transference of the Sun, every deity
will yield to you, to your decision nature will leave
which god you wish to be, where to set your kingdom of the universe.

This postmortem projection also has to do with the emperor's earthly life. Nero can choose to replace the Sun as driver of the fiery chariot after death; implied is his solar role *qua* emperor while alive. The role of the Sun, however, entails risks. The Earth is unperturbed by Nero's taking over the role of the Sun (Luc. 1.49). The Earth might be afraid because the last time someone replaced the Sun, that succession had disastrous consequences for her. Lucan's mention of a "wandering fire" [*igne uago*, Luc.1.50] may evoke Phaethon's straying from his path. The young Phaethon, unable to govern his father's chariot, burned the Earth and nearly destroyed it.

The hint at Phaethon has been taken as subtle critique of Nero; others deny its presence.[36] I believe that much of this passage's power lies in its ability to evoke anxieties at the same time that it suppresses them: The Earth should not fear, Lucan states, because *you* are no Phaethon. Still, the hint at the Earth's fear implies the possibility of a disastrous outcome and is there to warn the reader—and the emperor—that a mishandling of the office can have disastrous consequences.[37]

The Phaethon myth lent itself well to reflection on the emperor's ability to fulfill his duty.[38] Phaethon is a youth unable to take up his father's role; his task, driving a chariot, is an old metaphor for the government of state.[39] Roman readers are accustomed to see solar attributes ascribed to their rulers. In myth, Phaethon also needs to prove that he is the son of a god. The chariot of the Sun appeared in Augustan culture in connection with the emperor's apotheosis, and the solar monuments of Augustus in the Campus Martius were deeply intertwined with the topic of deification; as we saw, at the beginning of the *Bellum Ciuile*, Lucan conjures up the image of the solar charioteer with reference to Nero's apotheosis. Ovid's narrative of Phaethon, even if we are not prepared to read it as a political allegory, owes its appeal precisely to how it reflects on issues of great importance to the newly born empire: problems of paternity and succession, deification and access to immortality, as well as the disastrous consequences of a son's inability to fulfill his father's role.[40]

An explicit connection with Phaethon is found with reference to a famously unsuccessful emperor: Caligula. Suetonius tells us that Tiberius called his adoptive son a new Phaethon, and a similar comparison is implied in a passage by Seneca.[41] After 68 CE, it must have appeared to many that Nero had materialized Lucan's fears in the worst possible way.[42] More than other emperors, he had insisted on his solar nature and emphasized his ability as charioteer: He had claimed to be the equal of

---

[36] Hinds (1987) 26–9 and Rosati (2008) 186–7 see the ghost of Phaethon evoked by these lines. *Contra* Dewar (1994) 211. Champlin (2003a) 134–5 and Duret (1988) think that the Phaethon myth is implied but in a positive sense.

[37] On doubts about Nero's ability to take up the role of emperor see Tac. *Ann.* 13.6. Cf. also Sen. *Cl.* 1.1.7.

[38] On the political use of the Phaethon myth, with more materials and discussions: Degl'Innocenti Pierini (1990) 251–70; Rosati (2008) 187–92; Nauta (2002) 332–3.

[39] The idea of the chariot of state is at least as old as Plato: cf. e.g. *R.* 566d. In a Roman context one only needs to think of the metaphorical use of the term *habena* [rein], attested early and extremely common: see *ThlL* VI 3, 2393, 80ff. See the subsequent discussion in this section for other relevant Latin texts.

[40] Barchiesi (2005) 229–31; for a political interpretation of the episode with reference to the Augustan establishment see Schmitzer (1990) 89–107.

[41] Suet. *Cal.* 11.1; Sen. *Dial.* 11.17.3; see Degl'Innocenti Pierini (1990) 256–9.

[42] On the Phaethon myth as a Flavian reflection on Nero's inability to rule: Newlands (2002) 315–16; Heslin (2007) 18–19. That Valerius Flaccus' description of Aietes, a tyrant who closely associates his identity with the Sun god, hints at Nero has been plausibly suggested by Taylor (1994) 228–31. For hints at Nero through Phaethon in Valerius Flaccus see V. Fl. 5.429–32, with Heerink (2014) 89–92.

Apollo as a singer and of the Sun as a charioteer.[43] Reality proved him wrong: When he sought to drive a 10-horse chariot at Olympia, he was thrown off the chariot like Phaethon.[44] Like Phaethon, he was also considered responsible for burning down the Earth, through his involvement in the fire of Rome.[45]

Pliny the Elder hints that Nero acted as a new Phaethon when he calls Nero (and Caligula) the "torches of mankind."[46] That the topic of Phaethon was popular in official contexts under Domitian is confirmed by the evidence pertaining to Domitian's Capitoline games. In 94 CE, the boy Q. Sulpicius Maximus competed with an impromptu composition in Greek hexameters on the topic of Jupiter's reprimand to Helios for having lent his chariot to Phaethon.[47] The theme of the *agon* was always Jupiter. Domitian, who used to be identified with Capitoline Jupiter, presided in person and was a member of the jury.[48] Peter Heslin has advanced the suggestive hypothesis that Maximus' success was due to his ability to pick up on the allegory as promoted by the emperor: Phaethon for Nero, Helios for Augustus, Jupiter for Domitian.[49] The use of Phaethon as the subject of the compositions in the Capitoline games is particularly significant. Domitian's Capitolia restored the tradition of Nero's Greek games (Neronia), which was suppressed by Vespasian: The necessity of remarking the difference between Nero and Domitian must have been particularly pressing in that context.

There is a possibility that this use of Phaethon with reference to Nero and the fire of Rome is also attested in Statius. In his celebratory poem for Lucan's birthday (a poem in which Nero features as a tyrant and a monster), Statius comments on a juvenile poem by Lucan on the fire of Rome, *De Incendio Urbis*:[50]

dices culminibus Remi uagantes
infandos domini nocentis ignes.
Silv. 2.7.60–1

---

[43] Suet. *Nero* 53; on Nero's passion for chariot racing cf. also Tac. *Ann.* 14.14, 16.4; Suet. *Nero* 21.
[44] Suet. *Nero* 24.
[45] On the Flavian view of Nero see Chapter 1, Section 1.3. The belief that Nero set the city ablaze (mentioned cautiously by Tacitus *Ann.* 15.38, whereas Suetonius *Nero* 38.1 and Cassius Dio 62.16.2 are more inclined to believe it) is well established in the anti-Neronian vulgate of Flavian times. See e.g. Stat. *Silv.* 2.7.61–2 (cited in this section); *Oct.* 831, with Ferri's (2003) 363 note *ad loc.*
[46] Plin. *Nat.* 7.45; see Nauta (2010) 262.
[47] *CIL* 6.33976; *IGUR* 3.1336 with Nauta (2002) 330–5.
[48] Quint. *Inst.* 3.7.4; Suet. *Dom.* 4.4; Caldelli (1993) 65, 68. On Domitian's association with Capitoline Jupiter see Caldelli (1993) 62–7 and Chapter 6, Section 6.2. On the Capitoline games see Chapter 1, Section 1.3 n. 112.
[49] Heslin (2007) 19; but see the objections by Nauta (2010) 263. Sulpicius Maximus did not win the competition but gained the favor of the jury: see *IGUR* 3.1336.
[50] See van Dam (1984) 480–1; Newlands (2011) 237–8.

You shall tell of the monstrous fires of a guilty ruler wandering over the roofs of Remus.

Not only does Statius attribute the fire of Rome to Nero, but he also picks up the allusion to Phaethon in Lucan's proem. *Vagantes . . . ignes* possibly alludes to Lucan's *igne uago* [wandering fire, Luc. 1.50], one of the textual hints at the identification of Nero and Phaethon in the proem of the *Bellum Ciuile*. Through this allusion, Statius shows that Lucan's prophecy of Nero as a new Phaethon has materialized through his involvement in the fire.[51]

The myth of Phaethon could be used as a warning, as in Lucan, or to indict the failure of a former emperor, as in the passages on Caligula and the Flavian texts previously mentioned, especially—but not only—if that emperor made solar ideology central to his imperial persona. However, the myth of Phaethon was especially suited for the kind of distinction Flavian authors needed to make, for it entails the story of someone who claimed to be an equal of the Sun but failed. As we will see, the story allows Flavian authors to condemn Nero while rescuing solar ideology: Nero was the failed solar *auriga* and unsuccessful emperor, but later emperors can prove equal to the task; Domitian can be depicted in solar terms without the implication that he will be a second Nero. In addition, in post-Neronian Rome the myth of Phaethon became particularly attractive, since its admonitory power was heightened: Although the emperor must not necessarily fail, if he does he will replicate the disasters brought about by Nero.

2.3 THE SOLAR CHARIOTEER

This discourse on power centering on solar symbols and the Phaethon myth is woven into the narrative fabric of the *Thebaid*. First, at the beginning of the poem, Statius adapts the solar praise of Nero by Lucan. At the beginning of the *Thebaid*, Domitian is portrayed as the charioteer of the Roman state whom the Sun god invites to take his place in heaven:

(. . . licet ignipedum frenator equorum
ipse tuis alte radiantem crinibus arcum
imprimat aut magni cedat tibi Iuppiter aequa
parte poli), maneas hominum contentus habenis,

---

[51] That Statius read the *Bellum Ciuile* as an anti-Neronian work is clear from *Siluae* 2.7. He was thus prepared to look for ironic allusions to the *nocens dominus* [guilty ruler, *Silv.* 2.7.71] in Lucan's proem. See Nauta (2010) 264.

undarum terraeque potens, et sidera dones.
Theb. 1.27–31

... though he who controls the fire-footed horses himself set his high-shining crown on your locks or Jupiter yield you an equal portion of the broad sky, may you remain content with holding the reins of mankind, potent over sea and land, and surrender the stars.

In this passage, Statius bids the emperor to be content with the "reins of men": After death, Statius foresees for Domitian a natural evolution, in heaven, of his role as the political *auriga* of the Roman state. This image of postmortem succession to the role of Sun in the proem comes immediately after the description of Domitian's reception of power from his father Vespasian, that is, his earthly succession to the role of *auriga* of the Roman state. The passage is clearly modeled on Lucan's proem, and there may be hints at Ovid's narrative of Phaethon.[52] But Statius is hard at work here to reduce the unsettling effect of Lucan's address to Nero. Significantly, he glides over the two elements that conjured up the figure of Phaethon in Lucan's text: the reference to the wandering fire [*igne uago*] and to the fear of the Earth [*tellurem . . . timentem*].[53]

It is not difficult to construe this proem as subversive, especially after Nero's demise. Another possibility, however, emerges as we consider other texts. In *Siluae* 4.3, the emperor is praised in solar terms, but the reader is reassured that Domitian will not be a second Nero. This poem begins by contrasting Nero and Domitian, and goes on to proclaim that Domitian would be even better than the Sun himself in conducting the fiery chariot.[54] If he upsets the climate, it will be for the better:[55]

hic paci bonus, hic timendus armis;
hic si flammigeros teneret axes,
natura melior potentiorque,
largis, India, nubibus maderes,
undaret Libye, teperet Haemus.
Silv. 4.3.134–8

---

[52] Rosati (2008) 190.
[53] See the text quoted in Section 2.2; Rosati (2008) 190–3; Nauta (2010) 260–1.
[54] *Silv.* 4.3.1–19. On *Silv.* 4.3 see also Chapter 1, Section 1.3.
[55] On this passage see Rosati (2008) 187 and Nauta (2010) 262, with further references; a different interpretation is given in Newlands (2002) 314–16.

He is friend to peace, dreadful in arms; if he were to drive the fiery chariot, better and mightier than nature, you, India, would be wet with generous clouds, Lybia would be covered in water and Haemus warm.

Domitian outdoes Nero. To Nero's failure as solar charioteer, this poem juxtaposes the image of an emperor who is even better than the Sun. Domitian must not turn into a new Phaethon or a new Nero. Failure is possible, but, as the *Siluae* passage shows, success is not ruled out. The presence of Lucan in the *Thebaid*'s passage seems to heighten the admonitory power of the mythical comparison rather than implicitly condemn the emperor. In the *Thebaid*, Domitian is pictured as being in the same position as Nero at the beginning of his reign. It is up to him not to repeat Nero's errors and wreak havoc on humanity once again.

In the following section, we see that a similar dynamic is reflected in Statius' use of solar imagery and symbols in a number of passages of the *Thebaid*, especially in the chariot race narrated in book 6. The race narrative conjures up the story of Phaethon in order to hint at Nero and to construct an opposition between two solar figures. One is the successful *auriga*, beloved of Apollo; the second is a self-styled son of Apollo whom the Sun god throws off the chariot of power. This dichotomy allows Statius to employ solar imagery in a way that does not imply Domitian's identification with Nero, but in which allusions to Nero acquire an admonitory function. Statius' use of Phaethon and, more generally, his employment of solar symbols, is also part of a general reflection on a pressing problem of imperial politics: succession. By Statius' time, the question of succession was felt even more dramatically than under the Julio-Claudians. The Julio-Claudian dynasty proved how dangerous dynastic succession could be: It could produce a Nero or a Caligula. Statius wrote under an emperor who had no male heir and, for much of his life, did not appoint a successor.[56] As we will see, the *Thebaid*'s tour de force centering on solar imagery and chariot racing culminates in a scene of succession: In book 8, the good charioteer is replaced in a peaceful fashion by a worthy successor. Statius' construction of this episode reflects discussions alive in the elite circles of Flavian Rome and engages propagandistic versions of Flavian successions.

---

[56] Domitian's only son (born 73 CE) died before his accession to the throne (probably 83 CE); Jones (1992) 33 and n. 41; cf. also Mart. 6.5 with Grewing (1997) 84–6 and Nauta (2002) 434–6. Flavius Sabinus' sons are adopted by Domitian no earlier than 90 CE (probably 95 CE?); Jones (1992) 47–8.

2.4 A RACE AMONG THE STARS

The race episode begins with a catalogue of its participants: Polynices and Amphiaraus among the Argive Seven, Admetus, Thoas and Euneus (the twin sons of Hypsipyle), Chromis (a son of Hercules), and Hippodamus (son of Oenomaus).[57] When the race starts, Polynices, whose team is led by the divine horse Arion, wins first place. He is followed by Amphiaraus and Admetus, while Euneus and Thoas struggle for fourth place, and Chromis and Hippodamus for sixth. The situation changes suddenly at the fourth lap: Thoas falls from the chariot and has to retire; Chromis manages to push Hippodamus off the chariot but then stops his own horses to help him. At this point, Apollo intervenes in favor of Amphiaraus, who is fated to die shortly after the competition. The god raises a horrifying monster from the underworld to scare Polynices' horses. Polynices falls on the ground. His chariot goes on to finish the race, but according to ancient rules, a chariot without a charioteer is disqualified. The race is thus won by Amphiaraus, with Admetus coming in second.[58] As a prize, the seer receives a mixing bowl formerly belonging to Hercules.[59]

A race provides a good opportunity for political allusion. Not only is the chariot a metaphor for the state, but there is an important Roman poetic tradition of comparing chariot races to competitions for power. A crucial simile from Ennius' *Annales* involves chariot racing. Romulus and Remus are taking the auspices to decide who shall become the king of Rome; the people waiting for the outcome of the prophecy are compared to the crowds watching a chariot race.[60] In the *Georgics*, Virgil compares the chaos of civil war to a furious chariot race in which the drivers lose control of their chariots.[61] And in the *Aeneid*, Virgil's narrative of the ship race, no doubt one of Statius' main models for his chariot race, is open to political allusion and quasi-allegorical readings.[62] One of the competitors in Virgil's regatta, Sergestus, a mythical ancestor of the *gens Sergia*, crashes his ship against the rocks. It has been difficult for commentators to resist the temptation to see Sergestus as an image of Catiline, the reckless politician who, in his pursuit of power, crashes "the ship of state." Similarly, Cloanthus, the winner, has been seen as the ideal ruler, someone who wins thanks to his *pietas*.[63]

---

[57] The catalogue: *Theb.* 6.296–350.
[58] The race: *Theb.* 6.389–530. On this episode see Pavan (2009); Lovatt (2005) 23–40; Vessey (1973) 211–18.
[59] *Theb.* 6.531–39. On this passage see Chapter 3, Section 3.1.
[60] Enn. *Ann.* 79–83 Skutsch.
[61] *G.* 1.511–14.
[62] Virgil's ship race: *A.* 5.114–285. On Virgil's race as a model for Statius see Pavan (2009) *passim*; Lovatt (2005) 26–7; Vessey (1973) 211–18.
[63] Catiline was a member of the *gens Sergia*, allegedly descended from Sergestus (Serv. *A.* 5.121); Hardie (1987) 165–6; Delvigo (2001) esp. 16–33.

A further important factor for Statius' allusive construction of his chariot race is the metaphorical use of chariot racing as a symbol of the course of life. This *topos* is found in consolatory poetry.[64] On funerary reliefs it is common for the dead man to be represented as a charioteer who falls from his chariot during a race. The theme is used mostly on the sarcophagi of children and youths—of people, that is, who experience premature death. The allegorical meaning is clear: The inability to finish the race hints at the inability to reach maturity; the charioteer's premature fall alludes to the youth's premature death.[65] Finally, we need to add the solar connotations of the Circus and its symbolical value as a showplace of imperial power so prominent by Statius' time. Although links between the emperor's solar identity and the Circus were already present under Augustus, Nero had clearly made the Circus a symbol of his solar rule.[66]

All of these symbolical associations of chariot racing are relevant to Statius' narrative. They are combined with references and allusions to a myth that brings them all together: the story of Phaethon. Polynices is aligned with Phaethon at the very beginning of the race episode. When Adrastus lends his horse Arion to the young Theban hero, Statius compares the old king to Sol, entrusting his fiery chariot to Phaethon:[67]

> tunc rector genero Polynici indulget agendum
> multa monens, ubi feruor equo, qua suetus ab arte
> mulceri, ne saeua manus, ne liber habenis
> impetus. 'urge alios,' inquit, 'stimulisque minisque;
> ille ibit, minus ipse uoles.' sic ignea lora
> cum daret et rapido Sol natum imponeret axi,
> gaudentem lacrimans astra insidiosa docebat
> nolentesque teri zonas mediamque polorum
> temperiem: pius ille quidem et formidine cauta,

---

[64] Cf. e.g. *Epic. Drusi* 359–60 *tendimus huc omnes, metam properamus ad unam,* | *omnia sub leges Mors uocat atra suas* [we are all headed there, we hasten toward the same turning-post | dark Death calls everything under his laws]; Mart. 10.50.8.

[65] Zanker–Ewald (2008) 89–90. For the idea that a similar metaphorical sense may be in play in the Virgilian regatta see Hardie (2002) 344. The myth of Phaethon is also associated with premature death in funerary reliefs. In an important sarcophagus now in Florence, we find it coupled with a representation of a chariot race: Zanker–Ewald (2008) 86–90, 331–2. All the evidence discussed by Zanker and Ewald is later than Statius' poem and should therefore be taken with caution.

[66] One only needs to recall Nero's charioteering performances (Tac. *Ann.* 14.14–15; D.C. 61.19–20), or his dedications to Sol in the Circus after the capture of the conspirators of 65 CE (Tac. *Ann.* 15.74). See also Tac. *Ann.* 15.44 for Nero's sadistic charioteering performance during the persecution of Christians, with Champlin (2003a) 121–6. See Section 2.2.

[67] Lovatt (2005) 32–8; Vessey (1973) 212–13; Pavan (2009) 148–51.

sed iuuenem durae prohibebant discere Parcae.
Theb. 6.316–25

On this occasion the king lets his son-in-law Polynices drive him, with many an admonition: when the horse would get excited, with what art he was wont to be soothed, not to handle him harshly nor yet to let him speed free of the rein. 'Urge others,' he said, 'with goads and threats. He will go, and faster than you wish.' So when the Sun gave his child the fiery reins and placed him in the swift chariot, with tears he taught the happy youth of treacherous stars and zones which should not be entered and the temperate region between the poles; loving was he and cautious in his fear, but the cruel Parcae would not suffer the young man to learn.

As has been observed, there are remarkable correspondences with Ovid's narrative of Phaethon in the *Metamorphoses*.[68] Moreover, the vocabulary of horsemanship resonates with political advice: Adrastus' command on the horse is named *imperium* (6.315); his instruction to the youth, with its insistence on a middle way between excessive strictness and laxity, could well feature in recommendations to a monarch (see in part. *Theb.* 6.318–19).[69] Statius follows a thread of Ovidian imitation in the rest of the episode: Just as with Ovid's Phaethon, Polynices' horses soon deviate from the track, and they realize they are being driven by a different charioteer.[70] In Ovid's *Metamorphoses*, Phaethon eventually loses control of his chariot because of the appearance of a monstrous creature, the constellation of Scorpio.[71] Something similar happens to Polynices, who is thrown from his chariot when a monster sent by Apollo scares his horses.[72] On this occasion, Statius refers again explicitly to the myth of Phaethon, stating that Apollo's monster would have terrified even the Sun's horses.[73]

The comparison between Polynices and Phaethon is extended beyond the race. Polynices' fall from the chariot is described as a missed death: The youth would have died had it not been for Tisiphone, who wants to preserve him alive for the duel

---

[68] Vessey (1973) 212 n. 5; Pavan (2009) 148–51; Lovatt (2005) 33–4. Cf. *Met.* 2.126–40 and E. *Phaëth.* 168–70 Diggle.

[69] Pavan (2009) 133, 147.

[70] Statius gives a moral tinge to this latter detail, for the divine Arion senses not the lack of experience but the wickedness of his driver. Cf. *Theb.* 6.424–7; with Pavan (2009) 199–200.

[71] Ov. *Met.* 2.195–8 with Barchiesi (2005) 252–3.

[72] *Theb.* 6.491–512.

[73] *Theb.* 6.498–501. Moreover, Statius uses the same simile used by Ovid to describe the moment when the young charioteer loses control of his chariot: the naval simile of the helmsman who gives up his ship to the storm; cf. Ov. *Met.* 2.185–87; *Theb.* 6.450–3 with Pavan (2009) 208.

with his brother.[74] And when Polynices actually dies, the reader is directed back to the context of the race, for the young Theban is depicted as the dead Phaethon, whose burned body is washed by Argia and Antigone in their role as the *Heliades*, Phaethon's sisters:[75]

> sic Hyperionium trepido Phaethonta sorores
> fumantem lauere Pado; uixdum ille sepulcro
> conditus, et flentes stabant ad flumina siluae.
> *Theb.* 12.413–5

So his sisters washed burning Phaëthon, Hyperion's son, in the frightened Padus; he had just been buried, and the weeping trees already stood by the riverside.

The use of Phaethon to mark Polynices' death implies the idea of Phaethon as an image of the incapable political leader: Polynices' pursuit of power ends up in ashes, just like Phaethon's enterprise. In turn, the resurfacing of Phaethon at the point of Polynices' death increases our perception of the race as an image of the hero's life: The symmetry between Polynices' early fall and his early death is highlighted.

Statius' use of the metaphors previously discussed (the chariot as an image of the state and the race as the course of life) is not limited to the *Thebaid*. In *Siluae* 1.1, Statius praises the construction of Domitian's massive equestrian statue in the Roman Forum. The metaphor of riding a horse as an image of being in power lends itself easily to such a composition. Statius does not resist the temptation of shifting from the visual to the metaphorical in his description of the emperor's statue:

> hunc et Adrasteus uisum extimuisset Arion
> et pauet aspiciens Ledaeus ab aede propinqua
> Cyllarus; hic domini numquam mutabit habenas:
> perpetuus frenis atque uni seruiet astro.
> *Silv.* 1.1.52–5

Adrastus' Arion would have dreaded the sight of him, and Castor's Cyllarus trembles as he looks from his neighboring shrine. This horse shall never change his master's reins: forever at his bit, he shall serve one star only.

---

[74] *Theb.* 6.513–17; Vessey (1973) 216–17.
[75] Cf. Ov. *Met.* 2.340–66.

Domitian's horse is juxtaposed to two mythical horses: Castor's Cyllarus and Hercules' Arion, both famous for having had multiple owners. Arion belonged in succession to Neptune, Hercules, and Adrastus.[76] Cyllarus was held by Castor and Pollux in alternation. Unlike Cyllarus and Arion, the poet writes, Domitian's horse will have only one possessor. What does this mean? Statius is aware of what happens to equestrian statues of leaders when they are no longer in power. A few lines later, he mentions Caesar's equestrian statue.[77] The latter, formerly a statue of Alexander, had been reconfigured into a portrait of Caesar. For one thing, then, the poet reassures the emperor that he will never fall in disgrace and that his memory will remain untouched.[78] On a more symbolic level, however, the comparison is also meant to provide an image of continuity of political leadership. Domitian's permanence on the back of his horse signifies his ability to remain in power.[79] Intriguingly, these suggestions are reinforced by a direct allusion to *Thebaid* 6, for the two horses to which Domitian's horse is compared are both mentioned in the *Thebaid*'s chariot race. Arion is Polynices' horse, and Cyllarus is the father of Amphiaraus' horses.[80] Domitian is thus implicitly linked to the two riders who fight for first place in Statius' chariot race.[81] Statius' comment that Domitian will not be thrown off the saddle highlights Domitian's difference from Polynices.

2.5 AMPHIARAUS AND THE DEATH OF THE KING

We now return to the chariot race. Just as Polynices, who fails in the race, is presented as a failed solar charioteer, there are clear signs that the winning *auriga*, Amphiaraus, becomes Polynices' counterpart. As we will see, he is also involved in a discourse about succession that resonates with imperial discussions.

Amphiaraus too has solar connections. Throughout the poem, Statius makes constant use of the syncretism (and conflation) of Apollo and Sol. This is clear, for instance, in book 9, in which the encounter between Apollo and Diana in the sky is described as an eclipse: The two divinities correspond to the two main

---

[76] *Theb.* 6.301–15.

[77] *Silv.* 1.1.84–7.

[78] In spite of Statius' prophecy, the only preserved equestrian statue of Domitian, the one found at Misenum, has undergone exactly this destiny, for the face of the emperor in this statue was reconfigured into an image of Nerva after Domitian's *damnatio*. See Adamo Muscettola (2000); Flower (2005) 259–61.

[79] Later in the same poem, Statius compares Domitian to Marcus Curtius, a hero who, fully armed and riding his horse, plunged himself into a chasm to save the Roman state (*Silv.* 1.1.74–83). For the importance of this image for the *Thebaid* see Section 2.5 and Chapters 5, Section 5.9 and 6, Section 6.6.

[80] Arion: *Theb.* 6.301–13; Amphiaraus' horses: *Theb.* 4.214–15, 6.326–31.

[81] Newlands (2002) 64; Pavan (2009) 133; Geyssen (1996) 95–6. For a different interpretation see Ahl (1984) 95, who thinks the allusion is evoked to link Domitian with Polynices.

celestial bodies, the Sun and the Moon.[82] Amphiaraus, who is presented by Statius as a favorite of Apollo, is then, in fact, the favorite of the Sun.[83] The race in which Polynices proves to be a Phaethon, an unworthy driver of the Sun's chariot, is actually attended and directed by the Sun god himself, who engineers the victory of his protégé, Amphiaraus. This is appropriate of a god (Sol) who is so strongly associated with chariot racing and whose temple in Rome stood in the Circus.

Apollo's intervention in the race is in line with our reading of the race as a political contest. In the first book, Statius praises Apollo as the god who knows "what comets produce an alternation of scepters" [*quae mutent sceptra cometae*, 1.708]. During the race, Apollo's intervention is described as the falling of a star and, accordingly, produces a change at the top of this symbolical competition, with Polynices losing the first position to Amphiaraus.[84] Polynices falls from the chariot like Nero at Olympia, whose death was announced by a comet.[85]

Unlike Polynices, Amphiaraus is just and pious, and therefore he wins. And yet, even the pious Amphiaraus is destined to die shortly. But his death is very different from the death of Polynices, who dies under the gods' disfavor and goes to Tartarus.[86] As in the case of Polynices, there seems to be a symmetry between Amphiaraus' race and the scene of his death. Both feature a prominent use of solar imagery, and both imply the idea of chariot driving as an image of the hero's life. In contrast to what happens to Polynices, Apollo helps Amphiaraus until the very end. In the course of Amphiaraus' final *aristeia*, Apollo even assumes the role of Amphiaraus' charioteer and bestows his solar splendor upon him.[87] After the seer's death, the Sun eclipses in mourning.[88] More important, Amphiaraus' death is described with an insistence on how he remains on the chariot until the very end. This forms a stark contrast to Polynices' death, in which the Theban hero is compared to Phaethon knocked off his saddle by Jupiter's thunderbolt. When Amphiaraus dies, he goes to the underworld on his chariot and with the reins still in his hands: *non arma manu, non frena remisit: | sicut erat, rectos defert in Tartara currus* [he did not let the arms go from his hand or the reins. As he was, he brought the chariot upright down to Tartarus, *Theb.* 7.819–20].

---

[82] *Theb.* 9.647–9; see subsequent discussion.

[83] *Theb.* 9.637–69. On the syncretism of Apollo/Sol in Roman culture and literature see Pease (1955–1958) 727 on Cic. *Nat. Deo.* 2.27.68; Boyancé (1966) 149–70; Fontenrose (1939, 1940). On the relevance of the identification Apollo/Sol for Augustan ideology see Hardie (1986) 355–6.

[84] *Theb.* 6.385–8.

[85] Cf. Sen. *Nat.* 7.17.2, 21.3–4, 29.3; Plin. *Nat.* 2.92; Suet. *Ner.* 36; Tac. *Ann.* 14.22.1.

[86] Cf. *Theb.* 11.574–5.

[87] Cf. *Theb.* 7.752–3, 7.692–5, 7.700–1, 7.703–4; Statius is indebted to Hom. *Il.* 5.35–41 and Verg. *A.* 12.468–72; cf. also *Theb.* 7.779–88 with Hom. *Il.* 5.815–24. and Verg. *A.* 12.632–49; see Smolenaars (1994) 370.

[88] *Theb.* 9.647–49. Cf. Ov. *Met.* 2.329–31 with Barchiesi (2005) 265. More on this scene in a while.

And when he appears to Thiodamas after his death, he is still riding his chariot.[89] In sum, Polynices' inability to control his chariot is linked with his premature death, depicted in book 11. On the contrary, Amphiaraus' victory in the race is coupled with a description of his death (in book 7) in which the seer remains in control of his chariot until the very end of his life. The insistence on this detail is significant, especially in light of the metaphors we encountered in *Siluae* 1.1, where Statius tells us that Domitian will not be knocked off the saddle and will still be riding his horse in heaven.

Polynices is a failed charioteer and a failed leader. Amphiaraus is attributed some features of the dead king after his descent to the underworld. A first simile introduces the mourning of the troops after the seer's death, in which Amphiaraus is compared to Tiphys, the helmsman of the Argonauts.[90] The comparison is important: The helmsman is an old metaphor for the sovereign, and one that Statius is keen to use in his poem.[91] Likewise, the image of the death of a king and of political succession is found again just a few lines later, in a simile used to describe Thiodamas' role as substitute of Amphiaraus:

> sicut Achaemenius solium gentesque paternas
> excepit si forte puer, cui uiuere patrem
> tutius, incerta formidine gaudia librat
> an fidi proceres, ne pugnet uulgus habenis,
> cui latus Euphratae, cui Caspia limina mandet;
> sumere tunc arcus ipsumque onerare ueretur
> patris equum uisusque sibi nec sceptra capaci
> sustentare manu nec adhuc implere tiaran.
> *Theb.* 8.286–93

So if a boy from the Achaemenid dynasty, for whom it were safer that his father lived, happens to take over his father's throne and peoples, he balances joy with fear and doubt: are his nobles loyal, will the people not fight the reins, to whom shall he entrust Euphrates' bank or the Caspian border? Then he is afraid to take the bow and mount his father's very horse, thinks his hand still too small to wield the scepter and his head to fill the diadem.

---

[89] *Theb.* 10.202–6.
[90] *Theb.* 8.212–14. See Augoustakis (2016) 152–3. On this simile see also Conclusions, Section C.1.
[91] Cf. *Theb.* 2.105–8: Eteocles is compared to a helmsman; cf. also *Theb.* 8.267–70. The metaphor is indeed very old: With reference to Eteocles, it is found at the very beginning of Aeschylus' *Septem contra Thebas* (*Th.* 1–3).

The content of the simile is peculiar, for the reference is to an event beyond the chronological horizon of myth, the succession to the throne of Persia.[92] Although it is clear that Statius wants to evoke images of kingly deaths and successions in connection with Amphiaraus, one wonders about the role of Persia in this context. I submit that Persia is singled out because it offers a fitting parallel to Imperial Rome. Before Rome, Persia is the archetype of a great empire stretching over different lands and cultures. More important, Persia was traditionally regarded as the example of a kingdom destroyed by failure of succession mechanisms.[93] Contemporary Parthia, which the Romans often conflated with Persia and regarded as the extension of the Persian Empire, might also be hinted at. This great antagonist of Rome had also been plagued by succession-related turmoil and political instability by Statius' time.[94] Moreover, in Statius' simile there are specific elements that work toward linking Rome and Persia. In the simile, the young Persian king is uncertain as to whether the nobles will be loyal to him and whether the people will obey his rule. It is difficult not to recall that the Roman emperor's concerns were exactly the same, namely to gain the support of the Senate and of the people. And again, when Statius describes the newly appointed king's doubts as to whom to put in charge of the different territories, one cannot help but think of the new emperor's uncertainty regarding the distribution of the various provinces.[95]

Through this simile, Amphiaraus is then likened to the king of a great empire that in many respects resembles Rome. This Roman setting may be supported by another striking detail in Statius' account of the seer's death. After Amphiaraus' death, Statius presents a brief scene in which Apollo declares his grief at the death of his protégé to his sister Diana. The god has ceased his usual prophetic activities.[96] The suspension of prophecy is paralleled in the narrative by the interruption of the Sun's regular course; while meeting with his sister (Diana/Moon), the Sun (Apollo) is eclipsed.[97] The Romans have a tradition of associating the solar eclipse with the

---

[92] On this important simile see Augoustakis (2016) 183–4.

[93] There is an important Greek tradition of regarding the kingdom of Persia, in its early stage, as a somewhat idealized monarchy. This tradition, going back to Xenophon's popular *Cyropaedia* and echoed in Plato, is extremely influential on Roman culture (cf. e.g. Cic. *Sen.* 59.1; *Brut.* 112; *Q. fr.* 1.1.23). Importantly, central to this tradition was the problem of succession. Cyrus, although an ideal king, had not been able to provide a valuable successor, thus engendering the decay of his dynasty (Pl. *Lg.* 694c–95b)—hence, the necessity of reflecting on the problem of the education of the sovereign and the controversy between Plato and Xenophon on how this education should be undertaken. A useful starting point is Dorion (2003).

[94] Hollis (1994) suggests that the young king represented in the simile is the Parthian king Pacorus II, whose succession to his father Vologaeses I was marked by uncertainty and dynastic struggles.

[95] The relevance of the Roman imperial context already suggested by Vessey (1973) 266 n. 2. On this passage see also Hardie (1993) 111.

[96] Cf. *Theb.* 9.657–9; see also 8.195–205.

[97] *Theb.* 9.647–9. The idea that this is a description of an eclipse is already in Schol. Stat. 9.647 and has been endorsed by Feeney (1991, 373 n. 192), who also refers to the model of *Met.* 2.329–31. *Contra* Dewar (1991) 181.

disappearance of a political leader (or of a king): For instance, an eclipse follows Caesar's death in Virgil's *Georgics*.[98] In addition, Amphiaraus as a mythical character offers a good model for talking about the death of an emperor, for he was thought to enjoy a privileged position among the dead, and in Statius he goes to the Elysian fields, where Statius places the good Romans of the past in *Siluae* 2.7.[99]

2.6 SUCCESSION

The contrast between Polynices and Amphiaraus culminates in the episode of Amphiaraus' succession in book 8.[100] The simile of the Persian youth analyzed in the previous section, which Statius introduces in connection with Thiodamas' succession to Amphiaraus, describes dynastic succession. But in the narrative proper, Thiodamas is appointed by acclamation of the soldiers.[101] The scene is peculiar because there is no exact parallel in extant epics.[102] Thiodamas' reaction to his appointment is also strange and extremely unepic: He is humble and says that he is not equal to the task. Eventually, he has to be forced to accept the office:

illum ingens confundit honos inopinaque turbat
gloria et oblatas frondes summissus adorat
seque oneri negat esse parem, cogique meretur.
Theb. 8.283–5

The great honor confounds him and the unexpected glory upsets him. Humbly he reverences the proffered wreath and protests that he is unequal to the burden, deserving to be constrained.

It is difficult to imagine a Homeric hero, even a Virgilian hero, behaving in the same way. Humility is no epic virtue.

The odd scene can be explained by Statius' desire to allude to Roman political realities. Thiodamas' behavior finds parallels in accounts of imperial acclamations.

---

[98] *G.* 1.466–8.

[99] Amphiaraus in the Elysian fields: *Theb.* 7.776; cf. *Silv.* 2.7.111–19. For Amphiaraus' privileged position among the dead, witnessed by Statius' description at *Theb.* 10.202–6, see Section 2.7 and n. 116.

[100] In this section, I build on Hardie's (1993) 111–13 excellent analysis.

[101] *Theb.* 8.275–82.

[102] The closest parallel would be the scene in Apollonius Rhodius' *Argonautica* (A.R. 1.331–62), but there Hercules does not admit he is unequal to the task, and, unlike Thiodamas, he imposes his own choice of a different leader. Contrast also Erginus' succession to Typhis in Valerius (5.65–70), to which the *Thebaid* passage is related, where Erginus is appointed by the oak itself: Augoustakis (2016) 177.

One could compare, for instance, Vespasian's acclamation by his soldiers as narrated by Josephus (*BJ* 4.601). In this passage, the soon-to-be emperor, like Thiodamas, is acclaimed by his troops, protests against the election, and has eventually to be forced to accept the office. In fact, if Thiodamas' behavior does not fit the epic code, it is perfectly in line with the demeanor expected from a newly appointed Roman emperor. The act of *recusatio*, by which the emperor refuses to serve, is so common and has so few exceptions in accounts of imperial successions that scholars consider it almost a standard part of the ritual. Josephus' account is no different, for instance, from what Pliny the Younger recounts concerning Trajan's accession.[103]

There is another striking feature in Statius' account: the poet clearly contrasts the relationship between Thiodamas and Amphiaraus with that between Polynices and Eteocles. Thiodamas already holds a prominent position within the army, even before his appointment, and he is clearly presented as already fit to fulfill Amphiaraus' role before the priest's death:

> haud mora, cuncti
> insignem fama sanctoque Melampode cretum
> Thiodamanta uolunt, quicum ipse arcana deorum
> partiri et uisas uni sociare solebat
> Amphiaraus aues, tantaeque haud inuidus artis
> gaudebat dici similem iuxtaque secundum.
> *Theb.* 8.277–82

No delay, all want Thiodamas, the son of venerable Melampus, eminent in fame. Amphiaraus himself used to make him partaker in the secrets of the gods and share with him alone the birds he had seen. He was not jealous of so much skill and rejoiced that Thiodamas should be called his like and close second.

Amphiaraus is not envious of him and is happy that Thiodamas is considered his equal and close second. These lines clearly form a counterpart to Statius' description of Eteocles and Polynices at the very beginning of the poem.[104]

Unlike the brothers, Amphiaraus and Thiodamas are models of *concordia* [harmony] and of positive transmission of power. And if we read this succession scene in connection with Flavian panegyric, we find interesting parallels. Both Titus and Domitian had a prominent position within Roman society well before the deaths

---

[103] Plin. *Pan.* 5.5–6. A full list of imperial *recusationes* is found in Béranger (1953) 139, to whom I refer for discussion of this pivotal topic.

[104] *Theb.* 1.127–30; Augoustakis (2016) 181.

of their predecessors. Despite the potential for rivalry under such circumstances, Flavian ideology stresses the *concordia* within the royal family. Panegyrists of Domitian go so far as to say that Domitian voluntarily accepted being third, turning down his emperorship in favor of his father Vespasian and brother Titus.[105] The way in which Statius describes the relationship between Thiodamas and Amphiaraus could, then, reflect panegyric descriptions of the relationship among members of the Flavian family. The wicked Polynices, incapable of sharing power, is associated with Nero; the scene of Amphiaraus' succession contrasts the harmonious practices of the new dynasty with his rule.

There is another aspect of Statius' scene that can be read in connection with imperial discourses on succession. Thiodamas is elected by popular will, but he is also presented as a man whom Amphiaraus himself would have appointed, as we previously saw.[106] The new commander is then depicted as meeting both the will of the people and the desire of the former person in charge. This idea is mirrored in discussions of imperial succession and is the clear reversal of a common topic: The ruler chooses as his successor the man whom the people would have chosen.[107]

The scene's emphasis on the criteria for choosing a new ruler should also be understood in light of the specific situation of Domitian's family. Given Domitian's inability to produce a male heir, it must have seemed obvious to his contemporaries that he had to choose a successor from those around him. Here Statius provides a somewhat idealized model of how such a succession should take place: The new recipient of the office should be picked based on his merits and should be someone who meets popular approval and the will of the incumbent. Statius' position here might be aligned with that of his aristocratic patrons. Succession by election is the best that Roman aristocrats could have hoped for in the 80s and 90s, in the face of Domitian's lack of a natural heir, and is the practice that seemed more akin to the ideal of *libertas* under imperial rule.[108]

2.7 TALES OF IMPERIAL HARMONY: AMPHIARAUS AND THE DIOSCURI

Further reason to see the account of Amphiaraus' death as influenced by narratives of imperial *concordia* comes from the seer's constant association with the Dioscuri.

---

[105] Mart. 9.101.12–13. The same claim is made by Domitian in Suet. *Dom.* 13.1.

[106] *Theb.* 8.279–82.

[107] Cf. Plin. *Pan.* 7.6, 8.5–6.

[108] On *adoptio* as a surrogate for *libertas* see Tac. *Hist.* 1.16.1; Plin. *Pan.* 8.2. On the topic of adoption in relationship to *libertas* under the empire see Wirszubski (1968) 154–8.

Polynices' horse Arion, formerly a possession of Hercules, creates a connection between Polynices and Hercules.[109] The same applies to Amphiaraus. His horses are the offspring of Cyllarus, the legendary horse of the Dioscuri.[110] The origin of Amphiaraus' horses is mentioned again in book 4, in the catalogue of Argive forces, where we also learn that Amphiaraus is accompanied to war by the soldiers from Sparta, the fatherland of Castor and Pollux.[111] The Spartans' helmet, with its swan plumes, recalls Leda, the mother of Castor and Pollux, and her union with Jupiter in the form of a swan.[112] Other troops follow the seer from Amyclae, a city closely associated with the Dioscuri according to Roman poetic tradition.[113] The image of the Dioscuri surfaces again in the scene of Amphiaraus' death in book 7. The seer's chariot is compared to a ship abandoned by the light of the twin gods.[114] The link with the Dioscuri is fitting for Amphiaraus, whose mythical persona and cult have something in common with Castor. Castor is a famous horse tamer, a characteristic that is certainly important to Statius' depiction of Amphiaraus as a skilled charioteer. He is also known for his premature death and for his periodical permanence in the underworld, where he becomes a chthonic god.[115] In this he resembles Amphiaraus, who becomes an oracular god and has a special position among the dead.[116]

But there is more than this. I previously observed that Amphiaraus is presented as a ruler figure and that *concordia* is an important theme of Statius' description of Thiodamas' succession to Amphiaraus. The twin gods (especially Pollux) frequently feature as a divine counterpart of sovereigns. This panegyric use of the Dioscuri goes back to the Hellenistic world and has several precedents in Augustan literature and culture.[117] By Statius' time it had become a stock piece of imperial praise. We find

---

[109] See Chapter 3, Section 3.1.1.

[110] *Theb.* 6.326–9; see Pavan (2009) 151–2.

[111] *Theb.* 4.214–15. For the Dioscuri and Amphiaraus see Georgacopoulou (1996a) 446, (2005) 57; Parkes (2012) 145–6.

[112] *Theb.* 4.234–6 with Parkes (2012) 146, 152.

[113] See the passages collected by Parkes (2012) 146.

[114] *Theb.* 7.791–3.

[115] *RE* 5.1 1115.

[116] The idea of Amphiaraus' special status among the dead is found in Sophocles' *Electra* (836–41), where the chorus tries to console the heroine about her father's death by recounting the story of Amphiaraus, who, unlike the other dead, retains full power of his mind in the underworld; see Finglass (2007) 363 *ad loc.* Herodotus recounts that, as an oracular deity, Amphiaraus was honored by Croesus as much as the Delphic Apollo (1.46–52). His shrine at Oropus was famous throughout antiquity (Str. 9.1.22, 9.2.10–11; Paus. 1.34.1–5). See *RE* 18.1 834–5; Wilamowitz (1959) ii 12–13; *RE* 1.2 1886–93. Educated Romans are perfectly aware of the traditions about Amphiaraus as an oracular god: cf. Cic. *Div.* 1.88.

[117] *LIMC* III.1 592; the Dioscuri bring Arsinoe to heaven in Call. *Iamb.* 16, fr. 228 Pfeiffer; Theoc. 22 is also relevant in this context. On the Dioscuri and ruler ideology: Poulsen (1991). For Augustan uses, mainly featuring Pollux, cf. e.g. Hor. *Carm.* 3.3.10–13 with Nisbet–Rudd (2004) 41.

it as praise of Domitian in *Siluae* 4.2.47–8. But there is a more specific use of the comparison as a means to highlight the *concordia* of brothers within the imperial family. Valerius Maximus uses the example of the Dioscuri to describe the *concordia* between Tiberius and Drusus.[118] According to Cassius Dio, the elder Drusus' death was predicted by an apparition of the Dioscuri.[119] After Drusus' death, Tiberius restored the important temple of the Castores in the Republican Forum under his name and that of his brother.[120] This event is celebrated by Ovid, who is aware of the symbolic overtones of the restoration and does not fail to make explicit the connection between the two sets of divine brothers in his *Fasti*.[121] While restoring the temple, Tiberius appears as Pollux, willing to show his *pietas* for his deceased brother.[122] Later, other pairs of brothers within the imperial family are likened to the Dioscuri: Germanicus and Drusus *minor* ('Tiberius' sons),[123] and Nero and Drusus Caesar (Germanicus' sons).[124]

Martial, who frequently compares Domitian to Pollux, also tells us that the emperor, like Tiberius, restored the Dioscuri's temple in the Forum Romanum after Titus' death.[125] During Vespasian's life, Titus held the office of *magister equitum*, an office that was traditionally linked with Castor.[126] The identification of Domitian and Titus with the heavenly twins is visible in the coinage of Vespasian.[127] Valerius Flaccus' treatment of the Dioscuri may well resonate with this panegyric use of the gods under Vespasian.[128] The comparison predates Domitian's accession, but after Titus' death it could be used in a more specific way by identifying Domitian with Pollux and Titus with Castor, as a means of praising Domitian's *pietas* to his deceased brother. This political resonance of the Dioscuri comparison strengthens our perception of Thiodamas and Amphiaraus as an alternative to the Theban brothers,

---

[118] V. Max 5.5.3.26–8.

[119] D.C. 55.1.5 with Scott (1930a) 158–9.

[120] D.C. 55.27.3–4; Suet. *Tib.* 20.1. Tiberius also restored the temple of Concordia. On the temple of Castor and Pollux in the Forum see *LTUR* I 242–45; on its rededication and Tiberius' self-styling of his brother and himself as the heavenly twins, see now Champlin (2011).

[121] Ov. *Fast.* 1.705–8. See Green (2004b) 226–7; (2004a) on *Fast.* 1.706–7.

[122] Champlin (2011) 88.

[123] Cf. Ov. *Tr.* 2.167–68; *Pont.* 2.2.81–4; with Scott (1930b) 379; Champlin (2011) 93–4. Drusus the younger had been nicknamed Castor: D.C. 57.14.9; Champlin (2011) 93 n. 59. Cf. also *Epic. Drusi* 283, 409–10.

[124] The identification is plain in the coinage and inscriptions: *RPC* I no. 946; *RPC* I no. 171; inscriptions: *IGRR* 3.997; *IK Ephesos* VII 2.43 37; Scott (1930a) 158 n. 3, (1930b) 379; Poulsen (1991) 128–9; Champlin (2011) 93.

[125] Mart. 9.3.11, referring to the Dioscuri as the "pious Laconians."

[126] For the Dioscuri's traditional connection with the *Equites* [Knights] see Scott (1930a), especially 157–8.

[127] Cf. *RIC*² II no. 54: Domitian's and Titus' iconography recalls the traditional representation of the Dioscuri; cf. also *RIC*² II nos. 5, 64, 143–54 (coins of Vespasian); *RIC*² II nos. 159–60 (coins of Titus), obverse: Domitian and Titus clasping hands, with *concordia* between them; reverse: both riding right like the Dioscuri.

[128] Stover (2012) 59–60, 62–70, especially 69–70.

but also suggests their proximity to the latest pair of imperial brothers, Titus and Domitian.

2.8 APOLLO, OSIRIS, AND MITHRAS: DOMITIAN AND THE EAST

Statius' construction of the chariot race as a competition between ruler figures prepares the ground for his succession scene and for the description of Polynices' and Amphiaraus' deaths. The race pits Amphiaraus against Polynices and introduces the myth of Phaethon and the metaphor of the "race of life." It prepares the reader to understand the circumstances of both Polynices' and Amphiaraus' deaths, in which the imagery of chariot racing resurfaces. By means of the figure of Phaethon, the poet makes room for the phantoms of the Julio-Claudian age (Nero). Polynices-*qua*-Phaethon, the reckless youth incapable of leading the state, is contrasted with the seer whose success is associated with a seamless continuity that meets with the approval of the people. In addition to being a model of *concordia*, Thiodamas is the polar opposite of Phaethon in one important respect: Phaethon boasts he can carry his father's burden and proves unequal to the task, whereas Thiodamas, like the good emperors, professes that he is unequal to the task but, in the end, proves a worthy successor.

Statius' chariot race is a literary and ideological tour de force. The poet needs to create a dualism between two solar charioteers. Through this stratagem, he can show that there is a positive realization of the role of solar *auriga*—to be the new Sun does not necessarily imply turning out like Nero. Under these premises, solar imagery can be rescued and praise of Nero can be readapted. The *Thebaid* passages reinforce the conclusions we drew when considering the *Thebaid*'s praise of Domitian in connection with *Siluae* 4.3. The hints at Phaethon conjure up the figure of Nero, which retains its admonitory power: Nero becomes the emblem of a failed emperor, and his story reminds the emperor of the risks inherent in not living up to one's initial promises. But the possibility of success is not ruled out.

It remains for us to try to provide an answer to the vital question anticipated at the beginning of this chapter. Solar imagery was particularly important to Domitian. He invested much energy and resources in his pharaonic project in the Campus Martius, at the risk of being associated with Nero. Why was Domitian so attached to this set of symbols? Could he not have continued along the moderate lines set by his father? What exactly was at stake? These questions are too complex to be answered in full here. However, we can attempt a partial answer that opens new possibilities for the understanding of passages of Statius' major poem. This partial answer has to do with Nero and the East. Nero's Golden Day of 66 CE inaugurated a season of peaceful relations with Parthia. This season was not destined to last for long. Early in Vespasian's reign, at the invitation of the Hyrcani, the Alani invaded Parthian territory; they took captive Pacorus of Media Atropatene and almost captured Tiridates of Armenia.[129] Both Tiridates and Pacorus were brothers of Vologaeses of Parthia, and when Vologaeses asked Vespasian for help, he was told that it was not proper for Rome to interfere in others' affairs (D.C. 65.15.3). It is likely that Vespasian's response compromised the relationship between Parthia and Rome, particularly in light of how Parthian kings behaved on the occasion of the false Nero episodes.[130] When an impostor appeared in the eastern empire some 20 years after Nero's death and managed to cross into Parthia, he found the support of the Parthian king. This was due, according to Suetonius, to the great love Parthians had for the name of Nero.[131] The false Nero was finally surrendered and hunted down by Roman troops. The upheaval must have been serious: According to Tacitus, it nearly provoked a disastrous war with Parthia.[132] Domitian demanded the head of Civica Cerialis, the governor of Asia who underestimated the threat of the false Nero, and received a new imperial acclamation to celebrate his success against the impostor.[133]

The whole incident is revealing. The frontier with Parthia was vulnerable, diplomatic relations were minimal, and even the support of the eastern legions might have appeared to be at risk. Roman forces were concentrated on the Danube border as a result of Domitian's long Dacian campaigns. Domitian hardly had sufficient resources to face a threat from the East. Nero's popularity in the East was unshaken, and his name was the key to the relationship with Parthia. Domitian's reception of Nero's solar ideology must be understood in this context: Among other things, it had the East as its target. The identification of Mithras/Sol with the emperor had been inaugurated by Nero in an official context in 66 CE. Solar ideology was the connection necessary to link the Roman imperial cult with both Parthian royal ideology and Parthian religion. As we saw at the beginning of this chapter, part of the Flavian troops (Legio III Gallica) religiously saluted the rising Sun on the day of the decisive battle of Cremona II. Forms of solar cult were already spread among the eastern legions in the 60s. Those were the most important veterans of the 69 CE war, later redeployed to guard the Parthian border.[134] Archaeological evidence proves

---

[129] J. BJ 7.244–51; Jones (1992) 157.
[130] On the false Neros see introduction to Chapter 1.
[131] Suet. Nero 57.2.
[132] Tac. Hist. 1.2.
[133] Jones (1983), (1992) 158–9.
[134] Legio III Gallica, originally established by Julius Caesar, was stationed in the East after the battle of Philippi, from where it took part in important campaigns waged against the Parthians, first by Mark Antony and then by Domitius Corbulo under Nero. In 68 CE the legion was moved to Moesia, from where, after Otho's death,

that Mithraism spread early and found many followers among the troops stationed along the Danube and Rhine borders (the two key areas of military operation under Domitian).[135] Solar ideology of the type used by Nero, emphasizing syncretism of Apollo/Sol with eastern divinities, was central to Domitian's grip on his troops and was vital to relationships with Parthia. This cultural connection may be one of the motives for Domitian's decision not to relinquish the form of charismatic kingship centering on solar symbols so strongly emphasized by Nero.

Augustus' and Nero's harnessing of solar ideology anticipated by several centuries the cult of Sol Invictus, which was later to become an official cult of the empire. The principate of Domitian marks an important step in this process, which the poetry of Statius documents. The first book of the *Thebaid* ends with a hymn to Apollo, modeled on the hymn to Hercules in Virgil.[136] The entire section is rich in echoes of imperial propaganda, capitalizing on Augustan notions of Apollo as the god of empire. However, the hymn has an unexpected conclusion:

> . . . adsis o memor hospitii, Iunoniaque arua
> dexter ames, seu te roseum Titana uocari
> gentis Achaemeniae ritu, seu praestat Osirim
> frugiferum, seu Persei sub rupibus antri
> indignata sequi torquentem cornua Mithram.
> *Theb.* 1.716–20

> . . . oh come, mindful of our hospitality, and bestow your love and favor upon Juno's fields, whether 'tis best to call you rosy Titan in the fashion of the Persian people, or Osiris the grain-bringer, or Mithras who, in the rocks of Perses' cavern, twists by the horns the bull which refuses to follow.

Apollo is identified with three oriental gods: the Persian Titan, the Egyptian Osiris, and Mithras. The basis of the identification is the syncretism Apollo/Sol. The description of Mithras twisting the bull's horns accompanies Statius' mention of the god. It is possible that this was inspired by a real Mithraic monument observed in Rome.[137] More important, this same description is echoed at the end of the poem. The portrait of Theseus slaying the Minotaur that features on this hero's shield

---

it joined Antonius Primus in the civil war of 69 CE on Vespasian's side. After the war the legion was returned to Syria. See Dabrowa (2000) 309–10.

[135] Clauss (2000) 21–22. The earliest archaeological evidence for the cult of Mithras is found in Germania and is roughly coeval with the publication of the *Thebaid*.

[136] *A.* 8.293–302; *Theb.* 1.696–720.

[137] Clauss (2000) 22.

echoes the image of Mithras Tauroctonos at the beginning of the poem.[138] Theseus, the idealized sovereign who finally settles the civil war of the *Thebaid*, is thus an embodiment of the solar power of Apollo/Mithras described at the beginning of the poem in the hymn to Apollo.

The image of Theseus at the end of the *Thebaid* fuses allusions to Vespasian and to Domitian. The *Thebaid*'s civil war is settled by a Mithras-like sovereign who comes back from the Northeast, just like the 69 CE war was settled by Vespasian with the help of legions whose soldiers worshipped Mithras/Sun. But the image is also remindful of Domitian's triumphs on the Danube. Theseus comes back from a war against the Amazons in the Northeast, just as Domitian was victorious along the northeastern border.[139] Domitian's successes in this area were achieved with the help of legions among which Mithraism spread quickly and extensively. We now get a sense of why Domitian was so eager to retain the solar symbolism of Nero. Solar imagery was, among other things, a vital factor in shaping the emperor's relationship with the army. Statius' complex use of solar symbols, both in the chariot race and in his hymn to Apollo, is an extraordinary contribution to this complex ideological climate.

---

[138] *Theb.* 12.665–71; Vessey (1973) 313.
[139] See Chapter 1, Section 1.8.

3

Hercules in the *Thebaid*

NIGHT ON THE Palatine Hill. Statius is dining with the emperor in the imperial palace. The halls are splendid and so is the banquet, but Statius' eyes are for his beloved emperor only, whose calm countenance and serene majesty, tempered with modesty, command the admiration of the guests. Reclining at his table, Domitian is like Mars, Pollux, Bacchus, or Hercules after their triumphs:

> non aliter gelida Rhodopes in ualle recumbit
> dimissis Gradiuus equis; sic lubrica ponit
> membra Therapnaea resolutus gymnade Pollux,
> sic iacet ad Gangen Indis ululantibus Euhan,
> sic grauis Alcides post horrida iussa reuersus
> gaudebat strato latus acclinare leoni.
> *Silv.* 4.2.46–51

Not otherwise does Gradivus lie down in Rhodope's cold valley, his horses unharnessed; just so does Pollux lay down his oily limbs, relaxing from the boxing at Therapne, so Bacchus lies by the Ganges, while Indians howl, so ponderous Alcides, returning from his frightening labors, rejoiced to prop his flank upon the outspread lionskin.

The Hercules comparison is a traditional element of imperial panegyric, the greatest of heroes being a match for the emperor's power at war, an anticipation of his apotheosis, and a token of his close connection to the gods.[1] Yet what Statius has to say about imperial power through the figure of Hercules in the *Thebaid* is far from conventional and deserves further scrutiny.

3.1 HERCULES' CRATER

A passage from book 6 offers valuable insights into the relevance of Hercules for Statius' *Thebaid*. Amphiaraus wins the chariot race, the first competition in the games for the dead Opheltes; his prize is a golden mixing bowl, once a possession of Hercules, depicting one of the hero's feats, Hercules' participation in the fight between Centaurs and Lapiths:[2]

> huic pretium palmae gemini cratera ferebant
> Herculeum iuuenes: illum Tirynthius olim
> ferre manu sola spumantemque ore supino
> uertere, seu monstri uictor seu Marte, solebat.
> Centauros habet arte truces aurumque figuris
> terribile: hic mixta Lapitharum caede rotantur
> saxa, faces (aliique iterum crateres); ubique
> ingentes morientum irae; tenet ipse furentem
> Hylaeum et torta molitur robora barba.
> *Theb.* 6.531–9

Two young men brought him the prize of victory, Hercules' bowl, which the Tirynthian, victorious over monsters or in war, once used to lift with one hand only and tilt, foaming, into his upturned mouth. It has fearful figures in gold and Centaurs made savage by the artist's skill: here, in the confusion of the slaughter of the Lapiths, stones are hurled, and torches, and again other bowls; the great fury of the dying is represented everywhere; Hercules himself holds raging Hylaeus, and twisting his beard, he wields the club.

---

[1] See Section 3.2.
[2] Statius' picture of Centauromachy is indebted to Virgil's mention of the same episode in *G.* 2.455–7. On the *Thebaid*'s chariot race and its implications see Chapter 2, Sections 2.3 and 2.4.

Readers of epic are trained to explore connections between ekphrastic digressions and the narratives into which they are inserted. What is the relationship between this story and the *Thebaid*'s plot?[3]

3.1.1 A prize worthy of Hercules

The choice of Hercules and the Centaurs as the subject of the *ekphrasis* can be understood in light of Statius' characterization of the race. The crater is an appropriate prize for a very "Herculean" race, one that is envisaged as a competition to inherit Hercules' mantle. The race takes place in Nemea, the location of one of Hercules' toils (the killing of the Nemean lion).[4] The presence of Centauromachy on an object that belonged to Hercules is not surprising.[5] Some of the race contestants are related to the figures portrayed on the crater. Polynices' team is led by Arion, Hercules' divine horse, now a possession of Adrastus.[6] Chromis, a son of Hercules, drives the man-eating horses of King Diomedes, conquered by his father.[7] Admetus' horses, on the other hand, are the offspring of Centaurs.[8] Amphiaraus' horses have benign, though perhaps ill-omened, divine connections: They are born of Cyllarus, the horse of Castor, the one twin who died and became a god of the underworld.[9]

We are in a Herculean venue, Nemea, and the prize awaiting the winner is also Herculean. Yet, the two heroes most closely related to him cannot live up to Hercules. Chromis is a valuable charioteer, but his horses are too heavy and slow (*Theb.* 6.437–8); he ultimately struggles for the penultimate position.[10] Polynices' horse is worthy of Hercules; thanks to him, the hero immediately pulls into first place.[11] But Arion is difficult to control; even Hercules had trouble restraining him

---

[3] Interpretations of the *ekphrasis*: Vessey (1973) 216–17 connects Centauromachy with the centrality of *furor* in the *Thebaid* and notes the simile applied to Hippomedon in *Theb.* 4.139–44; Lovatt (2002) 80 argues that the *ekphrasis* should be seen as an allusion to Amphiaraus' *furor* in book 7 or, alternatively, as an anticipation of the episode of the night massacre by Thiodamas in book 10; Pavan (2009) 238–41 reads the *ekphrasis* in connection with the prominence of Hercules in the context of the race.

[4] A statue of Hercules strangling the Nemean lion is displayed at the beginning of the games (*Theb.* 6.270–1); see Section 3.4.

[5] Heroes often have their deeds represented on their possessions; cf. Theseus' shield (*Theb.* 12.665–71), depicting the killing of the Minotaur. Hercules used the crater to draw wine after his victories against monsters or in war (*Theb.* 6.534), and the mixing bowl is decorated with an image of one of Hercules' exploits against monsters, which is also a kind of war.

[6] *Theb.* 6.301–19.

[7] *Theb.* 6.346–50.

[8] *Theb.* 6.332–4.

[9] *Theb.* 4.214–6, 6.326–9. The story of Castor anticipates Amphiaraus' destiny as underworld oracular god: *Theb.* 8.329–38; cf. Chapter 2, Section 2.7.

[10] *Theb.* 6.436–8.

[11] *Theb.* 6.424–31.

(*Theb.* 6.313). Being no Hercules, Polynices very quickly loses control of his chariot.[12] Later, Apollo dispatches a monster from the underworld to scare Polynices' horses. Hercules drove Arion against several monsters (*Theb.* 6.311–13), but Polynices is helpless in the face of Apollo's creature and is thrown off the chariot.[13] Given his horse, Polynices is the one destined to win Hercules' crater. His failure opens up the possibility for other competitors to lay their hands on the prize. For a while, it seems as though Admetus' Centaur-born horses might have the upper hand, but Apollo intervenes to secure Amphiaraus' victory.[14] His success in a sense materializes the image on the crater: Like Hercules, Amphiaraus is victorious over (Admetus') Centaurs, yet he is also clearly a replacement for the failed Herculean hero. This sequence, as we will see, is reproduced several times and on various scales in the *Thebaid*: the failure of the Herculean hero, the appropriation of his role by a "new Hercules," and the risk that monsters might prevail.

3.1.2 *The seven Centaurs*

The relevance of the crater *ekphrasis* to the poem's main narrative is not limited to the chariot race episode.[15] An indication of how to read Centauromachy in connection with the *Thebaid*'s plot comes from Jupiter's prophecy in book 7, in which the king of the gods references the battle of Centaurs and Lapiths as a parallel for his current project of inflicting war on Argos and Thebes.[16] Statius adopts the version of the saga according to which the war between Centaurs and Lapiths is caused by Mars, who is angry at Pirithous for not inviting him to his wedding.[17] This version suits the action of the *Thebaid*, in which the war of Argos and Thebes is the result of Jupiter's punitive design (cf. *Theb.* 1.214–47). In the rest of the poem, repeated use of imagery and allusions to Centauromachy supports the analogy suggested by Jupiter.[18] During his fight with the 50 Thebans in book 2, Tydeus is compared to the Centaur Pholus hurling a crater at the Lapiths, a detail represented on Hercules' crater (*Theb.* 6.536–7).[19] Soon afterward, Tydeus is faced by a hero who carries the same name as Hercules' Argive son (Chromis) and is dressed precisely like the greatest of heroes

---

[12] *Theb.* 6.443–4.

[13] *Theb.* 6.491–506.

[14] *Theb.* 6. 431–3, 518–30.

[15] See Parkes (2009) 490–1.

[16] *Theb.* 7.203–5. Jupiter borrows here the words of Juno in the *Aeneid*: *A.* 7.304–7. The other story mentioned by Jupiter in Statius (the Caydonian boar) is harnessed by Statius in connection with Tydeus. See Section 3.5.

[17] The same version is implied by Virgil at *A.* 7.304; cf. Serv. *A.* 7.304.

[18] On Centaur-related imagery in the *Thebaid* see Parkes (2009) 485, 489–91, and Franchet d'Esperey (1999) 193–7.

[19] *Theb.* 2.559–64. On this passage's connection with Ovid's Centauromachy see Parkes (2009) 489.

(with lion skin, club, and all).[20] When the Centaur-like Tydeus meets the Herculean Chromis, the image on the crater finds a perfect parallel in the main narrative.

When Hippomedon first enters the poem, he is likened to Hylaeus, the Centaur engaged in close combat with Hercules in the crater scene.[21] The theme of Centauromachy is conjured up again at the time of Hippomedon's death. The hero's final *aristeia* is introduced by a simile comparing him to a Centaur.[22] The river god hits him repeatedly with the trunk of an oak tree, a gigantic version of the oak club used by Hercules against Hylaeus.[23]

The notoriously impious Centaurs are an appropriate foil for Capaneus, who is first introduced in the poem by a simile likening him to a Cyclops or a Centaur dwelling in the woods of Pholoe.[24] In book 1, Tydeus complains that Polynices acts more savagely than a Centaur or a Cyclops.[25] And in book 11, Eteocles, who is about to sacrifice to Jupiter in thanks for rescuing Thebes, is compared to Hercules, trying to sacrifice on Mount Oeta while the blood of Nessus is burning his flesh. Here Centauric blood is perhaps a symbol of the *furor* leading Eteocles to his final conflict with his brother.[26] In light of this imagery, it is ironic that Agave should use the argument that the dead Argives were not Centaurs in order to convince Theseus to intervene in favor of their deceased husbands.[27] She is on thin ice here, as has been noted, but this strengthens Statius' point. Even if the Argives have actually been as savage as Centaurs, they still deserve Theseus' clemency.[28]

The Hercules crater thus provides a miniature of the poem's action, with Centaur-like Argives pitted against Thebans in the role of Lapiths. It also foreshadows its conclusion. In the crater, Hercules resolves the conflict between two wicked peoples. The crater scene sets the expectation for the arrival of a Hercules-type figure who brings the conflict to an end. The Herculean role is thus associated with success in settling the poem's civil conflict. This expectation is fulfilled by Theseus' intervention. Theseus is similar to Hercules in many respects, and he is also known for having

---

[20] *Theb.* 2.613–19. For Chromis (the son of Hercules) see *Theb.* 6.346.

[21] *Theb.* 4.139–44. This echoes a simile employed by Virgil to introduce two Latin heroes from the city of Tibur (Catillus and Coras) in book 7 of the *Aeneid* (*A.* 7.670–7): Franchet d'Esperey (1999) 193; Parkes (2009) 485, (2012) 115. In Statius' simile, the Centaur terminates his run in the river Peneus, a gloomy omen for Hippomedon, who will conclude his life in the waters of Ismenus (*Theb.* 9.504–39).

[22] *Theb.* 9.220–2.

[23] *Theb.* 9.481–5.

[24] *Theb.* 3.604–7.

[25] *Theb.* 1.457–60.

[26] *Theb.* 11.234–8.

[27] *Theb.* 12.553–4.

[28] Feeney (1991) 361 n. 156. Soon after, the same principle is repeated when Creon is granted a burial, despite having acted inhumanly, like the Argives: *Theb.* 12.165–6.

taken part in the fight with the Centaurs.[29] As we will see, Statius highlights the similarities between the two heroes. In a way, Theseus is also similar to Amphiaraus in the chariot race; he is the outsider who replaces Hercules and achieves a victory against monstrous opponents. Both the race and its prize mirror the poem's narrative and anticipate its conclusion.

3.1.3 Roman Centaurs

There is more to Statius' choice of Centaurs and Lapiths than just mirroring the *Thebaid*'s main plot. Centauromachy functions figuratively as a foil for historical conflicts at least from the time of the Parthenon metopes, in which the myth works as a parallel for the recent conflict with the Persians, conceived as monstrous and uncivilized invaders. In Rome there are traces of adaptations of Centauromachy as a foil for civil war in Augustan culture. These are part of an attempt at refashioning civil war as a war against a foreign, barbarian enemy—a process that entails adaptation of fifth-century Athenian paradigms. A Centaur is at the bow of Antony's ship in Propertius' description of the battle of Actium (Prop. 4.6.47–50). In Horace, the fight between Centaurs and Lapiths seems to be related to the recent civil conflict, brought to an end by Hercules/Augustus.[30] In the *Aeneid*, Centaurus is the name of Sergestus' ship.[31] The latter is a Trojan, but his descendant, Catilina, will raise arms against his own country. It is no surprise that he, of all contestants, crashes his ship against the rocks.[32] Something similar can be said of Cupauo, the Ligures' chieftain.[33] His ship, like Antony's ship in Propertius, features a rock-hurling Centaur on the bow.[34] In the *Aeneid*, the Ligures are allies of the Trojans, but they should not be

---

[29] See e.g. Ov. *Met.* 12.189ff.

[30] *Carm.* 2.12.5–6. In his *recusatio*, Horace seems here to refer, through mythical and historical subjects, to recent feats by Augustus: Nisbet–Hubbard (1978) 188. In this context, Centauromachy is usually interpreted as a covert reference to Antony and his followers: The remark on the Centaurs' predilection for wine is consistent with the charge of leading a dissolute life often leveled at Antony and his party; moreover, Antony was head of the priestly college of the Luperci, a role that may have prompted associations with the hairy Centaurs. See also Hardie (1987) 165–6.

[31] *A.* 5.121–2. Propertius' ship of Antony is perhaps influenced by Sergestus' Centaurus. Hutchinson (2006, 162) notes that ships with a hundred oars (Prop. 4.6.47–50) would hardly have impressed a contemporary Roman reader—warships were commonly endowed with many more oars (up to 300). Most probably the detail conjures up an allusion to the world of epic, where 100 is the customary number (cf. Hom. *Il.* 20.247; Sil. 11.490), and specifically to the catalogue of ships in the *Aeneid*, in which a 100-oar ship is named soon after the mention of Cupauo's ship, decorated with a Centaur (*A.* 10.207–8).

[32] Cf. Hardie (1987) 165–6; Nisbet–Hubbard (1978) 188, Chapter 2, Section 2.4 and n. 63.

[33] Nisbet–Hubbard (1978, 188), Hutchinson (2006, 163–4), and Horsfall (2000, 441) find it hard to reconcile the use of the same imagery (Centaurs) at first for the ancestor of a prospective enemy of the state such as Catilina and later for Aeneas' allies. I argue that in both cases the imagery aims at foreshadowing a future betrayal by the person or people concerned, as I will show.

[34] *A.* 10.194–7.

trusted. We learn in book 11 that deceit [*fraus*] is their art.[35] They are "double," like Centaurs, with whom they share, according to Roman sources, a wild character and semicivilized lifestyle.[36] In historical times, the Ligures were fierce enemies of the Romans and faithful allies of Carthage.[37] Like Catilina then, they turned their arms against former friends. In the rest of his poem, Virgil consistently uses references to Centaurs to mark Aeneas' enemies.[38]

Centauromachy provides a particularly apt sets of images, for it recalls civil war on more than one level: It accompanies the war of Thebes and Argos, a civil war of sorts, but it also introduces a set of images that Roman readers were accustomed to considering in connection with their own historical civil conflicts. In this connection, Centauromachy works particularly well with respect to the 69 CE civil war. The image on the crater portrays a fight between two wicked parties that is resolved by the intervention of a third. Not only does it match the *Thebaid*'s plot, with Theseus' final intervention resolving the contest of the two armies and the two brothers, but it also balances Flavian representations of the conflict of 69 CE as a war motivated by divine anger and human impiety, fought by two wicked parties, and resolved by the intervention of a third (Domitian/Vespasian in the role of Hercules).[39] Domitian's reception of the model of Hercules is often connected with his claiming a role in the civil war of 69 CE.[40] And, as we see in Chapter 6, the idea of adapting fifth-century Athenian paradigms to the context of the 69 civil war, as a way of "barbarizing" the enemy, is an important feature of Flavian culture.[41] Centauromachic imagery helps place Statius' reflection on Hercules in a political context, inviting readers to consider the role of Herculean figures in connection with Rome's recent civil wars. This is an important leitmotif, which I follow in detail in the rest of this chapter.

---

[35] *A.* 11.715–17.

[36] They are commonly perceived as wild and violent; like the Centaurs, they are thought to live in caves and huts in the woods. See Cic. *Agr.* 2.95; Diod. 5.39; Cato *Origines* fr. 31 Peter; *RE* 13.1 533–4. A more positive view of the Ligures is adumbrated in the *Georgics* (2.168).

[37] The Romans fought the Ligures several times between 238 and 117 BCE. A triumph over them was celebrated in 117 BCE, but smaller conflicts are recorded under Augustus (14 BCE; see D.C. 44.24.3).

[38] Catillus and Coras, Latin warriors, are compared to Centaurs at *A.* 7.670–7.

[39] On the importance of the theme of the gods' anger in representations of the 69 CE civil conflict see Chapter 5, Section 5.2. On the 69 CE civil war as a war between two evil parties in Flavian perceptions see Chapter 4, Section 4.5. For links to the Flavian triumph in Theseus' portrait see Chapter 1, Section 1.8.

[40] See Section 3.2.

[41] See also Introduction, Section I.9.

3.2 HEROISM IN THE POLITICAL ARENA

Before we consider Statius' use of Herculean imagery more extensively, we need to cover some preliminary ground. The ideological resonances of Statius' reconfiguration of the Hercules paradigm can be fully grasped only if projected against the background of Augustan, Neronian, and post-Neronian uses of Hercules in imperial ideology. Hercules is associated with the sovereign in Hellenistic culture.[42] In Rome, his divine aura is invoked with special emphasis and insistence during the civil war period. Hercules was a symbol of the republican side under Pompey at the time of the war between Caesar and Pompey. On a grander scale, Antony made Hercules his counterpart in the years leading up to the battle of Actium. After his defeat, the hero was aligned with Augustus.[43]

The revival of the Hercules paradigm under Nero is particularly relevant for the *Thebaid*. Nero acted the role of Hercules in the theater. He let himself be represented as Hercules and was acclaimed as Hercules after his tour of Greece.[44] Here he claimed that he would kill a lion at the next games, imitating Hercules' feat.[45] The authorities at Delphi erected an elaborate frieze depicting the Labors of Hercules on the front face of the stage on which Nero was to perform at the Pythian Games; the emperor himself dedicated a purple robe and a golden crown on an altar to Hercules in the Temple of Hera at Argos.[46] Like Polynices, Nero took part in a chariot race in Greece and was thrown off the chariot.[47] His project of cutting the Isthmus of Corinth too was styled as one of Hercules' toils.[48]

The identification of Nero with Hercules was the target of Vindex's propaganda in 68 CE. When the governor of Gaul revolted against Nero, he issued coins portraying Hercules with the legend *Hercules Adsertor*, "Hercules the Liberator."[49] The message was clear: Hercules displaced the monster Cacus from his home on the Palatine on his way back from the West; Vindex too was on his way to displace the monster

---

[42] Huttner (1997).

[43] Hercules on the republican side in the war between Caesar and Pompey: App. *BC* 2.76. Hercules and Antony: Zanker (1988) 45–6; on Hercules and Augustus the bibliography is substantial. A starting point: La Penna (2005) 228–9, 270–1; Galinsky (1972) 144–5, and see Section 3.3 on Hercules, Aeneas, and Augustus in the *Aeneid*.

[44] Nero acting the role of the mad Hercules: D.C. 63.9.4–5, 63.10.2, 63.22.6; Suet. *Nero* 21.3, 46.3; Philostr. *VA* 5.7; Champlin (2003a) 103–7; Chapter 1, Section 1.6. Acclaimed as Nero Hercules: D.C. 63.20.5. Nero as Hercules on coins: *RPC* I n. 1278, cf. nos. 1275–81.

[45] Suet. *Nero* 53.

[46] Delphi frieze: Weir (1999). Dedication in the Temple of Hera at Argos: Paus. 2.17.6.

[47] Suet. *Nero* 24. Cf. Chapter 2, Section 2.2.

[48] Philostr. *Nero* 5. Cf. also *Her. O.* 82–4, with Champlin (2003a) 137–8, 307 nn. 83–5.

[49] *RIC*² I nos. 49, 62; Gallia (2012) 21–2.

Nero from Rome. Nero replied to Vindex's slogans. According to Suetonius, he planned in his last days to include in his projected campaign against Vindex the emperor's concubines with their hair shorn and armed with the axes and shields of Amazons. This was a reference to Hercules' own expedition against, and conquest of, the Amazons.[50] In a few months, however, this new Hercules was dead, and so was Nero. After Galba's short tenure, the state relapsed into civil war. By the time the Flavians stepped into the political arena, the image of Hercules was loaded with unfavorable associations. Vespasian famously laughed at a group of citizens who sought to prove that his family descended from one of Hercules' comrades.[51]

The question of success, or lack thereof, in the role of Hercules is particularly felt under Domitian, who recovers the association with Hercules abandoned by his father. Domitian's identification with the greatest of heroes is extensive and spans both literary and material evidence. We learn from Martial that in the temple on the Via Appia the cult statue of Hercules had been given Domitian's features.[52] In 9.101 Martial describes Domitian as a new Hercules in the context of his participation in the battle of the Capitol. He also compares Domitian's alleged success against Vitellius to Hercules' success over Cacus (ll. 13-4); note the key word *adseruit*, a reference to the tradition of Hercules Adsertor:

> haec minor Alcides: maior quae gesserit, audi,
> sextus ab Albana quem colit arce lapis.
> adseruit possessa malis Palatia regnis,
> prima suo gessit pro Ioue bella puer;
> solus Iuleas cum iam retineret habenas,
> tradidit inque suo tertius orbe fuit;
> Mart. 9.101.11–16

These were the exploits of the lesser Alcides: Hear now those performed by the greater Hercules whom the sixth milestone from the citadel of Alba honors. He set free the Palatine occupied by an evil king, as a boy fought his first war for his Jupiter; when he already held the Julian reins alone, he surrendered them and became third in the world that was his own;

Comparisons of Domitian and Hercules are also frequent in the *Siluae*, in which Domitian's military triumphs make him an equal to the greatest of heroes.[53] In

---

[50] Suet. *Nero* 44.1; Champlin (2003a) 136.

[51] Suet. *Ves.* 12.1.

[52] Mart. 9.101.1–2, 9.64.1–2, 9.65.2; for Domitian as new Hercules cf. also Mart. 5.65.

[53] See *Silv.* 4.3.155, 4.2.50–1.

the *Punica* Scipio is constantly compared to Hercules and Silius underscores the similarities among Hercules, Domitian and Scipio.[54] Statues of the young Hercules with Domitian's features were fashioned; the cuirass of the Misenum statue of Domitian portrays the child Hercules strangling snakes. The identification of Hercules and Domitian is also on coins and medallions.[55]

Domitian is also implicitly compared to Hercules in the *Thebaid*. At the beginning of the poem, Domitian is said to have taken part in the battle of the Capitol of 69 CE, helping the cause of his father Vespasian against Vitellius.[56] The phrase *bella Iouis* [wars of Jupiter] is a clear allusion to Gigantomachy. The only mortal known to have taken part in that war is Hercules, who helped his father Jupiter against the Giants.[57] Like Martial (9.101.14), Statius sees Domitian's youthful Gigantomachy as a Herculean labor. Right after these lines (*Theb.* 1.22–31), Statius announces Domitian's apotheosis: In perfectly Herculean fashion, the emperor will become a god in return for his service to mankind. The presentation of Domitian's youthful participation in the Capitoline battle as a Herculean feat, in both Martial and Status, is relevant. It may explain why in iconography Domitian is constantly represented as the *young* Hercules.[58]

3.3 HERCULES BETWEEN EPIC AND TRAGEDY

To better understand Statius' treatment of Hercules, we need to briefly consider the hero's literary pedigree, with particular attention to recent Roman adaptations in epic and tragedy. In Rome there is a rich literary tradition in which the figure of Hercules is used to explore notions of kingship and to discuss aspects of imperial

---

[54] Marks (2005a) 148–61, 222–7; for more bibliography on Scipio and Hercules in the *Punica* see Marks (2005a) 160 n. 136, 161 n. 139.

[55] Statues and medallions of Domitian as Hercules: Museum of Fine Arts, Boston n. 1978.227; Albertini Hercules, Parma, Museo Nazionale (this statue may originally have been placed in Domitian's throne room); Cornelian ringstone, Munich, Staatliche Münzsammlungen A2222; see Palagia (1986) 144–6; Laubscher (1997) fig. 8; Vermeule (1981) 300–1; Daltrop–Hausmann–Wegner (1966) 100. Misenum statue: Adamo Muscettola (2000); Flower (2005) 259–61. Coinage: *RPC* II, nos. 2709, 173, 362, 623, 1187, 1310, 1410; Hercules is much less present on provincial coinage of Titus and Vespasian: see *RPC* II Index s.v. Herakles on p. 381. Issues from cities traditionally associated with Hercules (e.g. *RPC* II no. 688, from Heraclea) do not count, for Hercules is a constant presence on coins from this city.

[56] *Bella Iouis: Theb.* 1.22.

[57] For this version of Gigantomachy see e.g. Pind. *Nem.* 1.67–8; E. *HF.* 178–80, 1193–4; Apollod. 1.6.1–2; Hor. *Carm.* 2.12.6–7; Sen. *Her. F.* 84–5.

[58] Silius too foregrounds Domitian's youth at the time of the Capitoline battle (3.607–10). The emphasis on youth provides an additional point of contact between Domitian and Scipio in the *Punica*. See Marks (2005a) 219–22.

ideology. Statius' redefinition of Herculean values responds and builds on some of these earlier uses of Hercules.

I begin with Statius' most important epic predecessor. The *Aeneid* stages a competition to inherit Hercules' mantle. Not all aspirants to Hercules' role are credible. Aventinus, Hercules' son, leaves no mark in the war narrative of *Aeneid* 7–12; heroes who simulate his dress, like Cysseus and Gyas, prove to be unworthy of the greatest hero.[59] Although others fall short of Hercules, Aeneas can be seen as gradually approaching the greatest of heroes.[60] Aeneas is compared to Hercules and invited to follow in the hero's footsteps when, upon his arrival at Pallanteum, he is prompted by Evander not to despise the humble abode that received the god.[61] But the connection of Hercules and Aeneas is also problematic, for the frenzied fury of Hercules in dispatching Cacus is echoed in the description of Aeneas' inability to spare Turnus at the end of the poem.[62]

Virgil's treatment has political and ideological undertones. Augustus too is compared to Hercules in the *Aeneid* (6.801–3). Virgil's Hercules moves to free Rome from a monster who resides on the Palatine, which will become the residence of Augustus. The severed heads hanging from Cacus' cave may have reminded Romans of gruesome scenes from the proscriptions—and the civil war period was the time when Hercules imagery had been employed most prominently.[63] Aeneas' progressive reception of the Hercules role as well as his opponents' inability to live up to the hero can be read as a commentary on attempts at embodying Hercules from the civil war period: After an array of self-styled descendants of Hercules (Pompey, Antony), a worthy successor of his power, Octavian, finally appears. Virgil's Hercules seems reminiscent of Octavian's civil war years, perhaps with special reference to his inability to contain anger at the time of his merciless vendetta against Caesar's assassins.

Other important suggestions come from the work of Lucan. Lucan too has an account centering on Hercules, and here too civil war is the stage for Herculean exploits. In book 4 of the *Bellum Ciuile*, the Caesarian Curio arrives in Africa, where

---

[59] Aventinus: *A.* 7.655–69; Cysseus and Gyas: *A.* 10.317–22. On Hercules in the *Aeneid*: Buchheit (1963) 122–31; Galinsky (1972) 131–52; Gransden (1976) 17–20; Feeney (1986), (1991) 156–61; Hardie (1993) 66–7, (1998) 82–3.

[60] Feeney (1986) 69–70.

[61] *A.* 8.362–8. Aeneas and Hercules are set beside one another in other passages of the *Aeneid*: Aeneas encounters traces of Hercules' journey from Spain to Italy and follows his path down to the underworld. The Trojan hero passes by Tarentum, one of Hercules' foundations (*A.* 3.551), sees Eryx's boxing gloves, used in the latter's fight with Hercules (*A.* 5.410–14), hears the story of Hercules' deeds (*A.* 6.392–93, 8.185–305), and witness the death of Hercules' comrade Antores (*A.* 10.777–82).

[62] See Hardie (1993) 66–7, (1997) 319–20; Labate (2010) 46–7. Cf. in part. *A.* 8.228–32 and *A.* 12.946–7.

[63] *A.* 8.196–7. Cf. for instance *Oct.* 510–14; Cornelius Severus fr. 13.1–2 Courtney; Luc. 2.166–8, 7.305; Sen. *Suas.* 6.17; Flor. 2.16 (4.6) 5.

a peasant tells him the story of Hercules' victorious fight against the African monster Antaeus.[64] The location is dense with heroic memories from the republican period, for here the Herculean Scipio defeated the African monster Hannibal. In an initial skirmish, Curio goes on to defeat a Pompeian garrison lead by Varus (Luc. 4.702–14), but this is no fulfillment of the Hercules story. For soon enough a descendant of Hannibal and a close connection of Antaeus, the monster-like Juba, comes to annihilate him. Officially, this is a victory of Pompey's side, but the reader should not be confused. In this poem, the Hercules–Antaeus paradigm is subverted: Victory will go to the monsters. The Pompeian side can win only when it enrolls monsters like Juba. In the rest of the narrative, we witness the progressive disintegration of Pompeian forces, historically associated with Hercules, while the impious and monstrous Caesar triumphs with the blessing of the gods, whose minds are set on the destruction of Rome.[65]

In Seneca's *Hercules Furens*, the political associations of the hero are played out in an imperial context.[66] Hercules is an ambiguous figure: very powerful, but also vulnerable and flawed. His ambition borders on megalomania and blasphemy.[67] More important, the characterization of the hero reflects elements of Seneca's political philosophy. Hercules' madness stems from his inability to resist passions, especially anger and desire for revenge.[68] In this respect, he is the opposite of the ideal sovereign whose portrait is sketched in Seneca's *De Clementia* and described by Theseus in his homily of *Hercules Furens* 735–47.[69] The ability to curtail punitive action is the key attribute of the ideal ruler presented in Seneca's *De Clementia*. This virtue, in turn, stems from the ability to resist irrational passions. Passions such as anger and desire for vengeance, if not controlled, can turn man into a beast:

> crudelitas minime humanum malum est indignumque tam miti animo; ferina ista rabies est sanguine gaudere ac volneribus et abiecto homine in silvestre animal transire. quid enim interest, oro te, Alexander, leoni Lysimachum obicias an ipse laceres dentibus tuis? tuum illud os est, tua illa feritas. o quam cuperes tibi potius ungues esse, tibi rictum illum edendorum hominum capacem!
> Sen. *Cl.* 1.25.1

---

[64] Luc. 4.589–660. On this episode: Ahl (1976) 97–103; Thompson–Bruère (1970); Asso (2010) 220–2.

[65] Ahl (1976) 268–74 argues that Cato, a stoic Hercules, forms a counterpart to the monstrous Hercules embodied by Caesar and his followers.

[66] Allusion to Roman imperial realities in Seneca's play: *Her. F.* 735–47, 58, 828, with Fitch (1987) 139, 311, 333–4.

[67] Fitch (1987) 24–8.

[68] Fitch (1987) 30–2.

[69] A passage heavily influenced by Seneca's *De Clementia*: Fitch (1987) 311.

Cruelty is an utterly unhuman evil and is not worthy of a spirit so kind; to rejoice in blood and wounds, to abandon human form and turn oneself into a wild animal, is the madness of beasts. I beg of you, Alexander, what difference does it make whether you throw Lysimachus to a lion or you yourself tear him to pieces with your teeth? That lion's mouth is yours, yours that bestiality. How you wish you had those claws yourself, those jaws big enough for devouring humans!

Bestiality is a trait of the tyrant. The good sovereign, on the contrary, becomes like a god.[70] Hercules' tragedy gives narrative substance to these ideas. In his exploration of continuity between the sane and insane mind, Seneca downplays the intervention of Juno by showing how Hercules' madness is rooted in certain flaws of his character while sane. Hercules is already prone to irrational passions: When these are stimulated by the achievement of immortality, Hercules turns into a beast. As sane, Seneca's hero has a tendency to resort to punitive action; his madness takes the form of a vindictive delirium (while killing his wife and children, the hero believes he is attacking Lykus' children) that results in the spilling of his own family's blood.[71] This too can be seen as the narrative counterpart to a notion found in *De Clementia*. In this treatise, the sovereign who cannot restrain himself from punitive action will eventually harm his fellow citizens, his extended "family." In Seneca, Hercules goes insane precisely after he has completed all of his labors, having virtually achieved immortality.[72] But instead of becoming a god, we see him become similar to the monsters that used to be his prey. In his hallucinations, Seneca's Hercules imagines leading the Titans in an assault against the gods. He passes from being the conqueror of the underworld to becoming an underworld creature himself, from monster slayer to monster.[73]

3.4 THE FAILED HERCULES: POLYNICES

In Virgil and Lucan, Hercules is the subject of the narrative asides of books 8 and 4, respectively; in Ovid's *Metamorphoses*, his adventures are recounted in book 9. In Statius he gets only a vignette in book 8 and a brief mention in book 10.[74] Hercules' status in the *Thebaid* is ambiguous in light of his connections with both cities at war (he was raised

---

[70] Sen. *Cl.* 1.1.2, 1.10.3, 1.5.7, 1.7.1.

[71] Fitch (1987) 28–32.

[72] On Hercules' imminent deification see passages listed by Fitch (1987) 22–3.

[73] Sen. *Her. F.* 955–91; Fitch (1987) 33–5.

[74] *Theb.* 8.500–18, 10.890–1; cf. also 11.45–8.

in Thebes by a family from Tiryns, in the region of Argos). The Argive army is filled with sons, relatives, and fans of Hercules, and the Argive city of Tiryns has a strong connection with its now-deified hero.[75] The Thebans too claim him as their foremost god, together with Bacchus.[76] Having ties to both cities, the hero does not know with whom to side.[77] It may be the presence of Juno, Argo's foremost advocate, that inhibits his willingness to help the Argives.[78] Hercules shows concern, on one occasion, for the destiny of the soldiers from Tiryns, but does nothing to help them.[79] On the contrary, he is seriously preoccupied with the survival of Thebes and actively protects the Theban Haemon.[80] Candidates to Hercules' role abound on both the Argive and Theban sides, none of them being particularly convincing.[81] Hercules' Argive son Agylleus is soundly beaten by Tydeus in a wrestling match that reproduces, yet subverts, the outcome of one of Hercules' deeds (the fight with the river Achelous).[82] Chromis, as we saw in Section 3.1.1, is far from living up to his father's standards during the chariot race. His Theban namesake, also a follower of Hercules, is easily dispatched by Tydeus in book 2.[83] Yet the most visible failure in this respect is Polynices.[84]

Polynices' arrival in Argos fulfills an arcane prophecy. Adrastus will marry his daughters off to a tawny lion and bristly boar (*Theb.* 1.390–7). The prophecy is obscure at this stage; it will be explained at 1.482–90, where we learn that Tydeus wears a boar's skin and Polynices a lion's hide, similar to the one worn by Hercules before killing the Nemean lion:

> ... tergo uidet huius inanem
> impexis utrimque iubis horrere leonem,
> illius in speciem quem per Teumesia tempe
> Amphitryoniades fractum iuuenalibus annis
> ante Cleonaei uestitus proelia monstri.
> *Theb.* 1.483–87

---

[75] A son of Hercules fights on the Argive side (Agylleus: *Theb.* 6.836–9 and 10.249); another takes part in the Argive games (Chromis: *Theb.* 6.346). Hercules appears among Argive ancestors in the procession of images that precedes the games: *Theb.* 6.271–3. Tiryns and Hercules: *Theb.* 4.156–7, 4.147–52.

[76] *Theb.* 10.899–901, 8.25–8, 11.223–5.

[77] *Theb.* 10.890–1.

[78] But then Hercules' patron goddess Minerva is also on the side of the Argives. For the embarrassment this causes Hercules see Section 3.5. For Juno's active support of Argos see *Theb.* 1.250–82, 9.510–19, 10.49–83, 12.291–311.

[79] *Theb.* 11.46–8.

[80] *Theb.* 8.456–520 (see Section 3.5).

[81] On the theme of true and false Hercules in the *Thebaid* see Ripoll (1998) 146–59; Brown (1994) 37–8; Parkes (2009) 483–8.

[82] See Section 3.5.

[83] *Theb.* 2.613–28; see Section 3.1.1.

[84] Hercules and Polynices: Parkes (2009) 485–6.

... on the back of one he sees on either side a lion's pelt, stiff with uncombed mane, similar to the lion which, in his youth, Amphitryon's son crushed in Teumesos' valley and with which he clothed himself before his fight with the monster of Cleonae.

Statius uses the lion skin detail to establish a connection between Polynices and Hercules. This connection is foreshadowed at the moment of Polynices' arrival in Argos. The first two places seen by Polynices upon his arrival in Argos are immediate reminders of the Hercules legend: On the one side is the Temple of Juno, Hercules' greatest enemy (1.383–4), on the other side the marshes where the Hydra was defeated by Hercules (1.384–5).[85] The topography sets the scene for the arrival of a young hero who is a match for Hercules. Hercules too, like Polynices, wandered far from his native city of Thebes.

In the preceding passage (1.483–7), we find a strange clarification. Polynices' mantel resembles the lion killed by Hercules before he killed the Nemean lion, whose hide was later to become Hercules' regular outfit.[86] This seemingly pedantic detail makes two important points. First, Polynices is a younger Hercules, a Hercules in the making, who still needs to prove his worth. Second, it points the reader's attention to the Nemea episode in book 6: In Nemea, Hercules conquered his lion, and here Polynices will be called to prove that he can live up to Hercules. Nemea is the first stop on the route to Thebes. Here Polynices takes part in the very first occurrence of the Nemean games, which were traditionally associated with Hercules' defeat of the Nemean lion. Statius follows an alternative tradition, the one connecting the games to the funeral of the child Opheltes, but he still opens the games with the statue of Hercules crushing the Nemean lion carried around in procession (6.270–1). The prize of the first and most important competition in the games, the chariot race, is the Hercules crater whose analysis opened this chapter. As we have seen, the race's outcome makes it clear that Polynices, unable to control Hercules' horse, is no match for the greatest of heroes.

Two aspects of Statius' use of Herculean imagery with reference to Polynices are relevant for my analysis. The first is the fact that Polynices' failure to be like Hercules is staged in the context of games. As we have seen, Nero was the most vocal aspirant to the role of Hercules in the years leading up to the principate of Domitian.

---

[85] The temple seen by Polynices is the Heraion of Argos, the same temple in which Nero made his offerings to Hercules. See Section 3.2.

[86] This lion of Tempe is most likely an invention of Statius: see Caviglia (1973) 141 *ad* 1.485–7; Parkes (2012) 89–90.

Unlike his predecessors, however, he had tied his Herculean impersonations not to military contexts but to performances in games. Polynices' failure to live up to Hercules takes place in the context of games. The mode of his failure, falling from a chariot, is reminiscent of Nero's famous failure in one of his exploits in the games at Olympia. Polynices' Herculean nature is emphasized at the time of his arrival in Argos, where he catches sight of the Heraion of Argos, the temple where Nero made his offerings to Hercules. The Hercules/Polynices relationship provides a commentary on the historical figure of Nero and his reception of Herculean imagery: Nero could not live up to the hero he sought to imitate.

The other particularly significant aspect of Statius' use of Hercules with reference to Polynices is the emphasis on the notion of Polynices as a "young Hercules." Herculean imagery, we have seen, was particularly linked to the young Domitian's participation in the 69 CE conflict (*Theb.* 1.21–2). In statuary, Domitian appeared as a young Hercules. Polynices' failure is the failure of a Hercules who cannot fulfill in maturity what he promised as a young man. We now understand that the Hercules paradigm, applied to Domitian at the beginning of the poem, is parsed in a way that is not purely panegyric. Like Polynices at Argos, Domitian is a young Hercules who needs to prove his worth, who needs to live up to the standards of the greatest hero after his juvenile exploits in the Capitol battle. The comparison of *Thebaid* 1.21–2 looks ahead to the future and sets demanding standards. The possibility of failure is real. If Domitian does not live up to his Herculean beginning, he will turn out like Polynices, or Nero.

The relationship of Hercules and Polynices highlights one of the aspects in which Nero could be seen to have fallen short of the hero he sought to equal. But Nero's failure in embodying Hercules was not limited to his fiascos in the arena. Many felt that he had turned into a polar opposite of Hercules, a bloodthirsty monster.[87] This second aspect appears clearly as we consider two other heroes with distinct Herculean associations in the *Thebaid*, namely Tydeus and Capaneus.

3.5 BETWEEN BEAST AND GOD: TYDEUS

Tydeus has a greater claim than Polynices to the title of Hercules, partly in light of his incredible *uirtus* and partly because, unlike the young Theban, he has a serious chance of achieving immortality. Suggestions from Seneca's *Hercules Furens* and Lucan's *Bellum Ciuile* conspire to highlight different aspects of Tydeus' relationship

---

[87] This is implied by Vindex's self-styling as Hercules Adsertor, a role later attributed to Domitian by Martial (with Vitellius in the role of the monster Cacus; see Section 3.2).

with Hercules. On the one hand, Tydeus can be seen as remaining caught in the "mad Hercules" paradigm as detailed by Seneca's play: Unable to control his passions, he is constantly at risk of going full circle, turning from near-god into beast.[88] On the other hand, Tydeus' heroism is influenced by Lucan's paradoxical representation of a world where monsters prevail in the face of a weak or nominal Hercules.

Contrasting imagery, in which Tydeus appears alternatively as a Hercules figure and as a beast, is a major attribute of Statius' representation of this hero.[89] In book 2, on his return from the failed embassy at Thebes, Tydeus is ambushed by 50 Theban warriors and manages to kill all of them, except for the seer Maeon, whom he sends back to announce his victory.[90] This is a Herculean *labor*, as Statius calls it at 2.689; Tydeus accomplishes it with the protection of Minerva, Hercules' foremost divine helper, to whom he dedicates the spoils. And yet, as we previously saw, Statius compares Tydeus to the Centaur Pholus in a simile recalling the scene on Hercules' crater.[91] In the same episode, Tydeus dispatches a Theban who seeks to emulate Hercules, Chromis.[92] In the *Aeneid*, Aeneas' success over followers of Hercules marks his gradual appropriation of the Hercules role. Tydeus too replaces a weak successor of Hercules (Chromis), but his appropriation is as disturbing as the victory of the monstrous Juba in Lucan.

Elsewhere, Tydeus' ambiguous nature is conveyed through the combination of a series of Herculean intertexts, as in the narrative of Tydeus' wrestling match with Agylleus (*Theb.* 6.824–910). In this passage, Statius engages three earlier accounts: Virgil's boxing match of Dares and Entellus in *Aeneid* 5, Ovid's wrestling match of Hercules and Achelous in *Metamorphoses* 9, and Lucan's fight of Hercules and Antaeus in *Bellum Ciuile* 4.[93] Statius' Agylleus is modeled after Virgil's Dares, the Herculean character who is surprisingly defeated.[94] However, Statius' main model for the match is Ovid's *Metamorphoses* 9.[95] Statius connects Tydeus and Agylleus, respectively, with Achelous and Hercules, the two characters of the Ovidian account. Agylleus is Hercules' son, and he has his father's physique, whereas Tydeus is related

---

[88] Feeney traces the importance of the beast–man–god series in Apollonius, Virgil, Ovid, and Statius: Feeney (1991) 94–8, 155–62, 194–8, 360–1; his treatment of Tydeus' death at 360–1 is particularly important for my subsequent analysis.

[89] The oscillation between bestiality and divinity, and the connection with Hercules, are relevant to the study of other characters in the poem (Hippomedon, and by contrast, Parthenopaeus, Amphiaraus and Theseus). See Conclusions, Section C.1.

[90] *Theb.* 2.527–743.

[91] *Theb.* 2.563–4. See Section 3.1.2.

[92] See Section 3.1.2.

[93] Ov. *Met.* 9.1–88; Luc. 4.593–660; Lovatt (2005) 197–204.

[94] Dares: *A.* 5.362–484.

[95] Lovatt (2005) 197–202.

The Fragility of Power

to Achelous.[96] The narrative of the match follows Ovid's text closely, the main difference being its outcome.[97] In Ovid, Hercules wins, whereas in the *Thebaid* the Herculean Agylleus is defeated. In both texts, the turning point occurs when the larger hero holds his opponent down with his heavy weight. In Ovid, this action leads to Achelous' final defeat. In Statius, it is the start of an offensive that allows Tydeus to win.[98] Significantly, this key moment in the narrative is signaled by a simile in which Tydeus, not Agylleus, is compared to Hercules:

Herculeis pressum sic fama lacertis
terrigenam sudasse Libyn, cum fraude reperta
raptus in excelsum, nec iam spes ulla cadendi,
nec licet extrema matrem contingere planta.
Theb. 6.893–6

So, as the story goes, sweated the Libyan monster, a son of Earth, gripped in Hercules' arms, when Hercules discovered his trick and lifted him up into the air; no hope now of falling, and he cannot touch his mother with the tip of his toe.

The simile refers to the myth of Hercules and Antaeus, narrated by Lucan in the *Bellum Ciuile*. There too Hercules' fight is styled as a wrestling match, and Tydeus' final maneuver, through which he is able to win, is the same move that allows Hercules to defeat Antaeus in Lucan.[99] In Lucan, the fight of Hercules and Antaeus

---

[96] For Agylleus and Hercules see *Theb.* 6.836–9. The connection between Hercules and Agylleus is mentioned by Statius also at *Theb.* 10.249, 259–61. Tydeus used to train on the banks of the river Achelous; the river god himself pointed out to him the appropriate sites for practicing (*Theb.* 6.830–9). Statius refers to the myth of Hercules' fight with Achelous at the moment of introducing Tydeus' soldiers (*Theb.* 4.106–9).

[97] Statius takes from Ovid the respective proportions of the two fighters: In both texts, a small but heavy hero faces a tall and slow one. On Hercules being taller than Achelous cf. the simile at *Met.* 9.56 (Achelous attacked by Hercules from behind likened to a man crushed by landslide; the simile is used by Statius too, see subsequent discussion in this note). On Achelous being small but heavy see Ov. *Met.* 9.39–41. Likewise, in Statius Agylleus is a giant, taller than all other men: *Theb.* 6.838–9. Tydeus instead is small but heavy: *Theb.* 6.844–5 (on the difference between the proportions of the two opponents see also *Theb.* 6.854–9, 878–80). Tydeus' small stature is a topos: cf. Hom. *Il.* 5.853–4. Other echoes: the lines describing the position of the fighters before starting the match (*Met.* 9.33–4; *Theb.* 6.850–1); the two fighters spreading sand on their bodies (*Met.* 9.35–6; *Theb.* 6.847–9); various incidents of the fight (*Met.* 9.37–9; *Theb.* 6.861–2); same simile to describe the same incident (*Met.* 9.46–9; *Theb.* 9.862–6); the simile of the man crushed by a landslide (*Met.* 9.54–6; *Theb.* 6.878–84); the conclusion of the match, with a hero pushed to the ground and kept down through a vice-like grip (*Met.* 9.60–1; *Theb.* 6.888–903).

[98] *Met.* 9.53–6; *Theb.* 6.876–80, 6.887–93.

[99] Lovatt (2005) 202–4. On the final maneuver see Luc. 4.649–53; cf. *Theb.* 6.890–3. On the identification of Agylleus and Antaeus see also *Theb.* 6.872–5 and Luc. 4.629–32 (Agylleus touching of the ground mimics the move through which Antaeus gains his strength in Lucan).

is the prelude to a surprising upsetting of Herculean narratives, with the monstrous Juba triumphing over Curio. In Statius, the Lucan intertext marks a similar upsetting of our predictions based on Statius' use of Herculean imagery. In the wrestling match, we see Tydeus transitioning into the role of Hercules and achieving victory, but he is a monstrous replacement for the greatest of heroes, just like Lucan's Juba.

Tydeus' fluctuation between the two extremes of beast and demigod is also conveyed through a strategic use of hunting imagery. Let us go back to the prophecy of the lion and the boar in book 1. As we saw, the detail of Polynices' lion hide develops into a complex system of Herculean allusions. In the same way, Tydeus' boar hide has important ramifications in later passages. In book 1, Tydeus appears in Argos wearing the skin of the legendary Calydonian boar, the one killed by Meleager (*Theb.* 1.488–90). It is not a good omen. The Calydonian boar's skin was the reason for the war between the Curetes and the Aetolians of Calydon, a fraternal war that led to the death of Meleager. The death of Meleager is a common mythical subject for funerary reliefs.[100] Tydeus is Meleager's half-brother; the boar's hide casts him as a new Meleager, who will soon be cut down by premature death.

A different way of looking at the Tydeus–boar pairing emerges in *Thebaid* 2.469–77. In this passage, Tydeus is compared to the Calydonian boar when, in a fit of rage, he abandons Eteocles' palace after publicly threatening the Theban tyrant. Imagery of boar hunting returns at the time of Tydeus' death in book 8. Tydeus' *aristeia* is marked by the hero's encounter with Hercules. The battlefield is dominated by two heroes, the Theban Haemon, supported by Hercules, and Argive Tydeus, helped by Minerva.[101] A duel between the two champions appears inevitable, but this ends up pitting Hercules and Minerva one against the other. The aberration is acknowledged by Hercules himself, who proceeds to stand down and abandon Haemon (*Theb.* 8.497–516). The awkward scene strengthens the notion that Tydeus, supported by Minerva in his *aristeia* and possibly on his way to final apotheosis, is a double of Hercules.[102] Right after the encounter of Minerva and Hercules, Heamon, now retreating, is described as a wild boar grazed by a spear.[103]

After being fatally wounded, Tydeus strikes Melanippus, whose body is compared to that of the monstrous boar killed by Hercules.[104] But before we begin to think that by slaying this boar/hero, Tydeus has turned into a new Meleager, or a new Hercules, Tydeus gnaws at Melanippus' head. This is the behavior of a beast, as the Thebans

---

[100] Zanker–Ewald (2008) 349–57. The evidence postdates the *Thebaid*.
[101] *Theb.* 8.456–9.
[102] On the connection between Tydeus and Hercules through the theme of apotheosis see Vessey (1973) 225, 288. See also Hardie (1993) 66.
[103] *Theb.* 8.532–5.
[104] *Theb.* 8.745–50.

say at the beginning of the following book.[105] The consequence of this action is Tydeus' loss of immortality. Minerva refuses to grant him what she helped Hercules achieve.[106] In the end, Tydeus comes full circle: When he is very close to achieving divinity he turns into a beast.[107] The transition from near-god to monster follows the pattern of Seneca's *Hercules Furens*, and the influence of Seneca's theory on passions is visible in the motivations leading up to Tydeus' metamorphosis into a beast.[108] In both incidents in which Tydeus turns into an animal (in book 2 and book 8), we see the hero falling prey to his immoderate passions, especially anger and desire for revenge. In book 2, the boar simile illustrates his angry outburst at Eteocles' words. In book 8, it accompanies his mad anger at the sight of Melanippus' head. At the beginning of the poem (1.41), Tydeus is described as *immodicus irae*, the one who has no measure in his anger. Tydeus lives up to this characterization in the rest of the poem: He is the one who thwarts Jocasta's attempt at reconciling the two brothers in book 7 (7.538–63), spreads hatred and anger in Argos in book 3 (3.336-44), and ultimately fails to achieve immortality because of his inability to restrain himself from vengeful action.

In the case of both Polynices and Tydeus, Herculean imagery is used to comment on notions of heroism in the political arena. In the case of Tydeus, we see something more alarming than Polynices' inability to play Hercules: a potential Hercules turning into a bloodthirsty monster. Men, and especially sovereigns, can become gods, but they can also turn into beasts: Nero, whom detractors often described as a beast (cf. e.g. *Silv.* 5.2.33), was an example. The tale of Hercules unfolds in the eyes of the readers, and the princeps, as a map of the dangers of political action. Although the sovereign can become divine, he can also turn into a monster.

3.6 KNOCKING ON HEAVEN'S DOOR: CAPANEUS

Tydeus' trajectory is also relevant for understanding Capaneus. He too has the potential of Hercules, and we see him attempting to enter heaven. But his heroism, marred by blasphemy and hubris, ends up turning him into a version of the monsters that Hercules defeated. The model of Seneca's *Hercules Furens* is central to the

---

[105] *Theb.* 9.8–20. Tydeus is compared to a beast and a monster; note especially 9.11 *monstris . . . crudelibus* [cruel . . . monsters]; 13–5 *morsibus . . . artus dilacerant* [with their fangs . . . they tear our limbs apart]; 16 *tigribus . . . leones* [tigers . . . lions]; 20 *feritas* [bestiality]. Statius tells us that Tydeus recognized himself in Melanippus (8.753). Hardie (1993) 66 suggests that, among other things, Tydeus recognizes himself in the beastly boar to which Melanippus has been compared.

[106] *Theb.* 8.751–64.

[107] Feeney (1991) 360–1.

[108] On the influence of stoic psychology on the *Thebaid* see Fantham (1997).

parable of this prospective Hercules as well. Elements of hubris and blasphemy are important features of Seneca's hero, and Capaneus' attack on heaven develops the delirious projects of Seneca's mad Hercules.

When Capaneus first appears in the poem, he is compared to a Centaur, one of the monsters fought by Hercules.[109] The description of Capaneus' armor in book 4 is endowed with the same ambiguity we have observed in Tydeus' characterization. Capaneus' shield portrays the death of Hydra, a monster slain by Hercules.[110] But before we start to think of Capaneus as a new Hercules, we notice some contrasting elements.[111] The hero's spear is made of cypress, the tree of the dead, and an infernal creature—a Giant—appears on his helmet.[112] His shield is covered with four layers of animal skins, a number encountered in rituals for the underworld gods.[113] On the shield, Statius has included the detail of how the unstoppable Hydra was finally defeated by Hercules—by fire—which is precisely the way Capaneus' unstoppable progression will be arrested by Jupiter in book 10.[114]

The same uncertainty features in the following episode focusing on Capaneus.[115] In book 5, Capaneus slays the snake that killed the child Opheltes. His speech on this occasion is illuminating. Capaneus says that he would kill the snake even if it were part of a Giant's body.[116] The fight takes on the colors of Gigantomachy, with Capaneus fighting Giants as Hercules did. The killing of the snake takes place in the woods of Nemea, the location of Hercules' legendary fight with the Nemean lion, and Hercules is credited with fighting both Giants and giant snakes. In spite of the snake's horrific nature, the killing of the monster is presented as an act of hubris, attracting the gods' vengeance. The snake is sacred to Jupiter; Capaneus attacks the monster explicitly to displease him (*Theb.* 5.668). His slaying of the monster (and Jupiter's reaction to it) foreshadows Capaneus' future attack on Heaven in book 10.[117] Capaneus appropriates the role of Hercules, yet he is a hubristic Hercules who directs his power against the gods.

---

[109] See Section 3.1.2.

[110] *Theb.* 4.165–77. The same myth is on the shield of Aventinus, a son of Hercules, in the *Aeneid* (*A.* 7.655–69). In the *Thebaid*, Parthenopaeus' shield depicts a heroic deed of his mother Atalanta (the hunt of the Calydonian boar: *Theb.* 4.267–8); Polynices has on his shield the Sphinx slain by his father Oedipus (*Theb.* 4.87); Theseus has his own slaying of the Minotaur (12.665–76).

[111] Parkes (2009) 486–7.

[112] Ancient spears were normally made of ash wood: Harrison (1992) 251.

[113] Cf. Verg. *G.* 4.550–3; *A.* 6.243, 10.518–20; *Theb.* 5.125, 6.218–19, 4.543–4; see Rebeggiani (2005) 152–3.

[114] *Theb.* 4.169–70; see Harrison (1992) 249.

[115] Parkes (2009) 487.

[116] *Theb.* 5.566–70. According to ancient representations, Giants were snake legged. See *LIMC* IV.1 191–6, 253–4.

[117] Jupiter nearly strikes Capaneus with his thunderbolt: *Theb.* 5.583–7.

Capaneus is again measured against Hercules in book 6, when he faces the young Spartan Alcidamas in a boxing match.[118] Here Statius relies in particular on Virgil's narrative of the boxing match between Entellus and Dares.[119] In Virgil, the younger of the two competitors, Dares, is linked to Pollux, whereas the older Entellus is a disciple of Eryx, the hero vanquished by Hercules in a boxing match. Statius appropriates from Virgil the idea of a younger competitor facing an older one: His Alcidamas, also a disciple of Pollux, is an equivalent of Dares, whereas Capaneus bears features of Entellus.[120] Thus Capaneus is associated with Eryx, an ancestral enemy of Hercules. The similes employed by Statius during the boxing match are consistent with these intertextual connections: The poet compares Capaneus to Tityos a monstrous creature and an enemy of the gods.[121] Two books later, however, this monstrous picture of Capaneus seems to dissolve, for when the hero picks up the body of the dying Melanippus and brings it to Tydeus, Statius compares him to Hercules bringing the Arcadian boar back to Argos (*Theb.* 8.745–50).

Statius' study of Capaneus' Herculean traits culminates in Capaneus' final *aristeia* in book 10. Here again we see Herculean feats mingled with bestiality as the scene enlarges on themes from Seneca's *Hercules Furens*. In Seneca, the mad Hercules dreams of leading legions of Giants and Titans to storm Olympus in order to seize immortality:

> recipis et reseras polum?
> an contumacis ianuam mundi traho?
> dubitatur etiam? uincla Saturno exuam
> contraque patris impii regnum impotens
> auum resoluam; bella Titanes parent,
> me duce furentes; saxa cum siluis feram
> rapiamque dextra plena Centauris iuga.
> iam monte gemino limitem ad superos agam:
> uideat sub Ossa Pelion Chiron suum,
> in caelum Olympus tertio positus gradu
> perueniet aut mittetur.
> Sen. *Her. F.* 963–73

---

[118] *Theb.* 6.722–825.
[119] *A.* 5.362–460; Lovatt (2005) 145–8.
[120] Alcidamas and Pollux: *Theb.* 6.740–6.
[121] *Theb.* 6.753–5.

Will you receive me and unbar the firmament? Or must I tear down the door of the stubborn heaven? Do you still hesitate? I shall strip off Saturn's chains, and against my unnatural father's unbridled rule I shall loose my grandfather. Let the Titans in rage prepare war under my leadership. I shall carry rocks and trees, and grasp ridges full of Centaurs in my right hand. With a pair of mountains I shall now construct a pathway to the world above: Chiron must see his Pelion set beneath Ossa. Then Olympus, placed as a third step, will reach to heaven—or else be hurled there.

Seneca presents Hercules' projected incursion into heaven as a necessary consequence of the hero's journey into the underworld: Every kingdom has yielded to Hercules' power; only heaven has not yet been subdued.[122]

This sequence provides a guideline for Capaneus' story: Books 8 and 10 are linked by a series of allusions to the *Hercules Furens* arranged in such a way so as to reproduce Hercules' incursions into the underworld, Earth, and heaven in Seneca. In book 7, Amphiaraus is swallowed alive by the Earth and enters the underworld. The next book opens with Dis' reaction to the intrusion, which the god takes as an attempt to conquer his kingdom on the part of the celestial gods.[123] He reacts by threatening to unleash his own legions (Giants and Titans) in return.[124] Dis' speech closes with a curse that introduces some of the actions later performed by the Seven Argives (*Theb.* 8.65–74). In particular, there will be someone who will wage war against the gods:[125]

praeterea ne sola furor mea regna lacessat,
quaere deis qui bella ferat, qui fulminis ignes
infestumque Iouem clipeo fumante repellat.
faxo haud sit cunctis leuior metus atra mouere
Tartara frondenti quam iungere Pelion Ossae.
Theb. 8.75–9

Furthermore, let the madness not challenge my kingdom only. Seek one to make war upon the gods and ward off the fires of the thunderbolt and angry

---

[122] Sen. *Her. F.* 955–70. The idea is found as early as the tragedy's prologue, uttered by Juno: *Her. F.* 63–74, with Fitch (1987) 141 *ad loc.*

[123] *Theb.* 8.34–42.

[124] *Theb.* 8.42–4.

[125] On the complex literary texture of this passage see Augoustakis (2016) 97–9.

Jove with his smoking shield. I shall see to it that all the world is no less afraid
to disturb black Tartarus than to join Pelion to leafy Ossa.

The person intended is Capaneus, whose subsequent attack on heaven is thus
presented as a fulfillment of Dis' curse. In book 10, Capaneus appears as a towering
Giant, climbing the mountain of Olympus, exactly as Dis had prophesied:[126]

> ... et alterno captiua in moenia gressu
> surgit ouans: quales mediis in nubibus aether
> uidit Aloidas, cum cresceret impia tellus
> despectura deos nec adhuc inmane ueniret
> Pelion et trepidum iam tangeret Ossa Tonantem.
> *Theb.* 10.848–52

... and step upon step rises exultant against the captive walls. So the heavens
saw the Aloidae amid the clouds when the impious earth rose to look down
upon the gods; vast Pelion had not yet come, and already Ossa touched the
frightened Thunderer.

Fulfilling the desires of his intertextual predecessor, Capaneus tries to make his
own way to immortality by attacking heaven. Statius' description of Capaneus'
actions as the consequence of *uirtus egressa modum* [valor that exceeds its limits,
Theb. 10.834] matches his description of Tydeus as *immodicus irae*. When *uirtus*
exceeds its measure, it can turn a man into a beast, a near god into an agent of the
underworld. Statius' close patterning of Capaneus' *aristeia* on the tragedy of mad
Hercules is tied to a specific political vision. In Seneca's play, the mad Hercules can
be envisaged as an opposite of the good sovereign of *De Clementia* and is contrasted
to Theseus, a merciful sovereign who intervenes to rescue Hercules, offering pardon
and purification. Statius' interaction with the *Hercules Furens* prepares Theseus' ar-
rival, and indeed, Theseus' characterization as merciful sovereign. It also reinforces
the notion that figures such as Capaneus and Tydeus embody different ways of
falling short of the ideals of *De Clementia*.

Capaneus and Tydeus fall short of Hercules and immortality in a way that is par-
ticularly disturbing. Their shortcomings connect with Seneca's depiction of Hercules
as an intrinsically flawed hero in his tragedy. The story of Capaneus develops the
hubristic traits of Seneca's Hercules and his delirious attack on heaven, whereas

---

[126] Cf. also *Theb.* 10.832–6, 11.5–11, 10.913–17.

Tydeus illustrates Seneca's emphasis on Hercules' inability to restrain his passions. Tydeus' adventure also recalls the world of Lucan, where the monstrous Caesar is unleashed by the gods and usurps the role of weak and ineffective Herculean figures. Statius' charting of Tydeus' and Capaneus' Herculean careers can be fruitfully understood against the background of Senecan theories on kingship and against a reading of Seneca's plays that interprets his tragedies—such as the *Hercules Furens*— as influenced by the vision of *De Clementia*.

The story of a hero who tries to become a new Hercules but ends up behaving like a monster is also a particularly apt commentary on historical appropriations of Herculean imagery by Nero.[127] The transition from the role of aspirant Hercules to that of monster matches perceptions of Nero's imperial career, both during the emperor's life and after his death, as shown by the aforementioned case of Vindex's propaganda. But before we assume that Domitian's appropriation of a Herculean role in the poem's opening will inevitably have the same outcome as Tydeus' and Capaneus' attempts at replacing the hero, we need to consider two more characters.

3.7 A NEW HERCULES

The first of these characters is Menoeceus, the only hero in the *Thebaid* who, together with Domitian, achieves immortality. Capaneus' *aristeia* is built as a confrontation between him and Menoeceus, even though the two heroes never meet. Capaneus consciously attacks Thebes from the tower from which Menoeceus has committed suicide; Menoeceus' mother declares that she feared her child would be killed by Capaneus.[128] Both protagonists of this duel are related to Hercules. The goddess Virtus, who has already worked out the deification of several mortals, inspires Menoeceus to sacrifice himself. When she appears to the Theban youth in the guise of Manto, she is compared to Hercules dressed in female attire. In return for his sacrifice, Menoeceus is granted apotheosis.[129] At the time of his funeral, he is compared to Hercules lying down on his pyre in happy expectation of the immortality he has already secured:

---

[127] For a view of the political implications of theomachy and of the role of Capaneus in the *Thebaid* see Chaudhuri (2014) 298–321. Chaudhuri shows that the topic of war against the gods is used as a mythical counterpart both for opponents of imperial power and for tyrants (at 305–11 Chaudhuri considers Capaneus' proximity to tyrannical figures such as Caligula). He also reads the *Thebaid*'s exploration of theomachy as reflecting pressing concerns felt under Domitian, namely the relationship between the emperor and the gods and the competition between different dynasties (see esp. 311–21).

[128] Vessey (1973) 123; Ripoll (1998) 232; *Theb.* 10.845–6, 10.811. On Menoeceus see also Chapter 6, Section 6.7.

[129] Virtus responsible for immortality of human heroes: *Theb.* 10.636–7; Virtus compared to Hercules dressed up as a woman: *Theb.* 10.646–9; Menoeceus' immortality: *Theb.* 10.664–5, 10.781–2.

... hostiles super ipse, ut uictor, aceruos
pacifera lauro crinem uittisque decorus
accubat: haud aliter quam cum poscentibus astris
laetus in accensa iacuit Tirynthius Oeta.
Theb. 12.64–7

... himself, as victor, his hair adorned with peace-bearing laurel and fillets, lies upon the amassed spoils, in the same fashion as the Tirynthian lay joyfully on burning Oeta while the stars were already summoning him.

Menoeceus' self-sacrifice for the sake of the city is a different act of heroism from the exploits of Tydeus and Capaneus. It is no ordinary act of courage and is one that is motivated by extraordinary circumstances. Statius shows how frightening and extreme the path to immortality, which Menoeceus choses to follow, really is.[130] But this extraordinary form of heroism is not unfit for an emperor. As we see in more detail in Chapter 6, Statius attributes to Domitian a willingness to sacrifice himself in a similar fashion in *Siluae* 1.1.[131] In this poem, Domitian's apotheosis is anticipated; Domitian is compared to Hercules and is put under the protection of Minerva, Hercules' patron goddess.[132]

The other successful recipient of the Hercules scepter in the *Thebaid* is Theseus. In Seneca's *Hercules Furens*, Hercules is rescued by the arrival of Theseus, who brings resolution to the play by convincing Hercules to follow him to Athens and to seek purification.[133] The *Thebaid*'s resolution also comes with Theseus, after a rash of less-than-successful Herculean figures. As we saw, the Herculean role of the hero who brings resolution to the *Thebaid* is foreshadowed by the *ekphrasis* of Hercules' crater.[134] Theseus has much in common with Hercules, and not only in light of his immense physical strength and military *uirtus*. Theseus, like Hercules, is helped and protected by Minerva. Statius describes him as someone who can perform actions equal to those of Hercules, building on a rich tradition that set the two heroes beside one another:[135]

---

[130] On Statius' complex depiction of Virtus and his tragic view of Menoeceus' sacrifice see Chapter 6, Section 6.7.

[131] See Chapter 6, Section 6.6.

[132] For Domitian and Minerva see Chapter 1, Section 1.8 n. 220.

[133] Sen. *Her. F.* 1138–44 (last act).

[134] See Section 3.1.3.

[135] On the relationship between the two heroes see Mills (1997) 136–9; on Theseus and Hercules in the *Thebaid* see Vessey (1973) 313; Ripoll (1998) 155–8; Bessone (2011) 156–63.

sic tibi non ullae socia sine Pallade pugnae,
nec sacer inuideat paribus Tirynthius actis . . .
Theb. 12.583–4

So may you never fight a battle without Pallas as your ally, and may the divine
Tirynthian not envy your equal exploits . . .

Theseus is known for killing tyrants and criminals, an attribute that Statius, in the
Siluae, attaches to Hercules.[136] Evadne invites Theseus to intervene in favor of the
Argives, mentioning his compassion for the aged Hecale, whose hospitality the hero
did not despise.[137] The parallel episode of Hercules' humble hospitality in the house of
Molorchus would not have been too far from the mind of readers, and Statius evokes it
at the end of the poem, through the filter of Virgil. After his victory over Creon, Theseus
is invited by the Thebans to accept their hospitality, a passage that recalls Evander's invi-
tation to Aeneas to follow in the footsteps of Hercules in book 8 of the *Aeneid*:[138]

accedunt utrimque pio uexilla tumultu
permiscentque manus; medio iam foedera bello,
iamque hospes Theseus; orant succedere muris
dignarique domos.
Theb. 12.782–5

From both sides the standards meet in friendly confusion; they grasp hands.
In the midst of battle comes a treaty; now Theseus is a guest. They beg him to
come inside their walls and not disdain their homes.

Theseus' final killing of Creon is the slaying of a monster, comparable to Hercules'
slaying of Cacus, evoked just at the end of it. There is no reference to *furor* in his final
duel against Creon: no gnashing of teeth in the style of Virgil's Hercules.[139] On the
contrary, there is an evident correction of Aeneas' final duel with Turnus.[140]
Theseus is, in many ways, a "better" Hercules: He outdoes Hercules' earlier literary
(and political) incarnations. Virgil's Hercules is tied to memories and propaganda

---

[136] *Silv.* 3.1.35; cf. Sen. *Her. F.* 271–2, 431, 920–4, 936–7. Bessone (2011) 157 n. 4.
[137] *Theb.* 12.582. On Statius' *Thebaid* and Callimachus' *Hecale* see Bessone (2011) 144–8.
[138] Bessone (2011) 158–9.
[139] The idea of Theseus as embodiment of *clementia* and in control of his passions is challenged by Ganiban
(2007) 222 and n. 60, who sees him falling prey to *misericordia* [compassion], but see Bessone (2011) 171–7
and Chapter 1, Section 1.8; in general Ripoll (1998) 432–40.
[140] Braund (1996a) 6.

of the civil wars; his anger looks ahead at Aeneas' inability to display *clementia* toward Turnus. Statius seeks to reintroduce within the epic discourse the more peaceful attributes of Hercules and does so by linking his Herculean hero to the imperial virtue of *clementia*. In Seneca, Hercules is unable to limit punitive action, and the same is true for Tydeus. But Theseus can grant a burial even to Creon, who, unlike Turnus or Mezentius, has not asked for mercy or burial. By connecting his Herculean hero (Theseus) with *clementia*, Statius attempts a reconfiguration of models of heroism, which is also a reconfiguration of the Hercules model. This redefinition, made necessary by the problematic pedigree of Hercules in light of his civil war connections and the recent exploitation by Nero, allows Statius to respond to the currency of the comparison with Hercules in Domitianic ideology without equating Domitian with Nero.[141]

Traces of a redefinition of Hercules in the same direction are visible in the *Siluae*. A suggestive example is *Siluae* 4.6, an ekphrastic poem on the small statue of Hercules owned by Novius Vindex. This Hercules is suitable for the peaceful times of the banquet. He is not endowed with a grim expression, but with the kind countenance that the god displayed on his visit to the house of Molorchus, or to the priestess Auge, or with the blessed expression of Hercules drinking ambrosia in heaven (4.6.50–4). This is a *mitis Hercules*, wielding the club in one hand and the cup in the other:

> . . . sic mitis uultus, ueluti de pectore gaudens,
> hortatur mensas. tenet haec marcentia fratris
> pocula, at haec clauae meminit manus; aspera sedes
> sustinet et cultum Nemeaeo tegmine saxum.
> *Silv.* 4.6.55–8

> . . . so does the gentle countenance, as though rejoicing from the heart, encourage the banquet. One hand holds his brother's languorous goblet, but the other remembers the club; a rough seat supports him, a stone adorned with Nemean hide.

Later, Statius provides the history of this Hercules statuette. There is an obvious contrast between the former owners and Novius Vindex. Earlier possessors of the statuette were great warlords: Alexander, Hannibal, and Sulla.[142] But the current owner of the statue is endowed with a kind nature that matches the peaceful

---

[141] Compare Statius' attempt at redefining *clementia* and detaching it from prior appropriations discussed in Chapter 1, Section 1.8 and Statius' redefinition of solar symbols discussed in Chapter 2.

[142] *Silv.* 4.6.59–93, 106–9.

disposition displayed by the statuette. Statius says nothing of Domitian in *Siluae* 4.6. Elsewhere in the *Siluae* the praise of Statius' patrons is modeled on that of Domitian.[143] Irrespective of possible connection between Domitian and Novius Vindex, Statius' creation of a new, peaceful Hercules makes the hero a suitable counterpart for his merciful sovereign. In *Siluae* 1.1, Statius contrasts Domitian with warlords such as Caesar, who feature as negative models in Seneca's *De Clementia*.[144] In the same poem, he remarks on the kindness of Domitian's facial expression, the same attribute praised in the Hercules statuette: The keyword *mitis* is attached to both Domitian and Hercules.[145]

This redefinition of the Hercules paradigm is also visible in Statius' fashioning of a hero, Coroebus, who can be seen as replacing Hercules in an important section of the *Thebaid*. In book 1, Statius introduces a direct equivalent to Evander's narrative of Hercules and Cacus in the *Aeneid*. Polynices is invited to a banquet, after which he receives a lengthy account—the story of Linus and Coroebus—that is meant to explain the rites in honor of Apollo performed after the banquet.[146] The scene has clear intertextual links with Evander's account of Hercules and Cacus in the eighth book of the *Aeneid*.[147] In Lucan's rewriting of the Hercules and Cacus episode, the protagonist is still Hercules.[148] Here, the monster slayer is Coroebus. The replacement of Hercules with Coroebus is a meaningful, deliberate gesture. In the *Aeneid*, Hercules represents a model of heroism against which other characters are measured. The same can be said of Coroebus, as we see in Chapter 5, but he differs from Virgil's Hercules in some significant respects. Coroebus kills a monster, but he has no divine father. He does not act in isolation, and *pietas* is emphasized as his main motivation. There is no uncontrolled fury in his heroism, no gnashing of teeth, no frightening outburst like those of Hercules in the *Aeneid*. Coroebus also does something Hercules never did in his life: He offers himself as a scapegoat to Apollo.[149] This is an important *trait d'union* with the only Herculean hero who achieves divine status in the poem, namely Menoeceus. Both Menoceus and Coroebus contribute to Statius' redefinition of the Herculean paradigm.

The time preceding Domitian's accession had seen the return of civil war and, in connection with it, a sequence of self-styled aspirants to the role of Hercules, just

---

[143] See Chapter 4, Section 4.2 and Chapter 1, Section 1.1 on *Siluae* 1.4.
[144] Domitian's superiority to Caesar: *Silv.* 1.1.25–7; cf. Chapter 1, Section 1.1.
[145] *Silv.* 4.6.55, 1.1.15, 1.1.25.
[146] *Theb.* 1.557–668. On this section of Statius' poem see Chapter 5.
[147] See Ganiban (2007) 13–15; Legras (1905) 38–9; Vessey (1973) 101; Brown (1994) 166–8; Taisne (1994) 245; Delarue (2000) 121; McNelis (2007) 27–9; Schetter (1960) 82–4.
[148] See Section 3.3.
[149] Coroebus' killing of Poine: *Theb.* 1.605–16; Coroebus offers himself to Apollo: *Theb.* 1.638–61. More on the Coroebus episode in Chapter 5.

as in the civil wars of the late Republic. The series of failed Hercules figures in the *Thebaid* resonates with attempts at seizing the role of Hercules by Nero and other actors during the civil war period. Domitian's appropriation of the Hercules character, which accompanies his claiming of a role in civil war, was problematic in light of the pedigree of the hero, his connection with late republican warlords such as Antony and Octavian, and his recent reception by Nero. It was vital to show that although Domitian was a new Hercules, he was not going to repeat the mistakes of former recipients of that role. Statius' solution is to accompany Domitian's appropriation of Hercules with a redefinition of the Hercules model, one that updates the traditional portrait of the hero through the reception of Seneca's political theory. This redefinition of heroism values self-sacrifice in place of megalomania, *pietas* in place of hubris, *clementia* instead of *ira*, and self-control as opposed to irrational passions. This new Hercules is fit for war and peace and has lost his most frightening, civil war aspects. Statius' redefinition of Herculean symbols can be connected with the need to differentiate Domitian from Nero, but there is more to it than this. The poem presents Domitian with a new paradigm. If he is able to follow this model, Domitian will surpass even Augustus, precisely as the ideal sovereign of *De Clementia* surpasses him.

The treatment of Tydeus, Polynices, and Capaneus in connection with Hercules should be understood in this light. In a sense, Statius' picture of these heroes complements his search for new models of heroism and his redefinition of the Hercules model. The parable of the failed Hercules in the *Thebaid* sketches a map of the dangers of political action. Men, and especially sovereigns, can become gods, but they can also turn into beasts. This is a powerful commentary on attempts at playing Hercules in the world of Roman politics. Figures such as Antony or the young Octavian may have been strong in war. But because of their inner flaws, lack of *clementia*, and inability to control passions, they were constantly at risk of turning into monsters. Like Seneca's Hercules in his madness, they became unable to tell enemy from friend and shed the blood of their own fellow citizens. This trajectory was exemplified by Nero, the man who claimed to be Hercules but turned into a bloodthirsty monster, materializing his own impersonation of the mad Hercules. Statius admits that Domitian might escape this pattern of bestiality. At the same time, the fragility of power and its inherent risks are presented in so emphatic a way as to form a warning. Is Domitian going to achieve immortality like Menoeceus? Or is he going to fail like Polynices, or worse, turn into a bloodthirsty monster like Tydeus? Will he display *clementia* like Theseus, or will he sink into a delirium of punishment and blood like Seneca's mad Hercules? The *Thebaid* leaves the reader with a vivid sense of what failure would entail. It also leaves the emperor with the imperative to provide an answer to these questions through his own political action.

4

Thebes and Rome

⌐⌐―――――――――――――――――――――――――――――――――――――――

FRATERNAS ACIES [FRATERNAL armies], the very first words of Statius' poem, detail the *Thebaid*'s indebtedness to Lucan's *Bellum Ciuile*, the poem on the clash of the *cognatae acies* [related armies] of Pompey and Caesar (Luc. 1.4).[1] Statius goes on to invoke Clio, the muse of history, for his mythical poem (*Theb.* 1.41): The intersection of myth and Roman reality is programmatic. The presence of Lucan in Statius is ubiquitous and has received much attention.[2] One of its effects is evoking Roman historical experiences. Reception of images and motifs from the *Bellum Ciuile* and recurring allusions to Lucan connect Statius' mythical narrative to Roman civil war.

The evocation of historical civil war, however, is not the only effect of the presence of Lucan. We should also ask how Lucan's vision of imperial power and its relationship to civil war affect the political outlook of Statius' text. What is the effect of Lucan on the *Thebaid*'s conception of imperial ideology? How does Statius deal with the presentation of imperial rule at the heart of Lucan's

---

[1] As noted by many scholars: see e.g. Vessey (1973) 61; Dominik (1994) 170; Delarue (2000) 102; Roche (2015) 393–4.

[2] Some important contributions on Statius and Lucan: Venini (1971) 45–83; Narducci (1979) 152–7, (2002) 457–70; Malamud (1995); Micozzi (1999, 2004); Lovatt (1999); Delarue (2000) 97–112; McNelis (2007) 32, 121–3, 131–2; Ganiban (2007) 36–8, 62–3, 204; Bessone (2011) 54–5, 58–9, 80–1, 85–92, 153–4; Roche (2015). A detailed discussion of the intertextual relationship between the *Thebaid* and the *Bellum Ciuile* can also be found in the commentaries: Augoustakis (2016), Parkes (2012), Smolenaars (1994), and Venini (1970) are particularly helpful.

Bellum Ciuile? As far as imperial power is concerned, the *Bellum Ciuile* appeared to a Flavian author as an ambiguous and possibly contradictory text. At the beginning of Lucan's poem, the emperor's power is presented as the price worth paying for the new sovereignty of Nero.[3] There is no question of returning to the Republic: Nero's rule is a new Golden Age, and even the great years of the Republic would pale in comparison. The kingship of Nero grants freedom from the horrors of civil war.[4]

And yet at the end of book 1 of the *Bellum Ciuile*, the prophecy of Nigidius Figulus casts quite a different light on the power of the emperor. The only hope for the Romans is to protract the civil war, for peace comes with slavery:

> et superos quid prodest poscere finem?
> cum domino pax ista uenit. duc, Roma, malorum
> continuam seriem clademque in tempora multa
> extrahe ciuili tantum iam libera bello.
> Luc. 1.669–72

> And what use is it to ask the gods to end it?
> The peace we long for brings a master. Rome, prolong your chain
> of disaster without a break and protract calamity
> for lengthy ages: Only now in civil war are you free.

This may be an effect of focalization: Nigidius is not Lucan, Nigidius may have had Augustus in mind, and Nero was presented as better than Augustus.[5] But later in book 7, Lucan speaks in his own voice:

> maius ab hac acie quam quod sua saecula ferrent
> uolnus habent populi; plus est quam uita salusque
> quod perit: in totum mundi prosternimur aeuum.
> uincitur his gladiis omnis quae seruiet aetas.
> Luc. 7.638–41

> From this battle the peoples receive a mightier wound
> than their own time could bear; more was lost than life

---

[3] Luc. 1.33–8, 60–2, cited in Section 4.1. On these contradictory aspects of Lucan's text see Narducci (2002) 33–6; for a survey of scholarly positions on these heavily debated passages see Roche (2009) 7–10, 129–31, and subsequent discussion in this section.

[4] I discuss in more detail the intellectual atmosphere from which this proposition stems in Section 4.1.

[5] Narducci (2002) 110–11. On Nero's superiority to Augustus see Section 4.1.

and safety: for all the world's eternity we are prostrated.
Every age which will suffer slavery is conquered by these swords.

The blow dealt by Pharsalus to freedom extends to all ages to come.[6] Such a statement must have seemed incompatible with support of Nero or any positive take on imperial power. And yet the episodes featuring Domitius in books 2 and 7 of the *Bellum Ciuile* could be read as an attempt to present Nero as the continuator of his ancestor's defense of republican values.[7]

To Flavian readers, Lucan offered a spectrum of—seemingly unreconciled—positions vis-à-vis imperial power. One could take at face value the praise of the emperor in the proem and use the ghost of civil war to uphold the harsh necessity of imperial power. Or one could focus on passages in which imperial power appears as an uncompromising degeneration and in which the gap between the tyrannical Caesar and his later successors seems to be closed. As we will see, Statius exploits both perspectives. In this chapter, I combine a study of the ways in which Lucan is used as a vehicle for historical allusion in the *Thebaid* with attention to the different ideological spins that reprises of Lucan are given within Statius' text. My aim is not to provide a comprehensive treatment of Statius' relationship to Lucan but to highlight some of the ways in which the presence of Lucan affects the political outlook of Statius' *Thebaid*. I try to locate Statius' intertextual operations within the ideological and cultural context of Domitianic Rome.

4.1 CIVIL WAR AND IMPERIAL POWER

Let us consider the first of the two positions offered by Lucan's text and the intellectual climate from which it stems. Civil war is an important prop of imperial ideology from the very beginning. Virgil closes the first book of the *Georgics* with a powerful description of the prodigies announcing civil war and a prayer imploring the gods to allow Octavian to bring peace to a broken world. At the beginning of the same book, Octavian's deification is imminent on account of his benefactions to humanity, but it is still unclear what position he will occupy once divine (a god of Earth, heaven, the sea or—god forbid—the underworld).[8]

Apotheosis and success in quelling civil war are also linked in the *Aeneid*. Jupiter's prophecy in book 1 announces Octavian's deification and foresees a time when the

---

[6] On this passage see Narducci (2002) 35–6; Leigh (1997) 79–80. More passages expressing a negative view of the principate are collected by Roche (2009) 4–5.

[7] Luc. 2.477–525. Domitius' death: 7.599–616. That praise of Domitius was meant to flatter Nero is flatly denied by Ahl (1976) 47–54, but see Braund (1992) xv–xvi.

[8] *G.* 1.24–42.

madness of civil war, finally defeated, will be locked inside the Temple of Janus, the world now living in harmony:

> hunc tu olim caelo spoliis Orientis onustum
> accipies secura; uocabitur hic quoque uotis.
> aspera tum positis mitescent saecula bellis:
> cana Fides et Vesta, Remo cum fratre Quirinus
> iura dabunt; dirae ferro et compagibus artis
> claudentur Belli portae; Furor impius intus
> saeua sedens super arma et centum uinctus aënis
> post tergum nodis fremet horridus ore cruento.
> *A.* 1.289–96

Him, one day, you, no longer anxious, will welcome in heaven loaded with the spoils of the East; he too will be invoked in vows. Wars will be abandoned; harsh ages will grow kind. White-haired Faith and Vesta, Quirinus with his brother Remus, will give laws; the grim, iron gates of War, with their close-fitting bars, will be closed; wicked Madness inside, sitting on savage arms, hands tied behind his back with a hundred knots of bronze, will roar dreadfully with his blood-stained mouth.

The praise of Augustus as the one who grants peace to the universe is transferred to the figure of Nero. We find it in texts that clearly advertise their debt to prophetic passages in Virgil centering on Octavian/Augustus (from the *Eclogues*, *Georgics*, and *Aeneid*). In the first eclogue of Calpurnius Siculus, a text that conflates elements from Virgil's *Eclogues* 1 and 4, Nero is described in terms that remind us of Virgil's *Aeneid*:[9]

> dum populos deus ipse reget, dabit impia uinctas
> post tergum Bellona manus spoliataque telis
> in sua uesanos torquebit uiscera morsus
> et modo quae toto ciuilia distulit orbe,
> secum bella geret: nullos iam Roma Philippos
> deflebit, nullos ducet captiua triumphos.
> Calp. *Ecl.* 1.46–51

---

[9] I agree on the Neronian dating of Calpurnius' works. See for discussion Vinchesi (2014) 15–20 with full references.

As long as he, a god himself, governs the nations, impious Bellona will let her hands be tied behind her back, and deprived of weapons she will turn her raving teeth into her entrails and will wage against herself the civil wars which she recently scattered all over the world: Rome will mourn no Philippi and will no longer lead triumphs in which she is a captive.

Bellona with hands tied is a variation on the image of Virgil's *Furor* in *Aeneid* 1, which Calpurnius sees as the instigator of civil war.[10] Under Nero, the civil wars that Bellona has recently scattered will be locked up with her forever. Nero is the new Augustus, and he is even better than Augustus. Although great, Augustus came to power after Philippi (and, we might add, Mutina, Perusia, Naulochoi, and Actium), but under Nero there will be no equivalent of Philippi (Calp. *Ecl.* 1.50).[11] What is the point of evoking civil war for an emperor who has never engaged in it? The first implication is that the power of Nero prevents the world from returning to civil war, keeping in check the forces of discord that vexed it until recently.

But there is another important aspect. Civil war did not disappear with Augustus. It was perpetrated, Calpurnius goes on to say, even at times of imperial peace:

> candida Pax aderit, nec solum candida uultu,
> qualis saepe fuit, quae libera Marte professo,
> quae domito procul hoste, tamen grassantibus armis
> publica diffudit tacito discordia ferro:
> omne procul uitium simulatae cedere pacis
> iussit et insanos Clementia contudit enses.
> nulla catenati feralis pompa senatus
> carnificum lassabit opus, nec carcere pleno
> infelix raros numerabit curia patres.
> Calp. *Ecl.* 1.54–62

Resplendent peace will come, shining not in her face alone, such as she often was, when, free from open wars and far from vanquished enemies, she none-theless scattered public discord through a silent sword amidst the tumult of arms: Mercy ordered every flaw of feigned peace to withdraw afar, she made blunt the raving swords. No funeral procession of senators in chain will weary

---

[10] *A.* 1.293–6; Vinchesi (2014) 130–1.

[11] Cf. Sen. *Cl.* 1.9.1, 1.11.1–2. On Nero's outdoing of Augustus cf. also Tac. *Ann.* 13.4; Vinchesi (2014) 132–3; Martin (1996) 24.

the work of the executioners; nor will the wretched senate house count just a few senators while the prison is full.

Earlier instances of peace were merely apparent. The sword kept striking citizens surreptitiously—with the execution of senators. The passage does not have a specific historical referent but extends to repeated instances of imperial repression (cf. 1.55 *saepe* [often]). The reader is free to supply the names: from Octavian's proscriptions to senatorial executions under Tiberius, Caligula, and most recently Claudius.[12] Tyranny and the killing of senators are equivalents of civil war, products of the same *discordia* [discord].[13] The new peace, brought about by the emperor's *clementia*, prevents civil war, but also saves the world from its equivalent—the execution of elite Romans.[14]

The advent of the new emperor is marked by the revitalization of republican offices and the return of the rule of law.[15] Thus Calpurnius:

iam nec adumbrati faciem mercatus honoris
nec uacuos tacitus fasces et inane tribunal
accipiet consul; sed legibus omne reductis
ius aderit moremque fori uultumque priorem
reddet et afflictum melior deus auferet aeuum.
Calp. *Ecl.* 1.69–73

The consul will no longer purchase the appearance of a shadowy office, or receive in silence worthless fasces and a meaningless judgement-seat; but, with the return of law, justice will be present; she will return to the Forum its previous appearance and customs, and a better god will remove the age of affliction.

A similar position is to be found in the second poem of the (anonymous) *Bucolica Einsidlensia* (also Neronian). This composition heralds the new era of Nero by turning to Virgil's prophetic texts (*Eclogues* 4 in particular):

sed procul a nobis infelix gloria Sullae
trinaque tempestas, moriens cum Roma supremas

---

[12] Vinchesi (2014) 135–40.

[13] The rare *discordia* in Calp. *Ecl.* 1.57 is a neuter plural from the adjective *discors*. See Vinchesi (2014) 136–7.

[14] On Claudius' lack of *clementia*, most visible in his numerous executions, see Sen. *Apoc.* 14.1; cf. *Apoc.* 10.4, 12.3.19–20. Nero criticized two qualities of Claudius in particular: stupidity and cruelty (Suet. *Nero* 33.1).

[15] See also Calp. *Ecl.* 1.43–4 with Vinchesi (2014) 127–8; on the return of law cf. also Sen. *Apoc.* 12.2, 4.24; Sen. *Cl.* 1.1.4.

desperauit <opes> et Martia uendidit arma.
Buc. Eins. 2.32–4

But far from us the unfortunate glory of Sulla and the threefold storm, when
dying Rome despaired of her last resources and sold her martial arms.

The glory of Sulla will not be a part of the new Golden Age of Nero. Sulla's luckless
glory, a subversion of Sulla's famous cognomen (*felix* [Lucky One]), is a reference to
the proscriptions that followed his victory over Marius.[16] It is unclear what the three-
fold storm [*trina tempestas*] in the following line refers to. With Housman and earlier
interpreters, I tend to believe it refers to the second triumvirate, characterized, once
again, by proscriptions.[17] Nero's principate will grant it that the world will not return
to the chaos of civil war, but the emphasis on Sulla and the triumvirs brings home an-
other point. Sulla and the triumvirs are a particularly powerful example in light of their
extermination of Roman aristocrats. The proscriptions are an apt parallel for imperial
executions. It is especially these horrors of civil war that Nero's regime will not replicate.

Lucan's praise of Nero at the beginning of the *Bellum Ciuile* shares a number
of elements with Calpurnius' *Eclogues* and the *Bucolica Einsidlensia*.[18] The praise
of Nero connects directly with Virgil's praise of Octavian in the *Georgics*, with its
prophecy of the emperor's apotheosis and the choice of a place in heaven.[19] On ac-
count of his benefactions, Nero is offered the place of Jupiter or that of the Sun god.
With such a god in charge, peace will reign in the world, between both citizens
and foreign peoples. The picture evoked by Lucan a few lines later recalls Jupiter's
prophecy of Augustus' suppression of civil war in Virgil:

tum genus humanum positis sibi consulat armis
inque uicem gens omnis amet; pax missa per orbem
ferrea belligeri conpescat limina Iani.
Luc. 1.60–2

Then may humankind lay down its weapons and care for itself
and every nation love one another; may Peace be sent throughout
the world and close the iron temple-gates of warring Janus.

---

[16] Lucan uses *infelix gloria* (2.221–2) to refer to Sulla's final victory and the ongoing proscriptions.

[17] That *trina tempestas* is a reference to the second triumvirate is implied by Housman (1910) 47; later interpreters
tend to relate the sentence to events in the 80s BCE and the war of Marius and Sulla; cf. Verdière (1954) 269;
Shackleton Bailey (1982) 126; a survey of the different positions in Piętka (2010) 177–80.

[18] Note especially Calp. *Ecl.* 1.151 and Lucan 1.12 for direct echoes; Narducci (2002) 32.

[19] Luc. 1.45–52, cited in Chapter 2, Section 2.2.

The power of Nero is weighed against war (both civil, we must assume, and against foreign enemies) precisely as in Calpurnius and the *Bucolica Einsidlensia*. But in Lucan the topic is hyperbolically augmented: Not only is Nero the alternative to civil war, as in those texts, but the subversion of every human and divine law in civil conflict is a price worth paying for Nero's rule:[20]

quod si non aliam uenturo fata Neroni
inuenere uiam magnoque aeterna parantur
regna deis caelumque suo seruire Tonanti
non nisi saeuorum potuit post bella gigantum,
iam nihil, o superi, querimur; scelera ipsa nefasque
hac mercede placent.
Luc. 1.33–8

But if the Fates could find no other way
for Nero's coming, if eternal kingdoms are purchased
by the gods at great cost, if heaven could serve its Thunderer
only after wars with the ferocious Giants,
then we have no complaint, O gods; for this reward we accept
even these crimes and guilt.

Lucan's comparison of civil war to Gigantomachy, in which Jupiter vanquished the Giants, is in tune with the praise of Nero *qua* new Jupiter introduced by Lucan

---

[20] There is a substantial scholarly debate on the sincerity, or lack thereof, of Lucan's praise of Nero in the *Bellum Ciuile*; it is aptly summarized by Narducci (2002) 22–6 and Roche (2009) 7–10, 129–31 with full references. Since antiquity there have been attempts at removing the contradictions in Lucan's text by positing that the praise of Nero is ironic, not sincere, or simply opportunistic. I hold that Lucan is aware of the risks connected to Nero's reception of imperial power (cf. Chapter 2, Section 2.2) and that these risks are hinted at through the ambiguous language of the address (see especially the reference to Phaethon: Chapter 2, Section 2.2) but the praise is not ironic and is perfectly acceptable as a piece of imperial praise, in accordance with the standards of the Neronian period; see Narducci (1979) 22, (2002) 23; Dewar (1994). I find it plausible that the praise of Nero is related to an early stage in Lucan's relationship with the emperor, at a time when Lucan was still aligned with the position found in other Neronian texts. Nero is projected as the emperor capable of surpassing all his imperial predecessors and bringing about *libertas* under imperial rule. This panegyric address, like Seneca's *De Clementia*, may contain protreptic elements: Nero is encouraged to live up to his beginnings. This position is later abandoned and contradicted by other passages in the text. In my view, the *Bellum Ciuile* remained a problematic and ultimately inconsistent text: No hermeneutic tool (ironic readings etc.) was immediately available to early readers through which they could work out the text's inconsistencies. As we see in this chapter, a post-Neronian perspective allows Statius to devise a way of reconciling Lucan's two opposing views of imperial power; at the same time, Statius makes the most of Lucan's inconsistent take on imperial rule.

later in the poem. We have seen how in contemporary Neronian texts Nero's control of civil *discordia* is accompanied by a restoration of republican freedom. After such an introduction to the *Bellum Ciuile*, we might expect a poem in which republican ideals are not tantamount to a rejection of imperial rule, but in which the power of Nero, unlike that of earlier emperors, is compatible with some form of *libertas*—as in Calpurnius. The *Bellum Ciuile* does not live up to its prologue in this respect: Darker images emerge in other parts of the poem.[21] However, the poem's opening lays out a way of interpreting the balance between civil war and imperial power that is favorable to the emperor.

How would Romans assess this praise after Nero's death? The post-Neronian *Octauia* provides an interesting answer, in the voice of Nero himself:

> quantum cruoris Roma tum uidit sui,
> lacerata totiens! ille qui meruit pia
> uirtute caelum, diuus Augustus, uiros
> quot interemit nobiles, iuuenes senes
> sparsos per orbem, cum suos mortis metu
> fugerent penates et trium ferrum ducum,
> tabula notante deditos tristi neci!
> exposita rostris capita caesorum patres
> uidere maesti, flere nec licuit suos,
> non gemere dira tabe polluto foro,
> stillante sanie per putres uultus graui.
> *Oct.* 503–13

Then what quantities of her own blood Rome saw, being wounded so often! He who earned a place in heaven by his virtues and sense of duty, the deified Augustus—how many noblemen *he* killed, young and old! They had scattered throughout the world in fear for their lives, in flight from their own homes and from the swords of the three leaders; a notice board listed those consigned to the horror of death! Sorrowing fathers saw the heads of the slain exposed on the Rostra, yet they could not weep for their own kin, nor lament in a forum polluted with horrible gore, as foul putrescence trickled down the rotting faces.

This speech takes place in an exchange between Nero and his former tutor Seneca. Seneca quotes from his *De Clementia* to convince Nero to recede from his

---

[21] See the passages collected by Roche (2009) 4–5.

intention of executing Plautus and Sulla, and mentions Augustus as an example of moderate kingship.[22] To this Nero replies in the passage just quoted with a picture of Rome's past civil wars, with special attention to the cruelty of Octavian's proscriptions. The unexpected twist is that Nero uses this historical precedent as *justification* for the necessity of repressing opponents—a legitimation for his own proscriptions. Nero's terror is presented as a continuation of the horrors of civil war.

The background of Seneca's *De Clementia* is necessary for making full sense of the exchange. In *De Clementia*, Seneca encouraged Nero to follow the example set by Augustus in his late years. Augustus had learned how to use *clementia* only after spilling the blood of citizens (here Seneca mentions the proscriptions and the wars of the 40s and 30s BCE).[23] The author of *Octauia* shows Nero doing exactly the opposite. Seneca's pupil purports to imitate the worst aspects of Augustus' early political career and to duplicate his proscriptions. In what seems like a pointed response to the Neronian passages just collected, Nero is shown doing the opposite of what panegyrists had announced of him: Instead of being the end of civil war, he is assaulting the very citizen body; he is bringing back the luckless glory of Sulla, the terror of the proscriptions. It is important to note that *Octauia*'s account of proscriptions by the triumvirs is indebted to Lucan's narrative of Sulla's proscriptions in book 2 of the *Bellum Ciuile*.[24] The analogy is relevant: The author of the *Bucolica Einsidlensia* conjoins the proscriptions of Sulla and those of the triumvirs as *exempla* of the crimes Nero will *not* repeat.[25]

From the texts discussed in this section we get a few elements that will be important for our reading of the *Thebaid*. The topic of civil war can be used as a panegyric element. The emperor who does not let civil war come back to the empire can be praised as emphatically as the one who rescued the world from it. But Neronian panegyric articulates another way in which the topic of civil war is relevant to imperial rule. There can be civil war hidden within imperial peace: the shedding of aristocratic blood. In this context too civil war is parsed in a pro-imperial way and joined with praise of *clementia*: Through his merciful attitude, the good emperor saves the state from this kind of war too.

---

[22] The exchange between Seneca and Nero: *Oct.* 437–592. Seneca's mention of Augustus: *Oct.* 477–81. On quotations from *De Clementia* in this section see Ferri (2003) 253ff. and his survey of the politics of *Octauia* (70–5); Boyle (2008) lxiv–lxxv.

[23] Sen. *Cl.* 1.9.1, 1.11.1–2.

[24] Ferri (2003) 271–2.

[25] Compare the *trina tempestas* (*Buc. Eins.* 2.33) with the "iron of the three leaders" [*ferrum trium ducum*] of *Oct.* 508.

4.2 IMPERIAL POWER AND CIVIL WAR IN THE *SILVAE*

This is, however, not the only position on imperial power present in Lucan. Flavian writers had to reckon with the other extreme on the spectrum, formed by passages in which the distinction between Caesar and his imperial successors, Nero included, is not preserved. As we will see shortly, an approach to this issue consists in reading the *Bellum Ciuile* as criticism of Nero, as an anti-Neronian rather than an anti-imperial text. Before considering the *Thebaid*, however, I would like to spend some time on the *Siluae*. In this work, both the notion of civil war as a source of legitimation for imperial power and a reading of Lucan as an anti-Neronian, but not necessarily anti-imperial, text find adequate space. Let us begin with the first point, appropriations of civil war as a way of legitimating imperial power. *Siluae* 1.1 details Domitian's successes in civil war:

> semel auctor ego inuentorque salutis
> Romuleae: tu bella Iouis, tu proelia Rheni,
> tu ciuile nefas, tu tardum in foedera montem
> longo Marte domas.
> *Silv.* 1.1.78–81

Once only did I find and offer salvation to the people of Romulus; you con-quer the war of Jupiter, the battles of the Rhine and civil war; you vanquish with a long war the mountain slow to accept a truce.

In this passage, Domitian is praised by the republican hero Marcus Curtius for rescuing the world from civil war not just once, but twice. Domitian contributed to Vitellius' defeat when he took part in the battle of the Capitol of 69 CE. That fight is described as *bella Iouis,* an allusion to Jupiter's battle against the Giants: The Capitoline, seat of Jupiter, was besieged by the Vitellians as Olympus was once attacked by Giants and Titans.[26] But Domitian also prevented the return of civil war by defeating Saturninus (1.1.80 *ciuile nefas* [civil crime]), who, like Vitellius, had moved his armies from the North to attack Rome.[27] Civil war is compared to Gigantomachy, as in Lucan's *Bellum Ciuile,* and its prevention is a prelude to

---

[26] For *bellum Iouis* as a reference to Gigantomachy cf. *Culex* 26–7; see also Mart. 9.101.14 and *Silv.* 5.3.195–8, in which the battle of the Capitol in 69 CE is explicitly compared to Gigantomachy. See also Chapter 3, Section 3.2.

[27] Saturninus found himself in the same position occupied by Vitellius (governor of Germania Inferior). His uprising involved one of the legions that supported Vitellius' bid for power (XXI Rapax) and probably started on the 20th anniversary of Vitellius' uprising; see Jones (1992) 144–9; Griffin (2000) 65–6; Syme (1988) 253.

Domitian's transformation into a new Jupiter and a new Sol, announced at the end
of the same poem, in a variation on the *Georgics* proem and its reception by Lucan
in the *Bellum Ciuile*:[28]

> utere perpetuum populi magnique senatus
> munere. Apelleae cuperent te scribere cerae
> optassetque nouo similem te ponere templo
> Atticus Elei senior Iouis, et tua mitis
> ora Tarans, tua sidereas imitantia flammas
> lumina contempto mallet Rhodos aspera Phoebo.
> certus ames terras et quae tibi templa dicamus
> ipse colas, nec te caeli iuuet aula, tuosque
> laetus huic dono uideas dare tura nepotes.
> *Silv.* 1.1.99–107

Enjoy for all time the gift of the people and the great Senate. Apelles' wax
would wish to inscribe you, the old man from Athens would have longed to
set your likeness in a new temple of Elean Jove, gentle Tarentum would have
preferred your countenance, fierce Rhodes, despising Phoebus, would have
preferred your eyes which resemble the heavenly flames. May you love Earth
without doubt and yourself frequent the temples we dedicate to you. Let not
heaven's palace delight you, and may you happily see your grandsons give in-
cense to this gift.

Here the inhabitants of Tarentum would prefer Domitian to Jupiter. This is a pan-
egyric exaggeration, but the idea that human kingship equals and even improves
on the Jovian model is well represented in the *Siluae*, which in turn draw on earlier
Roman traditions.[29] It is important to keep this in mind: As we will see, the idea of
human kingship improving on and even replacing the gods plays a key role in the
Thebaid.

In Calpurnius, Nero saves the world from the internal version of civil war thanks
to his merciful attitude, thus proving himself superior to all his predecessors on the
throne. We have seen in Chapter 1 that the idea of Domitian as superior to all of his
imperial predecessors is represented in various passages from the *Siluae*. That this
superiority is due, among other things, to Domitian's merciful attitude is implicit in

---

[28] On the identification of Jupiter and Domitian in this poem cf. also the preface (*Silv.* 1 *praef.* 18), where Statius
refers to *Siluae* 1.1 by writing that "he had to start from Jupiter" [*sumendum erat a Ioue principium*].

[29] Bessone (2011) 45–66.

Siluae 1.1. In this poem, Statius describes Domitian as an embodiment of *clementia*, extending even to foreign enemies the leniency usually reserved to citizens.[30] More specific echoes of Domitian's friendly attitude toward the Senate are found in *Siluae* 1.4, another poem strongly influenced by the vision of *De Clementia*. In this poem, Statius attributes to Rutilius Gallicus some of the virtues embodied by Domitian.[31] Statius' description of the Senate's anxious reaction to Gallicus' illness shows the Senate's love for this faithful administrator of Domitian (1.4.38–49; quoted in Chapter 1, Section 1.1). The poem echoes Calpurnius in comparing Gallicus to Numa. The tag *curia felix* [prosperous senate house, *Silv.* 1.4.41] is perhaps a deliberate inversion of Calpurnius' depiction of the sufferings of *infelix curia* [luckless senate house] under imperial repression.[32] The reason for this love is Gallicus' lenient attitude: He hates the sound of chains (1.4.43). In conclusion, in the *Siluae* we find both ideological uses of civil war observed previously in Neronian panegyric: The emperor guarantees peace by preventing the world from returning to civil war, and through his *clementia* he avoids enacting the internal version of civil war, the shedding of the blood of Roman citizens.

So far with the use of civil war as a prop for imperial power. But what to do with the rest of Lucan, especially those passages in which Lucan seems to close the gap between Caesar and his imperial descendants, and in which imperial power seems to be irreconcilable with *libertas*? In this respect, the *Siluae* once again offer important indications. The easiest way to reduce the unsettling power of Lucan was to read the *Bellum Ciuile* as an indictment of Nero in particular, not of imperial power in general. This is precisely the kind of reading implied in *Siluae* 2.7. In this poem, Statius has the soul of Lucan join Pompey and Cato in the underworld. They occupy the Elysian Fields and from there watch Nero tortured by Agrippina in the guise of a Fury in Tartarus.[33] The presence of Pompey in the Elysian Fields is prophesied by Lucan in book 6, while punishment in Tartarus awaits Caesar.[34] In *Siluae* 2.7, Caesar's place in Tartarus has been taken by Nero. Lucan and the cause of *libertas* on one side are opposed to Caesar and Nero on the other.

It is a remarkable reading that makes Lucan into a champion of freedom. This *libertas*, however, is not necessarily incompatible with the power of the emperor. The rule of Nero is incompatible with *libertas*, but this does not mean that every emperor should also be incompatible with it. The view of *Siluae* 2.7 is complemented by

[30] Chapter 1, Section 1.1.
[31] As we saw in Chapter 1, Section 1.1.
[32] Cf. Calp. *Ecl.* 1.62. The echo is noted by Vinchesi (2014) 139. For the happiness of the Senate cf. *Silv.* 4.1.10; the collocation *curia felix* is also at *Silv.* 4.4.76.
[33] *Silv.* 2.7.116–19.
[34] Luc. 6.804–5. Newlands (2011) 249–50.

Siluae 1.1. In this poem, as we saw, Domitian is contrasted with Caesar, on account of his leniency.[35] And he is also associated with Cato and Pompey:

> . . . te signa ferente
> et minor in leges gener et Cato Caesaris irent.
> *Silv.* 1.1.27–8

> . . . had you borne the standard, his lesser son-in-law and Cato would have submitted to Caesar's ordinances.

The corrupt text has been emendated here.[36] It seems clear enough, however, that, in contrasting Caesar and Domitian, this passage presented Cato and Pompey (the son-in-law: *gener*) as favorable to Domitian. Whereas Nero is the opposite of Pompey, Lucan, and Cato, the new emperor Domitian can be pictured on their side. The somewhat paradoxical idea of a principate that brings back the spirit of the Republic is paralleled in other imperial texts. As far as *libertas* is concerned, contemporaries of Statius were prepared to say of Domitian what Tacitus famously said of Nerva: that he had made possible the joint presence of principate and *libertas*, which were once irreconcilable.[37]

The notion of outdoing one's predecessors, which we have encountered in both Neronian panegyric and the *Siluae*, is implicit in Statius' reception of Neronian praise and in his projecting of the *Bellum Ciuile* as an anti-Neronian text. This concept is fundamental to understanding how certain ideas could be imported from earlier literature, and especially from Neronian texts. At the beginning of his imperial career, Nero was praised as the one who finally realized the promises of peace Augustus had only partially fulfilled. This turned out not to be true, yet the ideal did not have to be abandoned: Domitian could be presented as the one who managed to achieve what Nero had failed to bring about. In this context, elements of praise of Nero merely needed to be moved a few steps down the imperial ladder. The panegyric formulations could now be transferred to Domitian: After Augustus' and Nero's failure, the era of peace would finally start under the last Flavian.[38] In this perspective, the praise of imperial power at the beginning of the *Bellum Ciuile*

---

[35] On *Siluae* 1.1 see Chapter 1, Section 1.1.

[36] The text cited (Courtney) follows the emendations by Scriverius. The manuscript's text runs as follows: *et minor in leges iret gener et Cato castris.*

[37] Tac. *Ag.* 3.1; on *libertas* under the principate, Wirszubski (1968) 124–71 remains fundamental. Something similar to the passage from *Siluae* 1.1 previously quoted is said of Nerva by Martial at 11.5.9–12: Under this emperor, even Cato would become *Caesarianus* [a follower of Caesar].

[38] On this in general see Chapter 1, Section 1.1.

retained its value: It only needed a worthy emperor to be made a reality. As we see in the following section, the idea that Domitian surpasses all his predecessors allows Statius to transfer to Domitian in the *Thebaid* the praise of Octavian and Nero from Virgil's *Georgics* and Lucan's *Bellum Ciuile*.

4.3 IMPERIAL POWER, CIVIL WAR, AND COSMIC UPHEAVAL IN THE *THEBAID*

Let us now consider the impact of these ideas on the political outlook of the *Thebaid*. I begin by examining the idea of civil war as a prop of imperial power, which we have discussed in Sections 4.1 and 4.2 with reference to Neronian literature and the *Siluae*. I will show that the conception of imperial power as the only force capable of saving the world from civil war is not only programmatically stated at the beginning of the poem, but permeates the narrative design and the imagery of Statius' epic in a number of scenes. In addition, I will show that, while recognizing the necessity of imperial power, Statius also draws attention to its flaws, limits, and inherent fragility. The view emerging from this analysis is far from triumphalistic, imperial power appearing as a force which, though far from perfect, is still preferable to the chaos and destruction of political strife. I then move on to outline other uses of Lucan in the *Thebaid*, with particular attention to Lucan as a source of allusion to historical events and to Roman narratives of civil war. In the last section of this chapter, I consider the *Thebaid*'s exploitation of the potentialities of the *Bellum Ciuile* as an anti-Neronian text, in line with the position outlined in *Siluae* 2.7.

The apostrophe to Domitian in book 1 aligns the *Thebaid* with the tradition of Lucan's apostrophe to Nero and its Virgilian precedent in the *Georgics*.[39] Statius predicts Domitian's deification and his assumption of the role of Jupiter. The passage is modeled on the praise of Nero in the *Bellum Ciuile*.[40] Statius' praise of Domitian is preceded by a list of the emperor's achievements (*Theb.* 1.17–22), culminating, significantly—and in spite of chronology—with Domitian's participation in the *bella Iouis*. As we have seen, the phrase *bella Iouis* configures the battle of the Capitol as Gigantomachy, looking ahead to Domitian's reception of the role of Jupiter later in the apostrophe. As in Lucan's *Bellum Ciuile*, Domitian emerges as a new Jupiter after his triumph over the Giants, a war that, unlike Nero, he has fought in person.

The gesture seeks to inscribe Domitian in a tradition of texts that weigh imperial power against the chaos of civil war, presenting the emperor as the only salvation

---

[39] *Thebaid* 1.22–31.
[40] See Chapter 2, Sections 2.2 and 2.3.

from civil conflict. This is an apt proem for a poem on civil war; it sheds light on how to consider the *Thebaid*'s subject matter in relation to Domitian. Yet this is also a problematic tradition. Neronian literature questioned Octavian's success in bringing peace to the world. As for Nero, he had led the world to civil war again, and this after decimating the aristocracy. But before we construe this proem as subversive, we should remember that in the case of Nero, the reception of the *Georgics* proem arises in a context in which the new emperor is regarded as someone who will finally fulfill the promises made by Octavian. What makes this proem acceptable is the perspective that Domitian will be the one who finally fulfills the promises frustrated by Octavian and Nero. This, of course, does not deny the ominous weight of previous failed attempts: The risk of failure is greater and more dramatic after two (or more) unsuccessful efforts.

This conception of the role of the emperor as the only power that prevents the world from returning to the chaos of civil war is reflected in other scenes of the *Thebaid*. To this end, Statius builds on the parallelism between Jupiter and the power of the emperor suggested at the beginning of the poem and attested in the *Siluae*. The *Thebaid* also relies on a well-established epic tradition which highlights parallels between cosmic upheaval and civil war. The *Aeneid* begins with the description of a storm in which the cosmos is brought into connection with the political world. King Aeolus releases his control on the winds under pressure from Juno. Aeolus' power over the winds resembles the power of a king over defiant subjects. The result is a tempest that threatens to tear the cosmos apart (*A.* 1.50–123).[41] When Neptune intervenes and restores order, he is compared, fittingly, to an esteemed old citizen who calms down a riot (*A.* 1.124–156). The description of Aeolous' kingship and the final simile of the old man establish a parallelism between civil strife and cosmic upheaval. It follows that both cosmic and political chaos arise when the power controlling the forces from above is released or removed; and that order is possible only through the restoration of that power.

Post-Virgilian authors are sensitive to the political overtones of the Virgilian scene. Thus Ovid describes the clash of mighty winds at the beginning of the world with a collocation taken from Virgil's description of fraternal strife in the *Georgics*.[42] At the beginning of the *Bellum Ciuile*, the emperor is presented as a new Jupiter after the battle of the Giants. This cosmic role of the emperor goes hand in hand with a set of similes linking civil war to cosmic upheaval and subversion of the laws of the cosmos:

---

[41] On the cosmic aspects of this storm see Hardie (1986) 90–6.
[42] Ov. *Met.* 1.60; Verg. *G.* 2.496; Narducci (2002) 458–9.

> sic, cum conpage soluta
> saecula tot mundi suprema coegerit hora
> antiquum repetens iterum chaos, [omnia mixtis
> sidera sideribus concurrent,] ignea pontum
> astra petent, tellus extendere litora nolet
> excutietque fretum, fratri contraria Phoebe
> ibit et obliquum bigas agitare per orbem
> indignata diem poscet sibi, totaque discors
> machina diuolsi turbabit foedera mundi.
> Luc. 1.72–80

So, when the final hour
brings to an end the long ages of the universe, its structure dissolved,
reverting to primeval chaos, [all the constellations
will clash in confusion,] then fiery stars will plunge
into the sea, the earth will be unwilling to stretch flat her shores
and will shake the water off, Phoebe will confront
her brother and for herself demand the day, resentful
of driving her chariot along its slanting orbit, and the whole
discordant mechanism of universe torn apart will disrupt its own laws.

In this passage, civil war is compared to the final return to chaos, marking the end of a world cycle in stoic philosophy.[43]

At the beginning of the *Thebaid*, Eteocles and Polynices are presented as two bulls unable to share in the yoke (*Theb.* 1.131–38). But the phrase *illi indignantes* (*Theb.* 1.133) recalls the image of the Virgilian winds who do not submit to the power of Aeolus (*A.* 1.55–7). A few lines later, Statius builds again on the political overtones of storm imagery. In the words of the anonymous citizen of Thebes, Eteocles and Polynices, like the *Aeneid*'s winds, are ready to sink the ship of state:

> qualiter hinc gelidus Boreas, hinc nubifer Eurus
> uela trahunt, nutat mediae fortuna carinae,
> (heu dubio suspensa metu tolerandaque nullis
> aspera sors populis!) hic imperat, ille minatur.
> *Theb.* 1.193–6

---

[43] On cosmic imagery in Lucan see Lapidge (1979); Narducci (1979) 71, 109–10, (2002) 42–50; Hardie (1986) 381; Feeney (1991) 278; Hershkowitz (1998) 201–2.

Such as when freezing Boreas drags the sails one way and cloudy Eurus another, and the fate of the vessel wavers between (alas, harsh lot that hangs in doubt and fear, a lot no people should bear!); the one commands, the other threatens.

In Statius, the parallelism of cosmic and political order is continued in the scene of the divine council following immediately after the winds simile of *Thebaid* 1.193. Here Statius builds on a rich epic tradition. After Virgil, Ovid had made explicit the parallelism between the power of Jupiter and that of the emperor in his council scene of *Metamorphoses* 1. In Ovid, the sovereignty of Jupiter/Augustus is notably more autocratic than in the *Aeneid*.[44] Statius situates his Jupiter in this tradition, which he updates to the time of Domitian and the usages of the Domitianic *curia*. Statius' Jupiter, it has been noted, is an even more autocratic foil for the emperor than his Ovidian counterpart.[45] A sense of fear accompanies his entrance, which commands the lasting silence of the assembly.[46] It is no surprise that Statius' depiction of Jupiter has been taken as a derogatory portrait of Domitian's autocratic attitude, especially in regard to the Senate.[47] But considering the beginning of the scene yields a more complex picture. In Statius, the assembly includes minor gods such as the rivers and, more important, the winds:

> mox turba uagorum
> semideum et summis cognati nubibus Amnes
> et compressa metu seruantes murmura Venti
> aurea tecta replent.
> *Theb.* 1.205–8

Soon the golden palace is filled by a crowd of wandering demigods, by the Rivers, the kin of lofty clouds, and the Winds who restrain their roars out of fear.

Note the attitude of the winds: they restrain their roars out of fear (*Theb.* 1.207); *murmura* alludes to their roars in Aeolus' cave in the *Aeneid*.[48] Jupiter's power keeps the winds under control, and fear is an important ingredient in it. Remove this power and the world collapses into a war of elements; remove the power of the emperor and

---

[44] Ov. *Met.* 1.168–252; Barchiesi (2005) 179–81, 183, 187; Feeney (1991) 198–200.

[45] Feeney (1991) 353; Domitianic curia: Williams (1978) 251. On the political resonances of Statius' council: Schubert (1984) 76–7, 99, 102–3, 296–7.

[46] Schubert (1984) 77–8, 99.

[47] Dominik (1994) 7–15, 161–7; Ahl (1986) 2834–5.

[48] *A.* 1.55.

the world collapses into civil war again. An autocratic, even frightening, power is weighed against the menace of cosmic upheaval and civil war.

The symbolic power of these lines acquires its true relevance after Jupiter's speech (*Theb.* 1.214–47). The king of gods rehearses his own previous interventions against the crimes of humanity, noting that his former attempts at correction were unsuccessful. Although Jupiter's speech is visibly indebted to its counterpart in Ovid's *Metamorphoses*, in Statius, the king of gods speaks from a fictional standpoint that postdates Ovid's divine council.[49] In Statius, the flood—Jupiter's resolution after his speech in Ovid—and the fire of Phaethon (which Jupiter anticipates in Ovid) have already happened, and Jupiter complains that those punitive actions had no effect (*Theb.* 1.219–23). In Ovid, the crime of Lykaon, which prompts Jupiter to punitive action, forms a parallel to the crime of the tyrannicides, chastised by Octavian.[50] Statius adopts a fictional point of view in which humanity has already committed crimes akin to civil war and already received their punishment, to no avail, during the Augustan period. If we factor the political resonance of the Ovidian precedents into our reading of Statius, we see that Jupiter's heightened power in the *Thebaid* responds to a continuous relapse of humanity into civil discord, which is exactly what had happened again for the first time after Augustus in 69 CE. It seems as though from the time of Virgil the universe has become a lot more difficult to control. Statius' Jupiter might be more frightening and autocratic than his epic precedents. It is also true that his power is weighed against a universe with a chronic inclination toward evil. Is Statius saying that Rome's relapse into civil war warrants increasing the power of the emperor? Or that, if on one side of the scale we find a hypertrophic power, it is because on the other there is the ghost of (renewed) civil war?

Statius' discourse on the parallels between Jovian power and the emperor suggests that monarchical power, however imperfect, is inevitable. The complement to this view is offered by Statius' presentation of the people, the masses who are the flesh of the empire. An indication in this sense comes, again, from the voice of the anonymous speaker of book 1. This passage differs in important respects from its precedent in Lucan.[51] In Statius, the voice of the anonymous is undercut. What he says might be true, but he is presented as defiant to any kind of power, no matter its nature:

atque aliquis, cui mens humili laesisse ueneno
summa nec impositos umquam ceruice uolenti

---

[49] On Ovid's council as a model for Statius Feeney (1991) 353–4; Dominik (1994) 164; Ahl (1986) 2835, 2837–8.

[50] Ovid. *Met.* 1.199–205; Barchiesi (2005) 187 *ad loc.*; anticipations of the fire of Phaethon may be heard at *Met.* 1.253–8.

[51] For this passage's models see Section 4.5.

ferre duces . . .
Theb. 1.171–3

And one of them, a man always intent upon harming those at the top with lowly
venom, always unable to bear willingly on his neck the rulers placed over him . . .

We find scattered echoes of this position in passages of the *Siluae*. In *Siluae*
1.4.40, Statius speaks of the *plebs* as *ignara lugere potentes*—the commoners unable
to mourn the powerful—a close cognate of the envious *plebs* of the *Thebaid*, never
happy with a king and always awaiting *res nouae*. I find parallels to this representa-
tion of the populace in Valerius Flaccus; indeed, this notion is familiar from Roman
reflections on the necessity of imperial power.[52] One is reminded of the look cast
down by the sovereign on humanity at the beginning of Seneca's *De Clementia*:

iuuat . . . inmittere oculos in hanc inmensam multitudinem discordem, seditio-
sam, inpotentem, in perniciem alienam suamque pariter exultaturam, si hoc
iugum fregerit . . .
Cl. 1.1.1

It is pleasing . . . to cast one's eyes on this immense, discordant, riotous, restless
multitude, ready to run riot to its own destruction as well as to that of others,
if it will break this yoke . . .

By their own nature, the masses are riotous, restless, and ready for mu-
tual destruction if the yoke of imperial power is broken.[53] Something similar
is said by Galba in the famous speech reported by Tacitus at the beginning
of the *Histories*. The aged emperor reflects that imperial power is a necessity,
for the huge body of the empire could not stand on its own and be stable in
the absence of a single ruler.[54] The *Thebaid* seems aligned with the some-
what resigned position of imperial thinkers who envisage imperial power as
the only antidote to the self-destructive attitude of the masses. Implicit in this
position, as in the idea of imperial power as the only medicine against civil

---

[52] Cf. V. Fl. 1.71, 1.761; see McGuire (1997) 169.

[53] Cf. also Sen. *Cl.* 1.4.2–3. For other echoes of this view in Seneca see Braund (2009) 157. A different explanation
of Statius' weakening of the anonymous' voice is in Ahl (1986) 2829–34; Criado (2015) 303–4 draws attention
to the apparent contradiction in Statius' undercutting of the anonymous' words and his endorsement of the
anonymous' rejection of alternating kingship.

[54] *Hist.* 1.16; discussed by Gowing (2005) 102–3.

war discussed previously, is the notion that a return to the Republic is not feasible.[55]

The parallelism between imperial and cosmic power just discussed is also reflected in Theseus' portrait. The human hero who brings a resolution to the *Thebaid* extends to the world the power of Jupiter. The words with which he rallies his troops on the mission to Thebes sound like a pointed reply to Lucan's picture of civil war as cosmic chaos:[56]

> . . . terrarum leges et <u>mundi</u> <u>foedera</u> mecum
> defensura cohors, dignas insumite mentes
> coeptibus . . .
> *Theb.* 12.642–4

> . . . soldiers, who will defend with me laws of nations and the world's pacts, think as befits our enterprise . . .

In Jovian fashion, the thundering voice of Theseus accompanies the casting of the spear with which Theseus kills Creon, and finally restores peace to Thebes.[57] Theseus' resolution to attack Thebes is accompanied by a particularly significant simile in which Theseus is compared to Jupiter unleashing a storm.[58] This time, however, the mad thunderbolts, thunders, and winds act under the power of the king of gods, not against his will:

> . . . qualis Hyperboreos ubi nubilus institit axes
> Iuppiter et prima tremefecit sidera bruma,
> rumpitur Aeolia et longam indignata quietem
> tollit hiems animos uentosaque sibilat Arctos;
> tunc montes undaeque fremunt, tunc proelia caecis
> nubibus et tonitrus insanaque fulmina gaudent.
> *Theb.* 12.650–5

> . . . so when cloudy Jupiter takes his stand upon the Northern pole and makes the stars shake with the coming of winter, Aeolia's portals are cracked open and storms, no longer suffering the long idleness, take courage and the windy

---

[55] In Raymond Marks's view, a similar position is reflected in Silius' *Punica*: see Marks (2005a) 252, 269–83. Marks argues that Silius does not advocate a return to the Republic and regards one-man rule as the only solution to the woes of Rome, provided that the sovereign is endowed with certain characteristics.

[56] Luc. 1.80 cited previously in this section; Bessone (2011) 72.

[57] Bessone (2011) 191; *Theb.* 12.771 *intonat* [he thunders]; cf. Verg. *A.* 12.700.

[58] On this simile see Bessone (2011) 188–9.

Bear howls: then mountains and waves roar, then there are battles in the dark
clouds, thunders and mad thunderbolts rejoice.

In spite of Jupiter's control over the elements, there is something unexpected
about the king of the gods relying on those same forces that the poem has so far
associated with civil war. This, as we shall see at the end of this section, is related to
Statius' complex view of monarchical power. Monarchical power might be neces-
sary, it might even be the best one can hope for, but it is far from perfect. Imperial
rule cannot be effective unless it incorporates part of the terror it purports to fight.
Fear, as we saw, was part and parcel of Jupiter's control over the cosmos. Like Jupiter,
Theseus instills fear in those who look at him.[59] And the aforementioned simile sees
him channeling the powers of chaos into his military action. It is necessary to keep
in mind against what forces this fear is balanced. After 11 books on the destructive
power of civil war, it becomes clear that the amount of power necessary to keep these
forces under control is sizable and that fear is a necessary part of it.

Theseus has another dimension that is not fully realized in Statius' Jupiter. Statius'
Jupiter has hints of *clementia*—perceivable especially in his speech in book 7 (*Theb.*
7.199–209) in which the king of the gods admits that he is moved to punishment
against his will, seldom and sparingly.[60] But in the poem we do not see Jupiter's
mercy enacted, the god's action being limited to punishment. Theseus' reception
of Jovian power follows Jupiter's disappearance from the narrative.[61] The Athenian
hero can be considered a replacement for the king of the gods, and he is brought into
connection with a renewed understanding of *clementia*, as I discussed in Chapter 1.[62]
The idea of an earthly king endowed with *clementia* who acts on Jupiter's behalf and
even outdoes him in the rule of the cosmos is found with reference to Domitian
in the *Siluae*.[63] In conclusion, the poem casts doubts on Jupiter, but these extend
only partly to human kingship, which is understood as complementing and even
improving the Jovian model.[64] Theseus is superior to Jupiter in light of his *clementia*,
just as Domitian is superior to earlier emperors in the *Siluae* precisely in light of
this virtue.[65] Theseus' construction as a Jovian king allows Statius to refine and

---

[59] *Theb.* 12.672–4, 12.730–6.

[60] These words resonate with imperial discussions of *clementia principis*: See Bessone (2011) 70–1, who compares
Ov. *Pont.* 1.2.121–6. Cf. also *Theb.* 1.214–17.

[61] *Theb.* 11.122–35.

[62] Chapter 1, Section 1.8.

[63] See Section 4.2 in this chapter and Bessone (2011) 45–66.

[64] Bessone (2011) 58–74.

[65] Cf. also the simile comparing Theseus and Mars, with Bessone (2011) 187–8. In her response to Coffee (2009)
222–4, Bessone points out that Theseus is a version of Mars, yet he is deprived of the most disturbing aspects
present in Statius' other descriptions of the god.

improve earlier versions of the correspondence between Jovian and imperial power. This refashioning of Jovian power allows Statius to recuperate the comparison with Jupiter that he found in earlier Roman epic. The concept of the emperor's Jovian power emerging from civil war, already exploited by Octavian and Nero, can now be applied to Domitian without implying that Domitian will be a second Nero or that he will repeat the cruelty of Octavian's civil war exploits.

It is time to conclude. The beginning and end of the *Thebaid* match one another. The emergence of Domitian as new Jupiter after civil war in the beginning is complemented by Theseus' Jovian attributes and his resolution of the conflict in the end. Imperial power appears as the one restraint keeping in check a world always on the verge of returning to chaos. This power, it seems, is far from perfect and cannot dispense with fear. The view is hardly optimistic. To weigh the power of Domitian against the monstrosity of the recent civil conflict is an effective, if drastic, political doctrine. It entails a tragic alternative between the chaos of civil war and a hypertrophic, frightening, and fragile monarchical power. There is no third option: The nobles are unable to share power, and the people should not be trusted. To an extent, this is a position with which we are familiar from other imperial writers such as Seneca and Tacitus.[66]

The idea of mercy as the key attribute of the sovereign has an important precedent in Seneca's *De Clementia*, but Statius' sovereign is more problematic than Seneca's. In Statius' view, a completely benign version of power is not possible and not effective; power cannot renounce its dark aspects even when it pursues benign ends.[67] This is a disillusioned and somewhat pessimistic picture that is rooted in the experience of civil war and in Statius' own pessimistic view of human nature.[68] The influence of Virgil's tragic vision on this complex view of power is evident.[69] Statius does not dismiss the position advanced by Lucan at the beginning of the *Bellum Ciuile*, according to which imperial power comes to rid the world of strife and chaos. This position is restated at the *Thebaid*'s beginning and reinforced throughout the poem. But the *Thebaid*'s end differs from the Golden Age vision projected by Lucan's praise of Nero and by Neronian panegyrists. Statius' king brings in a much more limited and disillusioned solution, one that surpasses naïve Golden Age visions and sets the poem's finale within a tragic framework.

---

[66] See Sen. *Cl.* 1.1.1, cited before in this section, and nn. 53 and 54 in this section.

[67] On this aspect of the *Thebaid*'s political view see also Chapter 1, Section 1.8; Chapter 5, Section 5.4; Chapter 6, Section 6.7.

[68] See Introduction, Section I.8.

[69] See Chapter 5, Section 5.4; Chapter 6, Section 6.7.

One last point. The *Thebaid*'s beginning expresses the hope that Domitian will be the Theseus figure depicted by Statius, that he will secure peace by blocking the empire's regression to civil war. But Statius' placement of his text in a tradition of imperial praise that, stemming from Octavian/Augustus, had found its most emphatic application in recent times to Nero adds an element of warning to the comparison. Although Domitian's success is not ruled out, it becomes clear how easy it would be for him to fail after an auspicious beginning, just like Nero, and how dramatic such a failure would be. In other words, the idea of overcoming one's predecessors sets very high standards for the emperor: It requires him to be equal to the expectations frustrated by Nero and earlier emperors and equal to the ideal portrait of the sovereign formulated by Neronian writers at the same time as it equips the emperor with an eloquent portrayal of what failure in this endeavor would entail.

4.4 COMPLEX CHRONOLOGIES: BEING FIRST, BEING LAST

In the last section of this chapter (4.6), I will return to Statius' interaction with the anti-imperial elements in Lucan's text, and I will show that the perspective encountered in *Siluae* 2.7 offers important indications as to the strategies adopted by Statius to co-opt Lucan's vision to his own political project. But before I do that, I would like to consider other ways in which Lucan's text participates in Statius' political vision. In the next two sections, I explore intertextuality with Lucan as a source for historical allusion. In Section 4.4, I look at Statius' intertextual positioning of his own poem within Roman traditions about civil war. My point is to show that Statius adopts two seemingly opposing perspectives, presenting the *Thebaid* as both the archetype of civil war poetry and the latest installment in a long series of poems and wars. This second perspective facilitates allusions to the last civil war of Rome, the civil conflict of 69 CE. In the following Section (4.5), I look more closely at how Statius uses intertextuality, and especially interaction with Lucan, to allude to Roman narratives of civil war and to direct readers' attention to the last civil war of Rome (69 CE) as the most suitable parallel for Statius' mythical narrative.

References to earlier literature, and especially to Lucan and Ovid, are sometimes used to align the war of Eteocles and Polynices with the last in a series of Roman civil conflicts. In book 1, the anonymous Theban citizen investigating the causes of civil war mentions the *omen* of the fratricidal war of the Spartoi. As has been noted, he is unfolding in a Theban context the same idea applied by Horace and Lucan to the Romulus and Remus episode in connection with Roman civil wars: Both cities were marked by fratricidal war at the time of their foundation, and both saw civil war resurface again throughout the years.[70] It follows that, if the Spartoi are the Theban equivalent of Romulus and Remus, then the war between Eteocles and Polynices parallels Roman historical civil conflicts.[71]

The same connection between the war of Eteocles and Polynices and Roman civil wars is re-created in two sections centering on the past of Thebes. The first is the speech by Aletes in book 3. This speech adapts the long excursus by the anonymous citizen in Lucan's *Bellum Ciuile* 2. The latter recounts previous instances of civil war and compares them with the war at hand.[72] In Statius, earlier civil war episodes are replaced with a list of incidents from the history of Thebes. The list builds implicitly on Ovid's recasting of Theban history as the history of Rome in the *Metamorphoses*.[73] It follows that the conflict between Eteocles and Polynices should be aligned with Roman civil conflicts of historical times. Although Lucan concentrates on one phase of Roman civil conflict, the war between Sulla and Marius (the most suitable precedent among events predating the fight between Caesar and Pompey), Statius describes a whole series of incidents of divine displeasure. Statius' interaction with Lucan sets Aletes' speech in a Roman context and connects it with Roman civil wars. At the same time, Aletes presents the war between the Theban brothers as the last of a series of dramatic events encompassing the city, thus inviting Roman readers to align it with the latest episodes in their city's repeated civil wars. The same sequence of incidents from Thebes' history is found in the necromancy scene in book 4. The *Thebaid*'s necromancy (4.406–645), building on Ovidian material, again aligns the history of Thebes with that of Rome.[74]

Elsewhere the idea that the Theban war parallels recent Roman wars is conveyed in a subtler way, as in Statius' portrait of the fields of Mars. This is the portion of land that saw the fight of the Spartoi, and here Manto and Tiresias perform their necromancy.[75] In his description of this location, Statius adapts Virgil's and Lucan's topos of the farmer uncovering the bones of past civil conflicts after many years, which both Lucan and Virgil evoke in the context of the sequence of civil wars fought in Greece in the 40s (Pharsalus and Philippi).[76] Statius' evocation of this historical context gives the impression that the civil wars of the late Republic are equivalent to the war of the

---

[70] *Theb.* 1.180–5; Hor. *Epod.* 7.13–20; Luc. 1.93–5; Bessone (2011) 59–60; Micozzi (1999) 359–61; Hardie (1990) 230.

[71] The anonymous citizen's speech is also influenced by the speech by the anonymous citizens of Ariminum in Lucan, which likewise recalls past incidents in the history of the city: Luc. 2.248–57.

[72] Luc. 2.67–233. More on this passage and Statius in Section 4.6. For the relevance of another passage in Lucan for this section of the *Thebaid* see Roche (2015) 400–1.

[73] See Introduction, Section I.9.

[74] I discuss this important passage in more detail in Chapter 1, Section 1.7.

[75] *Theb.* 4.434–42, quoted in Section 4.7.

[76] Verg. *G.* 1.489–97; Luc. 7.851–68.

Spartoi and that the war of Eteocles and Polynices comes to renew past civil wars. The reader is invited to look at the latest civil war of Rome as a suitable parallel for the Theban war but also to consider it as a repetition of paradigmatic Roman conflicts immortalized by Virgil and Lucan. As we will see, the conflict of 69 CE resembled in a peculiar way the sequence of the wars culminating in the battles of Pharsalus and Philippi and was regarded as a "repetition" of those conflicts.[77]

In a sense, the "belatedness" of the Theban conflict narrated by Statius goes hand in hand with Statius' own position in Rome's literary history: He is the last in a series of poets dealing with Thebes and with civil war. But this "last" poet also seeks to establish himself as the "first." The strategy previously observed, in which the war of the Theban brothers is intertextually associated with the latest civil war of Rome, coexists, without being reconciled, with an opposite tendency that seeks to establish Eteocles and Polynices as the first, paradigmatic instance in a global history of civil war. There is a remarkable detail in Statius' description of Eteocles' and Polynices' enmity in book 1:

> et nondum crasso laquearia fulua metallo,
> montibus aut alte Grais effulta nitebant
> atria, congestos satis explicitura clientes;
> non impacatis regum aduigilantia somnis
> pila, nec alterna ferri statione gementes
> excubiae, nec cura mero committere gemmas
> atque aurum uiolare cibis: sed nuda potestas
> armauit fratres, pugna est de paupere regno.
> *Theb.* 1.144–51

And not yet did thick paneled ceilings of gold shine or lofty halls propped upon Greek marble, with space to spread assembled clients. There were no spears watching over the restless slumbers of monarchs nor sentinels groaning in alternating watch of iron, nor did people care to adorn cups with jewels and defile gold with food: naked power armed the brothers, their fight is for a poor kingdom.

Thebes is surprisingly presented as a poor kingdom. Acquisition of its riches is not a factor in the strife of the brothers—a detail that conflicts with traditional views.[78]

---

[77] See Section 4.7.

[78] Venini (1971) 72–3. Thebes' riches are an important factor in the fight of Eteocles and Polynices in earlier versions of the saga: cf. e.g. E. *Ph.* 80, 601; *Supp.* 14–15, 153–4; A. *Th.* 711, 727–30, 876–7, 902–8; Sen. *Phoen.* 54; cf. also Sen. *Her. F.* 332.

The target of Statius' polemic is the traditional Roman idea that civil strife is—among other things—the result of the corruption of morals engendered by wealth and love of riches.[79] Here Statius develops, and makes more radical, a point made by Lucan.[80] The latter evokes the strife of Romulus and Remus over a small *asylum* as proof that even possession of something small and insignificant warrants civil strife. There is no need for world power to be at stake in order for civil strife to arise:

> nec gentibus ullis
> credite nec longe fatorum exempla petantur:
> fraterno primi maduerunt sanguine muri.
> nec pretium tanti tellus pontusque furoris
> tunc erat: exiguum dominos commisit asylum.
> Luc 1.93–7

Search not the history of foreign nations for proof, nor look far for an instance of Fate's decree: the rising walls of Rome were wetted with a brother's blood. Nor was such madness rewarded then by lordship over land and sea: the narrow bounds of the Asylum pitted its owners one against the other.

Statius' *pugna de paupere regno* [fight for a poor kingdom] is a direct descendant of Romulus' and Remus' fight over a small *asylum* in Lucan.[81] The archetypical civil conflict in the Roman imagination is here transferred to the Theban brothers. Other echoes of Romulus and Remus can be perceived in Statius' account of the Theban brothers. Statius' use of the word *consors* [partner] to describe Polynices (*Theb.* 1.188) reminds us of Lucan's *potestas . . . impatiens consortis* [power that tolerates no partner, Luc. 1.92–3], but *consors regni* [partner of kingdom] is also often said of Remus.[82] The victorious contestant will get to plough the fields of Thebes (*Theb.* 1.152–4), a detail that evokes the foundational activities of Cadmus and presents Eteocles and Polynices as city founders.

Statius' association of Eteocles and Polynices with Romulus and Remus adds context to the point he goes on to make, also inherited from Lucan:

> quo tenditis iras,
> a, miseri? quid si peteretur crimine tanto

---

[79] Such a view is found, for example, in Virgil's *Georgics*; Statius may explicitly signal his correction of Virgil by alluding to a line from the relevant passage in the *Georgics* (cf. *Theb.* 1.449 and *G.* 2.506); Narducci (2002) 459.

[80] Venini (1971) 73–4.

[81] Narducci (2002) 460–1.

[82] Cf. e.g. Tib. 2.5.24.

limes uterque poli, quem Sol emissus Eoo
cardine, quem porta uergens prospectat Hibera,
quasque procul terras obliquo sidere tangit
auius aut Borea gelidas madidiue tepentes
igne Noti? quid si Phrygiae Tyriaeque sub unum
conuectentur opes? loca dira arcesque nefandae
suffecere odio, furiisque inmanibus emptum
Oedipodae sedisse loco.
Theb. 1.155–64

Alas you wretches, whereto do you lead your wrath? What if by such crime
you sought an empire limited by the two boundaries of heaven, that to which
the Sun looks when he is sent forth from the eastern gate and that to which
he gazes as he sinks from his Iberian gate, and those remote lands which he
touches from afar with slanting ray, the lands frozen by the North Wind or
warmed by the heat of the moist South Wind? What if the riches of Phrygia
and Tyre were amassed together in one place? A place of terror, a citadel ac-
cursed, sufficed your hate, monstrous madness did it cost to sit where Oedipus
had sat.

Lucan, too, had implicitly contrasted Romulus' and Remus' fight with the larger,
world-scale conflict of Pompey and Caesar (Luc. 1.96–7). Statius' speculation on a
kingdom encompassing the extreme East and West looks ahead to Imperial Rome,
the kingdom that will one day inherit the wealth of Troy (*Phrygiae opes* [the riches
of Phrygia]) and conquer the East but also appropriate Tyrian riches [*Tyriae opes*]
by way of its conquest of Tyrian Carthage. Statius' point modifies Lucan in a pro-
gressive sense: If *furor* accompanied the fight for a poor kingdom (Thebes), imagine
what the madness will be when the Roman Empire is at stake. Polynices and Eteocles
have replaced Romulus and Remus as the initial version of a conflict that is destined
to be replicated on a huge scale with the creation of the Roman Empire.

The placement of Eteocles and Polynices at the beginning of a history whose
continuation is Rome adds a global perspective to the *Thebaid*. For Statius there is
a larger story that transcends the geographic boundaries of Romanness. A Greek
myth of the birth of (Roman) civil war at the beginning of the poem accompanies
a Greek myth of the birth of Roman *clementia* at its end. Lucan saw the Theban
model as distant and somewhat weak. Statius responds by collapsing the boundaries
between Greece and Rome, myth and history: Eteocles and Polynices are the best
parallel for Roman civil wars, the archetype that predates even Romulus and Remus.
By addressing the archetype of all civil wars, Statius places himself above Lucan

and becomes the "archetypical" poet. The two tendencies just observed are contradictory, but Statius cares little for coherence here. He emphasizes the *Thebaid*'s belatedness when he wants to evoke the last civil war of Rome (the 69 CE civil conflict): The last poem is also the poem on the last civil war. He presents the Eteocles and Polynices story as the archetype of civil war to amplify its exemplary power and establish himself as the first poet, through his thorough tackling of the very beginning of a powerful tradition.

4.5 FROM AENEAS TO VITELLIUS

The first book of the *Thebaid* begins with an incredibly dense series of allusions to Lucan's first book, often combined with Virgilian intertexts. Tisiphone's intervention at the behest of Oedipus recalls Allecto's actions at the instigation of Juno in Virgil's *Aeneid*.[83] Yet the outbreak of fraternal strife that is the effect of her intervention recalls Lucan's survey of the causes of Caesar and Pompey's war. Take these lines in Statius:

> . . . gentilisque animos subiit furor aegraque laetis
> inuidia atque parens odii metus, inde regendi
> saeuus amor, ruptaeque uices iurisque secundi
> ambitus impatiens, et summo dulcius unum
> stare loco, sociisque comes discordia regnis.
> *Theb.* 1.126–30

> . . . the family madness invaded their minds, envy sick at another's good fortune and fear that generates hate, thence fierce love of rule, the alternation of power rejected, ambition intolerant of second place, the pleasure of standing alone at the top, and strife, the companion of shared sovereignty.

These lines are modeled on two passages in Lucan:[84]

> te iam series ususque laborum
> erigit inpatiensque loci fortuna secundi;
> nec quemquam iam ferre potest Caesarue priorem

---

[83] Cf. *Theb.* 1.56–130 and *A.* 7.323–562. On the influence of *Aeneid* 7 on *Thebaid* 1: Ganiban (2007) 30–3; on the Fury's intervention especially 31–3: Schetter (1960) 3–4; Vessey (1973) 75; Venini (1971) 70–1; Hardie (1993) 62–3; Hershkowitz (1998) 54, 247–8, and 261–2.

[84] See Venini (1971) 71–2, 81; Narducci (2002) 460–1; Roche (2015) 400–1. Cf. also *Theb.* 1.168.

Pompeiusue parem.

Luc. 1.123–6

Caesar, you are roused by your long chain
of tasks, experience of toil and your fortune not enduring second place;
Caesar cannot now bear anyone ahead
nor Pompey any equal.

nulla fides regni sociis, omnisque potestas
inpatiens consortis erit.

Luc. 1.92–3

There will be no loyalty between associates in tyranny
and no power will tolerate a partner.

A similar case is offered by the simile of Polynices and Eteocles as two bulls unable
to carry the yoke together, which follows immediately after the passage previously
discussed (*Theb.* 1.131–8). The content of the simile is Statius' creation, yet it stems
from a combination of suggestions from Virgil and Lucan. Two bulls fighting for a
female are described as kings at war in the *Georgics*; the *Aeneid* follows up with the
simile comparing Turnus and Aeneas to two bulls fighting for possession of the flock
and a female, and Lucan adapts the simile to Caesar and Pompey.[85] Statius has a first
attempt at the simile here, a variation on the topic attached to Adrastus, a reprise in
book 4, a culmination at the time of Eteocles' and Polynices' duel and a sequel in
the image of Theseus the bull slayer.[86] As far as the presence of Lucan is concerned,
a system of correspondences can be made out: Eteocles is associated with Caesar,
whereas traits of Pompey are given to Polynices and other characters on the Argive
side.[87] Echoes of the battle of Pharsalus are apparent at various point in the narrative,
especially leading up to the final fight of book 11.[88]

Another example of Statius' interlocking of Virgilian and Lucanian intertexts is
provided by the description of Adrastus in book 1:

---

[85] Verg. *G.* 3.219–28; *A.* 12.103–6, 12.715–22; Luc. 2.601–7; on this simile as a model of Statius see Ahl (1986)
2871–2.

[86] *Theb.* 1.131–8, 2.323–32, 4.69–73, 4.397–404, 11.251–6, 12.601–5; Micozzi (1999) 349; Narducci (2002) 464–5.
These are just some of the many bull similes in the *Thebaid*: see Parkes (2012) 212, with further references.

[87] On Caesar and Eteocles: Venini (1971) 55–67, esp. 65–7; Narducci (1979) 98; Roche (2015) 397; on Polynices
and Pompey: Micozzi (1999) 350–2. Roche (2015) is most helpful in documenting how Statius attenuates
this general system of correspondences by attributing traits of Pompey and Caesar to other characters and by
attaching traits of both Pompey and Caesar to Eteocles (see especially 396–7).

[88] See Micozzi (1999) 353–7 on the topic of *retardatio* [delaying], connecting Lucan's narrative of Pharsalus and
the *Thebaid*'s war. For Echoes of Lucan's narrative of Pharsalus in book 11 of the *Thebaid* see Venini (1971) 45–54.

rex ibi, tranquillae medio de limite uitae
in senium uergens, populos Adrastus habebat,
diues auis et utroque Iouem de sanguine ducens.
Theb. 1.390–2

There King Adrastus governed his people in tranquility, verging from life's
midway into old age. He was rich in ancestors, related by blood to Jupiter on
either side.

Readers will have recognized an allusion to Virgil's Latinus (*A.* 7.45–53); Adrastus,
like Latinus, is an aged king with unmarried children visited by a stranger who will
bring war to his country. As for Latinus, there is an impending prophecy involving
Adrastus' daughters, Argia and Deipyle. But there is another important character
behind Statius' Adrastus, Lucan's Pompey. Adrastus' introduction in the *Thebaid* is
modeled on Lucan's description of Pompey at *Bellum Ciuile* 1.129–31.[89] The merging
of Latinus and Pompey adapts and transforms a suggestion by Virgil. Virgil had al-
ready brought Latinus and Aeneas into connection with Caesar and Pompey. Juno's
famous words *socer atque gener coeant* [let father-in-law and son-in-law be joined]
refer to Latinus and Aeneas, but an allusion to the war of Caesar and Pompey, father-
in-law and son-in-law, respectively, is easily perceived.[90]

I could list many more instances of combined allusion to Lucan and Virgil (and
I provide some other examples in the rest of this chapter). It is important to reflect
on the effects of these intertextual links on the reader of Statius' poem. The first
effect of this conflation of the *Aeneid* and the *Bellum Ciuile* is to link the *Thebaid*'s
conflict with the first "civil war" in Rome's history (Latins and Trojans), but also
with one of the most important wars of the Republic, that of Caesar and Pompey.
But the range of historical allusion extends even further if we consider an aspect
that is usually overlooked by scholars. The war of Vitellius and Otho was generally
perceived as a replay of the war between Pompey and Caesar.

The German uprising of Vitellius began with a symbolic gesture: As he prepared
his invasion of Italy, he was awarded the sword of Caesar by his troops.[91] The dy-
namics of the two civil conflicts were similar, with an opponent located in Rome
(Otho and Pompey) facing an opponent who descended to invade Italy from

---

[89] Micozzi (1999) 346.
[90] *A.* 7.317; Horsfall (2000) 220; Caesar and Pompey are called *socer* and *gener* at *A.* 6.830–1. Virgil's allusion to
Pompey and Caesar connects Pompey with Aeneas (both are son-in-laws). By aligning Adrastus with Latinus
and Pompey, Statius transforms Virgil's hint, implicitly linking Pompey with the older member (Latinus) in
Virgil's pair.
[91] Suet. *Vit.* 8.1.

the North (Caesar and Vitellius). In addition, there was the infamous episode of Vitellius touring the field of battle covered with unburied bodies and rotting corpses after the victory of Cremona I, replicating Caesar's behavior after Pharsalus.[92] The other major factor equating the conflict of 69 CE to the war of Caesar and Pompey was the sequence of two battles fought in the same place: Pharsalus was followed by Philippi, which Romans tend to describe as being fought in the same region.[93] The decisive battle fought by Vitellius and Otho at Cremona was followed by a second engagement in the same place between the Flavians and Vitellius. The parallel does not escape Tacitus, who evokes the similarity of Caesar and Pompey to Otho and Vitellius in several passages and styles Cremona II as a repetition of Cremona I so that he can match the sequence of Pharsalus and Philippi, the two battles so powerfully impressed on the imagination of Romans.[94] Suetonius, on the other hand, is alert to the irony of a self-styled Caesar (Vitellius) who ends up defeated by a Gaul (Antonius Primus).[95] The parallelism between the two wars also contributed to the alignment of Vespasian with Augustus—the contestant who eventually emerged out of the sequence of wars initiated by the fight between Caesar and Pompey—and may have been encouraged by pro-Flavian sources.[96]

If we factor these elements and perceptions into our reading of the *Thebaid*, we realize the full potential of Statius' description of Adrastus as both a new Pompey and a new Latinus. In two lines, Statius can flash in front of the Roman reader the whole spectrum of Roman civil wars from Aeneas to Vitellius. This telescopic aspect is typical of Statius' artistry in the *Thebaid*, in which historical allusions are placed one behind the other so that the reader is always transported further back in time. Lucan in turn becomes a privileged tool for directing the reader's attention to the civil war of 69 CE.

This idea of multiple historical allusions, joining different seasons of Roman civil war up until the 69 CE conflict, provides a fruitful framework for reading Statius' modification of Lucan's passages in other parts of the poem. In particular, in the *Thebaid* Lucan's text is engaged in such a way as to evoke the latest of Rome's civil conflicts, a process that builds on perceptions of the civil war of 69 CE as a repetition

---

[92] Caesar: Luc. 7.789–99; Suet. *Jul.* 30.4. Vitellius: Tac. *Hist.* 2.70; D.C. 64.1.3. The return to the battlefield after the fight is a topos. Several instances, including passages from Statius, are discussed by Pagan (2000). The scenes involving Caesar and Vitellius have in common the sadistic enjoyment of the spectacle, which is not present in other occurrences of this topos. On Vitellius' tour of the battlefields after Cremona I see Morgan (1992). Echoes of Luc. 7.789–99 in the *Thebaid* are discussed later in this section.

[93] Cf. Verg. *G.* 1.489–97; Luc. 1.673–94, 7.847–54.

[94] Tac. *Hist.* 1.50, 2.38; Joseph (2012) 57–62 and 115–20 on Tacitus' highlighting of repetition in his accounts of Cremona I (*Hist.* 2.39–45) and II (*Hist.* 3.25–34).

[95] Suet. *Vit.* 9.1, 18.1.

[96] On Vespasian as new Augustus see Levick (1999) 73.

of Caesar's and Pompey's fight. The anonymous citizen's speech in book 1 (*Theb.* 1.164–96) is a good starting point. Among other things, this passage offers a sense of the cross-fertilization of epic and historiography. Statius' speech, a complaint about the present state of affairs, has models both in epic and historiography. Appian quotes the words of anonymous citizens recalling the conflict of Marius and Sulla in his account of the war of Caesar and Pompey.[97] Lucan may be drawing from the same historiographical source in book 2 of the *Bellum Ciuile*, in which an anonymous old man recalls the wars of Marius and Sulla and proclaims that the present conflict is worse, for the winner will not be content with revenge, as Sulla was, but will end the Republic. The topos, perhaps under the influence of Lucan, resurfaces in historiographical accounts of the 69 CE civil war. In Plutarch's *Life of Otho*, anonymous soldiers are imagined complaining about the present state of affairs. They state that the current civil war is worse than the previous ones, because this time the impiety of fighting one's fellow countrymen is to be endured to grant power to two impious individuals.[98] A similar passage is found in Tacitus: Here too the 69 CE civil war pejoratively replicates former conflicts, especially the sequence of Pharsalus and Philippi. Like Plutarch, Tacitus states that the contenders in this war are worse than those who fought for power before, and he especially underscores that neither is preferable. Tacitus also powerfully captures the condition of the city gripped by fear and contended between two tyrants, which is not emphasized in any of his precedents.[99] This set of passages testifies to a process of cross-fertilization between epic and historiography where it is difficult to determine who comes first and who borrows from whom.[100]

The speech by the anonymous citizen in *Thebaid* 1 belongs in this sequence of mutually influencing texts, and it implicitly links the war of the Theban brothers with the war between Caesar and Pompey by way of visible allusions to Lucan and the use of Roman political vocabulary.[101] The anonymous citizen can say that Eteocles will never again be a *privatus* [private citizen], which is what Caesar sees as impossible for Pompey in the *Bellum Ciuile*.[102] Statius' passage, however, combines these allusions to Lucan with emphasis on the fear of the city contended by two tyrants and the notion that neither is really preferable which we observed in accounts of 69 CE. It also clearly places the scene in an imperial context. Note in particular the

---

[97] App. *BC* 2.36; Luc. 2.67–233; Narducci (2002) 118.

[98] Plu. *Oth.* 9.4.

[99] Tac. *Hist.* 1.50. Cf. also Tac. *Hist.* 2.38 for a comparison of current and past civil wars of Rome.

[100] This process cannot be studied extensively here. On Statius and historiographical texts important indications now in Ash (2015). On the influence of Virgil and Lucan on Tacitus' *Histories* see Joseph (2012).

[101] For the influence of another passage in Lucan (Luc. 1.248–57) on *Theb.* 1.173–96 see Roche (2015) 400–1.

[102] Luc. 1.324; other relevant passages in Lucan: 4.188, 5.366, 5.668, 9.193–4; see Roche (2015) 401.

initial description of the crowd who *a principe ... dissidet* [is at odds with the prin-
ceps, *Theb.* 1.169–70] a phrase that would have invited Roman readers to connect it
to civil war episodes in an imperial context.[103] The closest historical parallel would
be the situation in Rome under Otho, described by Tacitus in the aforementioned
passage. Lucan's material is put into dialogue with historiographical accounts and is
recast in a way that invites comparisons with the 69 CE civil war.

A similar strategy seems to govern another string of Lucanian allusions in book
4. In this book, Statius compresses three sections of Lucan's first book: the passage
on false fears (Luc. 1.469–89), the section detailing the portents or *omina* (1.522–83),
and its conclusion, the prophecy of the frenzied *matrona* (1.673–95).[104] The motif of
terror provoked by false fears in the city has its counterpart in Statius: False sightings
of Argive cavalry on the Asopus evoke false accounts about Caesar's cavalry on the
Mevania.[105] Statius' prodigy section (4.374–7) likewise follows Lucan's passage in
detail, with several literary echoes. Note, for example, the mention of sweating Lares
(4.374), picking up the same phrase in Lucan (1.557), and the new monstrous off-
spring (Luc. 1.562 and *Theb.* 4.375).[106]

The close correspondence in the sequences of prodigies is a further link with
Roman civil wars and prepares for the insert on the frenzied Bacchant (*Theb.* 4.377–
405). The model for this passage is the analogous prophecy by a frenzied matron at
the end of *Bellum Ciuile* 1 (Luc. 1.673–95). Statius reverses the relationship of simile
and narrative: Lucan compared his *matrona*, inspired by Apollo, to a Bacchant;
Statius' prophetess is a Bacchant proper, coming down from the *uertice Ogygio* just
as the Bacchant in Lucan's simile comes from the top of Pindus under the influence
of Ogygian Bacchus.[107] The last picture in Statius' prophetic vision entails the fight
of two bulls, which replaces Lucan's vision of the different geographical locations
of war. Modeled on Virgil's simile of Aeneas and Turnus, it builds on the earlier
simile of Eteocles and Polynices as the two bulls who cannot share in the yoke.[108]

---

[103] On the Roman relevance of this phrase see Ahl (1986) 2832–3, (2015) 255. Cf. also Eteocles' own description
of the condition of *patres* and *plebs* when the person in power changes (*Theb.* 2.442–5).

[104] Narducci (1974) 106–7, 203–4; Micozzi (2004) 138–40; Parkes (2012) xxxii; Roche (2015) 402.

[105] Luc. 1.469–86 and *Theb.* 4.369–73. Cf. the collocation *fama pauores* [rumor ... fears, *Theb.* 4.369], alluding
to Lucan's *fama timores* [rumor ... fears, 1.469]; Parkes (2012) 203; Micozzi (2004) 138–40; Narducci (1974)
106–7; Roche (2015) 402.

[106] Parkes (2012) 203–4; Roche (2015) 402; Narducci (2002) 463.

[107] Once again, returning to the original context, Statius seeks to present the *Thebaid* as a prequel to Lucan.
Cf. Section 4.6. On this passage and Statius see Narducci (1974) 106–7, (2002) 463–4; Parkes (2012) 204–
5 (with further references to sections of her commentary); Roche (2015) 402; Ganiban (2007) 62–5; on
Lucan's frenzied matron see Roche (2009) 376–7.

[108] On the literary models of the simile: Parkes (2012) 211–12; cf. especially *A.* 12.715–24. Eteocles and Polynices
as the two bulls unable to share the yoke: *Theb.* 1.131–8.

In Lucan, both Pompey and Caesar's death are foreseen by the frenzied *matrona*; similarly, in Statius, both bulls will die. But there is a twist that is in neither Lucan nor Virgil: The two bulls will relinquish the power to a third contestant. Who is this third bull? Book 12 answers clearly: Theseus, a bull slayer, is also the third bull who comes to conquer (*Theb.* 12.601–5).[109] Statius' transformation of the Lucan scene resonates with traditions on the portents accompanying the last of Rome's civil wars. According to Suetonius, before the battle of Cremona I, two eagles were seen fighting in the sky; then a third arrived from the East and drove off the one who had survived, a prediction of the final victory of the Flavians after the war of Otho and Vitellius.[110]

In Lucan, the immediate response to the portents is the ritual and sacrifice performed by Arruns. In Statius, it is the necromancy of Tiresias and Manto, postponed after the scene of the frenzied Bacchant, which caps the *Thebaid*'s portents section. Statius' necromancy has several models; among these, Lucan's Erichto episode is particularly important.[111] The rites of Tiresias and Manto (*Theb.* 4.443–72), however, have nothing of the monstrous practices of Erichto (Luc. 6.667–94)— Tiresias' prayer to the underworld gods can actually be seen as a "canonic" version of Erichto's heretic prayer (*Theb.* 4.473–87; Luc. 6.695–718).[112] Yet Lucan's necromancy is repeatedly evoked, in a self-conscious manner, throughout Statius' scene. Tiresias and Manto do not fear the ghosts; Eteocles, on the contrary, like Pompey's son (Sextus), is terrified.[113] Tiresias is aware of his moral superiority to Erichto. He is upset that the spirits do not immediately respond to his prayer, whereas, he assumes, they would obey a Thessalian witch. I am no Erichto, he implies (he does not pick up bodies from the fields of battle like Lucan's character), but beware of despising me: I too can name that mysterious name mentioned by Erichto in Lucan, the name that no underworld god can resist (*Theb.* 4.500–18).[114]

At the end of his invocation in Statius, Tiresias requests that the ghosts come separated: on one side, the just from the Elysian Fields led by Hecate and Mercury, and on the other, the sinners from Erebus at the command of Tisiphone. The indication, which is not heeded in the rest of the narrative, follows Lucan's lead. In the Erichto episode, the dead soldier's underworld vision features two groups of souls, from the Elysian Fields and Tartarus, respectively. The enemies of Rome and

---

[109] The third bull cannot be Creon, who is never compared to a bull. *Contra* Parkes (2012) 213.
[110] Suet. *Vesp.* 5.7.
[111] *Theb.* 4.406–645. For the literary models of this passage see the commentary by Parkes (2012) 214–15 and her notes on lines 406–645 *passim*.
[112] For echoes of Lucan in Statius' prayer Parkes (2012) 234–5, 237.
[113] *Theb.* 4.488–93; Luc. 6.657–8; Parkes (2012) 238.
[114] Parkes (2012) 241ff. (see especially her notes on 4.504, 507–8, 510–11, 514, 515–16, 516, 517–18).

symbolic progenitors of Caesar (Catilina, Marius, Cethegus, the Gracchi, etc.) re-
joice, whereas the good Romans of the past are in despair (with the exception of
Brutus, who looks ahead at the tyrannicide by his descendant).[115] In the *Thebaid*
too we get ancestors from both sides of the conflict; what is missing is the moral dis-
tinction. The Theban part of the vision, recalling Seneca's *Oedipus*, is, for the most
part, a list of crimes.[116] The Argive souls are crying like the good Romans of Lucan
(4.587–92), for Thebes will be victorious. However, in Statius there is no sense of the
moral superiority of the Argives. The list of ancestors picked by Statius is not very
encouraging: Instead of the heroic Coroebus, we get guilty Proetus, grim Abas, the
famously treacherous Pelops (carrying the signs of his father's impiety), and the no-
less-cruel Oenomaus (only Phoroneus is *mitis*: perhaps a reflection of *mitis* Adrastus
in the company of the other impious Seven?). This is a pessimistic correction of the
Bellum Ciuile passage that resonates with perceptions of the 69 CE civil war as a
war between two wicked parties. In Lucan, the joy of criminals is connected to the
victory of Caesar, yet Caesar's punishment is also immediately mentioned, because
death and defeat await both. This in Lucan emerges clearly at 6.811: The leaders'
fight concerns their burial alone. In the *Thebaid* too there is little consolation for
Eteocles in the Theban victory. Immediately after the appearance of the Argive souls
a third group of ghosts appears for which there is no parallel in Lucan: the Thebans
whose death Eteocles has provoked, the 50 heroes slaughtered by Tydeus. The anger
of the Theban souls against Eteocles is the same as that of the ghosts of Pharsalus
at Caesar.[117] Once again, Lucan is adapted in such a way as to re-create the percep-
tion of a war between two wicked parties, thus matching widespread perceptions
of the war between Vitellius and Otho. The erasing of moral distinctions in the
underworld scene re-creates the same hopeless choice between wicked parties that
Tacitus and Plutarch work into their reconstruction of popular reactions to the war
of 69 CE.[118]

One last instance of Statius' interaction with Lucan deserves to be discussed in
this connection. The sense of accursed repetition is a traditional element of Roman
notions of civil war. It was made particularly strong in the case of the conflict be-
tween Caesar and Pompey and the wars that followed by the repetition of the key
battle in the same place (although Pharsalus and Philippi are actually quite distant
from one another). The key passage in this context is Virgil's *Georgics*, with its image
of the ploughing farmer digging up the bones of the two battles.[119] Lucan, whose

[115] Luc. 6.777–99.
[116] *Theb.* 4.553–78. Cf. Chapter 1, Section 1.7.
[117] *Theb.* 4.592–602; Luc. 7.771–6; Roche (2015) 397.
[118] See previous discussion in this section.
[119] Verg. *G.* 1.489–97.

poem, as we have it, does not include Philippi, alludes several times to the fateful repetition.[120] As we have seen, Statius adapts the topic to his description of the field of Thebes where the necromancy takes place.[121] More important, Statius evokes Lucan's description of Pharsalus on the eve of the actual conflict of Thebans and Argives:

> ... subeunt campo qui proximus urbi
> damnatus bellis patet expectatque furores.
> *Theb.* 7.238–9

> ... they enter a plain that spreads close to the city, doomed to battles and awaiting war's madness.

> hac ubi damnata fatis tellure locarunt
> castra duces ...
> Luc. 6.413–14

> When the leaders had pitched their camps in this land
> doomed by the Fates ...

The echoes of Pharsalus on both occasions emphasize the sense of repetition within Theban history: The fight of *Thebaid* 7–11 repeats the fratricidal war of the Spartoi. This sense of claustrophobic repetition is the same effect Lucan aims at through his insistence on the topos of the "two battles fought in the same place" (the Pharsalus/Philippi sequence). More directly, the description of the fields in *Thebaid* 7 has the effect of connecting the series of battles that Statius is about to narrate to Lucan's Pharsalus.[122] However, the *Thebaid*, unlike Lucan's poem, *does* go on to narrate the second battle fought in the same place, the "Philippi" after the "Pharsalus" of books 7–11. This is the fight between Theseus and Creon. Statius stops to describe the place where this last battle took place.

---

[120] Cf. the prophecy of the frenzied *matrona* previously quoted (Luc. 1.673–94) and the section that closes the narrative of the battle of Pharsalus (Luc. 7.847–54).

[121] See Section 4.4. In this passage (*Theb.* 4.434–42), Statius builds on a suggestion by Lucan concerning the fields of Pharsalus. Lucan described those fields by referring to the seeds of Mars, a likely allusion to Theban stories about the Spartoi (see Introduction, Section I.9). Statius, once again, writes the prequel to Lucan: In the *Thebaid* the fields where the Spartoi were sown echo the fields of Pharsalus; Micozzi (1999) 363–6. On Statius' attempt at establishing himself as "Lucan's predecessor" see Section 4.4.

[122] Micozzi (1999) 363; Venini (1971) 79. The equation is supported by other passages: for instance, Lucan's apostrophe at 7.552–6 is an important model for Statius' apostrophe at *Theb.* 11.574–9; see Bessone (2011) 86–8.

It is no surprise that his narrative is once again indebted to Lucan's momentous description of the aftermath of Pharsalus:

hunc saltem miseris ductor Thebanus honorem
largitur Danais, quod non super ipsa iacentum
corpora belligeras acies Martemque secundum
miscuit, aut lacera <u>ne</u> quid de strage nefandus
<u>perderet</u>, eligitur saeuos potura cruores
terra rudis.
Theb. 12.715–20

This respect at least the Theban chieftain paid to the hapless Danai, that he did not let the fighting battle lines clash in a second battle over the very bodies of the fallen; or, lest he lose something of the mangled corpses, the monster chooses untouched earth to drink cruel blood.

The passage echoes Caesar's sadistic observation of the unburied bodies of Pharsalus.[123] Neither Caesar nor Creon want to lose any part of the gruesome slaughter:

iuuat Emathiam non cernere terram
et lustrare oculis campos sub clade latentes.
fortunam superosque suos in sanguine cernit.
ac, <u>ne</u> laeta furens scelerum spectacula <u>perdat</u>,
inuidet igne rogi miseris, caeloque nocenti
ingerit Emathiam.
Luc. 7.794–9

He is delighted that he cannot see the Emathian land
and that his eyes scan fields hidden underneath the carnage.
In the blood he sees his fortune and his gods.
And not to lose the joyful sight of his wickedness, in a frenzy
he refuses those unfortunates the pyre's flame and forces on to guilty
heaven the sight of Emathia.

Caesar's sadistic tour of the fields of Pharsalus had been repeated by Vitellius; this was, together with the sequence of two battles fought in the same place, one of

---

[123] See n. 92 in this section.

the main points of connection between the civil war of 69 CE and the war between Pompey and Caesar. The detail is consistent with the echoes of Pharsalus in books 7 and 11. One might be tempted to see the final battle fought by Theseus and Creon as a new Philippi, reproducing the sequence initiated but not completed by Lucan and so powerfully impressed in the memory of Romans. But there is an important difference: The paradoxical effect of Creon's Caesar-like eagerness to revel in the sight of corpses is that the Thebaid's final battle is *not* fought in the same field as the earlier conflict (*Theb.* 12.719–20).

The idea of the two wars fought in the same place was regarded as a symbol of the endlessness and futility of civil war (thus, for instance, in Lucan). Statius' use of Lucan points in the opposite direction. This war is not a Philippi after the Pharsalus of books 7–11; it is not part of an endless repetition. The fight between Theseus and Creon is more like the death of Caesar, the tyrannicide announced by Lucan but not narrated in the text as we have it.[124] With this detail, Statius comes close to correcting the historical reality of Cremona II, a battle that was literally fought in the same area as the earlier engagement, and he does so to qualify his use of Lucan as a window onto the 69 CE civil war. Statius seems to be resisting the most pessimistic implications inherent in using the war between Caesar and Pompey as a foil for the 69 CE civil war. Although the two wars had followed a similar pattern, the victory of Cremona II and the subsequent fight in Rome did not equal Philippi. The Flavian triumph is not the last instance of an endless repetition, precisely as Theseus' battle is not inscribed in the series of Theban wars begun with the fight of the Spartoi.

4.6 TYRANNY AND CIVIL WAR

In the first part of this chapter, I considered the *Thebaid*'s valorization of the constructive aspects of Lucan's poem, namely the presentation of imperial rule as the only alternative to civil war articulated by the praise of Nero. I then examined Statius' use of Lucan as a means of historical allusion, with particular attention to the ways in which the *Thebaid* uses Lucan to evoke the most recent civil war of Rome. It is now time to consider a different facet of the *Thebaid*'s engagement with Lucan, which implies capitalizing on the antityrannical aspects of the *Bellum Ciuile*. As anticipated earlier, critical to this operation is a reading of Lucan as an anti-Neronian text, in which Lucan's Caesar stands as a foil for Nero in particular and not imperial

---

[124] On Creon's murder as tyrannicide see Bessone (2011) 155–6.

power in general. This is the reading of Lucan's epic projected by *Siluae* 2.7, in which Nero is aligned with Caesar and Lucan is a companion of Pompey in the underworld. As we see more clearly in this section, the emphasis on Nero as the object of Lucan's bias opens up the possibility of adapting the *Bellum Ciuile* to pro-imperial contexts. If Lucan's target was Nero's tyranny, then imperial power may not always be negative; a different emperor, perhaps someone who can be pictured as bringing back the spirit of the Republic, could be compatible with the poem's vision. Thus, Statius can appropriate both facets of Lucan's inconsistent vision of imperial rule, adapting both Lucan's constructive ideas from the proem and his fierce criticism of tyrannical rule from other parts of the *Bellum Ciuile*.

I would like to concentrate on the *Thebaid*'s engagement with a section of Lucan that was particularly amenable to this operation, one that attracted the interest of other Flavian authors. In book 2, Lucan presents a long excursus by an anonymous citizen recalling the experience of the wars of Marius and Sulla (2.64–233).[125] The anonymous citizen's narrative climaxes with the vivid portrait of Sulla's proscriptions—the gruesome images of bodies left to rot in the Forum—that the speaker remembers seeing in person: Lucan 2.169 *meque ipsum memini* [I remember that I myself . . .]. The conflict between Caesar and Pompey threatens to repeat and even to increase the horrors of that earlier conflict, and the reader is invited to explore similarities between the two sides then and at the time of the narrative. Lucan himself suggests connections between the protagonists of the two wars. In book 6, Lucan has Sulla lament the victory of Caesar, and yet the picture of Sulla glutting himself with the sight of the slaughter is recalled later in the portrait of Caesar watching the decomposing bodies on the fields of Pharsalus.[126]

The long speech by Aletes in book 3 of the *Thebaid* is a manifest rewriting of Lucan's excursus.[127] After Tydeus' slaughter of the 50 Theban warriors, the women and elderly of Thebes travel to the battlefield to retrieve the bodies of their loved ones, and here Aletes pronounces his speech. The whole episode is constellated by civil war allusions, mediated by the text of Lucan. Tydeus' *aristeia* is modeled on Scaeva's exploits in the *Bellum Ciuile*.[128] The insistent presence of the topic of civil

---

[125] On this passage see Fantham (1992a) 90–3; Conte (1968) 224–53.

[126] Sulla lamenting the victory of Caesar: Luc. 6.787; cf. also Luc. 1.324–35, where Caesar links Sulla and Pompey. Sulla's and Caesar's sadistic pleasures: cf. Luc. 2.207–9 and 7.786–94 (on this passage see also Section 4.5); Narducci (2002) 119. There are other correspondences between the two: The severed heads carried around on pikes during the Sullan proscriptions recall the head of Pompey displayed to Caesar. On Marius and Caesar see Narducci (2002) 119–20.

[127] *Theb.* 3.179–217; on this passage and Lucan see Micozzi (2004) 142–3.

[128] On Tydeus and Scaeva: Roche (2015) 396; McNelis (2007) 131–2; Williams (1978) 203; Vinchesi (1976) 50–1; Hardie (1993) 69 n. 23.

war through Lucan explains some odd aspects of Statius' narrative, such as the choice to compare Ide, the loving mother of two Theban twins, with a Thessalian witch, a clear allusion to Lucan's Erichto.[129]

This cluster of civil war allusions sets the stage for Aletes' account. Aletes is an old man, just like the speaker of Lucan. The anonymous figure of Lucan recalls previous instances of civil war. Statius' speaker also evokes past events, one of which, the story of the Spartoi, is a civil war of sorts (*Theb.* 3.180–3). Statius clearly signals the correspondence of one particular episode with the culmination of Lucan's account: At 3.195, Aletes repeats the pathetic exclamation of Lucan's anonymous citizen (*meque ipsum memini*). In Lucan, the collocation marks a vision of the horrors of the proscriptions. In particular, it introduces the furtive burial of the bodies of Sulla's victims. In Statius, the phrase marks the funeral of the children of Niobe; this is, in Aletes' view, the most appropriate parallel for the current events (*Theb.* 3.191–2).

There is, however, an important difference between the two accounts. In Lucan the past is evoked to complain about a present that resembles—and is even worse than—the past. But the *Thebaid*'s passage draws attention to an important difference between past and present tragedies. Earlier catastrophes were the consequence of divine wrath, says Aletes, but this time we suffer because of a tyrant:

> nunc regis iniqui
> ob noxam inmeritos patriae tot culmina ciues
> exuimus . . .
> *Theb.* 3.206–8

Now by the guilt of a wicked king we have lost so many innocent citizens, eminent in our fatherland . . .

This statement is slightly surprising: After all, the person immediately responsible for the slaughter is Tydeus. Yet the idea that Eteocles is the main culprit for the death of the 50 is repeated by Statius several times.[130] Aletes does not speak in general of the evil of civil war and does not mention Polynices' responsibility. In the *Thebaid*, a complaint about civil war (thus in Lucan) is recast as a lament over death under a tyrant. This begins to explain Statius' attention for the final picture of the account by Lucan, which deals with Sulla's proscriptions. That event provides the best parallel

---

[129] *Theb.* 3.140–6. Roche (2015) 398–9 emphasizes pathos as the main motivation for Statius' reprise of Lucan here.

[130] Maeon echoes this position, when, before killing himself, he publicly accuses Eteocles: *Theb.* 3.71–7; later in the necromancy, the ghosts of the 50 Thebans killed by Tydeus manifest their hatred of Eteocles: *Theb.* 4.592–8.

for what Aletes sees happening in book 3: a tyrant responsible for the death of many aristocratic youths. An important clue comes from the use of the word *libertas* that Statius applies to the two figures who accuse Eteocles during the episode. *Unde ea libertas?* [whence this freedom?] asks Statius of Aletes, echoing his own pathetic address to Maeon.[131] Suppression of *libertas*, as we previously saw, is the effect of imperial tyranny, and restoration of *libertas* goes hand in hand with the exercise of *clementia*.[132]

To fully make sense of this transformation, we need to recall our earlier discussion. Both Calpurnius and the anonymous author of the *Bucolica Einsidlensia* see senatorial executions as a continuation, under the empire, of the civil war of the late Republic, and both give particular attention to the proscriptions as an apt parallel.[133] They also make the point that Nero will keep the state safe both from civil war itself and from its imperial analog, the murder of aristocrats. An interesting parallel to this operation can be seen in *Octauia*. The anonymous author of this play shows Nero doing exactly the opposite of what Neronian panegyrists said of him. This Nero, while engaging in fierce repression of opponents, takes his example from the proscriptions (*Oct.* 503–13). Key to this passage in *Octauia* is a close engagement with the excursus in Lucan's book 2. As Rolando Ferri notes, the general atmosphere of this passage owes much to Lucan's account of the earlier proscriptions under Sulla.[134] Through his reprise of the Lucan account, the author of *Octauia* projects a reading of Lucan that sees Nero's repression encoded in Lucan's account of Sullan proscriptions.

This perspective explains why Statius is particularly interested in focusing attention on the proscriptions within his reprise of Lucan and provides the rationale for his strategy of recasting civil war allusions within criticism of tyranny. The story of the 50 is a civil war episode that at the same time is presented as an act of imperial repression, developing the analogy established by Neronian authors. Statius exploits the anti-imperial potential of the Lucan passage centering on the idea of proscriptions as a parallel for imperial repression. Significantly, Statius introduces Eteocles' resolution of sending the 50 heroes to ambush Tydeus with a reference to *tacito . . . ferro* [silent sword, *Theb.* 2.487]. The collocation echoes Calpurnius' description of the fake peace of Roman emperors prior to Nero, a peace that spread public discord through a silent sword [*publica diffudit tacito discordia ferro*].[135]

---

[131] *Theb.* 3.216, 3.102.
[132] See Section 4.2.
[133] See Section 4.1.
[134] Ferri (2003) 271.
[135] Calp. *Ecl.* 1.57.

Statius' engagement with Lucan's excursus associates Eteocles with a kind of imperial tyrant whom Neronian literature aligns with Nero's predecessors, but whom post-Neronian writers link with Nero.

Further details emerge as we examine Statius' emphasis on the story of Niobe as the closest parallel to the Sullan proscriptions in Lucan's text. Why is the episode of Niobe selected among the many myths of Thebes? For one, Niobe matches the incident mentioned by Lucan: The final scene of the funerals of the victims of Sulla can be coupled with the funeral of Niobe's children. Niobe also provides a good parallel for the figure of Ide. Ide is the mother of a pair of twins. The pathetic picture of her desperation and her moving speech are the centerpiece of Statius' scene of parental grief in the episode. Ide, like Niobe, boasted she could equal the gods thanks to her offspring.[136]

The choice of Niobe becomes clearer, however, if we consider uses of Niobe as a politicized myth in Rome. Niobe features prominently in Augustan culture as a mythical counterpart to Augustus' triumph over Antony and Cleopatra.[137] But the story had seen a revival under Nero, who made imitation of his ancestor Augustus a central tenet of his imperial ideology. Nero publicly sang the myth of Niobe at the Neronia of 65 CE, after his repression of the Piso conspiracy. The point in choosing Niobe must have been to suggest that Nero, who identified with Apollo, had struck down his impious enemies just as Apollo had punished Niobe. Nero publicly deposited garlands under the obelisk of the Circus Maximus after his repression of the Piso conspiracy in 65 CE, in thanksgiving to Apollo/Sun for helping him crush his opponents once again.[138] In the mind of educated Romans living under the Flavian emperors, the story of Niobe brought back memories of the cruel repression that had cost the lives of Lucan and Seneca, among many others.

Perhaps we can go even further. From the vantage point of Flavian observers, the story of Niobe had transitioned from being applied to a just king's (Augustus) victory against an impious foe (Cleopatra) to an impious king's (Nero) repression of his own pious enemies. This opposition between a wicked Niobe and a pious

---

[136] Ide: *Theb.* 3.133–68. Ide as a new Niobe: *Theb.* 3.154–6.

[137] Both in literary texts and iconography. Niobe appeared on the doors of the Temple of Palatine Apollo, dedicated in the aftermath of the triumph over Antony and Cleopatra: see Prop. 2.31.14; Zanker (1988) 87; Galinsky (1996) 219; on Cleopatra as Niobe in Ovid's account of Niobe (*Met.* 6.146–312) see Schmitzer (1990) 244–9.

[138] On the Neronia of 65 CE see Tac. *Ann.* 16.2–4; Suetonius' account of the event (*Nero* 21.2) is similar to the one in Tacitus, and Suetonius adds that the subject of Nero's singing within the citharodic contest was Niobe. However, Suetonius maintains that Nero begun the Neronia in 64 CE, then interrupted them and postponed them to the following year, an account rightly dismissed by the majority of modern interpreters, who think that the entire games took place in 65 CE. See Griffin (1984) 161, 280 n. 122; Champlin (2003a) 116, 309 n. 106, 317 n. 88. Offerings of thanksgiving to the Sun after the Piso conspiracy: Tac. *Ann.* 15.74.

Niobe might be reproduced in the text of Statius. In the past, an impious Niobe was punished by the gods for her foul speech. In the narrative at hand, a just Niobe (Ide) is suffering because of a human vengeful "Apollo" (Eteocles). Evidenced by the relationship between the Niobe of myth and the new Niobe, the contrast dramatically highlights Eteocles' wickedness. It also forms a counterpart to the historical sequence whereby Niobe/Cleopatra punished by Apollo/Augustus has been replaced by a tyrant (Nero) who claims to be Apollo and exterminates aristocratic houses.

In conclusion, Statius' reprise of the excursus in Lucan's second book details a different use to which the topic of civil war, and the text of Lucan, can be put. The *Thebaid* turns on Lucan to use civil war as a commentary on the experience of life under an evil emperor. Eteocles is a foil to the bad emperors of Rome, who repeated the horrors of civil war through their own repression of the aristocracy. In this context, the reader is free to supply the names of earlier emperors. The Neronian legibility of some of the mythological references in the passage (Niobe) might point in the direction of the position observed in *Siluae* 2.7, a reading aimed at detecting Nero under the tyrants of the *Bellum Ciuile*.

This anti-Neronian reading of Lucan's intertexts has some important implications. Pressing the anti-Neronian aspects of Lucan's text aligns the *Thebaid* with *Octauia*. Nero, who had a great start as an emperor, ended up repeating the massacres his panegyrists said he had rescued the world from. But pressing the anti-Neronian aspects of Lucan's poem also puts the *Thebaid* on the same footing as Nero's panegyrists. In Neronian texts discussed at the beginning of this chapter, former emperors are seen as having failed to fulfill their promises of clemency, but the new dynasty is pictured as being able to live up to them. A new start is made possible by the idea that the tyrannical aspects of imperial rule are tied to one specific individual, not to the institution per se. There is also an important ideological aspect that can be grasped by complementing the *Thebaid*'s account with Neronian panegyric and the *Siluae*. Although Eteocles is responsible for civil war and, figuratively, also for that imperial equivalent of civil war (repression of the aristocracy), the ideal sovereign rescues the state from civil war both by physical intervention in civil conflicts (like Theseus at the end of the poem) and through his own *clementia* in times of peace. In Neronian literature and in Domitian's panegyric, *clementia* goes hand in hand with *libertas*; in this light, Aletes' and Maeon's appeals to *libertas* are not necessarily in contrast with imperial power. The real question is whether Domitian will live up to these expectations and to this idealized portrait until the end of his kingdom. To this question, the *Thebaid* offers no final answer. The figure of Eteocles, with his Neronian allusions, shows how dramatic a failure in this area might be.

5

The unexpected savior

COROEBUS AND FLAVIAN IDEOLOGY

THIS CHAPTER FOCUSES on the Coroebus episode, the story recounted by
Adrastus to Tydeus and Polynices in book 1 of the *Thebaid*. Recent scholarship has
shed considerable light on this section of Statius' poem. Both Randall Ganiban
and Charles McNelis, for instance, have examined the episode's complex literary
texture, highlighting Statius' creative engagement with its literary models, namely
Callimachus, Virgil, Ovid, and Lucan.[1] My analysis builds on recent assessments of
the Coroebus story in an attempt to link Statius' formal gestures to the specific po-
litical and religious contexts of Domitian's Rome.

To explore the ideological background of this episode, I begin with a study of
religious attitudes connected to times of crisis in Rome, with specific attention to
civil war. I am particularly interested in highlighting the presence of a number of
religious elements and theological patterns that are typically associated with Roman
narratives of crisis and civil war. The idea that civil war is a punishment sent by the
gods and that involvement in civil war is in itself a crime, even if it brings about the
end of the conflict, is one of these elements. I also show that ideas of atonement
and purification typically accompany the return to normality after civil war, that
the topic of sacrificial substitution whereby an individual offers his life on behalf
of his fellow citizens surfaces frequently in connection with narratives of crisis, and

---

[1] Ganiban (2007) 9–23; McNelis (2007) 25–49.

that both notions are linked to the idea of civil war as a punishment by the gods. I then show that these elements are well represented in accounts of 69 CE. The civil conflict of 69 CE is seen as a punishment by the gods, and even after its resolution, the Flavian period is deeply troubled by religious anxiety, especially in light of the numerous natural catastrophes that plague the empire.

I then move on to look at the specific aspects of Statius' account of Linus and Coroebus by comparing it with its two most important models, Callimachus and Virgil. This analysis reveals that Statius emphasizes a few elements absent in his predecessors, namely the idea of atonement and purification and the notion of sacrificial substitution. It also appears that Statius builds on the possibility of regarding the royal house of Argos as a past version of the imperial house, an element that seems to underlie Callimachus' treatment. But Statius rereads Argive mythology through the lens of Virgil, and his post-Virgilian perspective adds a different nuance to his engagement with Argive myth. From Virgil he takes the idea of regarding Danaus as a symbol of civil war; he also relies on Virgil's play on the topography of Argos to characterize Adrastus' palace as the imperial palace of Rome and to link the past of Argos to the imperial past of Rome prior to the Flavian period.

Along the way, I stop to consider the *ekphrasis* of Adrastus' cup, featuring the myths of Ganymede and Perseus. This *ekphrasis*, I argue, sets the scene for the Coroebus excursus and allows us to appreciate Statius' innovations in that section of text. The *ekphrasis* also exemplifies, through a revealing use of imagery, Statius' complex, and to an extent pessimistic, view of imperial power and its limits. In conclusion, I try to show that Statius' selection of this mythical incident (the story of Linus and Coroebus) and his transformation of Callimachus and Virgil allow him to interact with the historical experience of civil war in Rome and its religious corollaries. I also show that the Greek material is translated by Statius into a Roman imperial context so that the poet can exploit the Coroebus episode as a mythical equivalent of a narrative, that of the "providential outsider," that was dear to both the Flavian house and members of the Roman elite under the empire.

5.1 RELIGION AND CIVIL WAR IN ROME

In Rome, as in many other ancient societies, religion and politics were inextricably linked. Successes and defeats in war depended primarily on the gods' favor. A defeat was an unmistakable sign of divine anger, which was typically traced back to some offense against the gods: negligence, the infringement of a divine law, or a general decline of morals. Because of this widespread religious attitude toward political events, a moment of crisis often resulted in an outbreak of religious hysteria, leading to public pursuit of the culprits of religious violations and inquiries into strategies for expiating the sin. A famous example is found in Livy's narrative of the catastrophe of Cannae. Livy recounts that the Roman defeat was followed by an outburst of religious terror. Two Vestal Virgins had been found guilty of acting unchastely that same year, and one was buried alive. The tension was not relieved until the Romans sent envoys to Delphi to enquire of the oracle "with what prayers and supplications they might placate the gods, and what would be the end of all their calamities." Extraordinary rituals were then performed, including the human sacrifice of a Gallic man and a Gallic woman and a Greek man and a Greek woman, who were buried alive in the Forum Boarium.[2]

This way of understanding the role of the gods with regard to political catastrophes is also visible in accounts of civil conflicts. Civil strife is perceived as a sign of divine displeasure and a punishment for religious violation or moral decline. This notion is often found in accounts of the civil wars of the late Republic.[3] The Romans have sinned against the gods, and the gods punish them by releasing civil war, which is characterized as a *poena* [punishment] or *ultio* [vengeance]. Accounts of civil war are typically introduced by lists of portents that manifest the gods' anger: *irae patuere deum* [the anger of the gods was revealed] is the sentence that opens one such section in Lucan.[4]

In poetry, the original sin that provokes the *poena* of civil war is often a mythical incident from the far past, like the sin of Laomedon, who defrauded Apollo and Neptune of their reward for building the walls of Troy, or Romulus' killing of Remus.[5] More often, however, the reason for the gods' anger is explicitly traced to the abandonment of religious piety. Thus, memorably, in Horace:

> delicta maiorum inmeritus lues,
> Romane, donec templa refeceris
> aedisque labentis deorum et
> foeda nigro simulacra fumo.
> dis te minorem quod geris, imperas.
> hinc omne principium, huc refer exitum:
> di multa neglecti dederunt
> Hesperiae mala luctuosae.
> *Carm.* 3.6.1–8

---

[2] Liv. 22.57.2–6.

[3] See e.g. Luc. 2.1–2 with Fantham's (1992a) 78–9; see also passages quoted in n. 4.

[4] Luc. 2.1–2. Lists of *prodigia* portending civil war in poetry and prose: Cic. *N.D.* 2.14; *Div.* 1.18.1–21.6; Verg. *G.* 1.464–88; Luc. 1.523–83 etc.; see Roche (2009) 318–19.

[5] Cf. Verg. *G.* 1.501–2; Hor. *Epod.* 7.17–20; *Carm.* 1.35.

Although innocent, Roman, you will pay for the crimes of your ancestors until you restore the temples and the collapsing shrines of the gods, and their statues made filthy by black smoke. You rule because you hold yourself inferior to the gods. Make this the beginning and the end of all things. The neglected gods gave many evils to sorrowing Hesperia.

Civil war ultimately stems from offenses against the gods. The return to normality after civil war must therefore be accompanied by a renewed emphasis on religious observance, so that further retaliation can be averted. The importance attributed to religious renewal, reconstruction of old temples, and reviving of old religious practices during the first years of Augustus' principate should be understood within this context.[6]

But, prior to emending one's mores and religious practices, expiation and atonement are required. Atonement settles the relationship with the gods; purification prepares a new beginning. Purification was an important element of the Ludi Saeculares in connection with the idea of new beginning.[7] Ideas of purification and atonement have left their mark on the art and poetry of the Augustan period. In the *Aeneid*, when Aeneas arrives at Cumae, he begs the gods to recede from their anger against the Trojans. He also promises that he will build a temple to Apollo in the city that he will found (*A.* 6.63–71). Scholars read this promise of a temple to Apollo as prefiguring the dedication of the Temple of Palatine Apollo built by Octavian after the victory of Actium.[8] The coupling of Palatine Apollo with the topic of divine forgiveness seems appropriate, for the themes of expiation and cleansing from sin were relevant to the Palatine temple. The god's cult statue in the Palatine Temple was shown pouring a libation, an act of expiation.[9] Insistence on expiation is also related to another problem. Civil war is a punishment for previous sins, and, at the same time, it is in itself the greatest sin. Whoever takes part in civil war is contaminated. This conception of civil war is reflected in the mythical narratives that accompany accounts of civil war. For instance, Propertius compares Octavian's crushing of Antony to Apollo's slaying of Python, the monstrous Earth-born snake.[10] But that killing, the Romans knew, had

---

[6] Zanker (1988) 101–6.

[7] On the *Ludi Saeculares* under Augustus see Latte (1960) 298–300; Beard–North–Price (1998) 201–6, esp. 203 on ties with rituals of purification; Miller (2009) 270–5.

[8] Harrison (2006) 171–2; Miller (2009) 138–9. The Apollo Temple of Cumae, where the encounter of Aeneas and the Sibyl takes place, has also been linked to the temple of Palatine Apollo: see Putnam (1998) 17; Miller (2009) 136–7.

[9] Galinsky (1996) 141.

[10] Prop. 4.6.35–6; Syndikus (1972–1973) 70.

to be expiated through a ritual pilgrimage to Delphi. Moreover, if the civil conflict is decreed by the gods, to stop it means to step in the way of the gods. This notion underlies Virgil's prayer to the gods that they permit Octavian to come to the help of a generation devastated by civil war at the end of *Georgics* 1 (*G.* 1.498–501).

The idea of sacrificial substitution typically accompanies Roman narratives of political crises and is connected to the gods' role in military and political setbacks. Divine anger demands punishment, but this punishment can be transferred to a man who offers himself as a scapegoat for the whole community. Such instances of self-sacrifice, at times explicitly configured along the lines of the ritual practice of *deuotio*, punctuate Roman history. For instance, when the city of Rome is on the point of being wiped out by the Gauls after the defeat of the Allia River (390 BCE), the nobles perform a *deuotio*, offering their lives to the gods as a substitute for the lives of their fellow citizens.[11] It is no surprise that this theme is adumbrated in the *Aeneid*, a poem that reflects on the establishment of the Augustan regime in the immediate aftermath of the civil conflict and that hints repeatedly at historical crises of the Roman state.[12] More explicit references to *deuotio* are in Lucan, who has Cato offer himself as a scapegoat to placate divine anger and grant salvation to the state:

> o utinam caelique deis Erebique liceret
> hoc caput in cunctas damnatum exponere poenas!
> deuotum hostiles Decium pressere cateruae:
> me geminae figant acies, me barbara telis
> Rheni turba petat, cunctis ego peruius hastis
> excipiam medius totius uolnera belli.
> hic redimat sanguis populos, hac caede luatur
> quidquid Romani meruerunt pendere mores.
> ad iuga cur faciles populi, cur saeua uolentes
> regna pati pereunt? me solum inuadite ferro,
> me frustra leges et inania iura tuentem.
> hic dabit hic pacem iugulus finemque malorum
> gentibus Hesperiis . . .
> Luc. 2.306–18

> O if only this head, condemned by heaven's gods
> and Erebus', could be exposed to every punishment!

---

[11] Liv. 5.41. On this episode and the religious climate underlying it see Chapter 6, Sections 6.3, 6.6, and 6.7. On *deuotio* see Versnel (1981); Beard–North–Price (1998) 35–6.

[12] Hardie (1993) 28–9; Leigh (1993).

When Decius offered his life, enemy squadrons overwhelmed him:
let me be pierced by twin battle-lines, let Rhine's barbarous
horde aim its weapons at me, let me, exposed to all the spears,
standing in the midst, receive the wounds of all the war.
Let this my blood preserve the people, let this my death
atone for all the penalties deserved by Roman morals.
Why should peoples ready for the yoke and willing to endure
cruel tyranny perish? With your sword attack me, me
alone, in vain the guardian of laws and empty rights.
This slaughter, this, will give the people of Hesperia peace
and an end of troubles . . .

This passage captures well the main features of the theological pattern previously described. Rome's decline of morals (cf. Luc. 2.313 *mores*) has earned the gods' anger, leading to the outbreak of civil war. The only way to avert the gods' destructive plan is for someone to offer himself as a scapegoat to redeem his people.[13]

5.2 ULTIO DEORUM

This understanding of the gods' punitive role with regard to political crises is found in accounts of the 69 CE conflict. This time, the sentiments are heightened by the notion that the Romans have fallen again into sin and so deserve another punishment through civil strife. The feeling is immortalized by Tacitus' epigrammatic sentence in his preface to the *Histories*:

> . . . nec enim umquam atrocioribus populi Romani cladibus magisue iustis indiciis adprobatum est non esse curae deis securitatem nostram, esse ultionem.
> *Hist.* 1.3

> . . . for never was it more fully proved by terrible disasters of the Roman people or by unquestionable signs that the gods cared not for our safety, but for our punishment.

The same notion is found in *Siluae* 5.3.195, where Statius describes the civil war of 69 CE as an Erinys or Poena, the traditional agent of the gods' retribution.[14]

---

[13] Note the reference to famous Roman *deuotiones* (2.308: Decius) and the religious language (312: *redimat . . . luatur*). See Fantham (1992a) 136–7 *ad loc*. For *deuotio* in Lucan see Hardie (1993) 30–1, 53–4; Leigh (1997) 128–43. More on *deuotio* in Statius in Chapter 6, Section 6.7.

[14] Cf. Luc. 1.572–7. In this passage a huge Erinys besieges Rome.

Attempts at appeasing the gods by way of sacrificial substitution are recorded for the 69 CE conflict as well. The most astonishing of them all is the attempted *deuotio* by Otho. When he received news of the defeat of Cremona I, Otho decided to take his own life. According to Dio, he explicitly characterized his suicide as a *deuotio* through which he hoped to put an end to the civil conflict. In Dio's version, he goes so far as to mention the precedents of Decius, Curtius, and other republican heroes who had given their lives on behalf of their fellow citizens.[15] The topic of self-sacrifice is also crucial to Tacitus' account of 69 CE. Russell Scott has drawn attention to the many references to *deuotio* in the *Histories*.[16] These allusions cluster around the figure of M. Curtius, leading man of the Roman state under arms, who made a religious *deuotio* of himself to expiate a portentous opening of the earth in the Forum.[17] A monument in the central area of the Forum, the Lacus Curtius, commemorated the place where the young hero had flung himself into the chasm. Galba is murdered in the Forum, and Tacitus makes the most of the proximity between the place of Galba's death and the Lacus Curtius. In this way, he can present the emperor's death as a sort of inverted *deuotio*.[18] The self-immolation of Curtius closed the chasm that threatened the destruction of Rome, but the murder of Galba cannot but symbolize its reopening, pinpointing a year of Roman self-destruction. Tacitus returns to this topic on the occasion of Otho's death, when he recounts that upon hearing of Otho's suicide, people in Rome went to the Lacus Curtius to offer flowers and wreaths in honor of the deceased Galba.[19] In Tacitus, Vitellius too ends up being forced to look at the Lacus Curtius before being killed.[20]

The 69 CE conflict involved massacres, catastrophes, and crimes previously unheard of.[21] These increased the sense of divine anger, irreparable sin, and contamination, which involved both the defeated and the victorious parties. When in 69 CE the Capitoline burned as a result of the civil conflict, people felt that the final destruction of Rome had been decreed, there being no greater sign of the gods' anger against Rome than the destruction of the gods' most sacred place in the city.[22] These widespread feelings explain the emphasis on the recovery of religious orthodoxy that

---

[15] D.C. 64.13. For the relevance of *deuotio* to (mythologized) accounts of the events of 69 CE see also Chapter 6, Section 6.6 and 6.7.

[16] Scott (1968) 56–62, 89.

[17] Liv. 7.6; Var. *L.* 5.148; V. Max. 5.6.2. The sacrifice of Curtius is included in traditional lists of Roman saviors, often in connection with Decius and other Romans who performed *deuotio*: cf. Prop. 3.11.61; *Culex* 363; Amp. 20; D.C. 64.13.

[18] Tac. *Hist.* 1.41; Scott (1968) 56–62.

[19] Tac. *Hist.* 2.55.

[20] Tac. *Hist.* 3.85.

[21] Cf. the eloquent prologue of Tacitus' *Histories* 1.2–3.

[22] Tac. *Hist.* 3.72.

accompanied the establishment of the Flavian regime. We gain a sense of this in Tacitus' description of the reconstruction of the Capitoline temples by Vespasian after the fire of 69 CE, which is carried out by the new emperor with great zeal and scrupulous observance of religious precepts.[23] A renewed attention to religion in all its traditional forms is a well-documented aspect of Vespasian's principate.[24]

But the Flavian period was anything but exempt from religious anxieties. Year 79 CE was marked by the catastrophe of Pompeii and Herculaneum, two cities completely wiped out by a volcanic eruption of incredible proportions. Pliny the Younger, who witnessed the event, wrote that during the eruption some people cried for help to the gods, but others thought that there were no gods at all and that the end of the world had come.[25] Statius is clearer about the role of the gods in that circumstance: He has Jupiter lift the top of Vesuvius and throw it over the wretched cities.[26] Another shock came the following year when a fire of great proportions struck the city of Rome.[27] Religious hysteria, we may presume, loomed large as a consequence of this incredible array of disasters. To alleviate the situation, Titus instigated the *supplicatio* of 80 CE, a traditional ritual aimed at imploring the gods for mercy on the occasion of a calamity.[28]

This religious tension explains Domitian's strict religious policy. This emperor, perhaps more than any of his predecessors, was obsessively fearful of offending the gods. He reconstructed the temples that were burned in 80 CE and established games (the Capitolia) to expiate the portent.[29] He was overwhelmingly preoccupied with the minutiae of rituals and religion. When the *flamen Dialis*, one of the most important priests in the state, wanted to divorce his wife, Domitian enjoined him to do it in the old-fashioned way, with "horrid rites and incantations."[30] He ordered the destruction of the tomb erected by one of his freedmen because the man had used stones meant for the Temple of Jupiter Capitolinus.[31] After the fire of 64 CE, Nero had promised to have altars erected to ward off future fires, a vow that was

---

[23] Tac. *Hist.* 4.53; Suet. *Ves.* 8.5. For the burning of the Capitol in 69 CE and its place within Flavian ideology see Chapter 6, Sections 6.2, 6.4, 6.5.

[24] Levick (1999) 65–6.

[25] Plin. *Ep.* 6.20.15. Cf. also Plin. *Ep.* 6.16. The eruption of Vesuvius: D.C. 66.22–3; Suet. *Tit.* 8.3.

[26] *Silv.* 5.3.207–8.

[27] Suet. *Tit.* 8.3–4; D.C. 66.24.

[28] The *supplicatio* may have left a mark on the coinage of the year: *BMCRE* II, lxxi–lxxiii; but see *RIC*[2] II nos. 117–25, with the objections by Buttrey and Carradice on p. 186. On *supplicationes* see Latte (1960) 245–6.

[29] On the Capitolia see Caldelli (1993), Jones (1992) 103–5, and Chapter 6, Sections 6.2, 6.5. Domitian's reconstruction: Martial 9.3.9 with Henriksén (2012) 31 *ad loc.*; see also Chapter 6, Section 6.5.

[30] Plu. *Quaes. Rom.* 50; see Jones (1992) 102; Syme (1958) 65, (1980) 117.

[31] Cf. Suetonius' eloquent explanation of the measure: *ne qua religio deum impune contaminaretur* [so that no ritual of the gods may be polluted without punishment, *Dom.* 8.5]. Jones (1992) 102 notes: "Presumably, he

long neglected. Domitian saw that it was scrupulously fulfilled.[32] Domitian's restrictive policy with regard to public morals should also be understood in this context.[33] Corruption of morals was traditionally regarded as a cause of divine anger, and it was therefore crucially important for the emperor to supervise his citizens' behavior. Terror of offending the gods also explains Domitian's attitude toward the Vestals.[34] He took very seriously his office of Pontifex Maximus, which involved supervision of the conduct of the Vestal Virgins.[35] Because they were technically daughters of the community, any moral transgressions on their part prompted divine retaliation against the entire state.[36] Domitian rigorously punished all crimes committed by Vestals and went so far as to resume the barbaric and long-abandoned custom of burying unfaithful virgins alive.[37] This scenario is important for understanding the role of the gods in the *Thebaid* and in the Coroebus episode in particular.[38] It allows us to appreciate some of this episode's interfaces with Roman realities, especially in connection with the recent experience of civil war. It also provides a different angle for considering Statius' emphasis on the punitive role of the gods in both the Coroebus episode and the *Thebaid* at large.

5.3 THE COROEBUS EPISODE: A SUMMARY

A brief summary of the Coroebus episode is in order before we proceed. By the middle of the *Thebaid*'s first book, Polynices, exiled from Thebes, arrives in Argos. After quarreling with Tydeus, Polynices is met by Adrastus, who offers him and Tydeus hospitality and invites them to a banquet. When the feast is over, Adrastus pours a libation and prays to Apollo, and his companions and servants join him in acclaiming the god.[39] Adrastus then explains to his guests the reason for the celebration. He recounts that Apollo, in search of expiation after slaying the giant snake

---

recalled the decision of the haruspices (at the time when Vespasian was restoring the same building) forbidding the builders to use stone that had been destined for some other purpose (*Hist.* 4.53)."

[32] *ILS* 4914.

[33] Suet. *Dom.* 8.3; Griffin (2000) 79–80; Jones (1992) 106–8.

[34] Jones (1992) 101–2; Griffin (2000) 79–80.

[35] Cf. Stat. *Silv.* 5.3.178, 1.1.36 with Geyssen (1996) 90–1.

[36] See the example from the Punic wars quoted at the beginning of this chapter.

[37] On a first occasion, the Vestals were allowed to choose their manner of death: Suet. *Dom.* 8.4; D.C. 67.3. The second time, the Vestal Cornelia was buried alive and her lovers beaten to death with rods, in the traditional way: Suet. *Dom.* 8.4; Juv. 4.9–10; Plin. *Ep.* 4.11; Griffin (2000) 79–80. For Domitian as inspector of religious practices cf. *Silv.* 5.3.178.

[38] For the influence of Domitian's religious policy on Silius' epic see Marks (2005a) 238–42.

[39] *Theb.* 1.364–556.

Python, reached Argos. Here he fell in love with Psamathe, daughter of Crotopus, king of the city, and raped her. She bore a divine son to Apollo, but, fearing her father's punishment, kept the baby secret, entrusting him to shepherds. When the child was killed by dogs, Psamathe, unable to conceal her grief, confessed to her father. Crotopus condemned her to death. Apollo, enraged at the death of his beloved, summoned a terrifying creature from the underworld—a snake-haired female monster called Poena (literally the personification of the god's punishment)—who ravaged the Argive cities, breaking into the houses at night and slaughtering babies. At last Coroebus killed the monster. Apollo sent a plague to avenge the death of Poena and subsequently demanded that the culprits of the monster's killing be handed over to him. Coroebus presented himself at Apollo's shrine in Delphi and willingly offered his life, but the god, moved by the hero's piety, decided to spare him.[40]

Statius' choice of this myth is striking. This is the only extant epic rewriting of an episode from Callimachus' *Aetia*.[41] Statius' excursus interacts substantially with Virgil's account of Hercules and Cacus in book 8 of the *Aeneid*, and yet both Statius' choice of myth and his depiction of heroic behavior differ substantially from Virgil's *Aeneid*.[42]

The choice of this myth and its relationship to the rest of the poem call for an explanation. Some scholars see the episode as having mainly thematic connections to the rest of the narrative. Others argue for more direct correspondences, with the episode seen as a miniature of the entire poem and interacting with some specific scenes of it.[43] As for the episode's general meaning, the story of Linus and Coroebus has been alternatively read as an exhibition of the power of *pietas* (Vessey) or of its insignificance in a post-Virgilian world (Ganiban).[44] Other scholars have drawn attention to Adrastus' inability to learn the lesson encoded in the tale of Coroebus: that the gods are intent on the city's destruction, which will soon be manifested through the impending war.[45] In addition, the story has been taken as a blueprint for Statius' conception of the gods. Both Dominik and Hill envisage the episode as a demonstration of the immorality and iniquity of Apollo and of the gods, following Lewis,

---

[40] The Coroebus episode: *Theb.* 1.557–672.

[41] Call. *Aet.* 25e–31b Harder. Mentions of the Coroebus myth in Roman literature also in Ovid's *Ibis* 575–6 and Martial 9.86.4.

[42] On the Coroebus episode and Virgil see Legras (1905) 38–9; Vessey (1973) 101; Brown (1994) 166–8; Taisne (1994) 245; Delarue (2000) 121; Hill (1990) 113; McNelis (2007) 27–9; Ganiban (2007) 13–17.

[43] Kytzler (1955) 186; Vessey (1973) 103–5; Brown (1994) 172; Dominik (1994) 63; Delarue (2000) 122.

[44] Vessey (1973) 106–7; Ganiban (2007) 9–23. On the Coroebus episode as demonstrating the value of *pietas* see also Ripoll (1998) 303–4.

[45] Dominik (1994) 69–70. On the Coroebus episode as a reflection on humans' misunderstanding of the gods and their relationship with justice see also Ahl (1986) 2853–7.

who saw the Coroebus narrative as asserting the moral superiority of humans to gods.[46] McNelis reads the episode in connection with Statius' general tendency to blur the distinctions between Olympian gods and the powers of the underworld; in this process, the *Thebaid*'s gods abandon their traditional role as agents of order and rationality, and Statius' radical destabilization of the gods opens up a void that must necessarily be filled by humans. It is the return of Theseus, with the importance given to *clementia*, that finally brings about order and stability.[47]

5.4 PERSEUS AND GANYMEDE

Before getting to the Coroebus episode, we should pause to consider another minia-ture narrative that is introduced just before Adrastus' account and that, in many ways, sets the stage for the narrative of Linus and Coroebus. The goblet used by Adrastus to pour a libation to Apollo is decorated with two mythical scenes, Ganymede's ab-duction and Perseus' return from the killing of Medusa:[48]

> tenet haec operum caelata figuras:
> aureus anguicomam praesecto Gorgona collo
> ales habet, iam iamque uagas (ita uisus) in auras
> exilit; illa graues oculos languentiaque ora
> paene mouet uiuoque etiam pallescit in auro.
> hinc Phrygius fuluis uenator tollitur alis,
> Gargara desidunt surgenti et Troia recedit,
> stant maesti comites frustraque sonantia lassant
> ora canes umbramque petunt et nubila latrant.
> *Theb.* 1.543–51

The carved goblet held sculpted figures: the winged hero in gold carries the snake-haired Gorgon's severed head, and even now, so it seems, leaps into the

---

[46] Hill (1990) 114; Dominik (1994) 67–70; Lewis (1998) 99.

[47] McNelis (2007) 25–49.

[48] The scene reworks a detail from *Aeneid* 1, in which Dido pours a libation from a goblet she inherited from her ancestor Belus (*A.* 1.728–30); Vessey (1973) 100; Newlands (2012) 75–6; Keith (2013) 305–6. Belus is Danaus' father, and Danaus is named by Statius as the former possessor of the cup used by Adrastus. Dido's cup, how-ever, is not decorated. An object with a representation of the Ganymede myth does appear in the *Aeneid* but in another context (*A.* 5.250–5; see subsequent discussion). I return later to the significance of Danaus for the Coroebus episode and the *Thebaid* in general. *Ekphraseis* featuring Ganymede are introduced both by Valerius Flaccus (2.408–17) and Silius Italicus (15.425–32). On these texts and the *Thebaid* see Newlands (2012) 77–80 and Ripoll (2000).

wandering airs; she almost seems to move her heavy eyes and drooping coun-
tenance and seems to grow pale even in the living gold. Here the Phrygian
hunter is raised aloft on golden wings, Gargara sinks as he rises and Troy
recedes; his comrades stand dismayed. In vain the hounds weary their
sounding mouths, pursuing the shadow and barking at the clouds.

Statius' choice to introduce his digression through this ekphrastic prelude
deserves attention. The myths of Perseus and Ganymede are connected to the nar-
rative of Linus and Coroebus in many ways. They shed light on how to understand
this short account's relationship to the *Thebaid*'s main plot and introduce us to the
political and historical resonances of Statius' digression. They also allow us to appre-
ciate some important peculiarities of the Coroebus episode. In addition, Statius' use
of the imagery connected with Perseus and Medusa reflects this author's complex
view of the limits of monarchical power, a concept that we have already discussed in
Chapter 4 and to which we will return in Chapter 6.

Let me start with the myth of Perseus and Medusa.[49] Perseus is a character fea-
tured in the *Thebaid*, although only for a short cameo in book 10 (to which I will
return). However, his myth is hinted at on several occasions. The house of Argos is
connected to Jupiter through Perseus, who is one of Adrastus' ancestors.[50] Statius
twice alludes to Perseus' presence in the dynasty of Argive kings, but he does so in
an oblique and indirect way. The *Thebaid* has two "catalogues" of Argive ancestors,
in books 1 and 6, respectively. In the first catalogue—a description of the ancestors'
statues in the royal palace of Argos—Statius mentions Perseus' grandfather
Acrisius. The second list (the pageant of images of Argive heroes during the funeral
games for the child Opheltes) features both Acrisius and Danae (Perseus' mother),
but Perseus himself is not mentioned.[51] Another indirect reference to Perseus is in
book 3, when Amphiaraus and Melampus take the auspices from the place from
which Perseus took flight for the first time.[52] Although Perseus is not named in the
lists of Argive ancestors, his place seems to have been taken by Coroebus. Without
regard for traditional chronology, in the second list just mentioned, Coroebus is

---

[49] Interpretations of the *ekphrasis*: Vessey (1973) 100 sees both myths as foreshadowing future events in the nar-
rative, namely Polynices' defeat by the Furies and the destruction of Argos; McNelis (2007) 41 n. 74 argues
that the severed head of the Gorgon indicates the ability of humans to eradicate evil, an idea that is, however,
countered by the power of the Gorgon that Vulcan adds to Harmonia's necklace (*Theb.* 2.278). Newlands
(2012) 82–3 emphasizes the *ekphrasis*' proleptic function in evoking the civil war themes of the *Thebaid* and its
ironic power in foreshadowing the evil Adrastus will bring to the city of Argos by welcoming his two guests.
She also highlights the *ekphrasis*' metaliterary power as an emblem of Statius' poetics.

[50] *Theb.* 1.225–6. Cf. also *Theb.* 3.441, in which Adrastus is named *Perseius heros*.

[51] *Theb.* 2.221–3 and *Theb.* 6.286–7. On both passages see Pavan (2009) 85–91.

[52] *Theb.* 3.460–5.

inserted between Perseus' mother (Danae) and his grandfather (Acrisius), and in the first list Coroebus follows after Acrisius.[53] The description of Coroebus in the first catalogue of ancestors (in book 2), with the head of Poine (a snake-haired monster like Medusa) in his hands, is clearly modeled on the traditional iconography of Perseus.[54]

Perseus' replacement with Coroebus in the two catalogues of Argive ancestors draws attention to the similarities between the two heroes and their stories: Both Perseus and Coroebus kill a snake-haired female monster; in both stories a god impregnates an Argive woman (Psamathe/Danae), who is eventually punished by her enraged father (Acrisius/Crotopus).[55] The description of Adrastus' goblet thus prepares readers for their encounter with Coroebus and invites them to appreciate similarities and differences between the two. One such difference emerges in book 10, in which we learn that Perseus resides together with Hercules and Bacchus (and other gods) on Olympus. Statius evidently conceives of Perseus as a deified hero in the manner of his companions Hercules and Bacchus.[56] After all, Perseus has a divine father just like Hercules and Bacchus. The Perseus myth establishes Coroebus as a double of Perseus, but with a difference: In the Coroebus story, a hero with no divine relations has replaced a child of Jupiter as the one who dispatches the snake-haired monster, and he achieves no immortality in the process.

The imagery related to the myth of Perseus reverberates throughout Statius' narrative. In the *Thebaid*, Perseus becomes a sort of heroic gauge by which to judge the action of other heroes. In book 6, Polynices' horses are frightened by the appearance of a Medusa-like female monster who is dubbed *anguicoma* [snake-haired], like Medusa at *Theb.* 1.544.[57] The scene is inspired by traditional accounts of Minerva scaring the horses of her enemies with the Gorgon's head on her shield: Statius may have had Lucan's simile of Minerva in book 7 of the *Bellum Ciuile* in mind.[58] Polynices, unlike Perseus or Coroebus, is helpless in the face of the monster. Polynices' failure to fight Apollo's monster in book 6 is a

---

[53] *Theb.* 6.286–7.

[54] *Theb.* 2.221. For Perseus' iconography see *LIMC* VII.1 332–48, esp. 347–8 (L. Jones–Roccos).

[55] However, unlike Psamathe, Danae eventually survives.

[56] This seems to be an innovation of Statius: see *RE* 19 978–92; Roscher 3.1986–2060. That Perseus is a god is also shown in book 7, in which the inhabitants of Argos pray to him in his temple: *Theb.* 7.417.

[57] *Theb.* 6.495–8: *anguicomam monstri effigiem, saeuissima uisu | ora, mouet siue ille Erebo seu finxit in astus | temporis, innumera certe formidine cultum | tollit in astra nefas* [the figure of a monster with snaky hair, a dreadful visage, he either summoned from Erebus or fashioned as a trick for the occasion; certain it is that he raised this abomination decked with countless terrors into the upper world.]

[58] Luc. 7.569–71; Fantham (1992b) 102–3. More on this passage in subsequent discussion.

prelude to his inability to resist Megaera, another snake-haired creature compa-
rable to Medusa, in book 11.[59]

The only hero who figuratively lives up to Perseus is Theseus. Theseus resembles
Perseus in many aspects: Assisted by Minerva, as Perseus always was, the Athenian
hero leads his troops against the standards of the *anguicomae sorores* (the Furies—
third and last occurrence of the word *anguicoma* in the poem) and the Poenae.[60]
Minerva herself supports Theseus by shaking her shield and menacing Thebes with
Medusa's head:

> ipsa metus Libycos seruatricemque Medusam
> pectoris incussa mouit Tritonia parma.
> protinus erecti toto simul agmine Thebas
> respexere angues; necdum Atticus ire parabat
> miles, et infelix expauit classica Dirce.
> *Theb.* 12.606–10

> Tritonia herself shook her shield, that Lybian terror, the Medusa that guarded
> her bosom. Straightaway the snakes reared up and their whole cohort looked
> toward Thebes. The Attic soldiers were not yet preparing to march, and hapless
> Dirce already trembled at the trumpet.

Theseus succeeds in defeating the Poenae and the snake-haired Furies (symboli-
cally), just as Perseus was able to kill Medusa. In sum, Statius particularly underscores
connections among Perseus, Theseus, and Coroebus, whereas Polynices appears not
to be on a level with these heroes.

The relevance of Perseus, however, is not limited to interactions with other
parts of the *Thebaid*. Statius' use of this mythical figure can be put in the right
perspective only by considering previous adaptations of this myth in Greece and
Rome. There is a Hellenistic tradition of using Perseus as a mythical counterpart
of kings, Perseus' killing of Medusa being a symbol of the sovereign's ability to
keep his monstrous enemies under control.[61] In Rome, traces of an ideological
exploitation of Perseus are visible in the Augustan period, chiefly as a reflection
on civil war. Medusa's severed head was represented on the breastplate of the cult

---

[59] *Theb.* 11.150–4, Vessey (1973) 100.

[60] *Theb.* 12.642–7.

[61] Perseus is harnessed in particular by Philip V, the Macedonian king defeated by T. Quinctius Flamininus at
Cynoscephalae in 197 CE, who went so far as to name his son Perseus and is constantly associated with Perseus
in the coinage. See the numismatic evidence collected by L. Jones–Roccos in *LIMC* 7.1 334.

statue in the Temple of Mars Ultor, the centerpiece of the Augustan Forum, which celebrated Octavian's revenge against his father's assassins at Philippi.[62] Perseus' fight with the Gorgon is one of the themes depicted on the terra-cotta plaques that decorated the Temple of Apollo on the Palatine, which was consecrated in the aftermath of the battle of Actium.[63] Imperial poets are alert to this imperial relevance of Perseus. Ulrich Schmitzer has argued that Perseus' victory over easterners in Ovid's *Metamorphoses* resonates with themes of Augustan propaganda, being particularly consonant with official representations of the battle of Actium.[64] In Lucan's *Bellum Ciuile*, the severed Gorgon's head features as a symbol of civil strife, and Medusa is ominously evoked in the context of the description of the battle of Pharsalus.[65]

In earlier Roman adaptations, the imperial dimension of Perseus is visible, and Medusa's head is associated with the terror of civil war. The connection between Medusa and civil war is influential on the *Thebaid* too, in which the Furies are figuratively associated with Medusa and the visual symbolism of Medusa accompanies Theseus' intervention against Creon. By Statius' time, the imagery connected to Perseus was particularly salient in light of its importance in the iconography of Domitian. Like Perseus, Domitian has Minerva as his patron goddess and is portrayed wielding the Gorgoneion on the most popular coin type issued during his tenure.[66] In *Siluae* 1.1, Domitian's massive statue holds in his hand a little Minerva. Brandishing the Gorgoneion, the goddess spurs Domitian's horse into action and frightens the emperor's enemies.[67] In this same poem, Statius mentions Domitian's ability to guarantee the security of the empire by conquering both civil war and foreign enemies. In conclusion, the story of Perseus sets the stage for the arrival of Coroebus by evoking a similar myth, a story that could be figuratively associated with imperial power and its control over the forces of chaos, be that civil war or assaults by foreigners. In the narrative proper, readers will find similarities between Coroebus and Perseus but they will also be surprised by important differences, for Coroebus has no divine parent and will not be deified.

---

[62] On the Forum Augustum see Zanker (1968); *LTUR* II, 289–95 (V. Kockel); Spannangel (1999).

[63] See Kellum (1985) 172; Zanker (1988) 199–200.

[64] Schmitzer (1990) 242–3. On the influence of Ovid's *Metamorphoses* on Statius' portrait of Perseus see Keith (2013) 305–7.

[65] Fantham (1992b) esp. 101–3. The relevance of Lucan's exploitation of Medusa's head as a symbol of civil war for Statius' *Thebaid* is well illustrated by Newlands (2012) 81–2.

[66] *RIC*[2] II nos. 56–63; description of types at pp. 263–5.

[67] *Silv.* 1.1.37–39. On the interconnections between the Perseus *ekphrasis*, the portrait of Domitian in *Siluae* 1.1 and the scene featuring Theseus in *Thebaid* 12.606–10 see Newlands (2012) 84.

However, the equation between Perseus and Theseus also tells us something about imperial power that is not entirely reassuring. As we have seen, in the *Thebaid*, the Gorgon's head is aligned with the power of the Furies: Medusa embodies the frightening reality—and the madness—of civil war. Polynices is overwhelmed by this monstrous presence. Theseus, on the contrary, can turn this source of terror against his enemies, transforming it into an instrument of order. This reflection is reminiscent of Virgil's characteristic use of the Furies in the *Aeneid*. In the *Aeneid*, the Furies are the powers behind the terror of fraternal war, yet it is by recourse to these powers and this terror that Jupiter finally settles the conflict of Trojans and Latins.[68] Statius seems to suggest that without recourse to these frightening forces power cannot be effective.

Let us now move to the second myth represented on Adrastus' goblet, Ganymede's abduction.[69] The myths of Perseus and Ganymede, as depicted by Statius, have some aspects in common: Both portray young heroes lifted from the ground: both heroes are destined to become immortal. Unlike Perseus, however, Ganymede has no connection with the Argive line. His presence on Adrastus' cup must therefore serve a specific purpose. Here, as in the case of Perseus, we can explore thematic links between this myth and the story of Coroebus. Ganymede is a child who is snatched away, provoking the anger of Juno. The connection of Ganymede with divine wrath is crucial to Virgil's *Aeneid*, in which the youth's abduction is mentioned as one of the reasons for Juno's hostility to the Trojans.[70] Likewise, Linus is the cause of Apollo's anger.[71] Second, just like Perseus, the figure of Ganymede had acquired a special significance in the political culture of the empire. Statius' Ganymede *ekphrasis* has an important model in the *Aeneid*, in which this myth is represented on the cloth that Cloanthus receives from Aeneas as a prize for his victory in the ship race.[72] Philip Hardie has convincingly shown that Virgil's *ekphrasis* is particularly concerned with the theme of apotheosis and with the dynastic propaganda of the Julian gens: The

---

[68] As apparent in Jupiter's recourse to the Dirae during Turnus' duel with Aeneas: *A.* 12.843–952; for this tragic notion of power and its limits see Chapter 4, Section 4.3 and Chapter 6, Section 6.7.

[69] On the Ganymede *ekphrasis* in the *Thebaid* and its proleptic function see Newlands (2012) 76–80.

[70] *A.* 1.28.

[71] Unlike Ganymede, Linus does not become a god. But later in the poem, another child, whom the poet connects with Linus and who undergoes a similar destiny, is said to have achieved apotheosis: Opheltes. Parallels between the Linus and Opheltes stories are discussed later in this chapter (Section 5.8). Opheltes' apotheosis is prophesied by Amphiaraus at *Theb.* 5.750–2. For the proleptic function of Statius' *ekphrasis* of Ganymede in connection with the topic of premature death in the poem see Newlands (2012) 79.

[72] *A.* 5.250–7. Statius' text bears a close resemblance to Virgil's *ekphrasis*: note in both cases the detail of the guardians who watch their master being taken away and the mention of the dogs barking; Caviglia (1973) 149–50. On Virgil's and Statius' *ekphraseis* see Newlands (2012) 77–8; Ripoll (2000) 485.

receipt of the young Trojan into heaven prefigures the divine future of the Trojan Julii.[73]

This political exploitation of Ganymede as a symbol of imperial apotheosis is not unknown to Flavian culture. The evidence for this comes from the exhibition of the famous Ganymede statue by the Greek master Leochares in the Templum Pacis, a monument inaugurated by Vespasian in 75 CE to celebrate his successes in Judaea.[74] The temple was decorated with a carefully chosen series of Greek works of art, including a statuary group portraying Ganymede lifted up by Jupiter's eagle.[75] The statue was very popular according to Juvenal and is described by Pliny. The eagle seemed to lift the boy gently, Pliny tells us; the bird seemed to be aware of who the boy was and to whom he was destined (Jupiter).[76] With its emphasis on Trojan ancestry, the statue was perhaps meant as a sign of continuity with the Augustan regime. Yet it was also very apposite for Flavian propaganda. The Flavians had come from the East to rescue Rome and Ganymede was an eastern hero. The statue portrayed an instance of deification, an apt reward for an emperor who rescued the empire from destruction.

In summary, the two myths share a number of features. Both allude to the theme of apotheosis, thematically (the two heroes are deified) and visually (both heroes are represented at the moment when they reach for the sky). Both stories anticipate themes of the Coroebus episode and of the *Thebaid*'s narrative. Perseus in particular is in many ways a version of Coroebus. In addition, both myths have an imperial dimension: Whereas Perseus can be regarded as a symbol of the emperor's power over his enemies, Ganymede emphasizes apotheosis.[77] The two stories prepare the reader for the upcoming narrative of Coroebus. The idea of an imperial dimension and of a connection with the rest of the narrative by way of anticipation and thematic links is crucial to the Coroebus excursus, as I try to show. The two myths also highlight some important differences in the Coroebus story: Coroebus has no divine origin, and, unlike Perseus and Ganymede, he does not achieve apotheosis.

---

[73] Hardie (2002) 341–7. For a different interpretation of this passage see Putnam (1998) 55–74.

[74] On the Templum Pacis see the relevant articles in Coarelli (2009a) 158–201 and *LTUR* IV 67–70 (F. Coarelli).

[75] See Bravi (2012) 167–81, esp. 173 on Ganymede.

[76] Juv. 9.22; Plin. *Nat.* 34.79.

[77] McNelis (2007) 41 n. 74 is on the right path when he notes that the myth of Ganymede in *Theb.* 1 suggests a less antagonistic relationship between Jupiter and humans than that at work in the *Thebaid*.

5.5 CALLIMACHUS, VIRGIL, AND STATIUS

Let us return to the story of Linus and Coroebus. To appreciate the ideological and political resonance of Statius' version of this story, we need to consider Statius' models, especially Callimachus and Virgil. Statius' divergences from Callimachus and Virgil tell us something important about the purpose of his narrative and its ideological undertones. In this section, I highlight some key features of Statius' rewriting of Callimachus; in the next, I reflect on the ideological background underlying Callimachus' interest in this story. I try to show that Statius recovers the imperial dimension of Callimachus' account and transfers it to a Roman civil war context. Thus, he is able to interact with aspects of Flavian ideology and with elite reflections on the role of aristocracy under the empire.

But let us proceed in order. It is an established point in scholarship that Statius is not simply treating the same episode as Callimachus but that he engages directly the *Aetia*'s text.[78] But Statius also experiments on Callimachus with some literary techniques that Callimachus himself applied to his literary predecessors.[79] In his rewriting of the Coroebus episode, Statius combines at least three Callimachean *aitia*. The Coroebus digression opens with Apollo's killing of Python in Delphi and his journey in search of expiation. This is the argument of Callimachus' *aition* on the Delphic Daphnephoria, from book 4 of the *Aetia*.[80] The reader is, however, surprised to find out that Apollo does not go to expiate along the banks of Peneus, as in Callimachus; rather he journeys to Argos, where he will set in motion the events leading to Linus' birth and the release of Poine, the topic of another episode in the *Aetia*, the one on Linus and Coroebus (from book 1).[81] In addition, the god's entry into Crotopus' house in Argos bears a resemblance to a third Callimachean passage: Hercules' visit to the humble house of Molorchus, described in the *Victory of Berenice* from the third book of the *Aetia*.[82] This last connection can also be seen as enacting a "window" allusion: The *Victory of Berenice* is one of the main models of Virgil's Hercules and Cacus episode, with which Statius' Coroebus story engages substantially. Statius' Coroebus episode looks at the *Victory of Berenice* both directly and through its relationship with Virgil.

---

[78] McNelis (2007) 34–5; Aricò (1960) 281–2; Vessey (1973) 101; Delarue (2000) 121–3.

[79] In this, Statius follows a pattern that is customary for Roman authors engaging with the great Alexandrian poet. See Barchiesi (2011) 513–14.

[80] Call. *Aet.* 86–89a Harder.

[81] *Theb.* 1.562–71; see McNelis (2007) 33.

[82] Call. *Aet.* 54–60j Harder; McNelis (2007) 33.

Statius' merging of more than one Callimachean episode transforms his narrative in important respects.[83] Statius' joining of the Delphic Daphnephoria with the Coroebus *aition* gives his narrative a sort of "ring composition": The story opens with Apollo killing a monstrous snake in Delphi and seeking expiation in Argos, and closes with Coroebus killing a snake-haired monster in Argos and seeking expiation in Delphi. Other differences are independent of Statius' combination of several episodes from Callimachus. In Callimachus, the story of Coroebus was recounted to explain the Argive ritual of killing dogs during the festival called Arneia.[84] In the *Thebaid*, the ritual celebrated by Adrastus has nothing to do with dogs.[85]

We may be tempted to think that for this detail, Statius is under the influence of his second great model, Virgil. In book 1, Polynices is provided with the story of Linus and Coroebus as an explanation for the rites in honor of Apollo performed after the banquet.[86] The sequence has clear intertextual links with Evander's account of Hercules and Cacus in *Aeneid* 8.[87] In the Hercules and Cacus episode, the citizens of Pallanteum perform a sacrifice of thanksgiving to Hercules, who has delivered them from the threat of Cacus. Yet in the *Thebaid*, the Argives do not sacrifice to Coroebus, who killed the monster, but to Apollo. And they do not praise Apollo for killing Python, but for sparing Coroebus and agreeing to quell his anger. Theirs is a sacrifice of expiation and atonement, working by the logic of substitution. They thank Apollo for accepting their victims instead of the life of Coroebus or the lives of the citizens of Argos (*Theb.* 1.667–8). Generally speaking, the topic of expiation, which is present in Callimachus and is emphasized by Statius, is absent from Virgil's account. In the episode of Hercules and Cacus, there is no sense that the killing of Cacus should be atoned for. The inhabitants of Pallanteum have committed no sin, and Cacus has not been released by the gods in order to punish them. To kill Cacus is no explicit offense to the gods and is not an obstacle to the fulfillment of a divine plan, as it is in the case of Poena. Cacus is Vulcanus' son (*A.* 8.198) but we hear nothing about his father's reaction to the murder.

The appeasing function of Adrastus' sacrifice is connected to a third and major divergence, concerning the nature of Coroebus' punishment by Apollo. In both Pausanias and Conon, Coroebus' punishment consists of being exiled from Argos. Coroebus is ordered to take a tripod with him and found a city (Tripodiscon) in the place where the tripod would slip from his

---

[83] McNelis (2007) 33.

[84] See Harder (2012) 259; 266.

[85] Harder (2012) 256–7.

[86] *Theb.* 1.557–60.

[87] See Ganiban (2007) 13–15; Legras (1905) 38–9; Vessey (1973) 101; Brown (1994) 166–8; Taisne (1994) 245; Delarue (2000) 121; McNelis (2007) 27–9; Schetter (1960) 82–4.

hands.[88] Coroebus' founding of Tripodiscon was recounted in Callimachus; it is then very likely that Callimachus' version did not differ from Conon and Pausanias in this respect. In all likelihood, the idea of Coroebus offering his life in the place of that of his fellow citizens is Statius' invention. The topic of self-sacrifice is also absent from Virgil's story of Hercules and Cacus. This innovation is of great importance for our understanding of this passage's historical and ideological implications.

Other differences from Virgil's account pertain to the characterization and the action of Coroebus. Both Hercules and Coroebus kill monsters, but Coroebus differs from Virgil's Hercules in some significant respects. Coroebus has no divine father and will not become a god. Unlike Hercules, Coroebus does not act in isolation, and *pietas* is emphasized as his main motivation.[89] There is no uncontrolled fury in his heroism, no gnashing of teeth, no frightening outburst like those of Hercules in the *Aeneid*.[90] In short, Coroebus is no *theios aner* (the individual of extraordinary charisma who achieves apotheosis as a reward for his actions); he is clearly kept at some distance from the most disturbing implications of the Hercules model in the *Aeneid*.

5.6 ARGOS AND ALEXANDRIA

In spite of all these differences, Statius seems to be receptive to the ideological function of the Coroebus episode within the project of the *Aetia*. Callimachus' passage has an important political dimension in connection with Ptolemaic ideology. Engaging the *Aetia* is not an occasion for avoiding politically sensible topics and the pressure to talk about kings and battles; Statius' engagement with this Alexandrian master is an attempt at adapting to a Roman context a tale that already in Callimachus lent itself to ideological appropriations.

The Coroebus story is a rather obscure myth even in Greek culture.[91] What elements played a part in Callimachus' decision to include it in his poem, besides this author's predilection for off-the-beaten-path mythical stories? Can we relate this story to the political dimension of the *Aetia*? A first important element is the story's setting: the city of Argos. Argos and its mythology have a special significance for Alexandrian culture.[92] From the time of Ptolemy I, the kings of Alexandria insisted on the close

---

[88] Paus. 1.43.7. In Conon (*FGrH* 26 F 1.19) it is Crotopus who is sent into exile from Argos, but Welcker suggests we read "Coroebus" for "Crotopus"; see Harder (2012) 258.

[89] *Theb.* 1.606–8. For Coroebus' *pietas* see *Theb.* 1.644.

[90] Cf. *A.* 8.219–32; on these aspects of Hercules' heroism and the difference between Hercules and Coroebus see Chapter 3, Section 3.7.

[91] On the Greek sources for the Coroebus story (Conon *FGrH* 26 F 1.19; Paus. 1.43.7–8) see Harder (2012) 255–6.

[92] See Bullock (1985) 12–13; Harder (1985) 129–37, (2012) 209–15, 234, 392.

connection between their family line (the Lagids) and the Macedonian royal family (the Argeads), which traced its origin back to the hero Argaeus.[93] Although the town of Argos with which the Argeads were linked was actually in Macedonia, a popular version of the genealogy made Peloponnesian Argos the homeland of the royal family, making it of pure Doric descent and providing a connection to Heracles and Dionysus.[94] This link between the Argeads and Argos is recorded as early as Herodotus, Thucydides, and, in a variant form, in Euripides' *Archelaos*.[95] A hero named Archelaos or Temenos—or, in some versions, his descendants—fled Peloponnesian Argos and established himself in Macedonia. Contemporaries of Callimachus emphasize this Argive connection: Theocritus stresses the descent of both Ptolemy I and Alexander from Heracles; in Theocritus 15, the Adonis song for the festival of the Ptolemaic palace is sung by an Argive; and in Theocritus 24, Argos is the most prominent place where Alcmene and Heracles are renowned.[96] Callimachus' fifth hymn is set in Argos and refers to the Argive festival of the baths of Pallas.[97] The centrality of Argos is also featured in the *Aetia*. In this work, Hercules plays a pivotal role, and it is his Argive ancestry (not his Theban connections) that is emphasized.[98] Argive stories are prominent throughout the *Aetia*: Besides the *aition* of Coroebus, there is the *Argive Springs* and, of course, the *Victory of Berenice*.[99]

Besides the prestige it offered through the dynastic tie with Hercules, Dionysus, and Alexander, Argive mythology was particularly useful for the Ptolemies for another reason. Through the figures of Io and Danaus, Argive mythology provided a connection between Greece and Egypt, establishing a mythic precedent for the Ptolemies' ambitions over both Egypt and the Greek mainland.[100] Io was a member of the Argive royal family who ended up settling in Egypt and achieving divine status as Isis. After Io's disappearance, Iasus (Io's father according to Callimachus) entrusted the reign to his son, Crotopus (the king of Callimachus' *aition* of Linus

[93] Bullock (1985) 12–13; Harder (1985) 129–37.
[94] For the genealogy of the Ptolemies see Satyros in *FGrH* 3c 631 F1.
[95] Herod. 8.137; Thuc. 2.99.3; Euripides *Archelaos: TrGFr* 228–64.
[96] Theoc. 17.16–27, 15.97, 24.78, 104ff.
[97] Bullock (1985) 12–13.
[98] See in particular the *Victory of Berenice*, with its emphasis on Hercules' connection to Argos (through Nemea): frs. 54–60j Harder; but also the *Sacrifice at Lindos* (frs. 22–23c Harder), which has an Argive setting, and the episode of Hercules and Theiodamas (24–25d Harder), concluded, probably, by the mention of Hercules' transferal of the Dryopes to the region of Argos, homeland of the hero; cf. also 76b–77d Harder on the nuptial rites in Elis; Massimilla (1996) 292; Harder (2012) 209–15, 232–4, 392.
[99] Coroebus: fr. 25e–31b Harder; *The Argive Springs* frs. 65–66 Harder; *The Victory of Berenice* 54–60j Harder. Callimachus drew on the prose work by Argive mythographers (the *Argolica* of Agyas and Dercylus: Call. *Aet.* 31a Harder); see D'Alessio (2007) 383; *FGrH* 305 F8.
[100] On the ideological importance of Danaus for the Ptolemies see Harder (2012) 400–1.

and Coroebus).[101] Crotopus was succeeded by Sthenelas and then Gelanor. At this point, Danaus made his first appearance in Argos, and, as a response to an oracle, gained the throne of Gelanor.[102] The Danaus myth thus encompassed both the story of how a dynasty of Greek kings had established itself in Egypt and of how these same Greek/Egyptian kings had returned to impose their dominion over the Greek mainland. Furthermore, the Danaus myth could be pressed for even more precise correspondences. Danaus was a cadet member of the royal family, a descendant of a female daughter of the king, who, coming from Egypt, had finally acquired power in his homeland. The Ptolemies too, like Danaus, were cadet members of the royal family through a female member (Arsinoe), with a connection to Egypt, who claimed to have proved the true heir to the Argive line of Alexander.[103] This dynastic relevance of Danaus and Io explains the importance attributed to these figures in Callimachus.[104]

The Ptolemies' interest in Argive dynastic lines offers a first suggestion as to how to read the *aition* of Coroebus with reference to the Ptolemaic establishment. Crotopus, Psamathe, and Linus were the royal ancestors of the kings of Alexandria. The Coroebus *aition* told of how in the past, the royal house from which the Ptolemies came had undergone a great calamity because of divine hostility, and of how a peaceful relationship with the gods had been regained thanks to a courageous hero. As I previously noted, after killing the monster, Coroebus went to Delphi, where he was ordered to take a tripod and go into exile. He was to found a new city, sacred to Apollo, in the place where the tripod would fall from his hands.[105] The sequence resembles that of the myth of Temenos/Archelaos, the mythical founder of the Argead line. He too was an Argive hero, who, involved in a murder, had to go into exile; in some versions he too received the order from Apollo to found a new city.[106] Even apart from the connection to the story of Archelaos, the theme of the foundation of new cities was of great importance for the Ptolemies.[107]

---

[101] On Iasus father of Io cf. Call. *Aet.* fr. 66.1 Harder, with Harder (2012) 533.

[102] A detailed genealogy is found in Paus. 2.16.

[103] On the Ptolemies' attempt to link themselves to the line of Alexander see Tarn (1933) 57; Beloch (1927) 176–7.

[104] Callimachus wrote a poem titled *The Arrival of Io*. Danaus and Io play a central role in one of Callimachus' most popular and widely imitated episodes from the *Aetia*, the *Victory of Berenice*. Cf. especially Call. *Aet.* 54.1–6 Harder, with Harder (2012) 400–1.

[105] Call. *Aet.* frs. 31–31b Harder; Paus. 1.43.7–8; see Section 5.5, n. 88.

[106] Herod. 8.137; Thuc. 2.99.3; Euripides *Archelaos TrGFr* 228–64. On this myth, see Harder (1985) 129–37.

[107] Fantuzzi–Hunter (2002) 69–70; on *ktisis* stories in the *Aetia* see Harder (2012) 300–1. A comparable story to that of Coroebus' foundation is found in A.R. 4.522–36, 4.1547–50.

The Coroebus episode entails a mythical pattern represented in other passages of the *Aetia*, that of a hero who kills a monster.[108] Besides the Coroebus episode and the story of Apollo and Python, Callimachus' *Aetia* also features Hercules killing the Nemean lion. This story type provides a good place to look for political relevance. Ridding the earth of monsters works well as a symbol of the civilizing activities of a savior king. Hercules, one of the heroes favored by the Ptolemies, was awarded apotheosis for performing just that. Scholars have argued that stories of monster killing in the *Aetia* should be understood in this panegyric context, although there is no consensus on this point.[109] Whatever we make of Callimachus' interest in monster slaying, there is no doubt that the Romans were alert to this mythical pattern's potential for political allegory, as demonstrated, for instance, by Virgil's ideological reception of the *Victory of Berenice* centering on Hercules as a model for Augustus and Aeneas.[110]

5.7 ARGOS AND ROME

The Coroebus episode's potential for political allusion is already in Callimachus. This explains why Statius turned to this story as an alternative to the more conventional pattern represented by stories about Hercules. The *aition* of Coroebus was suitable for ideological appropriations in the same way as the Hercules stories, but it allowed constructions of royal identities to be tied to a very different kind of heroism and a different mythical pattern. Like the Hercules stories, the myth of Coroebus was set in the mythical past of the royal house, and it involved a hero who had something in common with the Ptolemies' mythical ancestors and had killed a monster. But the tale of Coroebus displayed a few elements that were foreign to the Hercules myth. The hero did not have a divine father, and he was not a member of the royal house; divine hostility, atonement, and expiation, which do not feature in accounts of Hercules' monster killing, were central to the story.

Between Statius and Callimachus, an important mediation is offered by Virgil's *Aeneid*. The story of Coroebus acquires further ideological potential in light of Virgil's interaction with Callimachus and Argive myth. Virgil's use of Argive mythology in the *Aeneid* is variously connected to Callimachus' *Aetia*, but it develops

---

[108] Also present in other works by Callimachus: cf. Call. *Ap.* 97–104, Apollo killing Python, with possible allusions to Ptolemy and Berenice; see Depew (2004) 121–5; Call. *Del.* 165–87, Ptolemy defeating the Giant-like Celtoi; see Bing (1988) 128–31.

[109] See the survey in Harder (2012) 712–13.

[110] For the political resonances of the Hercules episode in the *Aeneid* and the connections among Hercules, Aeneas, and Augustus see Chapter 3, Section 3.3.

two points that are important for Statius' treatment. The first is the adaptation of Danaus to Roman contexts in connection with the topic of Roman civil war. The second is the potential of topographical descriptions for creating a sense of a layered past within the royal house. A third indirect effect of Virgil's text stems from the centrality acquired by Apollo as god of empire under Augustus. Writing about the suffering of a royal house that entertains a special relationship with Apollo acquires a different poignancy in a post-Augustan and post-Virgilian context. It seems fitting to bring these three aspects into the picture before considering the Coroebus episode in the context of Statius' poem.

Argive myth plays an important role within Augustan ideology. In the aftermath of the conquest of Alexandria and the victory of Actium, Octavian inaugurated the Temple of Palatine Apollo and its surrounding buildings.[111] The iconography of the Apollo Palatinus Temple employed elements of Argive myth. A portico within the temple complex comprised statues of the Danaids and of their enemies, the sons of Aegyptus. Danaus too was represented, threatening his enemies with drawn sword.[112] The interpretation of this iconographical choice has involved much debate. One possible way of reading it sees Danaus as an image of Augustus, with Antony in the guise of Aegyptus.[113] This reading would be consistent with panegyric uses of the figure of Danaus in Hellenistic contexts—these, as we previously saw, may lie behind Callimachus' interest in this hero.[114] Be that as it may, there is little doubt that, no matter how they unpacked the myth of Danaus (whether in connection with Augustus or his enemies), Roman viewers understood the strife of Danaus and Aegyptus as related to the civil wars of Rome, especially the one between Antony and Augustus. Although Danaus may have had a primarily dynastic relevance in Callimachus, in Augustan culture his story is inextricably linked to civil war.

Virgil's interaction with Argive mythology should be read against this background of adaptations of Argive mythology in political contexts. Through a number of Callimachean allusions Virgil brings Argos in connection with Rome, and especially with the future location of Augustus' palace, the Palatine. In *Aeneid* 8, the episode of Hercules' visit to the house of Evander and his killing of Cacus is deeply influenced by the Callimachean account of Hercules' visit to the house of Molorchus

---

[111] On this complex see "Apollo Palatinus" in *LTUR* I 54–7 (P. Gros); Sauron (1981) 286–94; Zanker (1983); Simon (1986) 20–4; Kellum (1985) 172–5; Galinsky (1996) 213–24; Gurval (1995) 111–31; Miller (2009) 185–252.

[112] Prop. 2.31.3–4; Ov. *Trist.* 3.1.62; cf. also *Ars* 1.74.

[113] Galinsky (1996) 220–2.

[114] Other Argive myths were represented on the Campana plaques of the temple, and the cult statue of Apollo Palatinus seems to have been distinctively linked with the Argive cult of Apollo; Spawforth (2012) 184; see Section 5.4 for the presence of the Perseus myth on the Campana plaques.

before killing the Nemean lion, recounted in the *Victory of Berenice*.[115] Apart from lexical reminiscences, general correspondences between the two passages can be highlighted: In both episodes Hercules is hosted in a humble house; the Nemean lion lives in a cave and ravages the local cattle, exactly like Cacus; like Cacus, the Nemean lion is strangled by Hercules; and in both stories, the monster's killing is celebrated by a sacrifice performed by the humble character who gives Hercules hospitality. Callimachus' intertext thus encourages the reader to relate the Palatine to the city of Argos.

This play on the interconnections of Rome and Argos is coupled with a tantalizing use of Argive mythology, involving in particular the figure of Danaus. Virgil presents the war in Latium as a repetition of the war of Troy, with the Latins in the role of the Greeks.[116] Significantly, the poet stresses the Latins' connection with Argos. Turnus is a descendant of the royal house of Argos.[117] His city, Ardea, was founded by Danae, Perseus' mother.[118] Turnus' shield is decorated with images of the myth of Io, the Greek/Egyptian heroine who played such an important role in Ptolemaic ideology.[119] Given the Egyptian connections of Io, we may see this element as providing a link between Turnus and Antony, whom Augustan propaganda styled as an egyptianizing descendant of the Ptolemies. Furthermore, Turnus is supported by Argive allies such as Catillus and Coras, descendants of the Argive priest Amphiaraus, and by a son of Hercules, Aventinus.[120] The Latins seek the aid of a Greek hero from Argos, Diomedes.[121] Moreover, in the *Aeneid*, the Greeks are usually referred to as the Argives or the Danai, a label that brings to mind their mythical ancestor Danaus.[122]

This chain of allusions culminates in book 10 of the *Aeneid*. Here, Turnus kills Pallas and strips off his baldric, which portrays the sons of Aegyptus slaughtered by the Danaides.[123] Because Turnus is related to the royal house of Argos and is presented as an Argive, perhaps the prophecy on Pallas' baldric has been fulfilled: A descendant of Danaus puts an end to the life of the young and inexperienced Pallas, just as the Danaides killed their cousins.[124] Yet, as the Virgilian narrative unfolds,

---

[115] George (1974) 43–70; Gransden (1976) 26.

[116] Cf. *A.* 6.89–90; see Anderson (1957).

[117] *A.* 7.371–2.

[118] *A.* 7.409–12; very possibly a Virgilian invention, see Horsfall (2000) 280–1.

[119] *A.* 7.789–92. Cf. also 794, in which Turnus' soldiers are labeled *Argiua pubes*.

[120] Catillus and Coras: *A.* 7.670–4; on their descending from Amphiaraus see Plin. *Nat.* 16.637 and Horsfall (2000) 441.

[121] *A.* 11.243–5.

[122] Cf. for instance *A.* 2.254–9.

[123] On this much-discussed *ekphrasis* see Galinsky (1996) 221–2; Harrison (1991) 198, (1998), (2006) 173–4; Putnam (1998) 189–207; Fowler (2000) 212–14.

[124] This line of interpretation, with different nuances, in Conte (1985); Harrison (1991) 198, (2006) 173–4.

the possibility of a different reading of the baldric emerges. Aeneas' endeavors throughout the poem are accompanied by a progressive rapprochement with Achilles and with the Greek side of the Trojan War. This process culminates in the final duel, in which Aeneas plays the role of Achilles. This transition of Aeneas from the role of the Trojan to that of the Greek allows us to read the baldric differently: Turnus is the slaughtered bridegroom, the son of Aegyptus, whereas Aeneas is one of the Greek daughters of Danaus.[125] The transition from one possible reading to the other marks the progressive appropriation of Greek/Argive mythology by Aeneas. Regardless of what we make of Danaus, it is clear that in the text of Virgil, the murder of the Danaides is related to the war of Trojans and Latins, a war involving peoples who will one day be related and that foreshadows Roman civil wars.

Let us turn to the *Thebaid*. The three features of Virgil's reception of Argive myth that I have just outlined are central to Statius' weaving of connections between the Coroebus myth and historical realities. Statius builds on Virgil's use of Argive stories to link the house of Argos with Imperial Rome and, more specifically, to identify the past of Argos with the imperial past of Flavian Rome, especially the Augustan period. If in Callimachus the Argive myth is an occasion for looking into the past of the royal house through the veil of myth, in Statius the story of Danaus becomes a way of looking into the civil war past of Rome. But let us proceed in order. For one, Statius builds on Virgil's play on the equivalence between Rome and Argos, fueled by engagement with Callimachus' *Victory of Berenice*. In the *Thebaid*, the palace of Argos at the time of Crotopus and Coroebus is described as a poor dwelling.[126] This detail alludes to Hercules' visit to Evander's house in book 8 of the *Aeneid*, Statius' main intertext for this section, itself reworking Hercules' visit to the humble house of Molorchus.[127] In the Hercules episode, Virgil describes a poor house on the Palatine that by the Augustan period has become a rich palace. This transformation is mirrored within Statius' narrative: Crotopus' house is a humble dwelling, but by the time Adrastus tells his story, it too has become a wealthy palace. This palace is very similar to the Palatine palace of Augustus. Adrastus' house is particularly linked to the cult of Apollo, containing an altar to the god, exactly like the Palatine palace.[128] Moreover, Adrastus' palace hosts a portico with statues of ancestors.[129] This detail is taken from the *Aeneid*'s description of the house of Latinus, a passage that scholars

---

[125] Keuls (1974) 116.

[126] *Theb.* 1.570.

[127] Evander's poor house, visited by Hercules and later Aeneas: *A.* 8.362–8; Vessey (1973) 101; McNelis (2007) 27–9; Ganiban (2007) 13–17 with references.

[128] *Theb.* 1.553–6, 668.

[129] *Theb.* 2.214–23.

interpret as alluding to the future palaces of Augustus.[130] Adrastus' palace, like the
Palatine complex, includes statues of Danaus.[131]

Statius also inherits from Virgil the idea of using the story of Danaus as a parallel
for civil war. As we have previously seen, the Coroebus episode is introduced by the
ekphrasis of the cup of Danaus.[132] References to Danaus pervade the narrative of
the *Thebaid*, and nearly every mention of the Argive king is accompanied by a re-
minder of his crime. Danaus occupies a climactic position at the end of the two lists
of Argive ancestors introduced by the poet (*Theb.* 2.222, 6.292–4). The Danaus myth
is also evoked in other contexts. The "night of Danaus" is depicted on the shield of
Hippomedon.[133] The myth of Danaus is hinted at during the Hypsipyle episode in
book 5, an independent narrative excursus that, in many ways, mirrors the *Thebaid*'s
main plot.[134] Finally, there is an allusion to Danaus and his daughters at the end of
the poem, in Statius' description of the Argive women's pledge to Theseus at the
altar of Clementia in Athens.[135] Here the women from Argos present themselves as
a "throng of women, not aware of crime" [*nec conscia noxae | turba*, Theb. 12.548–9].
Like the Aeschylean Danaides, they are innocent suppliant women of Argive de-
scent, gathered around an altar, imploring an Athenian king.

Statius' use of Danaus follows in the footsteps of Virgil: It is a story of fraternal
strife that can work as an analog for the poem's main conflict.[136] Like Polynices,
Danaus fought against his brother Aegyptus for the throne and went to Argos as an
exile. His *nefas*, that of ordering his daughters to kill their promised husbands after
pretending to have made peace with Aegyptus, reminds us of the broken covenant
between the two Theban brothers. The story of Danaus is an Argive myth of civil
war that forms a counterpart to stories of civil conflict plaguing the royal house of
Thebes before Eteocles and Polynices.[137] It makes clear that fraternal war is in the
DNA of the royal house of Argos, just as it is in the history of the royal house of

[130] *A.* 7.170–8; see Horsfall (2000) 146–8 and Harrison (2006) 177.
[131] *Theb.* 2.222.
[132] *Theb.* 1.542.
[133] *Theb.* 4.132–5. On Hippomedon's shield see Parkes (2012) 112; Klinnert (1970) 82–3; Fernandelli (1996) 88–90; Taisne (1994) 280.
[134] There are obvious thematic parallels between the story of the Danaides and the events at Lemnos (a group of women slaying their husbands); the story is mentioned as a model by the mastermind of the Lemnos crime, the aged Polyxo: *Theb.* 5.117–19. On the Lemnos episode's similarities and thematic affinities with the *Thebaid*'s main narrative see Conclusions, Section C.1.
[135] *Theb.* 12.546–59.
[136] Georgacopoulou (1996b) 108.
[137] A similar point, on the Theban side, is conveyed by the poet's insistence on the story of the Spartoi (cf. e.g. *Theb.* 1.180–5); see Chapter 4, Section 4.4.

Thebes. Both the house of Thebes and that of Argos have a predisposition to fraternal hatred.

Unlike the story of Eteocles and Polynices, for Roman readers the myth of Danaus is particularly related to the civil war fought by Augustus. In this sense, the story is singularly apt for establishing a connection between the house of Argos in the poem and the imperial house after Augustus. The visitors of the Palatine palace under Domitian saw the statues of Danaus and Aegyptus in the portico of the Apollo Temple, and, whatever their interpretation, there is little doubt that they related the iconography to the civil conflict that had led to the establishment of the Augustan regime. In a similar manner, the Argives visiting Adrastus' palace on the occasion of Polynices' wedding see the statue of Danaus in the portico, a reminder of the civil strife that affected their royal house in the past.[138] The Danaus statues bid the Argives remember that civil war is engrained in the history of their city, just like those in the Palatine reminded viewers that civil war was an inescapable part of Rome's past. Danaus is to Adrastus what Augustus was to Domitian. Just as the 69 CE conflict came to renew the civil wars of the late Republic, the civil war of Eteocles and Polynices comes to reiterate Danaus' crime. Adrastus' Argos is a city on the brink of falling once more into civil war, just like Rome in the last years of Nero. But Adrastus, who pours wine for Polynices from Danaus' goblet, is tragically unaware of this.

5.8 COROEBUS IN THE *THEBAID*

The last necessary step before analyzing the political texture of the Coroebus episode consists of considering the story's intratextual allusions and thematic links with other parts of the poem. These shed fundamental light on how to read this portion of Statius' text in connection with the topic of civil/fratricidal war, helping us in turn to bring into focus some of the episode's political resonances.

There is some degree of correspondence between the Coroebus story and the plot of the *Thebaid*. In the poem's main narrative, Jupiter is infuriated with the houses of Thebes and Argos because of their impiety and decides to punish them through civil war.[139] By doing this, he fulfills the desire of Oedipus, who has invoked Tisiphone as avenger and has asked her to punish his sons.[140] Jupiter has blood ties with both houses (in the case of Argos through his love affair with Danae, and in the case of Thebes through his relationship with Europa).[141] He is then in the same position as

---

[138] *Theb.* 2.222.

[139] *Theb.* 1.197–302.

[140] *Theb.* 1.80–1.

[141] *Theb.* 1.224–6.

Apollo, related to Argos by his affair with Psamathe. The task of inflicting war on Thebes and Argos is carried out by the Erinyes, snake-haired monsters, whose description matches Statius' portrait of Poena. The Erinyes are traditionally regarded as an instrument of the gods' punishment and are often called Poenae in Rome.[142] In Coroebus' story, Poena prematurely kills a number of young Argives: In this she is very similar to the war that snatches away so many Theban and Argive youths.[143] Poena is called *lues* [plague, *Theb.* 1.601], a term used by Statius to refer to the damage inflicted on Thebes through civil war.[144] Finally, as in the Coroebus story, in the *Thebaid*, the monster of civil war is forestalled by the intervention of a hero, Theseus, whose fight against Thebes is explicitly presented as a battle against the snake-haired Erinyes.[145]

In addition to these thematic resemblances, there are several other connections between the Coroebus episode and other sections of the poem. The *Thebaid* features heroes who fight chthonic monsters as well as mortals engaged in combat against female creatures who carry out destructive plans on behalf of the gods. Several characters seem to be measured against Coroebus in the course of the narrative, all of them proving unequal to the task, with the sole exception of Theseus. To begin with, the story of Linus and Coroebus is distinctly evoked in the Nemean episode in books 4 and 5, which can be read as a consciously distorted and controversial replay of the Coroebus story. Statius recounts how the child Opheltes was killed by a giant snake, a monster sacred to Jupiter, that inhabited the woods of Nemea. The child had been carelessly abandoned by Hypsipyle, his nurse, while she recounted her past adventures to the Argives.[146] Opheltes is explicitly connected to Linus. At the child's funeral, Opheltes' body is laid on an embroidered cloth representing the death of Linus.[147] Moreover, Opheltes carries within his other name his destiny of being the beginning of all evils for the Argives (Archemorus).[148] In this he resembles Linus, whose death marks the start of all evils falling upon Argos. Correspondingly, Hypsipyle, Opheltes' nurse, shares many traits of Psamathe. Both Hypsipyle and Psamathe have suffered violence.[149] Psamathe was raped within the woods of Argos,

---

[142] For the identification of Poine and Erinys in Greek culture cf. e.g. Aeschin. 1.190; Str. 3.175; in Roman culture: Luc. 6.695; V. Fl. 1.796; Cic. *Pis.* 91, *Ver.* 5.113. For connection of Poena and Erynis in Statius cf. *Theb.* 8.24–5, 12.646; see *RE* 22 1212–15.

[143] There is, however, an important difference: Whereas Poena in the Coroebus episode acts at Apollo's behest, in the poem the Furies have a greater degree of freedom and, although their plan overlaps with Jupiter's designs, they do not act under the god's supervision.

[144] *Theb.* 11.273–5; see also *Theb.* 10.854–5; McNelis (2007) 47; Vessey (1973) 104.

[145] See subsequent discussion in this section.

[146] *Theb.* 5.499–540.

[147] *Theb.* 6.64–6; Vessey (1973) 104–5; Brown (1994) 161–87.

[148] *Theb.* 4.726, 5.609; Parkes (2012) 301–2.

[149] For Hypsipyle's rape cf. *Theb.* 5.463.

along the banks of a river. Hypsipyle, in turn, is compared several times to Amymone, a nymph who, like Psamathe, was raped by Poseidon in the woods of Nemea.[150]

Statius encourages his readers to see the Nemean snake as an image of the civil war that Jupiter has unleashed against Argives and Thebans. Just as Poena was a personification of Apollo's wrath and was his own possession, this monster belongs to Jupiter. Jupiter's snake takes the first victim of civil war, and can thus work well as an image of Jupiter's *poena*, the civil conflict itself. In addition, Statius compares the snake of Nemea to Python, the monster slain by Apollo at the beginning of the Coroebus section. This provides a further connection between Jupiter's snake and the Coroebus episode.[151] In the Coroebus episode, Coroebus marvels that a monster such as Poena is dearer to Apollo than the life of the innocent Argives (*Theb.* 1.648–50); Statius evokes this same sense of marvel when he reminds his readers that the snake of Nemea was dear to the gods.[152]

Capaneus faces the snake and kills it and therefore incurs divine wrath, just like Coroebus after the killing of Poena. Jupiter nearly strikes him with his thunderbolt, a clear foreshadowing of the hero's future death by Jupiter's fire in book 10.[153] Capaneus is a perverted version of Coroebus: The latter deserves to be spared by Apollo (1.661–2) because of his piety (1.644), but Capaneus is anything but pious. True, there are some elements of provocation in Coroebus' words to Apollo, but Capaneus goes far beyond that when he expresses his hope that the snake is a toy of the gods, so that, by killing it, he can offend them.[154]

Whereas Capaneus proves to be a sort of monstrous, and in the end ineffective, version of Coroebus, Theseus looks like a worthy replacement for Coroebus. Like Coroebus, he is the one who interrupts the chain of violence released by the gods

---

[150] In the Amymone myth, the land of Argos is struck by a draught sent by Poseidon. Danaus sends his daughters to look for water in the Nemean woods. One of them (Amymone) asks Poseidon to show her a running spring. The god reveals the place but then takes advantage of Amymone in the woods. The story is recounted by Callimachus in the *Aetia*: Frs. 65–6 Harder (Amymone mentioned at 66.2); see Parkes (2012) 305. Amymone appears among the Argive ancestors in the sixth book: *Theb.* 6.287–8. In this scene, although she has found the spring, she is *tristis* [gloomy]. In book 4, Argos is again struck by drought (this time because of Bacchus), and Adrastus, like Danaus before him, sends the Argive warriors in search of water in the woods of Nemea. They approach Amymone's fountain but find it dry (*Theb.* 4.742). However, another Amymone type comes to their help: Hypsipyle. She too is *tristis* when they encounter her (4.721; cf. also 4.747), and she too has been raped, like Amymone and Psamathe, and lost her children (*Theb.* 5.452–7, 463, 644). In book 5, Statius compares the women of Lemnos to the Danaides several times (see preceding discussion, and cf. *Theb.* 5.116–18), thus strengthening the link between Hypsipyle and Amymone.

[151] *Theb.* 5.531–3.

[152] Cf. the snake description (*Theb.* 5.505–33) and Statius' mention of the gods' heartfelt grievance at the snake's death (*Theb.* 5.579–87).

[153] *Theb.* 5.583–7.

[154] *Theb.* 5.566–70.

against Thebes and Argos. Theseus himself presents his war at Thebes as an expedition to conquer the Poenae and the "snake-haired Sisters," just like Coroebus' mission involved killing Poena:

... terrarum leges et mundi foedera mecum
defensura cohors, dignas insumite mentes
coeptibus: hac omnem diuumque hominumque fauorem
Naturamque ducem coetusque silentis Auerni
stare palam est; illic Poenarum exercita Thebis
agmina et anguicomae ducent uexilla sorores.
Theb. 12.642–7

... soldiers, who will defend with me the laws of nations and the world's pacts, think as befits our enterprise. It is plain that the favor of all gods and men, the multitudes of silent Avernus, and Nature, our leader, stand on our side. On the other are the hosts of the Poenae, long in service at Thebes, and the snake-haired Sisters will lead the standards.

Statius underscores that Creon is a descendant of the Theban snake killed by Cadmus. Thus his death is a powerful symbol of Theseus' ability to extinguish the seeds of civil war in Thebes. And just before being killed by Theseus, Creon is compared to a snake.[155] Theseus' victory over Creon is hence likened to Coroebus' defeat of Poena and to Apollo's slaying of Python.

Echoes of Adrastus' hymn to Apollo in book 1 connect Theseus to Apollo. Long ago, David Vessey drew attention to the intertextual links between the passage describing Apollo *qua* Mithras in book 1 and the images on Theseus' shield.[156] Theseus has traits of both Coroebus and of Apollo. The idea is partly anticipated by the Coroebus episode itself, in which, as we have seen, the hero and the god are brought into close connection, as they both kill chthonic monsters and journey in search of expiation. This merging of Coroebus and Apollo in the figure of Theseus is reinforced by Statius' use of the theme of *clementia*.[157] *Clementia* consists in pardoning one's enemies, interrupting the sequence of retaliations initiated by the violation of a human or divine law. The bloodshed at Argos is forestalled by Apollo's *clementia*, and this central virtue is transferred to Theseus at the end of the narrative. Divine *clementia* is replaced by human *clementia*, while the gods disappear from the

---

[155] *Theb.* 11.652–4.

[156] *Theb.* 1.717–20, 12.666–71; Vessey (1973) 313. On this passage see also Chapter 2, Section 2.8.

[157] McNelis (2007) 45, 48–9.

scene. Unlike in the case of Coroebus, there is no formal divine sanction of Theseus' achievement, nor is there any indication that the gods will cease from their anger against the Argives and Thebans, that they will pardon Theseus' killing of the snake of civil war just like Apollo forgave Coroebus' stepping in the way of his vengeance.

Allusions to Adrastus' hymn to Apollo are perceptible in other sections of the *Thebaid*. Adrastus ends his hymn by listing a number of deeds accomplished by the god. The list includes punishments inflicted by Apollo on famous sinners: Marsyas, Niobe, Phlegyas, and Tityos.[158] Images of these punitive actions accompany the narrative of the Theban war, providing a further, indirect link between Apollo's vengeance at Argos and the *Thebaid*'s civil war. Capaneus is compared to Tityos in book 6, during the boxing match with Alcidamas, and again on the occasion of his death.[159] In book 5, after the hero's killing of the Nemean snake, it seemed as though Capaneus could somehow be a new Apollo, triumphing over chthonic monsters. Here we discover that Capaneus is more similar to those monsters than to the god: His dead body occupies a huge portion of land, like that of Python, and is compared to Tityos' body pierced by Apollo's arrows.[160] In book 7, a Theban warrior killed by Amphiarausis is significantly named Phlegyas; though he is a priest of Apollo, he carries the name of one of Apollo's traditional enemies, listed in Adrastus' hymn.[161]

The myth of Niobe is evoked during Parthenopaeus' *aristeia* in book 9. With the aid of Diana, Parthenopaeus kills a number of Theban youths with his bow, thus repeating Apollo's and Diana's attack on the sons and daughters of Theban Niobe. The framework of Niobe's myth is explicitly suggested at the beginning of the section (*Theb.* 9.679–82). The goddess gives her special arrows to the youth, so that he can shoot at Theban enemies infallibly, repeating the slaughter of Niobe's sons.[162] The motif of the "invisible arrow," by which Diana kills Dryas, Parthenopaeus' murderer, is another characteristic motif of the Niobe myth.[163] Although Parthenopaeus' *aristeia* entails a massacre of Theban warriors, the theme of Apollo's punishment on the Argives is also present. The first victim of Parthenopaeus' arrows is a Theban called Coroebus.[164] The idea that the topic of Apollo's anger is reflected in Parthenopaeus' *aristeia* is confirmed by the following names in the list of Parthenopaeus' victims: the

---

[158] *Theb.* 1.709–15.

[159] *Theb.* 6.753–5, 11.12–17.

[160] Cf. *Theb.* 1.567–8.

[161] *Theb.* 7.711. Phlegyas is also the name of one of Eteocles' servants: *Theb.* 3.80, 8.688.

[162] *Theb.* 9.728–31.

[163] Cf. Ov. *Met.* 6.148–310 and *Theb.* 9.875–6.

[164] *Theb.* 9.745.

sons of Abas (one of the Argive ancestors named by Statius in book 6) and a hero significantly called Argus.[165]

In conclusion, thematic connections between Adrastus' account and the rest of the poem suggest Theseus as an equivalent of Coroebus and link Poena to the *Thebaid*'s fraternal war. Theseus, like Coroebus, is an outsider who brings an end to the war decreed by the gods as a punishment for wicked kings. Although figuratively both Theseus and Coroebus can be aligned with Perseus, neither Theseus not Coroebus enjoys apotheosis. As we will see, a character who becomes divine within the poem, Menoeceus, has many ties with Coroebus.[166] However, the lack of divine reward for Coroebus has something in common with the atmosphere at the poem's end, in which Theseus' victory is achieved in the absence of any divine ratification. It is important to keep these thematic connections in mind as we move on to reflect on the Coroebus episode's interaction with the political and historical reality of Flavian Rome.

5.9 COROEBUS AND FLAVIAN ROME

We have now gathered the necessary elements to tease out the political and ideological implications of Statius' narrative of Linus and Coroebus. At the beginning of this chapter, I sketched the theological pattern surrounding Roman narratives of political crisis and the elements accompanying it, such as the idea of divine hostility, sacrificial substitution, and the necessity for atonement. I then considered the *ekphrasis* of Adrastus' cup; it appeared that both Perseus and Ganymede have imperial dimensions and achieve apotheosis, and that Coroebus, though similar to Perseus in many respects, does not obtain the same reward for killing a monster. I then examined the differences between Statius and his two main models, namely Virgil and Callimachus. Statius introduces the idea of sacrificial substitution, absent in his models, and emphasizes the topic of atonement already present in Callimachus. The story of Coroebus has the potential for working as a reflection on the past of the imperial house in light of the role of Argive myth within Ptolemaic ruler ideology. This dimension is present in Callimachus; Statius enhances it and refines it by building on Virgil's own adaptation of Argive mythology in the *Aeneid*, in which the dynastic dimension of Argive myth is transferred to a civil war context. The Coroebus episode also functions as a cameo image of the plot of the *Thebaid*, with many textual and structural links with the rest of the poem. In particular,

---

[165] *Theb.* 9.758. For Abas as Argive ancestor see *Theb.* 2.220.
[166] Chapter 6, Section 6.7.

Statius highlights links between Theseus and Coroebus and fashions Poine as an embodiment of the civil conflict.

It is in light of this equivalence between civil war and Poine that a first set of correspondences emerges between Statius' excursus and Roman reflections on civil war. In the Coroebus story, the gods, angry with a wicked royal house, unleash a monster on the city. This monster, a personification of divine vengeance (Poena) is brought into close connection with fratricidal/civil war, which is also presented as divine punishment. Poena is stopped by a hero (not a member of the royal house) who dares to face her. But to arrest divine vengeance is in itself a sin and attracts further retaliation. Thus other catastrophes fall on the city, proving that the gods have not ceased from their anger. In the end, however, upon witnessing Coroebus' self-sacrifice, the greatest act of *pietas*, Apollo consents to spare the city. If we build on Statius' twinning of Poena with civil war, a number of significant correspondences appear with perceptions of the 69 CE conflict. I have shown in a previous section that the Romans tend to interpret the outbreak of civil war as divine retribution for previous sins. These sentiments are particularly present in accounts of 69 CE. In popular perception, that civil war was caused by the gods' hostility to a wicked royal house (the Julio-Claudians, and especially Nero). In the Coroebus story, catastrophe is visited on the entire city because of Crotopus' impious deeds. Divine anger, manifesting itself as civil war, had been stopped by the intervention of the Flavians. Although it served a positive purpose, the Flavians' involvement in civil war entailed pollution. It was far from ensured that the gods would leave this unnoticed. In spite of Vespasian's attempts at atonement, other catastrophes befell the city and the empire under Titus and Domitian (especially the eruption of Vesuvius and the fire of 80 CE), arousing the suspicion that the gods' anger had not been placated. Under Domitian, scrupulous religious observance coexisted with constant fear of provoking the gods again, and the need for expiation and atonement was acutely felt.

These interactions with coeval religious outlooks offer new ways of understanding the role of the gods within the Coroebus episode and within the *Thebaid* in general. I observed in the introduction that Statius emphasizes in particular the punitive role of the gods at the expense of more balanced views of the gods such as the one in Virgil's *Aeneid*. In particular, the *Thebaid*'s gods know little about rewarding the pious, they are slow and ineffective at protecting their friends, and they are very successful at wreaking havoc on their enemies. The *Thebaid*'s emphasis on the punitive nature of the gods is particularly amenable to Statius' search for the tragic effect.[167] However, it can also be related to coeval perceptions of the gods.

---

[167] See Introduction, Section I.8.

The providential elements of religion are more likely to be emphasized in constructive contexts, in an atmosphere of optimism and new beginning. But Statius' poem looks primarily at the experience of civil war. In these circumstances, the terrifying and punitive aspects of the divinity are more likely to emerge than its providential aspects. Apollo's relentless cruelty in the Coroebus episode seems less a purely literary creation when read against an historical context in which the fear of divine retaliation drives Domitian to resume the capital punishment of unfaithful Vestals. And Apollo's decision to visit punishment on all of Argos solely because of the sins of Crotopus looks less exotic when set against widespread perceptions that Rome's ruin had been motivated by Nero's impiety.[168]

Even when Statius considers the possibility of a new beginning—chiefly through the poem's finale and the figure of Theseus—he is still influenced by the somewhat pessimistic religious climate that accompanied the reign of Titus and the early portions of Domitian's reign, a time of great uncertainty, religious anxiety, and recurring catastrophes. Statius does not feel he can vouchsafe divine benevolence for the Flavian political project (which explains why the gods are absent from the poem's close). This does not mean that criticism of the gods is foreign to Statius' poem, or that Statius approves of the gods being so cruel and arbitrary. Regardless of his personal likes or dislikes, Statius is painting a picture of the divine with which his troubled readers can connect while looking back at the experience of civil war, a context in which the harsh and somewhat arbitrary nature of the gods emerged in full force, overshadowing more optimistic conceptions.

Earlier in this chapter I noted that one of the main differences between Statius and his models is the emphasis on expiation and the notion of sacrificial substitution. Both are absent from the Virgilian excursus of Hercules and Cacus, whereas Callimachus does not seem to have included the idea that Coroebus offered his life in exchange for that of the Argives. The idea of self-sacrifice is tied to the topic of divine hostility: It is an attempt at placating the gods by way of substitution. It is a behavior particularly attached to Roman narratives of situations of extreme crisis, moments when divine hostility brings the city close to doom. During the republican period, the self-sacrifices of the Decii were famous; another example was the *deuotio* of Marcus Curtius, discussed earlier in this chapter, which forestalled the city's ruin. Ideas of sacrificial substitution also appear during the civil war period, precisely because this catastrophe too is usually perceived as stemming from divine hostility; we have previously observed that the topic of *deuotio* is central to Lucan's take on civil war but is also evoked by Tacitus' narrative of 69 CE. Unlike the story of

---

[168] For this notion cf. e.g. *Oct.* 235–7; Chapter 1, Section 1.6.

Apollo and Python, or Hercules and Cacus, the Coroebus myth could be modified to accommodate a cluster of religious ideas (divine hostility, punishment, sacrificial substitution) that were particularly attached to Roman narratives of crisis, including the crisis of 69 CE.

There exists a piece of imperial panegyric in which behavior consistent with that of Coroebus is attributed to Domitian. In *Siluae* 1.1, Domitian is addressed by the republican hero Curtius, who made a *deuotio* of himself to expiate the portentous opening of the earth in the Forum. Curtius says that had he lived in Curtius' time, Domitian would have offered his life, but, unlike Curtius and very much like Coroebus, he would have been spared.[169] Curtius, as we have seen, is a crucial figure in accounts of 69 CE, and it is possible, as we will see in Chapter 6, that Statius' comparison of Curtius and Domitian is connected to Domitian's participation in the war of 69 CE.[170] Domitian had been the only member of the Flavian family to actually engage in combat with Vitellius, and he did so when he was very young.[171] It is possible that Coroebus, this courageous youth who first faces the monster and then offers his life, is meant, among other things, as a mythical counterpart of the young emperor to be, who is credited by Statius with an attempt to offer his life for his fellow citizens. Domitian faced the monster of civil war, just like Coroebus, and he was spared by the gods because of his *pietas*.

In this context, the differences in characterization and action between Coroebus and Virgil's Hercules become particularly significant. As we saw, Coroebus is deprived of some of the most disturbing aspects of Hercules' heroism. He remains in control of his sentiments and is not prey to a sudden fury. His cold-blooded murder of Poena anticipates Theseus' dispatching of Creon at the end of the poem. Coroebus has no divine father and does not achieve apotheosis. Within Statius' mythical narrative, the model of the *theios aner* is replaced by something more secular and more civil.[172] This is a form of heroism that does not require the supernatural charisma stemming from divine origins. The city of Argos is not saved by a divine savior but by the courage of an extraordinary human outsider.

Perhaps the historical correspondences should be articulated in more general terms. A passage in Juvenal is particularly instructive. In his eighth satire, written under Hadrian, Juvenal declaims upon the theme *quid stemmata faciunt* [what difference does lineage make?]. At 8.198–230, he introduces Nero as the clearest

---

[169] *Silv.* 1.1.66–83.

[170] Chapter 6, Section 6.6.

[171] Tac. *Hist.* 3.63–74; Suet. *Dom.* 1.2 Both Titus and Vespasian never personally met the Vitellians in battle. The major victory against Vitellius' armies (Cremona II) was obtained by Antonius Primus. More on this in Chapter 6, Section 6.2.

[172] See also Chapter 3, especially Section 3.7.

example that lineage does not matter: He was high-born, yet he stained himself with countless crimes. And indeed, had the people been given free vote, they would have chosen Seneca over Nero as their emperor (8.211–12). Then Juvenal moves on to list a number of situations of extreme danger in which Rome was rescued by a morally upright outsider. The list references, among others, Cicero, Marius, Servius Tullius, and the Decii, who gave up their lives for the state (236–68). Juvenal makes no explicit reference to the dynasty in power, but this type of rhetoric could easily be applied to Hadrian and to his predecessor on the imperial throne.

To articulate Roman history in terms of a succession of repeated crises and last-minute saves is no novelty. For instance, Virgil's narrative of the history of Rome on Aeneas' shield seems to be arranged precisely around this principle; as we will see more clearly in Chapter 6, the idea of Roman history as characterized by a series of recurring crises is a pattern Roman politicians were wont to exploit to portray themselves as the last in a chain of saviors of the state.[173] What is new in Juvenal is the emphasis on the social extraction of the savior, the fact that he is an outsider, and the importance given to self-sacrifice. At times of crisis, Rome was saved by low-born outsiders, who risked or lost their lives in the process. This type of rhetoric was central to the Flavian triumph. The Flavii embodied precisely the type of the low-born outsider who brings salvation at times of crisis.

More generally, this rhetoric was also dear to the new elites of the Roman Empire, families that had risen to the top but could not boast an aristocratic pedigree.[174] Some of Statius' patrons clearly fell into this category. The Annaens, for instance, for whom Statius writes *Siluae* 2.7, were newcomers from Baetica, and it is significant that Juvenal inscribes one of this clan's heroes, Seneca, in the tradition of low-born outsiders who come to the help of the state at times of crisis. It seems clear that the Coroebus episode allows Statius to recreate this type of dynamic within a mythical narrative. Statius recovers the imperial potential in the version by Callimachus and sets it in a Roman civil war context so that he can replace the Virgilian tale of Hercules—a story of salvation coming from a child of Jupiter— with a mythical equivalent for the kind of stories mentioned by Juvenal, the tales of Rome saved by the worthy outsider, which appealed both to the Flavians and to his patrons.

---

[173] On the shield of Aeneas as a collection of "crisis" narratives see Harrison (1997). On the appropriation of narratives of crisis by Roman politicians, with particular reference to the Gallic sack of 390 BCE, see Chapter 6, Section 6.3.

[174] Habinek (2000) 292–4.

6

The Gauls on the Capitol

⌒ ───

IN CHAPTERS 3, 4, and 5, I have explored a number of different strategies adopted
by Statius to interact with the recent experience of civil war. Both Argos and Thebes
are brought into connection with Imperial Rome, and the past crimes of both Argos
and Thebes bring to mind images of the civil wars of the late Republic. In Chapter 4,
we saw that one of the effects of Statius' interaction with Lucan is to connect the
poem's civil war to the 69 CE conflict. Likewise, the Neronian allusions we explored
in Chapter 1 encourage the reader to relate the *Thebaid*'s narrative to the context of
the last years of Nero's principate and its immediate aftermath.

   In this chapter, I continue to focus on the *Thebaid*'s interaction with the 69 CE
war, and I concentrate on a section of the poem to which I have referred only in
passing so far: the siege of Thebes in book 10. My starting point is a difficult pas-
sage from this book, and I try to show that to explain it, we need to explore Flavian
presentations of Vitellius' invasion of Italy and of the Flavian triumph of 69 CE.
How was Vespasian's civil war success presented to the people of Rome and the
empire? And how could Domitian, who came to power in 81 CE and could boast
no military success, link himself with his father's victory against Vitellius? In what
follows, I consider some features of mythologized versions of the 69 CE war, and
I show that they can shed new light on our understanding of passages of the *Thebaid*
and their historical and political resonances. This investigation allows me to explore
the *Thebaid*'s engagement with some aspects of Domitian's ideology that have not
been considered so far: Domitian's appropriation of his father's Jovian propaganda,

as well as Flavian uses of Celtomachy, Gigantomachy, and the theme of the rebirth of Rome.

So far, particularly in Chapter 4, we have seen that Statius relies on a rich Roman tradition that regards the conflict of Eteocles and Polynices as a suitable parallel for Roman civil wars. However, alongside this type of interaction, Roman culture knows of a simpler way of considering the war of Thebes in connection with political and historical contexts. This tradition looks back at important Greek models, such as Aeschylus' *Septem contra Thebas*. In this foundational play, the characterization of the Argive heroes and the description of their assault on Thebes is meant to evoke frightening experiences of barbaric threats against Greek cities (the Persian invasions of the first quarter of the fifth century are very much in the background). In republican Rome, and in the poetry of Virgil, there are traces of this simplified ideological exploitation, and there are signs that the Argive assault on Thebes is associated with memories of legendary battles for the survival of Rome.[1] In the *Thebaid* these two uses of the story (the Theban war as a mythical analogue of civil war and the Theban war as a projection of foreign assaults) coexist and can be employed as complementary ways of looking at the history of Rome because of the special circumstances of the 69 CE conflict. This last civil war of Rome had been marked by the clash of Roman armies, but one of these armies (Vitellius') could also be conveniently construed as a barbaric horde.

6.1 A GAUL AT THEBES

Let us begin with the siege of Thebes, recounted in book 10 of Statius' *Thebaid*. In this book, the Argives break the siege of their camp and reverse the situation by attempting to storm the city of Thebes. When the Argives rush to attack, the city gates are closed with all haste. But the Theban Echion is slower than the others. Some Argive heroes manage to slip in before he shuts the gate. Finding themselves trapped within the walls once the gate is closed, they are soon overwhelmed by their opponents. Among the trapped Argives is a hero named Amyntor, whose death is described in some detail:

> par operis iactura lucro, quippe hoste retento
> exclusere suos; cadit intra moenia Graius
> Ormenus, et pronas tendentis Amyntoris ulnas
> fundentisque preces penitus ceruice remissa

---

[1] See Introduction, Section I.9.

uerba solo uultusque cadunt, colloque decorus
torquis in hostiles cecidit per uulnus harenas.
Theb. 10.513–18

The labor balanced gain and loss, for keeping the enemy within, they shut their
comrades out. Greek Ormenus falls inside the walls. As Amyntor stretched
forth his upturned arms and poured out entreaties, his neck is cut right off,
words and face fall to the ground, his handsome necklace dropped from his
neck through the wound onto the hostile sands.

At first sight there is nothing remarkable in this scene. The sequence is modeled
on a passage from the *Aeneid*, in which a similar incident occurs.[2] There is, however,
a strange detail in Statius' picture. Amyntor, an Argive soldier, is wearing a *torquis*.[3]
This kind of collar is no Greek garment. Instead, it was known to the ancients
for being an attribute of barbarians, and especially of Gauls. The *torquis* is often
mentioned as the most typical spoil from a Gallic victory, and in the primary use of
the term to denote a physical object (that is, when it is not used metaphorically to
describe something in the shape of a *torquis*), the word usually refers to the garment
worn by barbarians or Gauls.[4] The famous Manlius Torquatus, for instance, owed
his name to his victory in a duel with a Gallic chieftain, from whom he took the
torquis as a spoil.[5] Archeological evidence shows that Roman subjects from Gaul
advertised their ethnic origin by portraying themselves with *torquis*-style collars,
and a *torquis* is commonly the hallmark of defeated Gauls in public and private
reliefs.[6]

Why this apparently unnecessary detail? Is this just an attempt to make the pic-
ture more exotic? Clearly not. The *Thebaid* passage also contains an allusion to a
famous poem by Propertius dealing with the defeat and death of a Gallic warrior:[7]

---

[2] *A.* 9.722–7.

[3] Or *torques*; spelling varies: see *OLD* p. 1951 s.v. *torques*. That Amyntor is a Theban is suggested by Shackleton
Bailey (2003) 163, unconvincingly.

[4] Cf. Lucil. 11.409 Marx; Quad. *Hist.* 10b Peter; Hor. *Carm.* 3.6.12; Prop. 4.10.44 (quoted subsequently in this
section); Curt. 3.3.13; V. Fl. 2.112; see *D–S* 5.375–8; *RE* 6A 1800 ff. For the *torquis* as a Gallic spoil cf. Liv.
24.42.8 and subsequent discussion in this section on Manlius Torquatus. *Torques* were conferred to Roman
soldiers as military awards (cf. e.g. *CIL* 1.709.4.5; *OLD* s.v. *Torques* p. 1951; *D–S* 5.377); this use stems from the
fact that this object was associated with victories over Celtic enemies.

[5] For the story of Manlius Torquatus see Quad. *Hist.* 10b Peter; Cic. *Fin.* 1.23; *Tusc.* 4.49.10; *Off.* 3.112.

[6] For the *torquis* as an ethnic marker under Roman rule see e.g. the Vachères warrior: Barruol (1996). The dying
Gaul from Pergamon, whom Statius probably saw in person in Rome, also wears a *torquis*: see discussion of this
famous statue and its display within Vespasian's victory monuments in Section 6.4.

[7] Williams (1972) 94.

genus hic Brenno iactabat ab ipso,
mobilis e rectis fundere gaesa rotis.
illi uirgatas maculanti sanguine bracas
<u>torquis</u> ab incisa <u>decidit</u> unca gula.
Prop. 4.10.41–4

This one boasted descent from Brennus himself, quick at throwing Gallic javelins from the chariot he drove. His twisted necklace fell from his severed throat as he stained his striped trousers with his own blood.

In this passage, the Roman Marcellus wins *spolia opima* by killing Virdomarus, a Gallic chieftain claiming to be a descendant of the legendary Brennus, the leader of the Gauls who sacked Rome in 390 BCE. Statius' choice is then deliberately aimed at assigning his Argive hero barbaric features. What is the purpose of this strategy? What is a Gaul doing at the gates of Thebes in the middle of the heroic age?

6.2 *BELLA IOVIS*

To answer this question, we need to go back to an important episode from 69 CE: the siege of the Capitoline. We need to consider how this episode is constructed in Flavian sources and its interaction with Roman traditions of (real or imaginary) barbaric assaults against the city of Rome. Vitellius' last days in Rome were marked by a dramatic episode. After his troops surrendered to Antonius Primus at Narnia, Vitellius, upon receiving promises of immunity from the Flavian entourage, agreed to step down and attempted to resign his imperial *insignia*. His soldiers and the people of Rome did not allow him to surrender his title, but the news of his intention spread. In response, Flavius Sabinus, Vespasian's brother and prefect of the city, decided to place the city under the control of his urban cohorts. On the Quirinal, Sabinus and his retinue were intercepted by a group of Vitellians and attacked. Defeated, they were forced to retreat to the Capitoline, where they spent the night. During the night, the young Domitian joined his uncle on the hill. The following day, the Vitellians launched an attack against the Flavian garrison. The Capitoline was captured and set on fire. Sabinus was slaughtered, but Domitian managed to escape thanks to the help of an attendant of the Jupiter Temple (an *aedituus*) who first concealed him and then helped him go through the enemy lines disguised as a priest of Isis.[8]

---

[8] My summary follows the account by Tacitus at *Hist.* 3.63–74; cf. also Suet. *Dom.* 1.2; *Vit.* 15.3. Josephus' version (*BJ* 4.645–55) is considerably more favorable to the Flavians. Tacitus (perhaps in a deliberate reaction to pro-Flavian sources) plays down the importance of the episode and Vitellius' responsibility (in Tacitus, Vitellius'

This episode was not decisive for the outcome of the war. Its importance is due in large part to its subsequent exploitation by the Flavian entourage, especially Domitian. When he became emperor at the age of 30, Domitian, unlike his brother, could boast no military success. In spite of his strong desires, he had not been given a chance to lead a military expedition before his accession to the throne. One thing, however, he could pride himself on: He had played an active role in the events of 69 CE, being the only surviving member of the Flavian family to fight Vitellius in person. True, the future emperor was not credited with any particularly heroic deed during the siege, but the story could be used to underline his courage (in spite of his young age when he had joined his uncle to fight Vitellius) and to demonstrate that he enjoyed the gods' favor. Domitian made no secret of his conviction that he had been saved by Jupiter, whose attendant had concealed him and helped him to escape. In return for the aid received, Domitian first built an altar and a small shrine to Iuppiter Conservator [Jupiter the Savior] where the house of the *aedituus* stood. Then, after his accession, he replaced the small shrine with a new temple to Iuppiter Custos [Jupiter the Protector].[9] In short, the episode is the source of Domitian's predilection for Jupiter Capitolinus, which is reflected in his identification with the god in poetry and coinage and in his institution of the Capitoline games in honor of Jupiter Capitolinus.[10]

The story soon became a special topic in panegyric of Domitian. In Josephus, whose version is clearly influenced by pro-Flavian sources, Sabinus' initiative upsets Vitellius more than Antonius Primus' earlier (and much more important) victory; Domitian's role in the siege is enhanced, and there is no mention of his disguise as a priest; Sabinus displays none of the flaws and weaknesses Tacitus attributes to him; and the responsibility for burning the Capitol rests firmly with the Vitellians, who go so far as to plunder the temples on the hill.[11] In the *Thebaid*'s prologue, a mention of Domitian's participation in the siege emphatically closes the list of the emperor's military achievements.[12] Similarly, Martial never tires of praising Jupiter for having saved the life of his beloved sovereign on that occasion.[13] The episode of the Capitoline siege was also employed as the subject of historical epics. One such

---

troops act against his orders). In Josephus, the battle is a vital incident and the assault on the Capitol is directly ordered by Vitellius, who also witnesses Sabinus' execution. More on Josephus' version subsequently in this section.

[9] Tac. *Hist.* 3.74; Suet. *Dom.* 5.2. Both titles of Jupiter feature prominently in the emperor's coinage; Iuppiter Conservator: *RIC*² II nos. 489, 218, 301–2, 381, 416, 190; Iuppiter Custos: *RIC*² II nos. 635, 751.

[10] See further discussion in this section.

[11] In *Hist.* 3.71, on the contrary, Tacitus holds that the general account made the Flavians responsible for setting the buildings on fire in an attempt to repel the assailants.

[12] *Theb.* 1.17–22. Cf. also Stat. *Silv.* 1.1.79; Sil. 3.609–10.

[13] Mart. 5.1.7–8, 7.60.1–2; cf. also Mart. 2.91.2. On Domitian protected by Jupiter see also Mart. 9.20.9–10.

poem was written by Statius' father, the elder Papinius, as Statius himself informs us.[14] Another epic on the Capitoline battle was composed by Domitian. This poem is praised by Martial, who urges that Domitian's epic be placed right beside the *Aeneid* in the Palatine library (Mart. 5.5.7–8). We do not know when such a poem was composed. Our sources agree that Domitian dedicated himself considerably to poetry when he was young, so it seems reasonable to suppose that the poem was composed before Domitian's accession, in the immediate aftermath of the events of 69 CE.[15]

Be that as it may, Domitian's participation in the 69 CE siege is also likely to have been celebrated in the poetry and *declamationes* recited at the Capitoline games. We know from Quintilian that the subject of the compositions for the oratory contests at the games was always Jupiter Capitolinus, the god who saved the emperor.[16] And the one poem that has survived from the poetry contests has Jupiter as its subject.[17] Domitian presided in person over the games and was a member of the jury, and the ritual of the games seems to have encouraged the emperor's identification with the god.[18] As we will see, the games were instituted to atone for the fire that destroyed the Capitoline in 80 CE, but there are some indications that a connection to the former destruction of the Capitoline by fire during the 69 CE siege was also perceived. It is unlikely that in such a context the *aition* of Domitian's predilection for Jupiter was left unmentioned.

Regrettably, nothing is left of the epics of the elder Papinius or of Domitian. Such works raise intriguing questions, both from a literary and a historical point of view. What literary models could be harnessed for such poems? And how was Domitian's participation in the siege mythologized? Unfortunately, there is nothing to prove Penwill's fascinating speculation that Domitian's poem on the Capitoline battle was indebted to Virgil's narrative of the sack of Troy.[19] However, Statius' description of his father's poem on the siege provides some important information on how such an event could have been made the subject of poetry. It is worth examining in detail:

---

[14] Stat. *Silv.* 5.3.196–204, on which see subsequent discussion in this section.

[15] Quintilian praises Domitian's poetic ability in *Inst.* 10.1.91–2; that Domitian engaged in poetry at a young age is noted by V. Fl. 1.12–14; Tac. *Hist.* 4.86 and Suet. *Dom.* 2.2. Praise of Domitian's poetic ability also appears in Sil. 3.618–21; Stat. *Ach.* 1.14–8; Mart. 8.82; see Penwill (2000).

[16] Quint. *Inst.* 3.7.4; cf. also Plin. *Pan.* 54.1; Caldelli (1993) 68–9.

[17] The subject of Sulpicius Maximus' impromptu poem was Jupiter's reprimand to Sol for lending his chariot to Phaethon: see *CIL* 6.33976; *IGUR* 3.1336 with Nauta (2002) 330–5; cf. Chapter 2, Section 2.2.

[18] Domitian wore a crown with the Capitoline triad, and perhaps the ritual of the games stressed this connection further; see Momigliano (1935). Martial on Domitian as Jupiter: 14.1, 4.8.12, 5.6, 6.10, 7.56, 7.99, 8.14, 8.24, 9.28, 9.39, 9.86, 9.91.

[19] Penwill (2000) 69.

talia dum celebras, subitam ciuilis Erinys
Tarpeio de monte facem Phlegraeaque mouit
proelia. sacrilegis lucent Capitolia taedis
et Senonum furias Latiae sumpsere cohorts.
Silv. 5.3.195–8

Such was your occupation when the Fury of civil war suddenly raised her torch
from the Tarpeian hill and stirred battles as of Phlegra. The Capitol was alight
with sacrilegious brands, and Roman armies took on the fury of the Senones.

Statius connects the siege carried out by the Vitellians with Gigantomachy and
with the Gallic sack of Rome by Brennus in 390 BCE. Both *comparanda* seem wholly
appropriate: Gigantomachy (*Phlegraea . . . proelia, Silv.* 5.3.196) is an obvious parallel
for a battle fought on the Capitoline (the seat of Jupiter), and the story of the Gallic
sack refers to the most famous occasion in which the Capitoline was besieged prior
to 69 CE.[20] Moreover, the association of Celtomachy and Gigantomachy had illus-
trious literary models. It occurs in Callimachus' *Hymn to Delos* (171–6), in which the
Galatae attacking Delphi are compared to Titans. Gigantomachy and Celtomachy
were also associated in the monuments dedicated by the Attalids in Pergamon and
Athens.[21] Statius is describing his father's poem; it is possible that these two leg-
endary counterparts of the siege of 69 CE were already featured in the elder Papinius'
epic. Be that as it may, particularly interesting for us are the implications of such
comparisons, to which we now turn.

6.3 *MAGNUS ANNUS*

Let me start with the second of Statius' *comparanda*: the Gallic sack. It seems useful
at this juncture to provide a brief outline of this event.[22] In 390 BCE, a group of
Gauls descends into Italy and threatens to invade the Etruscan city of Clusium. The

---

[20] Gigantomachy is also implicitly evoked by Statius' two other references to the Capitoline battle: *Theb.* 1.21–2,
previously quoted, and *Silv.* 1.1.79.

[21] See Section 6.3.

[22] The fullest narrative account of the Gallic sack of Rome and its aftermath is Livy 5.32–55, on which the sub-
sequent summary is based; other sources: D.H. 13.6ff.; Plu. *Cam.* 15–30; D.S. 14.113–17; Plb. 1.6.2–4, 2.18.1–4,
2.22.4–5; App. *Gall.* frs. 1.1, 2–9; *Ital.* fr. 8.2; D.C. fr. 25, with Zonar. 7.23; Flor. *Epit.* 1.7.4–19; Eutr. 1.20. See
the discussion by Williams (2001) 142–50. There are several variants to the story [Ogilvie (1965) 720]; impor-
tantly, in one version of the legend the Capitol is actually conquered (see following discussion). The date of
390 BCE is dubious, even in terms of the Romans' own account of their history; I retain it for convenience
in my subsequent discussion.

inhabitants of Clusium ask for the aid of Rome. Rome sends a delegation, consisting of three members of the gens Fabia, to negotiate with the Gauls. But diplomacy fails, and the council eventually degenerates into a fight between Etruscans and Gauls. The Roman ambassadors, transgressing the laws of nations, join in battle, and one of the Fabii kills the Gallic chieftain. The Gauls are outraged and send an embassy to Rome, demanding that the Fabii be surrendered to them. Upon Rome's denial, the Gauls move against the city and defeat the Roman army in the proximity of the Allia River. Rome is panic stricken: Many flee to the countryside, but those able to fight encamp on the Capitoline, while the majority of the old patricians decide to wait for the enemy in their homes. According to some sources, the old nobles perform a ritual *deuotio* of themselves, led by the Pontifex Maximus, offering their lives for the salvation of the city. Once in Rome, the Gauls massacre the elders and set the city on fire. However, in the prevailing version of the story, they fail to conquer the Capitol because of the strenuous resistance of its defendants. In the end, the besieged Romans manage to negotiate the retreat of the Gauls by paying a generous ransom. In the meantime, Camillus, who had been previously sent into exile at Ardea, is nominated dictator. A Roman army is gathered at Veii and put under his command. Camillus drives it against the Gauls, defeating them in two consecutive battles. The general is then triumphantly welcomed back into Rome and acclaimed as a new founder—a second Romulus—and a savior of the city.

The story of the Gallic sack had an enormous impact on the imagination of the Romans of subsequent generations. For one thing, it highlights the role of the Capitoline as a means of Rome's survival: Rome endured because the Capitoline was not captured.[23] Moreover, because the Gallic siege marked the first "destruction" of Rome, this event tends to be evoked whenever the Romans give voice to their fears and anxieties about the final destruction of their city. Therefore, during the late Republic and for some time afterward, the people most frequently envisaged as the agents of Rome's final doom are the Gauls.[24] This apocalyptic mentality regarding the story of the Gallic sack is encouraged by quasi-millenarian calculations of the "years" of the city. The Gallic sack occurred at the end of Rome's first *magnus annus* (that is, after a "year of years" had passed from the city's foundation).[25] As we will

---

[23] Cf. Hor. *Carm.* 3.30.8–9 and Verg. *A.* 9.446–9 for the two *loci classici* of the Capitoline as a symbol of the eternity of Rome.

[24] Williams (2001) 170–1.

[25] The idea that the sack occurred 365 years after the foundation of Rome is found in Livy (5.54.5), who is likely to imply the concept of *magnus annus* [a year of years], though the calculation does not work for the time between Rome's foundation and the Gallic sack according to most Roman chronological schemes. Livy himself contradicts it in other passages (cf. 5.40.1, 5.45.4). To make things more complicated, some of these *magnus annus* calculations may not work around 365 days/year cycles. The question is complex and deserves more

see, fears of an approaching catastrophe that would coincide with the end of Rome's second *magnus annus* appear on several occasions in Roman history; the end of the second great year is at times expected to bring about a Gallic invasion. Moreover, the story of the Gallic siege is the source of the so-called *metus Gallicus*, Rome's special fear of Gallic enemies, which was clearly dependent on Gaul's connection to the city's apocalypse.[26] The day of the Allia battle is proclaimed a *dies religiosus*, and it remains such throughout Roman history.[27]

This symbolic meaning of the Gallic sack is perceivable when one examines the numerous appropriations of this legend that punctuate Roman history.[28] One important element that adds to the significance of this story is that it was often seen as a parallel of the Gallic attack against Delphi by the Galatae in 279 BCE.[29] Historians draw a connection between the two events, and the name of the Gallic chieftain, Brennus, is the same for both incidents.[30] The Gallic sack of Delphi was immortalized by Callimachus, and the Pergamene statues that celebrated the victory over the Galatae were famous.[31] In Rome, the legend of the Gallic sack is appropriated on several occasions. At times, the emphasis is on the Gauls as the agents of Rome's destruction. On other occasions, the focus is more on Camillus, the Roman hero who engenders the resurrection of Rome. For instance, Gaius Marius is hailed as a new Camillus after his victories over the Cimbri, whose previous successes stoked the terror of a barbaric invasion.[32] In a similar manner, in the *Catilinarians*, Cicero accuses the conspirators of planning a destruction of Rome by fire, thus achieving what the Gauls failed to achieve in 390 BCE, and makes the most of their involvement of Gauls in the plan.[33] Thus, Cicero can present himself as a new Camillus, the *pater patriae* who averts the city's catastrophe and begins the moral resurrection of

---

discussion than is possible here. For Livy see Miles (1986) 19–20; for an attempt at interpreting the whole of Livy's history in terms of the detailed working of these year-of-years cycles see Mineo (2006).

[26] See the materials collected by Williams (2001) 181 n. 109. In turn, the *metus Gallicus* explains the existence of legal procedures such as the *tumultus Gallicus*, the special measure that allowed the consuls to immediately levy troops, calling to duty even the elderly and the priests, in the case of a Gallic threat. Cf. App. *BC* 2.150; Cic. *Font.* 46; *Att.* 1.19.2; and see Williams (2001) 171.

[27] Gel. 4.9.5; cf. also 5.17.2; Macr. 1.16.23.

[28] For this section, I rely on Williams' (2001, 172–82) excellent discussion.

[29] Williams (2001) 158–70.

[30] See especially Plb. 2.20.6–7, with Williams (2001) 167. On the influence of the stories of the Galatae's attack on Delphi on Roman versions of Celtomachy, including the Capitol siege, see Ogilvie (1965) 719.

[31] On the prestige of the Pergamene Gauls in Rome see the following discussion. For the Galatae's attack on Delphi see Call. *Del.* 171–87.

[32] Plu. *Mar.* 27.9; Rawson (1974) on Marius as the new Camillus, hailed as the third founder of Rome.

[33] Cic. *Cat.* 4.12–13; Stockton (1970) 126; cf. also Cic. *Cat.* 3. 19–22, with Williams (2001) 177–8. Cicero used the same strategy against Antony in 44–3 BCE when he insinuated that the latter was collaborating with the recently conquered Gauls to bring about the destruction of Rome: Cic. *Phil.* 5.37, 7.3, 13.37.

Rome.[34] Cicero uses the same strategy in Caesar's favor when he builds on the Roman fear of Gaul to present the dictator as the one who finally delivered Rome from the Gallic threat, thus implicitly removing the cause of the city's final destruction.[35]

The legend of the Gauls' capture of Rome had other important implications. Livy offers an imperial perspective on the events surrounding the Gallic sack of 390 BCE that is particularly helpful for my analysis. In Livy, the story of the Gallic sack is handed down to future generations not just as the account of a military catastrophe, but as an exemplary story of how impiety and the decline of morals can bring the city to the brink of its destruction.[36] In Livy, the entire event of the Gallic invasion is summarized in religious terms by Camillus himself, in his final speech to the Senate after his return to Rome:

> quid haec tandem urbis nostrae clades noua? num ante exorta est quam spreta uox caelo emissa de aduentu Gallorum, quam gentium ius ab legatis nostris uiolatum, quam a nobis cum uindicari deberet eadem neglegentia deorum praetermissum? igitur uicti captique ac redempti tantum poenarum dis hominibusque dedimus ut terrarum orbi documento essemus.
> Liv. 5.51.7–8

> What about this recent catastrophe of our city? Did it not happen after we despised the voice sent from heaven announcing the coming of the Gauls? After the law of nations was violated by our envoys, after we neglected to punish this violation because of the same neglect of the gods? Therefore, vanquished, captured, and ransomed, we paid so great a penalty to gods and men that we are today an object lesson for the world.

According to Livy, the ultimate reason for the catastrophe of the Gallic sack lay in the Romans' neglect of the gods.[37] Initially, they fail to expiate the portent of the voice speaking on the Capitoline. Later, the Fabii commit sacrilege in attacking the Gallic envoys, and the consular tribunes fail to take the auspices before the Allia battle.[38] What is also relevant in Livy's account is the connection between divine anger and civil discord, for Livy underlines the fact that, among other things, it is the Romans' break with civil harmony that engenders divine displeasure.[39] Accordingly, after the Romans have been defeated and nearly destroyed, only the recovery of

---

[34] See Vasaly (1993) 77–80 on Cicero as the new Romulus and new Camillus, with Cic. *Pis.* 6; Plu. *Cic.* 23.3.

[35] Cic. *Prov. Con.* 34; Williams (2001) 179.

[36] The religious element is emphasized by Livy considerably more than other sources: see Levene (1993) 175–203.

[37] On this passage see Levene (1993) 200–1.

[38] Liv. 5.32, 36, 38.

[39] Levene (1993) 177–9.

religious orthodoxy begins to turn the tide of war.[40] The nobles make a ritual *deuotio* of themselves, offering their lives to atone for the sins committed. The besieged Romans piously observe the sacrifices in honor of the gods. And when Camillus returns to Rome, his first provisions are aimed at reestablishing a proper relationship with the gods. He rebuilds the temples and performs rituals of purification and atonement.[41] Then he provides an interpretation of the events leading to the sack in religious terms in his speech, as we have seen.[42]

6.4 THE GALLIC SACK IN FLAVIAN CULTURE

The story of the Gallic sack has a considerable influence on Flavian culture, too. Tacitus attests to the shared notion that 69 CE was almost the last year of Rome.[43] This idea would be enough to suggest a connection with the aforementioned prophecies of Rome's apocalypse. In fact, evocations of the Gallic sack and of the end of Rome's *magnus annus* even predate the start of the 69 CE conflict. According to Tacitus, the great fire of 64 CE, which nearly destroyed the city under Nero, was thought by many to be a repetition of the fire of 390 BCE. People even ventured to say that the 64 fire occurred on the same day as the Gallic fire and that the same number of years had passed from the foundation of the city to the Gallic fire as from the Gallic fire to the fire of 64.[44] By what sort of calculations this result could be obtained is far from clear. What matters for us is that millenarian fears were already hard at work in the last years of Nero's principate and that the story of the Gallic sack was evoked in the context of prophecies involving Rome's destruction.

The events of 69 CE conspired to materialize Rome's apocalyptic fears with a remarkable degree of precision. Not only did Vitellius' campaign climax in the destruction of the Capitoline, it was also carried out by an army—and a commander—whom contemporary sources depict as a barbaric horde. Vitellius was governor of Germany. Many of his auxiliaries were ethnically Germans and he was joined by a number of Celtic tribes.[45] One of Vitellius' generals, Caecina, went so far as to appear in public dressed as a Gaul (with *bracae*, the traditional Gallic garment).[46] The barbaric nature of Vitellius and his troops is emphasized by the pro-Flavian Josephus, who remarks on the German origins of the Vitellians and has them plunder the temples on the

---

[40] Levene (1993) 197–202.

[41] Liv. 5.50.1–8; Plu. *Cam.* 30.3.4.

[42] On Camillus' pious characterization (cf. e.g. Liv. 5.50.1) see Levene (1993) 192–3 and 199–201.

[43] Tac. *Hist.* 1.11.

[44] Tac. *Ann.* 15.41.

[45] Tac. *Hist.* 1.53–4; 57.

[46] Tac. *Hist.* 2.20.

Capitoline, precisely as one would expect of barbarians.[47] Once in the city, Vitellius ignored the prohibition against performing civic duties on the day of the battle of the Allia River.[48] This escalation of bad portents culminated in the Capitoline siege, when Vitellius' soldiers brought to completion what Brennus had failed to achieve in 390 BCE. Tacitus stresses that, more than anything else, this event made people believe that the end of Rome's *imperium* had arrived, for even when the city had fallen to the Gauls, Jupiter's Temple had survived intact. In addition, rumors circulated of Druidic prophecies announcing the end of Rome's *imperium* and the transferal of supreme power to the peoples north of the Alps.[49]

In spite of all these negative predictions, however, the city survived. Just as in the case of Camillus, Rome was ultimately saved by the return of a Roman general (Vespasian). This, of course, gave the Flavians the opportunity to emphasize and turn to their advantage the connection between Vitellius and the Senones. Besides Josephus' version, indirect evidence for this comes from the statuary collection preserved in the Templum Pacis, the monument erected by Vespasian in 75 CE to celebrate his victory over Judaea. This innovative complex consisted of a large square portico encircling a temple to the goddess Peace.[50] The portico was adorned with a collection of carefully chosen Greek masterpieces, whose selection reflected the ideological function of the building, namely the celebration of the Flavian victory.[51] For instance, a massive statue of the Nile reminded viewers of the beginnings of Vespasian's ascent to power, when in Alexandria a number of miracles, including an overflow of the Nile, had announced that he had been chosen by the gods as the new emperor.[52] The Templum Pacis collection also included the famous statues of the Galatae from Pergamon.[53] These Greek masterpieces, originally placed in the Pergamene Temple of Athena Nikephoros, represented the Gauls defeated by Attalus I.[54] The inclusion of these statues, previously kept in the Domus Aurea as a private treasure of Nero, conveyed a clear message: Vespasian advocated for himself the role of Attalus. He had defeated the sacrilegious barbarians (the Vitellians) who attacked the seat of Jupiter (the Capitoline), just as Attalus defeated the Galatae, the same tribe that some decades before had dared to attack Apollo's Temple in

---

[47] *BJ* 4.647–9.

[48] Tac. *Hist.* 2.91; Suet. *Vit.* 11.

[49] Tac. *Hist.* 3.72, 4.54.

[50] On the Templum Pacis see the relevant articles in Coarelli (2009a) 158–201 and *LTUR* IV 67–70 (F. Coarelli).

[51] On Greek works of art in the Templum Pacis see Bravi (2012) 167–81.

[52] Bravi (2012) 170–2. The Nile miracle: D.C. 65.8.1.

[53] Plin. *Nat.* 34.84; Bravi (2012) 175–8; Rebeggiani (2017).

[54] The Greek originals did not survive, but a number of Roman copies have been identified: These include the famous Dying Gaul, now in the Capitoline Museum, as well as the Ludovisi Gaul in the Museo Nazionale Romano, Palazzo Altemps. See Wenning (1978) 1–36.

Delphi.[55] Appropriating Greek versions of Celtomachy allowed Vespasian to style
his success over Vitellius as a war against a foreign enemy, thus avoiding the scandal
of civil war.[56] As we saw, in his coupling of Gigantomachy and Celtomachy as a par-
allel for the Vitellians' attack on the Capitoline, Statius may have been influenced by
Callimachus' use of Gigantomachy in his lines on the sack of Delphi. Statius' passage
can also be seen as responding to Vespasian' reception of Hellenistic paradigms of
victory over Celts.

The appropriation of the Gallic sack by the Flavians was favored by a corre-
spondence in the religious climate: the same sense of religious decline leading to
catastrophe that we saw in Livy's account of the Gallic sack colors perceptions of
the events of 69 CE, and in both cases reconstruction is marked by an insistence
on atonement and the recovery of religious orthodoxy.[57] Vespasian took care to re-
build the temples destroyed by fire, and did so with scrupulous attention to religious
prescriptions, repeating the reconstruction first made by Camillus.[58] In addition, the
ideas of a rebirth and new foundation of the city (Camillus as the new Romulus)
are well documented in Vespasian's ideology. A clear specimen of these motives is
offered by the coinage, on which images of renewal and rebirth abound, coupled
with evocation of the mythical origins of Rome and its foundation.[59]

6.5 THE GAULS ON THE CAPITOL UNDER DOMITIAN

After his accession to the throne, Domitian appropriated many aspects of his father's
ideology. Key to this appropriation was the narrative of the Capitoline siege, for it
allowed Domitian to share in his father's self-promotion as the one who had put
an end to civil war and rescued Rome from a crisis that threatened the city's very
survival. Panegyrists make the most of Domitian's participation in the siege to pre-
sent him as the party responsible for Vitellius' defeat, and myths are adapted to

---

[55] For this interpretation see Rebeggiani (2017). A different explanation of the ideological significance of the
Pergamene Gauls is in Bravi (2012) 175–8. For appropriations of Celtomachy and the Gallic assault on Delphi
in Augustan culture see Hardie (1986) 120–43; Rebeggiani (2017) 73–4.

[56] I surmise that the celebratory monuments erected by Vespasian, including the Templum Pacis, although nom-
inally celebrating Vespasian's victory over Judaea, also adumbrated his more important triumph, the victory
over Vitellius, through which he had restored peace to the world: see Rebeggiani (2017) 76.

[57] For religious orthodoxy as a response to the crisis of 69 CE see Chapter 5, Section 5.2.

[58] Cf. the accounts on the reconsecration of the Capitoline temples: Tac. *Hist.* 4.53; Suet. *Ves.* 8.5. See Chapter 5,
Section 5.2.

[59] Cf. for instance *RIC*[2] II no. 109: reverse with the personification of Roma, kneeling, raised by Vespasian, with
the legend ROMA RESURGE(N)S. Images of prosperity and the return of Fortune: *RIC*[2] II nos. 1, 33–4, 36,
61–2, 64. References to the Romulus legend and the foundation of Rome: *RIC*[2] II 960–2 (she-wolf with the
twins, struck under the name of Domitian).

make room for Domitian's participation in the event. A key feature of Pergamene monuments was the association of Gigantomachy and Celtomachy.[60] These two myths are present both in Callimachus' description of the Galatae's attack on Delphi and in Statius' lines on the Capitoline siege. Alongside Celtomachy, Gigantomachy is also an important theme in panegyric of Vespasian. Flavian culture seems to have favored a version of Gigantomachy according to which the fight of Jupiter against the Giants was seen as the event that consolidated Jupiter's reception of power, thus marking the beginning of the Jovian era.[61] This version of the myth joined the defeat of one's enemies to the idea of a new beginning and could thus work well as a parallel to the inaugural dimensions of Vespasian's reign. Moreover, it promoted the equating of Vespasian and Jupiter.[62] This political exploitation of Gigantomachic themes has an impact on coeval poetry: Tim Stover has recently shown that the proliferation of Gigantomachic imagery in the poetry of Valerius Flaccus could be read in this context.[63]

If panegyrists of Vespasian think of his victory in the civil conflict in terms of Gigantomachy, with Vespasian in the role of Jupiter, Domitianic poets adopt a specific version of Gigantomachy whereby Jupiter is significantly helped by his son Hercules (Domitian) in his war against the Giants.[64] However, Domitian was soon regarded as Jupiter himself fighting the Giants. Martial uses references to Gigantomachy to praise Domitian, and Statius compares Domitian to Jupiter enjoying hearing the Muses tell of Gigantomachy.[65] On coinage, Domitian is represented wielding thunderbolt and aegis, the weapons employed by Jupiter against the Giants.[66]

This appropriation of Vespasianic ideology was soon extended to the Camillus paradigm. In fact, Domitian sought to replace his father as the new Camillus in

---

[60] Gigantomachy was represented on the frieze of the Great Altar of Zeus, Celtomachy featured in the monuments in the precinct of Athena; Celtomachy and Gigantomachy were also associated in the monument dedicated by Attalus at the south wall of the Athens Acropolis (Paus. 1.25.2); see Palma (1981) and Stewart (2004). It is still debated whether the Great Altar of Zeus in Pergamon was directly associated with a Gallic victory: see Stewart (2000) for a recent discussion.

[61] Val. Fl. 1.563–5; with Stover (2012) 52–5, and Zissos (2008) 323–4.

[62] Stover (2012) 51–70.

[63] On Gigantomachy and imperial ideology under Vespasian see Stover (2012) 80–1; on Gigantomachic imagery in Valerius Flaccus see Stover (2012) 79–110, 113–48.

[64] Cf. e.g. Stat. *Theb.* 1.22 previously quoted: the phrase *bella Iouis* implicitly compares the Capitoline battle to the battle of gods and Giants (cf. Chapter 4, Section 4.2), and the image of Domitian at work to help Jupiter against the Giants is likely to evoke Hercules' participation in Gigantomachy. Cf. Mart. 9.101.14, discussed in Chapter 3, Section 3.2. For this version of Gigantomachy see passages quoted in Chapter 3, Section 3.2 n. 57. For Domitian and Hercules see subsequent discussion and Chapter 3, Section 3.2.

[65] Mart. 8.49; Stat. *Silv.* 4.2.55–6, with Coleman (1988) 99.

[66] Cf. e.g. *RIC*² II nos. 177, 181, 185–6, 190–1, 194, 197–8, 206–9 etc. (with *aegis*); nos. 283, 362, 404 etc. (with thunderbolt).

the same way that he replaced Vespasian as the new Jupiter and the hero of civil war. A chance to appropriate the Camillus story was offered by the fire of 80 CE, which destroyed the sacred buildings of the Capitoline. A new destruction of the Capitoline at such a short distance from the previous catastrophe was certainly a great tragedy. However, it gave Domitian the chance to appropriate his father's role as the one who rebuilt the Capitoline temples. The emperor lavishly reconstructed the Capitoline buildings.[67] And, unlike his father, Domitian decided to celebrate the event with games. The choice to name the games "Capitoline" (Agon Capitolinus or Ludi Capitolini or Capitolia) is relevant: An earlier version of the Ludi Capitolini is attested during the Republic. In some sources, their institution is attributed to Camillus (either after the capture of Veii or after the Gallic sack), while in others, the founder is Romulus.[68] In either case, the name forged a connection with Rome's first founder (Romulus) or with his savior and second founder (Camillus). Domitian made the celebration of the games coincide with the ceremony of the Lustrum, which was traditionally connected to the idea of purification and new beginning.[69]

The Flavian appropriation of narratives of the Gallic sack and of Camillus left its mark on the poetry of the time. In Silius, Camillus stands as a parallel for Scipio, the hero of the *Punica*, and as such also for Domitian.[70] This is clear, for instance, in the final scene of the poem:

salue, inuicte parens, non concessure Quirino
laudibus ac meritis non concessure Camillo:
nec uero, cum te memorat de stirpe deorum,
prolem Tarpei mentitur Roma Tonantis.
Sil. 17.651–4

Hail, O unconquered father, not inferior in glory to Quirinus, no second to Camillus in your merits: Rome does not lie when she calls you a son of gods, the offspring of Tarpeian Jupiter.

---

[67] Martial 9.3.7–9 with Henriksén (2012) 31 *ad loc.*

[68] Liv. 5.50.4, 5.52.11 (Camillus establishes the games after the Gallic sack); Plu. *Quaest. Rom.* 277C–D; Fest. 430L; Plu. *Rom.* 25.5; Tert. *De Spect.* 5.

[69] Domitian's coupling of the Ludi with the Lustrum is connected to Domitian's taking up the office of Censor Perpetuus in 85/86 CE in concomitance with his institution of the Capitoline games, but it also contributes to transferring to the games the notion of purification and new beginning associated with the Lustrum; see Caldelli (1993) 60–2.

[70] For Scipio's connection with Domitian see Marks (2005a) 218–44.

Scipio is here brought into connection with Romulus and Camillus, the two founders of Rome. The mention of Scipio as a descendant of Tarpeian Jupiter—that is, of Capitoline Jupiter—is a panegyric hint at Domitian's identification with the god.[71]

The comparison of Camillus and Scipio is found in other passages of the poem. Notably, Silius favors a rather minor version of the story of the Gallic sack according to which the Capitoline is captured. This version is found as early as Ennius' *Annales*.[72] Although it is not easy to explain why Ennius preferred this version to the more common one in which the Capitol survives, Silius' choice is easier to account for. The fact that in Silius the Gauls actually conquer the Capitol makes the Senones' sack resemble what happened during the Capitoline siege of 69 CE more closely. That this version is favored by Silius is clear, for instance, in a passage from the first book:

> hic galeae Senonum pensatique improbus auri
> arbiter ensis inest, Gallisque ex arce fugatis
> arma reuertentis pompa gestata Camilli . . .
> Sil. 1.624–6

> Here are the helmets of the Senones and the wicked sword that settled the dispute about the weight of gold, and the arms carried by Camillus when he came back in triumph, after the Gauls had been driven away from the citadel . . .

This passage comes from an *ekphrasis* on the temple in which the Senate meets, most likely the temple of Jupiter on the Capitol, and Silius' description is likely to allude to Domitian's lavish restoration of the same temple.[73] Silius says that the Gauls have been chased away from the *arx*—here a metonymy for the Capitoline—of which they have taken hold. Silius' mention of Camillus' triumphal entrance into Rome after his victory over the Senones sets the scene for the final return of Scipio in book 17, in which Camillus is explicitly mentioned once again.

---

[71] For Scipio's relationship with Domitian through their shared association with Jupiter see Marks (2005a) 230–5.

[72] Enn. *Ann.* 227 Skutsch; see Skutsch (1953) and (1978). The Capitol is not only conquered but even burned down in Luc. 5.27–8.

[73] Feeney (1982) 307.

6.6 *CORONA CIVICA*

Let us now return to the 69 CE siege. I have examined the centrality of this episode for Domitian's ideology. I have also focused on one of the narratives that Statius associates with it, namely the story of the Gallic sack of 390 BCE, and have shown that this story plays an important role in Flavian ideology as a way of mythologizing Vitellius' descent into Italy and his assault on the Capitoline. There are, however, some important questions pertaining to this event that I have not yet answered. How exactly did panegyrists carve a heroic role for Domitian during the battle of the Capitoline? What strategies could be adopted in poetry to mythologize and amplify the resonance of his participation? Unfortunately, a direct answer to this question is impossible. But there are some indications in Flavian texts of how this problem may have been tackled.

There is an aspect of Domitian's self-representation that can set us on the right track. On statues predating his accession, the young Domitian is portrayed wearing an oak wreath.[74] The oak wreath, or *corona ciuica* [civic crown], is an ornament awarded to those who "saved the lives of their fellow citizens" [*ob ciues servatos*]. A *corona ciuica* being awarded to an emperor is not surprising: Both Augustus and Vespasian were given this honor, and we know that Domitian also bore a *corona ciuica* during his reign.[75] However, Domitian's receipt of a *corona ciuica* before his accession calls for an explanation. In which context could he have been awarded such an honor? Because no relevant deed of Domitian before his accession is recorded except for his participation in the 69 CE siege, it is likely that his reception of the award was connected to some kind of narrative appended to this episode. But what kind of narrative exactly?

Perhaps the answer can be found in a passage of Statius that features Domitian addressed by a man who wears a *corona ciuica*. In *Siluae* 1.1, Statius describes the colossal statue of Domitian erected in the Republican Forum. At one key point in the poem, the poet portrays the emperor's statue being addressed by a hero from Rome's past, Marcus Curtius, a young man who offered his life to save his fellow citizens.

---

[74] The most important of these is the one in the Museo Archeologico Nazionale di Napoli, inv. 6058. See description in Gasparri (2009) 81. This statue depicts an adolescent Domitian wearing the *corona ciuica*. The bust, clearly predating Domitian's accession to the throne, seems to belong to the second portrait type of Domitian, attested on coins from 75 CE onward; see Bergmann–Zanker (1981) 360–3. The portrait with *corona ciuica* is replicated later, after the emperor's accession, as a portrait from the Museo Nazionale Romano (Rome) proves. This second portrait dates from around 85 CE; see Amadio in Giuliano (1987) 198; Varner (2004) 251–2; Bergmann–Zanker (1981) 349–52, no. 12, figs. 25a–d.

[75] For Vespasian's *corona ciuica* see *RIC*[2] II nos. 121–5. For Domitian wearing a *corona ciuica* after his accession to the throne cf. Martial 8.82 and the statuary evidence mentioned in the preceding note.

A chasm had suddenly opened in the Forum, and Curtius threw himself into it to expiate the portent, thus earning the survival of the city.[76] In the *Siluae*, Curtius speaks to Domitian from the Lacus Curtius, the fountain that stood on the spot where the young Roman had sacrificed his life:

> ... salue, magnorum proles genitorque deorum,
> auditum longe numen mihi. nunc mea felix,
> nunc ueneranda palus, cum te prope nosse tuumque
> immortale iubar uicina sede tueri
> concessum. semel auctor ego inuentorque salutis
> Romuleae: tu bella Iouis, tu proelia Rheni,
> tu ciuile nefas, tu tardum in foedera montem
> longo Marte domas. quod si te nostra tulissent
> saecula, temptasses me non audente profundo
> ire lacu, sed Roma tuas tenuisset habenas.
> *Silv.* 1.1.74–83

> ... hail, offspring and father of great gods, a deity announced to me long ago. Now is my pond blessed, now it is worth worship, now that I have been allowed to know you from close at hand and contemplate your immortal splendor from a nearby place. Once only did I find and offer salvation to the people of Romulus; you conquer the war of Jupiter, the battles of the Rhine and civil war, you vanquish with a long war the mountain slow to accept a truce. But if you had been born in my time, you would have attempted to plunge into the deep pool, when I dared not venture, but Rome would have held your reins.

Before this passage, Curtius is introduced by Statius with a reference to his *corona ciuica* (1.1.69–70 *mouet horrida sancto | ora situ meritaque caput uenerabile quercu* [he raises his visage, unkempt in sacred squalor, and a head sanctified by a well-earned wreath of oak]), and his words to the emperor are clearly meant to establish a connection between him and Domitian. The emperor is presented as a new Curtius, someone who would be willing to give his life for his fellow citizens. More important, this behavior of Domitian is brought into connection with his participation in the Capitoline battle (*Silv.* 1.1.78–9): "Once only did I find and offer salvation to the people of Romulus; you conquer the war of Jupiter [i.e. the Capitoline battle]." What is remarkable is the fact that Curtius saved his country not by fighting but

---

[76] Liv. 7.6; Var. *L.* 5.148; V. Max. 5.6.2. On Curtius and his relevance for accounts of 69 CE see Chapter 5, Section 5.2.

by offering his life as a scapegoat. The context of Curtius' sacrifice is that of Roman rituals of *deuotio*, a religious practice that works by the logic of sacrificial substitution: An individual offers his life to the gods instead of that of his fellow citizens.[77] This is exactly the kind of behavior Curtius envisages for Domitian in *Silv.* 1.1.82–3: "You would have attempted to plunge into the deep pool, when I dared not venture, but Rome would have held your reins." Domitian is thus like Curtius, with only one difference: Rome does not allow him to die.

The idea of linking the *corona ciuica* with self-sacrifice is the key aspect of the Curtius story, and one sees the obvious advantage of this notion when it comes to praising Domitian. But in which circumstance of Domitian's life could such an act be imagined? The reader already knows the answer: in 69 CE. As we noted in an earlier chapter, the topic of *deuotio* is central to accounts of 69 CE and is deeply tied to the religious climate of those years.[78] We can now try to imagine a context for the stories concerning Domitian's receipt of his *corona ciuica*. The context should be that of accounts of his behavior in 69 CE, in which the young emperor's decision to join his uncle on the Capitoline was presented as a decision to give up his life for his fellow citizens. It is possible that images of legendary *deuotiones* were attached to these accounts. Panegyrists may have hinted that Domitian was ready to offer himself but that in the end, just as *Siluae* 1.1 suggests, the gods prevented him from doing so in light of the role he was later to perform as emperor. Panegyrists recounting the 69 siege avoid mentioning Domitian's flight, instead saying that the young emperor-to-be was saved by the gods. This position is found in Silius' speech of Jupiter in book 3 of the *Punica*, where Domitian is saved at the last moment by the gods, exactly as Statius says that the goddess Roma would not allow Domitian to give up his life:[79]

> nec te terruerint Tarpei culminis ignes:
> sacrilegas inter flammas seruabere terris . . .
> Sil. 3.609–10

> Let the fire of the Tarpeian hill not frighten you: Among the impious flames you will be saved for the world . . .

---

[77] On *deuotio* see Versnel (1981); Beard–North–Price (1998) 35–6.

[78] See Chapter 5, Section 5.2.

[79] Cf. also Josephus *BJ* 4.649, in which Domitian, whose disguise is not mentioned, is said to have escaped providentially. The topic of *deuotio*—evoked by Statius in *Siluae* 1.1 and, as I discuss in Section 6.7 of this chapter, also in *Thebaid* 10—is also central to Silius' narrative of the second Punic war. See Marks (2005b).

That narratives of self-sacrifice and *deuotio*, thwarted at the last moment by divine intervention, were part of panegyric strategies of pro-Domitianic mythologizing of the Capitoline siege cannot be proved. But further encouragement to proceed in this direction is given by the story of the Gallic sack, the legend that Statius, and others, connect with the incident. For this story also featured a famous *deuotio*. Livy and other sources tell us that the sack of Rome in 390 BCE was characterized by the ritual *deuotio* of the elderly nobles, who offered their lives so that the state could be saved.[80] This *deuotio* was famous as the first in a number of sacrifices by Roman citizens on behalf of the state.[81]

6.7 SELF-SACRIFICE AND THE SURVIVAL OF THE CITY

It is now time to return to the *Thebaid*. So far, we have considered a number of elements that emerge in connection with Flavian presentations of the last phases of the 69 CE civil war: apocalyptic ideas about the end of the city and evocations of former crises involving barbarian assaults (especially the Gallic sack); the topic of salvation achieved through a legendary savior and of a new beginning marked by religious renewal; and adaptations of Hellenistic paradigms of victories against Celts and of mythological narratives such as Gigantomachy. I have also suggested that the notion of self-sacrifice or *deuotio* may have been part of strategies to mythologize Domitian's participation in the Capitoline battle of 69 CE. In short, a constellation of elements traditionally attached to Roman narratives of crisis and reconstruction are substantially harnessed by Flavian ideology. Let us now move on to observe how this reconstruction affects our reading of *Thebaid* 10. We will see that this cluster of elements is distinctly evoked by Statius during the siege of Thebes in book 10. They contribute to aligning the Argive assault with threats to the city of Rome, including the latest assault by Vitellius. Statius builds on Roman traditions of harnessing the Argive assault on Thebes as a foil for barbaric assaults on the city of Rome.[82]

As we have seen repeatedly in the previous chapters, in the course of his epic poem Statius plays considerably on the idea of Thebes as an image of Rome. In book 10, these suggestions acquire a more specific poignancy, for Statius' narrative of the siege of Thebes evokes many of the elements traditionally associated with Roman narratives of crisis. To begin with, the Argives' assault on Thebes is presented through a sustained engagement with the same two myths that feature in Statius' description

---

[80] Liv. 5.41.

[81] As such, it features in the list of Roman *deuotiones* in the schoolbook by Ampelius, right after the *deuotiones* of the Decii and before that of Curtius: Amp. 20.7.

[82] See Introduction, Section I.9.

of the 69 CE siege, namely Gigantomachy and the Gallic sack. As for the latter, we have seen that Statius commences his narrative of the siege of Thebes with the unexpected introduction of an Argive hero in Gallic guise, a passage that also alludes to a text by Propertius describing a descendant of Brennus at war against the Romans. This unseemly evocation of Celtomachy should be read in light of the traditions previously surveyed about the Gallic sack of Rome and its centrality to Roman culture. Statius is harnessing a theme that, in the Roman imagination, was connected to narratives of mortal threats to the city of Rome. This tradition becomes particularly salient for contemporaries of Statius in light of the apocalyptic context that surrounds the events of 69 CE, and more specifically in light of Flavian appropriations of the traditions on Camillus and the Gallic sack. Statius' portrait of his dying Gaul (Amyntor), with visible *torquis* on his neck, is a literary materialization of the dying Gaul of Pergamon (the latter likewise wears a *torquis*) that the *Thebaid's* readers could admire in the Templum Pacis. This tactic of connecting the mythical narrative to the historical context through a well-calculated use of names and identities of otherwise irrelevant characters should not surprise readers of Statius, who are familiar with similar strategies employed by Statius' foremost model, Virgil.[83] In general, the idea of exploiting the Argive assault on Thebes to interact with memories of a terrifying foreign assault looks back at some earlier adaptations of the Eteocles and Polynices myth, especially Aeschylus' *Septem contra Thebas*.

The historical resonance of Statius' Celtomachic allusions is reinforced by the massive exploitation of Gigantomachic imagery, the second myth Statius associates with the battle of the Capitoline in the *Siluae*. In *Thebaid* 10, the main agent of the Argive attack, Capaneus, is compared several times to a Giant.[84] It is sufficient to read the first grand simile that marks the start of Capaneus' *aristeia*.[85] This connection with the Giants belongs to the traditional picture of the hero, but in Statius it is heightened by the fact that it is not just the author who likens Capaneus to a Giant: Capaneus himself understands his attack as an assault on Jupiter.[86]

Let us now consider the other great protagonist of book 10, Menoeceus. Menoeceus is a young Theban prince who sacrifices himself in response to an oracle. Upon consulting the gods, Tiresias proclaims that the city will be saved if the

---

[83] Cf. Virgil's story of Thymbraeus killing Osiris at *A*. 12.458, analyzed by Reed (1998).

[84] Besides the passage subsequently quoted, cf. also 10.909–10, 10.915–17, 11.7–8; see McNelis (2007) 142–3; Franchet d'Esperey (1999) 197–203, 333–4. On comparison of Capaneus and the Giants earlier in the poem see Lovatt (2005) 128–33; Harrison (1992) 251–2.

[85] *Theb*. 10.848–52; text quoted in Chapter 3, Section 3.6. For Capaneus and his *aristeia* see now Chaudhuri (2014) 256–97; see also 298–321 for the political implications of theomachy in the *Thebaid*.

[86] For Capaneus as a Giant cf. *A*. *Th*. 422–4; E. *Ph*. 1128–33; for Capaneus' characterization and his project of attacking heaven see Leigh (2006) 225–8; Chaudhuri (2014) 256–97.

last descendant of the snake killed by Cadmus is sacrificed.[87] In spite of its mythical setting, Menoeceus' self-immolation draws on accounts of Roman *deuotiones*.[88] This has been convincingly argued by David Vessey, who also points out Statius' indebtedness to Livy's account of the death of the older Decius:

> at pius electa murorum in parte Menoeceus
> iam sacer aspectu solitoque augustior ore,
> ceu subito in terras supero demissus ab axe,
> constitit, exempta manifestus casside nosci,
> despexitque acies hominum et clamore profundo
> conuertit campum iussitque silentia bello.
> 'armorum superi, tuque o qui funere tanto
> indulges mihi, Phoebe, mori, date gaudia Thebis
> quae pepigi et toto quae sanguine prodigus emi.
> ferte retro bellum captaeque impingite Lernae
> reliquias turpes, confixaque terga fouentes
> Inachus indecores pater auersetur alumnos.
> at Tyriis templa, arua, domos, conubia, natos
> reddite morte mea . . .'
> *Theb.* 10.756–69

But pious Menoeceus took his stand on a chosen part of the walls. Sacred now in his aspect, more august than his usual countenance, as though he had been suddenly sent from heaven down to earth. Taking off his helmet and manifest for all to recognize, he stood still, looked down upon the ranks of men, and with a deep cry he turned the field upon himself, calling the war to silence: "Gods of war and you, O Phoebus, who grant me to die so great a death, give to Thebes the joy that I have covenanted and bought with the lavishing of all my blood. Drive back the war and thrust the ignominious survivors upon captive Lerna. Let father Inachus turn away from his inglorious nurslings as they tend their wounded backs. But to the Tyrians restore temples, lands, homes, wives, and children at the price of my death . . ."

---

[87] That is, the last descendant of the Spartoi through Echion; see *Theb.* 10.610–15.

[88] Allusions and references to *deuotio* in Roman epic have been identified by several scholars. For Virgil see Hardie (1993) 28–9 and Leigh (1993). For Lucan see Hardie (1993) 30–1, 53–4; Leigh (1997) 128–43. For Statius see Vessey (1971) 239–40; Heinrich (1999) 180–90; Bernstein (2013). For Silius see Marks (2005b).

When he is about to sacrifice his life, Menoeceus is said to look "more august" than usual, exactly like Decius in Livy.[89] Moreover, Menoeceus' speech before his suicide has a number of striking connections with the *deuotio* speeches we find in Livy.[90] In Livy, Decius' *deuotio* is significantly anticipated by an earlier sacrifice, the *deuotio* of the patricians during the Gallic invasion:[91]

> adeo haud secus quam uenerabundi intuebantur in aedium uestibulis sedentes uiros, praeter ornatum habitumque humano augustiorem, maiestate etiam quam uoltus grauitasque oris prae se ferebat simillimos dis.
> Liv. 5.41.8

> Indeed, they contemplated as in veneration the men sitting in the vestibules of their homes. These men, besides their ornament and clothes, which surpassed those of mortal men, seemed most similar to gods in the majesty expressed by their countenances and the gravity of their faces.

This passage likewise has strong correspondences with Statius' account. The nobles look more august than usual, and they resemble gods, exactly like Menoeceus. What is the point of this Roman setting for the Menoeceus sacrifice? Self-sacrifice, as we saw, was part of Roman narratives of extreme danger and miraculous salvation. Statius' alignment of Menoeceus with Roman authors of *deuotiones* activates this tradition within Statius' narrative. A more specific reference was available in light of recent appropriations of the topic of *deuotio* by Domitian's panegyrists. In presenting the figure of a young prince ready to offer his life for the salvation of his country in the manner of a Curtius or a Decius, in the context of a siege that evokes threats to the city of Rome, the *Thebaid* comes very close to creating a mythical equivalent for *Siluae* 1.1, in which Domitian is paired with the author of a famous *deuotio*. The portrait of this young prince inflamed by love for his country who goes on to become a god may well contain some panegyric hints of Domitian's behavior in 69 CE. Interestingly, Menoeceus, just like Domitian, is the younger of two brothers belonging to the royal house, and he preempts his older brother in sacrificing his life on behalf of the state.[92] Domitian, and not Titus, had risked his life fighting on the Capitoline in 69 CE. This interpretation is also supported by

---

[89] Liv. 8.9.10. See Vessey (1971) 239.
[90] See Vessey (1971) 239.
[91] See Levene (1993) 196.
[92] *Theb.* 10.670–1. On this passage, usually read as undermining Statius' presentation of Menoeceus, see subsequent discussion.

the fact that the figure of Menoeceus has strong links with another character of the poem who attempts to offer his life for his fellow citizens, namely Coroebus. As I tried to show in an earlier chapter, the latter is also part of the *Thebaid*'s attempt at finding mythical equivalents for Roman narratives of crisis resolved by heroic self-sacrifice.[93]

Encouragement to read the episode along these lines is given by the description of the Thebans' reaction to Menoeceus' sacrifice. Once the hero makes it known that he is prepared to offer his life, Menoeceus is acclaimed with titles that resonate with the political language of Rome:

> . . . tum uulgus euntem
> auctorem pacis seruatoremque deumque
> conclamat gaudens atque ignibus implet honestis.
> *Theb.* 10.683–5

> . . . then, as he goes, the rejoicing people hail him as peace-bringer, savior, and god, and fire his heart with noble passion.

The title *auctor pacis* [peace-bringer] is a common attribute of Roman leaders, especially emperors. Cicero, who, as we have seen, liked to style himself as a new Camillus, uses it several times to refer to himself.[94] Ovid employs it with reference to Augustus, and the anonymous author of *Octauia* presents it as a title of the emperor.[95] Later, Menoeceus is acclaimed as a second founder of the city:

> iamque intra muros nullo sudore receptum
> gaudentes heroa ferunt: abscesserat ultro
> Tantalidum uenerata cohors; subit agmine longo
> colla inter iuuenum, laetisque fauoribus omni
> concinitur uulgo Cadmum atque Amphiona supra
> conditor; hi sertis, hi ueris honore soluto
> accumulant artus patriaque in sede reponunt
> corpus adoratum.
> *Theb.* 10.783–90

[93] On Coroebus and Domitian see Chapter 5, Section 5.9. On Menoeceus and Hercules see Chapter 3, Section 3.7.
[94] Cf. e.g. Cic. *Phil.* 7.8, 14.20; *Att.* 9.11a.2.
[95] Ov. *Pont.* 1.1.32; *Oct.* 488; cf. also Sen. *Her. F.* 250, with Fitch (1987) *ad loc.* 199.

And now, rejoicing, they bear the hero within the walls, recovered with no labor. The Tantalid army had withdrawn of its own accord, in reverence. He comes in a long procession on the neck of warriors, and all the folk with joyful favor acclaim him as their founder above Cadmus and Amphion. Some heap his limbs with garlands, some with loose spring flowers, and place the venerated body in the ancestral tomb.

These are the most typical titles of Camillus: He was the *conditor alter* [second founder] par excellence of Roman history.[96] After Camillus, other Romans claimed the title of "second founder" after rescuing the city from extreme danger.

In addition, Statius tells us that Menoeceus achieves apotheosis.[97] The Theban hero is the only character who manages to conquer immortality in a poem that starts with a prophecy of Domitian's transformation into a god.[98] Menoeceus' apotheosis is emphasized by a simile in which he is likened to Hercules at the time of his deification.[99] The comparison brings home the theme of apotheosis, but the mention of Hercules is also relevant for another reason. When Flavian panegyrists say that Domitian fought the "war of Jupiter," as we saw, they imply a special version of the myth of Gigantomachy according to which Jupiter was helped by Hercules to fight the Giants.[100] Menoeceus' sacrifice wards off Capaneus' attack, precisely as Domitian's participation in the Capitoline siege preceded the Flavian victory over the Vitellians.[101] Just like Curtius, Menoeceus is a young hero who has given his life to save his fellow citizens. Like Curtius, he would deserve a *corona ciuica*, an oak wreath like the one awarded to the young Domitian. But, of course, unlike Curtius and Menoeceus, and very much like Coroebus, Domitian in the end had been spared by the gods. Just like Menoeceus' sacrifice, Domitian's intervention in the Capitoline battle was not able to bring an end to the fight. In the *Thebaid*, it is necessary to wait for Theseus' return from his victorious campaigns to see the city finally delivered from tyrants, just as, in the case of Rome, people had to wait for Vespasian's triumphal entry into the city. The hints at *deuotio* and the topic of the second founder sets the story of Menoeceus alongside Roman narratives centering on the city's rescue by an outsider at times of extreme crisis. Such a narrative, as we saw in Chapter 5, was applied to the Flavian victory, but it was also part of a

[96] Cf. e.g. Liv. 5.49.7 *Romulus ac parens patriae conditorque alter urbis haud uanis laudibus appellabatur* [with fitting praise [Camillus] was called a new Romulus, a father of the country and a second founder of the city].
[97] *Theb.* 10.665, 780–1; Chapter 3, Section 3.7.
[98] *Theb.* 1.22–31. On this passage see also Chapter 2, Section 2.3 and Chapter 4, Section 4.3.
[99] *Theb.* 12.64–7.
[100] See Section 6.5 and n. 64.
[101] See Chapter 3, Section 3.7.

rhetorical tradition that was regarded favorably by members of the Roman elite in Statius' time.

Yet the account of Menoeceus' sacrifice is far from a naïve piece of panegyric. Scholars have drawn attention to some disturbing elements in Statius' presentation of Menoeceus' ritual suicide and have questioned its effectiveness.[102] Arguments about the sacrifice's lack of effectiveness do not persuade me. In his speech, Menoeceus asks two things of the gods in return for his sacrifice: to drive the Argives back to their native city and to preserve the city, its temples, and its citizens. All of these requests materialize a few narrative moments after his suicide: Immediately after Menoeceus' death, Jupiter neutralizes Capaneus' assault, and the city is not conquered; in book 11, the Argive armies lift their siege of Thebes and ingloriously run away to Argos, which is precisely what Menoeceus asked (*Theb.* 11.21–6). That Capaneus attacks Thebes after Menoeceus' speech, deliberately challenging Menoeceus' sacrifice, cannot be taken to prove the sacrifice's ineffectiveness. Quite the opposite, in fact: By placing Capaneus' assault immediately after Menoeceus' suicide, Statius provides an emphatic demonstration of the sacrifice's effectiveness when Jupiter does not allow Capaneus to storm the city.[103] True, soon Creon will be king, and soon another army will assault Thebes, but Menoeceus begs the gods to ward off the *present* danger; his prayer does not concern every future danger the city might incur. Nor is Menoeceus concerned with halting the strife of the Theban brothers, whose subsequent duel bears no consequence for the city's salvation. Statius follows Euripides in separating the destiny of Thebes from that of the royal house.

As far as the immediate danger incumbent on Thebes is concerned (the Argive siege), Menoeceus' prayer is heeded. Statius joins Euripides' *Phoenissae* with his *Supplices* through the addition of book 12 to his narrative. As a result, the resonance of Menoeceus' sacrifice appears limited by the fact that the sacrifice ends up being juxtaposed to the narrative of a new conflict motivated by Creon's impiety. But this is a side effect that Statius turns to his advantage by using Menoeceus' sacrifice to underscore Creon's wickedness. That Creon manipulates the memory of his son's sacrifice is undeniable, but the fact that Creon partly nullifies Menoeceus' sacrifice by causing a new war only heightens Creon's impiety; it hardly voids the sacrifice.[104] The sacrifice remains effective as far as its immediate object is concerned, and even in the long run its effects will only partly be invalidated by Creon's mindlessness: Although

---

[102] Fantham (1995); Heinrich (1999) 180–93; Ganiban (2007) 139–44; Bernstein (2013) 239–44.

[103] *Contra* Heinrich (1999) 184–93. Jupiter does not characterize his intervention against Capaneus as being motivated by Menoeceus' sacrifice, but this indetermination is already in Statius' model, Euripides' *Phoenissae*, in which the causal mechanism underlying Thebes' salvation is equally left undefined; see Heinrich (1999) 186.

[104] *Contra* Ganiban (2007) 139; Bernstein (2013) 242–4.

it is true that a few Thebans die in the war against Athens, without Menoeceus' sacrifice there would be no Thebes. The citizens who happily welcome Theseus within their walls in book 12 would simply not be there—nor would their walls, for that matter—had Jupiter not granted salvation to the city by forestalling Capaneus' assault.

The sacrifice's effectiveness, however, does not erase the episode's complexities and ambiguities. These are connected to the pessimistic framework within which instances of constructive action in the *Thebaid* are set. Scholars have rightly highlighted some problematic elements in the Menoeceus episode. The scene of Menoeceus' encounter with Virtus—the personified goddess who drives Menoeceus to commit suicide—and the characterization of Virtus herself are far from reassuring. Virtus is a terrifying figure who appears to Menoeceus in disguise. To convince the Theban hero, Virtus relies on the youth's craving for glory and his desire to outdo his brother Haemon.[105] Virtus' encounter with Menoeceus is modeled on Allecto's apparition to Turnus in *Aeneid* 7, in which the Fury infects the young Rutulian with madness.[106] The presence of this intertext is undeniable. However, I do not think Statius' point is to undermine the value of Menoeceus' act. It seems to me that Statius is here expressing a tragic view of power and human nature that parallels his depiction of Theseus.

First, we need to take into account that the circumstances are extraordinary and extreme. *Deuotio*, a self-administered human sacrifice to the underworld gods, remains a terrifying act, a last resort that only extraordinary circumstances warrant. In addition, there is an aspect of the connection with Turnus that should not be forgotten. In the *Aeneid*, the topic of *deuotio* is substantially hinted at in connection with Turnus. On several occasions, Turnus displays the kind of heroic behavior that Romans associated with the Decii, the republican heroes who famously committed *deuotiones*.[107] On the other hand, Virtus' positive aspects should not be forgotten. Virtus is connected with Hercules, and she allows Menoeceus to achieve apotheosis: He is the only hero to be awarded such a gift in the whole poem, though many others strive for it.[108] And even in terms of Aeneadic models, Menoeceus is equally associated with Aeneas, as Statius' insistence on his characterization as *pius* shows.[109]

This does not eliminate the unsettling potential of the connection between Virtus and Allecto. The point, however, seems to me to be a tragic view of power and

[105] *Theb.* 10.671; Ganiban (2007) 139–40; Bernstein (2013) 242.
[106] Feeney (1991) 383; Fantham (1995); Ganiban (2007) 142–3. Cf. in part. *Theb.* 10.672–3 and *A.* 7.456–7.
[107] Leigh (1993).
[108] See Chapter 3, Section 3.7.
[109] Ganiban (2007) 138–9. Cf. in particular *A.* 4.576–7 and *Theb.* 10.680–1; as Menoeceus throws himself from the Theban walls, his body is carried gently to the ground by Virtus and Pietas (*Theb.* 10.780–1).

human nature, one that has parallels in Statius' depiction of Theseus' intervention. We have seen in earlier chapters that there is a Virgilian paradox activated by Statius in his account of Theseus' campaign against Creon in book 12. Just as at the end of the *Aeneid* Jupiter turns to the Dirae to crush down Turnus, in the *Thebaid* it seems as though, to be successful, Theseus has to tap into the same irrational forces that the poet has associated with civil war up to that point.[110] Not by chance is Statius' depiction of Virtus also modeled on Virgil's account of the Dirae in *Aeneid* 12.[111] Purely benign power cannot be effective: The terror embodied by Medusa's shield and the frightening war frenzy of Mars, channeled by Theseus against Creon, are necessary to rid Thebes of its tyrant. Although the end is positive, the means are far from perfect, and it seems—and here one touches Statius' pessimism—that they can never be.

Menoeceus' sacrifice remains a great heroic act, but one that can be achieved only by an infusion of irrational powers, by channeling toward a good end the same frightening forces that loom large behind the poem's acts of *nefas*. It is a tragic paradox from which the poet does not want to exempt his readers: Both Theseus' intervention and Menoeceus' sacrifice are vital for Thebes, both bring a positive resolution, and yet neither action can really be successful without appropriating a certain portion of the terror embodied by the forces against which the two characters are pitted. It is the tragic paradox in which Statius' contemporaries live: The best imaginable form of power is one that cannot do without terror. And yet living under this power is preferable to living outside its purview, for at least it channels frightening forces toward the pursuit of a certain amount of peace and security from which the community benefits.

---

[110] See Chapter 4, Section 4.3 and Chapter 5, Section 5.4.
[111] Ganiban (2007) 143; Fantham (1995). Cf. *Theb.* 10.632–3 and *A.* 12.845, 859–60.

Conclusions

C.1 BEYOND THE SCOPE OF THIS BOOK

In this last chapter, I recapitulate some of this volume's achievements. Before I do that, however, let me take some time to first consider some possible ways of expanding the analysis carried out in this book. I would like to draw attention to some sources that might help us put the *Thebaid*'s vision into perspective and to highlight how my approach could be applied to sections of the poem that I have not covered in detail in my analysis.

One of this book's main points is the emphasis given to the influence of Neronian culture and the historical figure of Nero on the ideological world of the *Thebaid*. In this area, much could be gained by putting the *Thebaid* in dialogue with other Flavian epics. Valerius Flaccus is particularly relevant, as the Neronian implications of his poem seem to me to have only been partly teased out. It would have been difficult for readers of Valerius not to think of Nero when presented with the picture of Aietes, a tyrant who closely associates his identity with the Sun. At the beginning of the poem, the executions commanded by Pelias have several points of contact with the literature on the martyrs of Nero that started to circulate in the Flavian period, discussed in Chapter 1.[1]

---

[1] For the connection to the Sun god as forging a link between Nero and Aietes see Valerius Flaccus' description of the temple to the Sun god where Aietes meets the Argonauts (5.407–454); see in particular V. Fl. 5.429–32,

It is also worth considering Valerius in connection with other topics addressed in this book. One of these is the issue of succession.[2] In book 8, Statius' description of Thiodamas' succession to Amphiaraus intersects with accounts of imperial successions and military acclamations.[3] In that passage (*Theb.* 8.212–4), Statius compares Amphiaraus' death to that of Tiphys, the helmsman of the Argonauts, whose death is recounted by Valerius in book 5 of the *Argonautica*; Statius is influenced by Valerius' account of Tyhypis' death and succession and partly models Amphiaraus on Typhis.[4] The helmsman is a common metaphor for a ruler.[5] In Valerius, Tiphys' death is preceded at a short distance by the death of the seer Idmon.[6] The sequence has a particular resonance for Flavian readers who had witnessed Titus passing away a mere 2 years after Vespasian. I suspect that Statius' succession scene, with its echoes of Flavian presentations of succession within the imperial family, might be responding to Valerius' own construction of a mythical equivalent for the death of Vespasian and the premature passing of Titus in his *Argonautica*.[7]

To go back to the *Thebaid*, the question of succession can also be explored from another point of view. In Domitianic Rome, as well as earlier and later during the Roman Empire, adoptive succession was made necessary by the lack of a natural male heir. Domitian's son died prematurely, before his accession to the throne.[8] The death of a royal child is a key topic of Statius' *Thebaid*. Two royal children, Linus and Opheltes, die prematurely in the *Thebaid*, and Statius brings them into close connection (the story of Linus is embroidered on the cloth placed on Opheltes' funerary pyre).[9] Amphiaraus' prophecy hints at the child's deification.[10] Domitian's child too was proclaimed divine. Earlier imperial history had

---

with Heerink (2014) 89–92. The death of Jason's parents: V. Fl. 1.730–851. On allusions to Nero through Aietes and Pelias see Taylor (1994) 228–31; on Pelias' executions and the end of the stoic martyrs see Taylor (1994) 233–35. Taylor's argument is weakened by her interpretation of Valerius' historical allusions in a narrowly symbolic and allegorical fashion. For the literature on the martyrs of Nero see Chapter 1, Section 1.4.

[2] On succession in Valerius and in Flavian Rome see Taylor (1994) 219–22, 226–8, whose symbolic interpretation of facts and characters of the poem I do not find convincing.

[3] See Chapter 2, Section 2.6.

[4] See Augoustakis (2016) 152–3 with further references.

[5] See e.g. *Theb.* 2.105–8 (Eteocles is compared to a helmsman); cf. also *Theb.* 8.267–70 and A. *Th.* 1–2; Chapter 2, Section 2.5.

[6] V. Fl. 5.1–72.

[7] This suggested reading implies that Valerius was still alive to witness the death of both Vespasian and Titus. This is possible: Valerius' poem hints at the eruption of Vesuvius in 79 CE, which occurred after Vespasian's death. Whether the poem actually contains references to events after 79 CE is, however, a matter of dispute among scholars; see now Stover (2012) 7–26, with full references.

[8] See Chapter 2, Section 2.3 n. 56.

[9] *Theb.* 5.64–6.

[10] *Theb.* 5.733–52.

known far too many untimely deaths of prospective emperors, some of whom ended up being replaced by unworthy peers.

In Chapter 1, I deal with the political undertones of Statius' interactions with Seneca's tragic corpus. I contend that a particular approach to Seneca's tragedies, based on a reading of his tragic poetry as a reflection on the principate of Nero and as deeply influenced by Seneca's political theory, may help us capture some of the ideological implications of Statius' reception of Seneca. I also maintain that the special confusion between reality and myth engendered by Nero's aggressive use of the theater has relevance for our understanding of the *Thebaid*'s use of certain characters for political allusion. I focused in particular on Seneca's *Oedipus* (Chapter 1) and his *Hercules Furens* (Chapter 3). But other Senecan tragedies have great relevance for the *Thebaid* and deal with characters whom Nero made central to his public persona. One is certainly Seneca's *Thyestes*. Thyestes was one of Nero's favorite tragic roles.[11] Whether his interest in this tragic subject implied identification with either of the play's main characters (Atreus or Thyestes) is not clear. Brotherly rivalry was certainly relevant for his kingdom, given the murder of Britannicus—which happened at a banquet, like Atreus' frightening revenge on Thyestes. Alongside Oedipus, Atreus is one of Nero's mythical counterparts in *Octauia*.[12] Seneca's Thyestes is absolutely central to Statius' *Thebaid*. Seneca's tragedy is invoked as a programmatic model in Oedipus' first speech.[13] The enmity of Atreus and Thyestes is constantly evoked as a parallel for the crimes of Eteocles and Polynices.[14] The fact that this mythical story was brought into connection with the events of the Julio-Claudian dynasty by Nero's critics, and even by Nero himself, should certainly be factored into our analysis of the political implications of Statius' interaction with this text. Another obvious candidate is Seneca's *Phoenissae*, a major model for Statius at the close of the *Thebaid*. This text too was amenable to politicized readings in the aftermath of Nero's death.

---

[11] D.C. 63. 9.4–5, 10.2.

[12] Ferri (2003) 70 n. 170, 360 etc. (see index of passages discussed s.v. Seneca, Thyestes on p. 440).

[13] Cf. *Theb.* 1.80–7; Sen. *Thy.* 23–67, 193–5; the whole sequence of Laius' return from the underworld at Jupiter's command to encourage enmity between his descendants is influenced by the prologue of Seneca's *Thyestes*, with the Fury forcing Tantalus out of the underworld to spread madness and drive his descendants to *nefas*: cf. e.g. *Theb.* 2.65–70 and *Thy.* 67–73 (Laius' and Tantalus' hesitation); *Theb.* 2.116–19 and *Thy.* 201–4.

[14] There are several references to the enmity of Atreus and Thyestes and to Atreus' revenge, which caused the Sun to turn back: *Theb.* 1.324–6, 2.184–5, 11.127–9, 8.742; Augoustakis (2015) 386–9 detects an allusion to Atreus' revenge in Tydeus' cannibalistic attack on Melanippus. For other allusions to Seneca's *Thyestes* see Venini (1971) 76–7.

Another area where expansion is in order pertains to the study of divine figures. In Chapter 3, I tried to show that there are ideological implications to Statius' use of heroic/divine models such as Hercules. In particular, I suggested that Statius' redefinition of the Hercules character should be read in connection with recent appropriations of Hercules by Nero and Vindex and against the background of the new currency given to the Hercules comparison under Domitian. A similar approach could be adopted with regard to Bacchus. In a series of passages in the *Thebaid*, Bacchus is cast in the role occupied by Venus in the *Aeneid*. In book 7, the scene of Bacchus' entreaty to Jupiter is clearly modeled on Venus' plea to her father in *Aeneid* 1. Similarly, in the Hypsipyle episode in book 5 (a section strongly influenced by Virgil's narrative of the fall of Troy in *Aeneid* 2), Bacchus replaces Venus as the god who leads his protegé to safety through the ravaged city.[15] The *Thebaid*'s Bacchus is a much more warlike figure than we would expect, borrowing some traits from Mars.[16] And Bacchus is brought into close connection with the *Thebaid*'s most credible kingly figure, for Bacchic imagery accompanies the final triumph of Theseus in book 12.[17]

There is some evidence that Bacchus may be associated with Domitian in panegyric contexts.[18] One fruitful approach to the *Thebaid*'s interest in Bacchus would be to look at the importance of Bacchus within Neronian ideology. How relevant a model was this god of revelries for the emperor who made enjoyment and pleasure at public expense a central part of his ideology? Besides the Neronian influence, there is a long-standing tradition, going back to Alexandria and its kings, of regarding Bacchus as a model of the sovereign, a god who wages war for the sake of expanding civilization and can at the same time guarantee his subjects a life of pleasure. This notion of the Bacchic king is, I suspect, active in Domitianic culture, and complements the somewhat more austere portrait of the "merciful" king reflected in *Siluae* 1.1 and influential on the *Thebaid*.

---

[15] *Theb.* 5.265–86 and *A.* 2.589–621; *Theb.* 7.151–226 and *A.* 1.227–96. Statius uses the scene of Venus' entreaty to Jupiter in the *Aeneid* multiple times: see Hershkowitz (1997).

[16] Cf. the portrait of Bacchus and his comrades coming back from a military expedition in the Northeast (*Theb.* 4.652–63) and the portrait of Mars' retinue, also returning from a military campaign, at *Theb.* 7.48–52.

[17] *Theb.* 12.786–8.

[18] In passages from the *Siluae*, Bacchus appears as a model for Domitian's eastern triumphs: 4.3.154–9, 4.2.47–51; cf. also 4.1.40–3, with Coleman (1988) 79. At *Silv.* 4.2.35–7, Bacchus is a model for Domitian's ability to provide his guests with wine and pleasure. A survey of the evidence for the comparison between Domitian and Dionysus is found in Sauter (1934) 88–9; see also Scott (1936) 147.

The Lemnos episode in book 5, which I have not discussed in this book, is another section that deserves to be considered by readers interested in the *Thebaid*'s interfaces with Flavian ideology. The story of the massacre at Lemnos, narrated by Queen Hypsipyle to the Argive chiefs, is dense with historical allusion, and, like other inset narratives in the *Thebaid*, reproduces at the microscopic level some of the dynamics that govern Statius' narrative at large. The Lemnos episode provides another lens through which to look at the reality of civil war, both within the poem and outside it in the world of Roman history. In Chapter 5, I argue that the Coroebus episode in book 1 functions as a miniature image of the plot of the *Thebaid* but that it is also configured in such a way as to channel allusions to the 69 CE civil war. The same is true, to a lesser extent, of the *ekphrasis* of Hercules' crater in book 6, which I explore in Chapter 3.

This dual function is also visible in the Lemnos episode. The massacre of Lemnos is instigated by a divinity (Venus) who acts with the help of underworld powers and causes enmity and eventually separation within members of a family. This initial intervention is followed by a second mediation, this time by a human (Polysso), whom Venus inspires to deceive the Lemnian women into attacking their husbands. This echoes the sequence setting in motion the action of the poem: Oedipus' anger triggers the intervention of the Furies and leads to the enmity between Eteocles and Polynices; angry Jupiter makes use of Laius to heighten Eteocles' hostility to his brother.[19] There are also important thematic connections. The slaughter of the men at Lemnos is compared to the fight of Centaurs and Lapiths, which Statius brings into connection with the action of the poem on several occasions.[20] Scenes from the massacre of Lemnos return in the narrative of the war of Thebes.[21] In addition, the story of Lemnos is made to intersect Roman narratives of civil war through its connection with Virgil's account of the sack of Troy. Statius' text follows Virgil in detail.[22] By Statius' time, the end of Troy is often evoked in connection with the destruction of Rome.[23] In Chapter 6, I showed that narratives of the end of Rome influence Flavian pictures of the last part of the 69 CE civil war, in particular with reference to the destruction of the Capitol by Vitellius' soldiers. In this context,

---

[19] Venus' anger and her intervention through underworld powers: *Theb*. 5.57–69; Polisso: *Theb*. 5.85–142; Oedipus' curse and Tisiphone's intervention: *Theb*. 1.56–122; Laius is sent to Eteocles by Jupiter: 1.292–311, 2.1–133.

[20] Allusions to Centauromachy in the Lemnos episode: *Theb*. 5.261–4 (cf. also *Theb*. 5.257 and Ov. *Met*. 12.324–5); for references to Centauromachy in the *Thebaid* outside of the Lemnos episode see Chapter 3, Section 3.1.2.

[21] Cf. *Theb*. 5.183–5 and *Theb*. 11.125–35; *Theb*. 5.202–3 and *Theb*. 11.403–4; *Theb*. 5.265–86 and *Theb*. 7.151–226; 5.85–142 and *Theb*. 10.156–218.

[22] Ganiban (2007) 71–88.

[23] The fall of Troy is what Nero allegedly sung during the devastating fire of Rome in 64 CE: Suet. *Nero* 38. 2; Tac. *Ann*. 15.39; D.C. 62.18.1.

Statius' night of Lemnos, with a royal figure saved from the city in flames, lends it-self to panegyric readings through its many points of contact with Flavian accounts of Domitian's legendary escape from the fire of the Capitoline in 69 CE.[24]

In Chapter 3, I considered Statius' study of passions in connection with notions of bestiality and divinity. Statius' ideas about how heroes can turn into beasts or gods are influenced by a certain way of applying stoic theories of passions to the field of polit-ical behavior. In this line of thought, uncontrolled passions such as anger can turn a man into a beast. At the opposite side of the spectrum is the sovereign depicted in *De Clementia*, a man who, through his illuminated behavior, approaches the status of a god. This paradigm seems to underlie Statius' depiction of the earthly parable of some of his heroes. Figures such as Tydeus and Capaneus are seen as an unstable mix of good and evil, constantly oscillating between beast and god. Ultimately, their search for im-mortality fails, and in Tydeus' case this is related to his inability to resist passions.[25]

This paradigm provides an interesting lens though which to look at other characters in the poem. Book 7 features a particularly effective concentration of the imagery re-lated to bestiality. The start of hostilities between Thebans and Argives is caused by an incident that is nearly symbolic of the relationship among passions, bestiality, and war in Statius' poem. Jocasta enters the Argive camp and addresses Polynices, asking him to join her in the city and parley with Eteocles (7.470–538). When it seems that Polynices might yield to the proposal, Tydeus intrudes to remind Polynices of Eteocles' treachery, which he experienced at the time of his embassy to Thebes (7.539–63). At this point, two tamed tigers, formerly part of Bacchus' retinue, are struck by the Fury. Going back to their old habits, they attack Argive soldiers. The tigers' attack dispels the gathering and precipitates the war (7.564–607). Tydeus' role as the one who prevents the possibility of a peaceful settlement is in tune with this hero's personality, as depicted in other scenes. It is only fitting that his action is twinned by the tigers' return to their old savagery.

The same pattern of bestiality is visible with reference to Hippomedon, a char-acter whom I have discussed only in passing. This hero's *aristeia* starts with an inter-vention by Tisiphone, who deceives Hippomedon into following her, causing him to lose Tydeus' body to the Thebans. Hippomedon then launches on a solitary fight at the beginning of which he is compared to a Centaur.[26] As is the case with Tydeus and Capaneus, bestial imagery creates a certain ambiguity concerning the status of

---

[24] Valerius Flaccus' parallel version of the episode (2.78–431) is similarly amenable to panegyric readings in con-nection with the events of 69 CE. In Valerius, Hypsipyle manages to save her father by disguising him, just as Domitian escaped in disguise from the Capitoline siege.

[25] See Chapter 3, Sections 3.3, 3.5 and 3.6.

[26] *Theb.* 9.220–2. Cf. *Theb.* 4.139–44.

this hero. Imagery connecting Hippomedon to monsters or beasts is combined with allusions to the greatest of heroes, Hercules. At some point during this hero's *aristeia*, we may think Hippomedon has something in common with Hercules (9.640), yet his death reminds us that he is actually more similar to the monstrous Centaurs. After his impious challenge to the river god, Ismenus beats him into submission in a way that reminds us of Hercules' punishment of the Centaurs.[27]

The fact that Statius presents these three heroes as occupying an unstable position in the spectrum between god and beast draws attention to the difference in the characterization of other heroes among the Seven, namely Parthenopaeus and Amphiaraus. In Chapter 2, I argued that Statius' Amphiaraus is in some important ways unlike the other Seven and that his peculiar characterization is instrumental to Statius' construction of a discourse on kingship and succession. This difference is remarked on at the time of Amphiaraus' death, but is also clearly visible in the heroic exploits that precede it. The hero's final *aristeia* presents the audience with an aspect of Amphiaraus that we have not seen previously, his war valor. Yet Amphiaraus is not associated to the beast–god pattern that Statius activates with regard to other heroes. Even in his final fury, Statius makes sure we notice that Amphiaraus' victims are prevalently impious.[28] His descent to the underworld is not a punishment but a reward for his piety.[29] The same treatment applies to Parthenopaeus. Statius does not compare him to beasts or monsters, but pits him against a monstrous and impious hero in his final *aristeia*.[30] The young Arcadian interests Statius as a tragic figure of the youth who dies prematurely, unable to make a transition into the world of adults. His story expands Statius' reflection on the topic of premature death. How about Theseus? What is his position in the beast–god spectrum? I discussed Theseus' playing the role of a god in Chapter 4. As for animal imagery, the Athenian sovereign, at war with Thebes, is compared to a lion who despises worthless, weak prey. As Federica Bessone has shown, this simile recalls the *leo mansuetus* [tamed lion] topic, a conventional subject used to praise the emperor's merciful attitude in imperial panegyric.[31] The animal comparison is used in a way that underscores the nobility and control of the Athenian hero. Yet it reminds us

---

[27] *Theb.* 9.481–5. See Chapter 3, Section 3.1.2.

[28] For example, Hypseus, who is characterized with reference to Asopus, the river god who dared to challenge Jupiter (*Theb.* 7.723–35); Polites, who murdered his brother (7.757); Lampus, who sought to rape the priestess Manto (7.758–9).

[29] He goes to Elysium. At *Theb.* 8.90–1 he refers to himself as *sanctus manis* [sacred shade], and at 8.101 he states that he enters the underworld without having committed any crime. See Augoustakis (2016) 104, 109.

[30] Cf. Statius' description of Dryas, the hero who kills Parthenopaeus, at *Theb.* 9.841–4 (cf. also 7.254–8).

[31] See Chapter 1, Section 1.8 n. 213.

of the tragic paradox on which I have reflected several times in this book: To bring an end to the conflict, Theseus needs, to an extent, to step into his enemies' footsteps and draw from the same dark energies by which their actions are fueled.[32]

C.2 THE *THEBAID*'S POLITICAL VISION

In the course of this book, I have advanced the hypothesis that the *Thebaid*'s political vision is best understood from a didactic perspective. Rather than simply praising or blaming, Statius is interested in outlining the factors that grant success or failure to a leader. The poet highlights features that drive rulers to cruelty and those that can instead make them approach the role of benevolent deities. However, Statius does not vouchsafe for his imperial addressee: Success is presented as a possibility, never as certainty. Even when, at the beginning of the poem, Statius explicitly depicts Domitian as successful in his imperial role, the picture is constellated by reminders of the failure of Domitian's predecessors in a way that calls attention to the fragility of the emperor's position and to the risk that he himself might turn into one of them. Similarly, as examined in Chapter 3, Statius' study of heroic models presents the emperor and his audience with a spectrum of possibilities, involving both success and failure. Heroes who aspire to play the role of Hercules may end up turning into monsters or beasts; they may also, alternatively, achieve immortality on account of their benefactions to humanity, like Hercules. At the beginning of the *Thebaid*, Statius hints that Domitian possesses divine qualities, that he acts like a savior of humanity, but the poem also vividly brings to mind the precariousness of his position, the possibility of regression, deviation, or failure. Statius presents success as a fragile balance, always at the risk of being overturned, rather than as a permanent achievement.[33]

Within this perspective, the question about the poem's stance toward the power of Domitian does not afford a simple answer. Nothing in the text seems to suggest that Domitian is precluded from realizing the illuminated form of kingship the poem allows us to perceive. Ultimately our answer to this question will be shaped by the view of Domitian we entertain. If we picture Domitian as a tyrant and a second Nero, the panegyric parts of the poem will look like desperate and insincere flattery, and it will seem impossible to detach the poem's tyrants from this emperor. If we allow for a less one-sided perception of Domitian, and if we take into account the *Thebaid*'s interaction with the cultural atmosphere of Domitian's early reign, then

---

[32] See Chapter 4, Section 4.3 and Chapter 5, Section 5.4.
[33] This holds true for the poem's finale too: see Introduction, Section I.8.

the ideal of the princeps inspired by *clementia* will look like a reasonable attempt at directing the emperor toward a certain model, and we will become receptive to the elements that connect the *Thebaid*'s tyrants with earlier phases of the principate.

In Chapter 1, I drew attention to Domitian's attempts at building a new relationship with the senatorial elite based on the behavior recommended by Seneca's *De Clementia*, visible in his policy of pardoning and advancing the careers of survivors of earlier emperors. I connected the revival of some aspects of Neronian ideology introduced by Domitian's panegyrists to these concrete acts by the emperor. Panegyrists of Domitian transfer to this emperor the praise of Nero as the emperor who introduces a new era of peace marked by *clementia* and the restoration of *libertas*. I tried to demonstrate that the atmosphere surrounding Domitian's accession to the throne, reflected in later panegyric poetry, was remarkably similar to the one accompanying Trajan's succession and reflected in Pliny's *Panegyricus*. In this context, the *Thebaid* can be seen as an attempt at constraining the emperor to abide by his auspicious beginnings. This initial phase was obscured by Domitian's denigration by the following dynasty, a process that also contributed to transforming Domitian into a second Nero. In this book, I have tried to show that constructive visions of Domitian's power should be considered as possible responses to Statius' poem by early audiences. I also argued that less-than-optimistic readings became more and more appealing with the deterioration of Domitian's rapport with the elite.

Let us consider some specific aspects of the construction of kingship that Statius envisages as an ideal for Domitian. This construction is strongly influenced by the notion of merciful king as elaborated by Seneca's *De Clementia*. According to Seneca, the sovereign endowed with *clementia* limits his recourse to punishment in the conducting of public affairs; centers his power on the love of his subjects, not on their fear; and never lets his judgment be clouded by passions such as anger or fear.[34] He gains the support of his subjects by granting pardon to those who plotted against him.[35] Such a ruler grants peace and welfare to his community, performing the role of a benevolent deity.[36] Seneca's notion of the ideal sovereign is influential on Statius' portrait of Domitian in *Siluae* 1.1. In this poem, the poet praises Domitian for his mildness and his inclination to forgiveness while contrasting him with figures such as Caesar and Alexander.[37]

---

[34] For example, *Cl.* 1.1.3–4 (Nero's merciful behavior); 2.3.1–2.7.5 (definition of *clementia*); 1.3.3–4 and 1.11.4–1.13.5 (*clementia* grants security). See Chapter 1, Section 1.1.

[35] *Cl.* 1.9.1–11.

[36] *Cl.* 1.5.7, 1.7.1–3; cf. also 1.10.1–4; Chapter 1, Section 1.1; Chapter 3, Section 3.3 n. 70.

[37] *Silv.* 1.1.25–7, 85–91; Chapter 1, Section 1.1.

The influence of this ideal is visible in the *Thebaid*, most clearly in the centrality attributed to *clementia* in the poem's finale.[38] This key concept for Roman imperial politics is redefined in the poem's close. *Clementia* is no longer solely conceived as restraint in administering punishment: Statius' altar of *clementia* is a place where suppliants and the oppressed find refuge, and *clementia* becomes the virtue of defending the rights of humans against tyranny and oppression. The scope of *clementia* is broadened in connection with Roman notions of *humanitas*. The strategic Roman value of *clementia* is given a Greek background and is linked to the traditional role of Athens as guardian of the oppressed and defender of freedom. Theseus' action brings these values into effect, as he heeds the request of the Argive women and proceeds to deliver Thebes from the tyranny of Creon. Theseus' short military intervention is accompanied by images that surface in Roman discussions of imperial *clementia* (such as the simile of the tamed lion), and the Athenian sovereign is prepared to grant a burial even to Creon, displaying the promptness with which he offers pardon.[39]

The influence of Seneca's thought is not limited to book 12. In *De Clementia*, the sovereign who is not able to resist irrational passions such as anger and vindictive drive is unfit to rule. These passions are capable of turning him into a beast, whereas the sovereign inspired by *clementia* approaches the gods.[40] This theory of passions and their effects on those in power forms the counterpart to Statius' view of *clementia* as the central virtue of a sovereign. Stoic approaches to passions and their effect on those in power underlie Statius' reflection on heroic virtue and are particularly visible where Statius observes the adventures of certain heroes through the prism of the Hercules myth. Tydeus is endowed with great courage and martial valor, but he is dominated by passions that eventually deprive him of immortality and turn him into a beast. Capaneus' valor is equally extraordinary, but the hero's impiety mars his actions and relegates him to the role of a monster. Seneca's *Hercules Furens* becomes a powerful tool for expressing these concepts. Underlying Statius' use of Seneca's play is a reading of the *Hercules Furens* in a political light as a portrait of a sovereign who in many ways falls short of the dictates of Seneca's *De Clementia*. Statius' picture of Theseus as an embodiment of *clementia* complements his view of other heroes as impaired by the same flaws that compromise Seneca's Hercules.

The *Thebaid*'s vision of power is also deeply influenced by the political culture of the Neronian period. Statius is genuinely critical of the former season of Roman governance. He joins in the indictment of Nero that is current in Domitianic Rome

---

[38] Bessone (2011) 128–99. See Chapter 1, Section 1.8.

[39] See Chapter 1, Section 1.8, with full references.

[40] Chapter 3, Section 3.3.

and is influenced by the Flavian construction of Nero as the quintessential Roman tyrant. He is also influenced by what I have called martyrology, the idealized presentation of the sufferings of Roman aristocrats crushed by imperial repression. The condemnation of the former dynasty, especially in the person of Nero, has more profound implications. For Statius, Neronian Rome provides an *exemplum*: It details the consequences of tyrannical rule and the connection between the latter and civil war. The picture of an emperor who started as a champion of *clementia* and ended up as a monster is a powerful warning for an emperor who made eloquent gestures of *clementia* at the beginning of his reign.

Whatever we make of the *Thebaid*'s presentation of monarchy, Statius' poem does not envisage any feasible alternative to one-man rule. In Statius' view, the story of the Theban brothers exemplifies a universal law: Supreme power cannot be shared.[41] This position is complemented by a negative view of the masses. Seneca and other imperial authors stress the uncontrollable, riotous, and self-destructive nature of the masses, which can find peace only under the protective kingship of an illuminated sovereign.[42] Statius seems to adumbrate a similar view in his *Thebaid*. A negative view of the commoners is perceivable in the anonymous citizen's speech in book 1.[43] This anonymous individual voices the same criticism of brotherly *discordia* introduced by Statius earlier in book 1. Yet his credibility is undercut by Statius' remarks on him: The anonymous Theban is always ready to criticize those in power, no matter who they are. In a comparable fashion, in the *Siluae*, Statius describes the *plebs* as "unable to mourn the powerful."[44]

Statius' point seems to be the same as Seneca's: Monarchy is the only form of government that can grant order to the unruly masses of imperial citizens. Whether this is, as in Tacitus, a condition of the Roman Empire at a certain point in its history or a general law valid for human societies irrespective of time and place we are not told.[45] In an important scene from book 8, the army seems to be pictured in a more favorable light than the citizens of Thebes. The troops, unlike the commoners, are able to mourn the loss of a just commander like Amphiaraus; they act unanimously and display the right instincts in selecting and acclaiming his successor.[46] But that scene is remindful of imperial acclamations: To deny that the troops can have the right instinct in selecting their beloved general for power would be tantamount to

---

[41] Cf. *Theb.* 1.130 and Chapter 4, Section 4.3 and 4.4.

[42] For example, Sen. *Cl.* 1.1.1. Other sources in Chapter 4, Section 4.6.

[43] *Theb.* 1.168–73; see Chapter 4, Section 4.3.

[44] *Silv.* 1.4.40.

[45] Tac. *Hist.* 1.1.1, 1.16.1.

[46] *Theb.* 8.271–85.

denying the legitimacy of Vespasian's acclamation. I doubt that the scene in book 8 can be taken as a general view of the ability of the soldiers, as opposed to the urban population, of producing sound judgments.

Statius' endorsement of imperial power rests on another ideological prop, namely the fear of civil war. The *Thebaid* builds on a tradition of texts in which imperial power is presented as the only option for a world torn apart by civil conflicts. Such a view underlies Virgil's address to Octavian in the *Georgics* and is implied in the praise of Nero at the beginning of Lucan's *Bellum Ciuile*. The formulas used by Virgil and Lucan to celebrate Octavian and Nero as providential figures are transferred to Domitian at the beginning of the *Thebaid*, in which Statius also references Domitian's participation in the civil war of 69 CE.[47] In Chapter 6, I showed that appropriating Vespasian's success in civil war played an important role in Domitianic ideology.

The idea that imperial power is the only force able to grant peace to the Roman state is reflected in Statius' metaphorical use of the cosmos as a mirror for human action. The *Thebaid* builds on an epic tradition (especially present in Virgil's *Aeneid*, Ovid's *Metamorphoses*, and Lucan's *Bellum Ciuile*) in which the power of the emperor is likened to the cosmic dominion of Jupiter and in which chaos and the struggle of the elements are parallels for civil war.[48] In the *Thebaid*, images of cosmic upheaval accompany the strife of Eteocles and Polynices to the point at which a clear parallelism is delineated between civil war and cosmic disorder.[49] The winds and other elements threaten to overturn the order of the universe in the same way as the forces of civil strife threaten the cohesion of human communities. In the natural world, Jupiter's power keeps the elements under control, thus guaranteeing peace. In the poem's beginning, Jupiter's control over the universe is linked to the power of the emperor, and Theseus is compared to Jupiter in a key passage of book 12.[50] The implications of this parallelism are evident: just as the cosmos would naturally return to chaos without the power of Jupiter, the world would naturally be torn apart by civil war without the power of the emperor. Imperial power appears as the one form of authority that can keep in check a world always on the brink of dissolution.

Connected to the idea that monarchical rule is unavoidable is the poem's reflection on *libertas*. In imperial reflections, *libertas* is no longer understood as the political freedom inherent in the republican constitution. *Libertas* for the Roman elite consists in its capacity to preserve its dignity and freedom of speech, and for

---

[47] *Theb.* 1.17–31: the reference to Domitian's participation in the siege of Capitoline in 69 CE is at line 22 (*bella Iouis*). Cf. also *Silv.* 1.1.74–83. See Chapter 4, Sections 4.1–4.2.

[48] Chapter 4, Section 4.3.

[49] *Theb.* 1.193–6; see also *Theb.* 1.133, discussed in Chapter 4, Section 4.3.

[50] *Theb.* 12.650–5. Chapter 4, Section 4.3.

the citizens in their protection against the abuses of the king when he respects the rule of law. The *Thebaid* seems to be aligned with this understanding of *libertas*. Statius has no doubt about the necessity of monarchical power, yet he remarks on the importance of *libertas* under monarchical regimes. He uses this politically loaded term in two key scenes to define the behavior of characters opposing tyranny: The word seems to denote the freedom to speak the truth in front of the tyrant.[51] Such freedom of speech is impossible under a regime that bases its power on the fear of subjects, but a sovereign endowed with *clementia*, we assume, is compatible with it.

The *Thebaid* reflects on a particularly controversial problem of the Roman Empire, that of succession. The fact that he had two adult children helped Vespasian's credibility as an aspirant to the imperial throne.[52] The same could not be said of Domitian, whose only child died before his accession and who did not appoint a successor for much of his life.[53] Statius' view on this delicate issue can be grasped in the scene of Amphiaraus' succession in book 8. The seer's successor is elected by the troops in a context that is strongly evocative of narratives of imperial acclamations. After the fashion of Roman emperors, Amphiaraus' successor performs a *recusatio*, proclaiming himself unequal to the task. Eventually, he has to be forced into accepting the office. The new chief is chosen because of his merits. He fulfills popular will and the will of the former holder of the office.[54] Here Statius stresses the role of public *consensus* as a determining factor in imperial succession. Moreover, by emphasizing the *concordia* between Amphiaraus and Thiodamas, he argues for the necessity of *concordia* among members of the imperial family.[55] In short, Amphiaraus' succession is given the traits of an idealized imperial succession. Pliny's description of Trajan's accession in his *Panegyricus* provides an important term of comparison and shares some of Statius' themes.[56]

Imperial power might be necessary, but it is by no means perfect or purely benign. Key to the *Thebaid*'s political view is the portrait of the sovereign endowed with *clementia*, an ideal figure shaped by the reflection of post-Augustan thinkers such as Seneca. Yet *clementia* is not sufficient. Force, and one of its correlates, fear, are required too. In a different world, perhaps matters could be settled in a different way. But given what Statius has shown us about human nature, force cannot be avoided.[57]

---

[51] *Theb.* 3.102 (Maeon); *Theb.* 3.216 (Aletes). Cf. also *Theb.* 11.264.

[52] Tac. *Hist.* 2.77.

[53] See Chapter 2, Section 2.3 n. 56.

[54] *Theb.* 8.275–82, discussed in Chapter 2, Section 2.6.

[55] Chapter 2, Sections 2.6 and 2.7.

[56] Cf. Plin. *Pan.* 7–8. See Chapter 2, Section 2.6.

[57] For Statius' pessimistic view of human nature see Introduction, Section I.8.

The poem's crisis could not have been resolved without force. The poet is explicit about this: There is no dialogue with a tyrant like Creon; only through force can he be led to behave as a human.[58] But this is not all. To succeed, Theseus needs to inspire fear. He needs to appropriate some elements of the terror deployed by the forces he seeks to oppose.

In this respect, the *Thebaid* follows in the footsteps of the *Aeneid*. At the end of the *Aeneid*, Jupiter dispatches the Dirae against Turnus. The king of gods taps into the same underworld powers harnessed by Juno as he drives the poem toward a resolution.[59] In a similar way, in the *Thebaid*, Theseus—the human who in a sense replaces Jupiter as an agent of order—brings the narrative to an end by channeling some of the energies that up to this point have been a resource of his enemies. Statius conveys this through particularly effective imagery. Medusa, the snake-haired monster whom the poet associates with the Furies and with the madness of civil war, is emblazoned on the hero's shield. Theseus turns the terror inspired by Medusa against his enemies.[60] Storm imagery is constantly associated to chaos and civil war in the poem. At the poem's climax, Theseus becomes an embodiment of the threatening power of the storm, but he channels the cosmic upheaval represented by the storm into an action against his enemies.[61]

This complex nature of the forces wielded by Theseus has given rise to much discussion among scholars. It is true that Theseus borrows some traits from Mars, the god whose war fury the poet associates with the most gruesome moments in the civil war.[62] However, this does not undermine Theseus' portrait. The power of Mars is necessary. The same power that dispenses chaos and slaughter can become the instrument of a good cause. The question is who is using this power, how, and for what ends. The difference between Theseus and Aeneas does not lie in the forces that are at their service as they approach their enemies. Rather, the difference seems to be control. Whereas Aeneas is swept away by his anger at the end of the poem, Theseus does not lose his rational control. Not by chance, Theseus' heroic exploit is introduced by a simile in which the natural elements participating in the storm are presented not as revolting against the power of Jupiter, but as firmly under his control and directed by him. In the *Aeneid*, such control is a prerogative of Jupiter and not Aeneas; in the *Thebaid*, the earthly Jupiter Theseus brings to Earth the virtue of his divine counterpart. In spite of his control, Theseus' channeling of the terror

---

[58] *Theb.* 12.165–6.
[59] *A.* 12.843–952.
[60] *Theb.* 12.606–10; see discussion in Chapter 5, Section 5.4.
[61] *Theb.* 12.650–5, discussed in Chapter 4, Section 4.3.
[62] Coffee (2009) 222–4.

associated with the forces of madness and civil war is not encouraging. Although necessary, monarchical power cannot be purely benign. This is a disturbing view of power, one that is rooted in a pessimistic view of human nature. A purely benevolent form of power is impossible and would be ineffective. And yet it is better for humans to live under this power's purview than to be swept away by the centrifugal forces of chaos, for Theseus channels the poem's dark energies toward a positive resolution.

The *Thebaid* complicates the somewhat more optimistic conception of the illuminated sovereign from Seneca's *De Clementia* with this pessimistic and tragic view of power that we can trace back to Virgil's *Aeneid*. This differentiates the *Thebaid* from the position of Seneca's *De Clementia* and from the portrait of Domitian in the *Siluae*. In the *Siluae*, this darker dimension of power is obscured: Although it is true that Domitian is praised for his ability to frighten his enemies while also looking benevolently on his friends, there is no sense of the inherent necessity for the emperor of tapping into these obscure forces in order for his power to be effective. Nor do we find in the *Siluae* the precarious isolation of the sovereign at the end of the *Thebaid*. Unlike Domitian's rule in the *Siluae*, Theseus' success is not accompanied by any promise of a Golden Age and is not ratified by divine powers. Theseus' victory is a purely human achievement, fragile and reversible as every human success.

C.3 STATIUS' *THEBAID* AND THE SURVIVORS OF NERO

In the previous section, I listed a number of elements that characterize the *Thebaid*'s political view. Some aspects of this position are in tune with the views of the senatorial elite. Certainly the senatorial class had everything to gain from Domitian's policy of lenience toward the upper classes and from his promises of restoring *libertas*. The ideal of the merciful king inspired by *clementia* and Statius' ideas about succession were in line with the position of the elite. Even Statius' resignation to monarchy as the only option for a world troubled by civil war has parallels in the position of elite imperial thinkers. Indeed, Statius' notion of an ideal ruler has much in common with the presentation of illuminated kingship as reflected in the works of authors active under the following imperial dynasty, such as Pliny the Younger.

More specific aspects of Statius' view fit particularly well the concerns of narrower groups within the Roman elite at the time of the poem's publication. In particular, survivors of Nero would have found much in the *Thebaid* that reflected their attitude to the power of Domitian. Domitian had close ties to survivors of Nero even before ascending to the throne, and they are the ones who most directly benefited from Domitian's *clementia* until late in his reign.[63] For these survivors, it was vital that Domitian live up to his promises of a new season marked by *clementia*. Anti-Neronian ideology was relevant for them in a more direct way: Indeed, for members of this group it was a form of self-advertising and self-promotion. Some of these intellectuals had a vested interest in promoting the reputation of the Annaeans and the diffusion of their thought and poetry. The *Thebaid* is not only influenced by Seneca's political thought; it is also an indirect attempt at rehabilitating the memory of Seneca and establishing both Seneca and Lucan as models of behavior under tyranny and defendants of the traditions of *libertas*.

Statius' connection with survivors of Nero can be documented. The *Siluae* provide evidence for Statius' tie with the house of Argentaria Polla, Lucan's widow.[64] Statius was an acquaintance of Polla and attended her house.[65] At Polla's instigation, Statius and Martial wrote poems to keep alive the reputation of Lucan almost 30 years after his death.[66] Polla may have been remarried to Pollius Felix, a rich Campanian landowner and patron of arts. Statius dedicates to Pollius book 3 of the *Siluae; Siluae* 2.2 deals with Pollius' Surrentine villa; *Siluae* 3.1 deals with Pollius' Hercules shrine; and *Siluae* 4.8 is dedicated to Pollius' son-in-law Julius Menecrates.[67] Pollius, possibly a poet himself, was a devotee of Greek culture and a sophisticated reader.[68] Statius wrote poetry at Pollius' house and profited from his advice.[69] Pollius and his family do not seem to belong to the opposition to Domitian's regime. Pollius held magistratures in Naples and Puteoli.[70] In *Siluae* 4.8, his son-in-law Julius Menecrates appears as a rich and prominent Neapolitan aristocrat, possibly the holder of a number of priesthoods and the recipient of Domitian's favor.[71] Statius' ease in advertising his connection to this family at a time when he also enjoys imperial favor seems to corroborate the view that attachment to the house of Polla was not compromising. It is likely that Statius' poem on Lucan (*Siluae* 2.7) reflects the outlook of Polla and her affiliates. In this poem, unsurprisingly, the vulgate on Nero as a monster has consolidated: Nero is a matricide and a crazed tyrant, responsible for the fire of Rome.[72] Lucan is presented as a hero who dies for the sake of *libertas* and a model for behaving under tyranny. Because Polla is committed to preserving the memory

---

[63] Chapter 1, Sections 1.2 and 1.4.
[64] See Chapter 1, Section 1.4.
[65] Cf. *Silv.* 2 *praef.* 23–6.
[66] Stat. *Silv.* 2.7; Mart. 7.21, 22, 23.
[67] On Pollius and Polla see Chapter 1, Section 1.4 and bibliography given in n. 119 in Chapter 1.
[68] Poet: *Silv.* 2.2.137 with Hardie (1983) 67, 217 n. 76; devotee of Greek culture: *Silv.* 2.2.95–6.
[69] *Silv.* 3 *praef.* 4–8.
[70] *Silv.* 2.2.133–7, 3.1.91–3.
[71] *Silv.* 4.8.45–62, 4.8.20–1; Hardie (1983) 68, 217 n. 79.
[72] *Silv.* 2.7.58, 60–61, 100–1, 117–19.

of members of the Annaean clan, it is likely that this group was acquainted with the political thought of Seneca.

Traces of the influence of patronage activities by survivors of the Annaeans can be recovered in another Flavian text. In his commentary, Rolando Ferri has advanced the hypothesis that the pseudo-Senecan *Octauia* may be related to patronage activities supported by the Annaeans.[73] *Octauia* aims to rehabilitate the memory of Seneca, another member of the Annaean family.[74] This play shares a number of features with Statius' political vision and with some of the elements we can trace back to the house of Polla through *Siluae* 2.7. And there are remarkable similarities in the textual strategies through which political meaning is developed in both the *Thebaid* and *Octauia*. *Octauia* is an important document for the reception of Seneca's *De Clementia*, a text that, as I previously argued, has an important influence on both the *Siluae* and the *Thebaid*.[75] Moreover, both Statius and the author of *Octauia* seem to have assimilated the vulgate of Nero the monster and the idea of his direct responsibility for the fire of Rome.[76] Both the *Thebaid* and *Octauia* capitalize on a politicized reading of Seneca's plays.[77] The author of *Octauia* may be acquainted with the poetry of Statius, and his portrait of Nero shows important similarities with Statius' depiction of Nero in *Siluae* 2.7.[78] Another common feature is the importance given to the role of *consensus* in the exercise of imperial power.[79]

The number of correspondences among *Octauia*, the *Thebaid*, and the *Siluae*; the fact that the author of *Octauia* seems to be acquainted with Statius' poetry; and the notice that Statius attended meetings at Polla's house, make the suggestion attractive that both the *Thebaid* and *Octauia* originate from an active participation of the two poets in cultural activities orchestrated by survivors of Nero. However, too much is uncertain about this scenario. The correspondences between the *Thebaid* and *Octauia* may be taken to reflect the common orientation of the Flavian regime toward Nero and his principate; the interest in Seneca's political theory may stem from individual acts of reception rather than from involvement in a shared cultural environment. We have no clear idea of the extent of the patronage activities orchestrated

[73] Ferri (2003) 26. The date of the play is debated; see for discussion Ferri (2003) 5–30; Boyle (2008) xiv–xvi. I agree on the Flavian date of the play.

[74] Ferri (2003) 71–2.

[75] Ferri (2003) 70–1.

[76] For the vulgate on Nero the monster in Statius cf. *Silv.* 2.7.58, 60–1, 100–1, 117–19; Degl'Innocenti Pierini (2007) 142–5. For the presence of this tradition in *Octauia* see Ferri (2003) 9–11.

[77] On *Octauia*'s ideological reading of Seneca's tragedies see Ferri (2003) 73–4.

[78] The suggestion that *Octauia*'s author is acquainted with the poetry of Statius is in Ferri (2003) 17–27. For correspondences in the depiction of Nero cf. *Silv.* 2.7.108–9 and *Oct.* 23–4; see Newlands (2011) 250–1.

[79] For *consensus* in *Octauia* see Ferri (2003) 73–4. For the role of *consensus* in the context of imperial succession in the *Thebaid* see Chapter 2, Section 2.6.

by Polla. That Statius had extensive connections with this family (besides the request to compose *Siluae* 2.7) rests on our identification of Argentaria Polla with Pollius' wife, an attractive possibility but not a certainty. The real degree of influence and interconnection between the *Thebaid* and the house of Polla must therefore remain a subject of speculation.

However, exploring these connections is worthwhile, for it allows us to individuate a portion of Rome's elite that would have been particularly receptive to the political vision expressed by the *Thebaid*. The greatest advantage of connecting the *Thebaid* to the cultural activities of groups of survivors from the Neronian period consists in achieving a better sense of the agency behind the *Thebaid*'s political message. It allows us to envisage certain groups of Romans who had a stake in the cultural mission and didactic enterprise that Statius sets up for himself.

Adamo Muscettola, S. (2000) "The Sculptural Evidence," in P. Miniero, ed., *The Sacellum of the Augustales at Misenum*, Naples: Electa Napoli: 29–48.

Ahl, F. (1976) *Lucan: An Introduction*, Ithaca/London: Cornell University Press.

———(1984a) "The Rider and the Horse: Politics and Power in Roman Poetry From Horace to Statius," *ANRW* II 32.1: 40–110.

———(1984b) "The Art of Safe Criticism in Greece and Rome," *AJPh* 105: 174–208.

———(1986) "Statius' *Thebaid*: A Reconsideration," *ANRW* II 32.4: 2803–912.

———(2015) "Transgressing Boundaries of the Unthinkable: Sophocles, Ovid, Vergil, Seneca, and Homer Refracted in Statius' *Thebaid*," in W. J. Dominik, C. E. Newlands, and K. Gervais, eds., *Brill's Companion to Statius*, Leiden, The Netherlands/Boston: Brill: 240–65.

Anderson, W. S. (1957) "Virgil's Second Iliad," *TAPhA* 88: 17–30.

Aricò, G. (1960) "Sul mito di Lino e Corebo in Stat. *Theb.* I 557–668," *RFIC* 88: 277–85.

Ash, R. (2015) "War Came in Disarray . . ." (*Thebaid* 7.616): Statius and the Depiction of Battle," in W. J. Dominik, C. E. Newlands, and K. Gervais, eds., *Brill's Companion to Statius*, Leiden, The Netherlands/Boston: Brill: 207–20.

Asso, P. ed. (2010) *A Commentary on Lucan, De Bello Civili IV*, Berlin/New York: De Gruyter.

Augoustakis, A. (2015) "Statius and Senecan Drama," in W. J. Dominik, C. E. Newlands, and K. Gervais, eds., *Brill's Companion to Statius*, Leiden, The Netherlands/Boston: Brill: 377–92.

———ed. (2016) *Statius, Thebaid 8. Edited with an Introduction, Translation, and Commentary*, Oxford: Oxford University Press.

Barchiesi, A. ed. (1988) *Seneca, Le Fenicie, traduzione e commento a cura di A. B.*, Venice: Marsilio.

———ed. (2005) *Ovidio, Metamorfosi. Vol. I: libri I–II*, Milan: Mondadori.

———(2009) "Phaethon and the Monsters," in Ph. Hardie, ed., *Paradox and the Marvellous in Augustan Literature and Culture*, Oxford: Oxford University Press: 163–88.

————(2011) "Roman Callimachus," in Benjamin Acosta-Hughes, Luigi Lehnus, and Susan Stephens, eds., *Brill's Companion to Callimachus*, Leiden, The Netherlands/Boston: Brill: 511–33.

Barruol, G. (1996) "La statue du guerrier de Vachères (Alpes-de-Haute-Provence)," *RAN* 29: 1–12.

Bartsch, S. (1994) *Actors in the Audience*, Cambridge, MA: Harvard University Press.

Beard–North–Price (1998): M. Beard, J. North, and S. Price, *Religions of Rome*, Cambridge: Cambridge University Press.

Beloch, K. J. (1927) *Griechische Geschichte*, vol. IV 2, 2nd ed., Berlin/Leipzig: De Gruyter.

Béranger, J. (1953) *Recherches sur l'aspect idéologique du principat*, Basel: Reinhardt.

Bergmann, M. (1993) "Der Koloss Neros, die Domus Aurea und der Mentalitätswandel im Rom der frühen Kaiserzeit," *Trierer Winckelmannsprogramme* 13: 3–37.

————(1998) *Die Strahlen der Herrscher: theomorphes Herrscherbild und politische Symbolik im Hellenismus und in der römischen Kaiserzeit*, Mainz: von Zabern.

Bergmann–Zanker (1981): M. Bergmann and P. Zanker, "Damnatio Memoriae. Umgearbeitete Nero-und Domitiansporträts. Zur Ikonographie der Flavischen Kaiser und des Nerva," *JDAI* 96: 317–412.

Bernstein, N. W. (2008) *In the Image of the Ancestors: Narratives of Kinship in Flavian Epic*, Toronto: University of Toronto Press.

————(2013) "Ritual Murder and Suicide in the *Thebaid*," in A. Augoustakis, ed., *Ritual and Religion in Flavian Epic*, Oxford/New York: Oxford University Press: 233–48.

Bessone, F. (2006) "Un mito da dimenticare. Tragedia e memoria epica nella *Tebaide*," *MD* 56: 93–127.

————(2008a) "Epica e potere. Forma narrativa e discorso politico nella *Tebaide* di Stazio," in R. Uglione, ed., *Arma virumque cano ... L'epica dei Greci e dei Romani*, Alessandria, Italy: Edizioni dell'Orso: 185–208.

————(2008b) "Teseo, la *clementia* e la punizione dei tiranni: Esemplarità e pessimismo nel finale della *Tebaide*," *Dictynna* 5 (http://dictynna.review.org/200).

————(2009) "*Clementia* e *philantropia*. Atene e Roma nel finale della *Tebaide*," *MD* 62: 179–214.

————(2011) *La Tebaide di Stazio. Epica e potere*, Pisa/Rome: Fabrizio Serra.

Bing, P. (1988) *The Well-Read Muse. Present and Past in Callimachus and the Hellenistic Poets*, Göttingen, Germany: Vandenhoeck & Ruprecht.

Blänsdorf, J. ed. (2011) *Fragmenta Poetarum Latinorum Epicorum et Lyricorum Praeter Enni Annales et Ciceronis Germanicique Aratea* post W. Morel et K. Büchner editionem quartam auctam curavit J. B., Berlin/New York: De Gruyter.

Bönisch-Meyer et al. (2014): S. Bönisch-Meyer, L. Cordes, V. Schulz, A. Wolsfeld, M. Ziegert, eds., *Nero und Domitian: Mediale Diskurse der Herrscherrepräsentation im Vergleich*, Tübingen, Germany: Narr.

Boyancé, P. (1966) "L'Apollon Solaire," in *Mélanges d'archéologie, d'épigraphie et d'histoire offerts à J. Carcopino*, Paris: Hachette: 149–70.

Boyle, A. J. ed. (2008) *Octavia: Attributed to Seneca*, Oxford/New York: Oxford University Press.

————ed. (2011) *Seneca: Oedipus*, Oxford/New York: Oxford University Press.

Braund, S. ed. (1992) *Lucan. Civil War*, Oxford: Clarendon.

————(1996a) "Ending Epic: Statius, Theseus and a Merciful Release," *PCPhS* 42: 1–23.

————ed. (1996b) *Juvenal. Satires Book I*, Cambridge: Cambridge University Press.

——(1998) "Praise and Protreptic in Early Imperial Panegyric: Cicero, Seneca, Pliny," in M. Whitby, ed., *The Propaganda of Power: The Role of Panegyric in Late Antiquity*, Leiden, The Netherlands/Boston: Brill: 53–76.

——(2006) "A Tale of Two Cities: Statius, Thebes, and Rome," *Phoenix* 60: 259–73.

——ed. (2009) *Seneca. De Clementia*, Oxford/New York: Oxford University Press.

Bravi, A. (2012) *Ornamenta Urbis. Opere d'arte greche negli spazi romani*, Bari, Italy: Edipuglia.

Brown, J. (1994) *Into the Woods: Narrative Studies in the Thebaid of Statius with Special Reference to Books IV–VI*, PhD dissertation, Cambridge University.

Buchheit, V. (1963) *Vergil über die Sendung Roms. Untersuchungen zum Bellum Poenicum und zur Aeneis*, Heidelberg: Winter.

Buchner, E. (1982) *Die Sonnenuhr des Augustus: Nachdruck aus RM 1976 und 1980 und Nachtrag über die Ausgrabung 1980/1981*, Mainz am Rhein: von Zabern.

Bullock, A. W. ed. (1985) *Callimachus. The Fifth Hymn*, Cambridge: Cambridge University Press.

Burgess, J. F. (1972) "Statius' Altar of Mercy," *CQ* 22: 339–49.

Caldelli, M. L. (1993) *L'Agon Capitolinus: Storia e protagonisti dall'istituzione domizianea al IV secolo*, Rome: Istituto Italiano per la Storia Antica.

Caviglia, F. ed. (1973) *La Tebaide–Libro I*, Rome: Edizioni dell'Ateneo.

Champlin, E. J. (2003a) *Nero*, Cambridge, MA: Harvard University Press.

——(2003b) "Nero, Apollo, and the Poets," *Phoenix* 57: 276–83.

——(2011) "Tiberius and the Heavenly Twins," *JRS* 101: 73–99.

Chaudhuri, P. (2014) *The War With God: Theomachy in Roman Imperial Poetry*, Oxford/New York: Oxford University Press.

Citroni, M. ed. (1975) *M. Valerii Martialis Epigrammaton liber primus*, Florence: La Nuova Italia.

Clauss, M. (2000) *The Roman Cult of Mithras: The God and His Mysteries*, translated by R. Gordon, New York: Routledge.

Coarelli, F. ed. (2009a) *Diuus Vespasianus, il bimillenario dei Flavi*, Rome: Electa.

——(2009b) "I Flavi e Roma," in F. Coarelli, ed., *Diuus Vespasianus, il bimillenario dei Flavi*, Rome: Electa: 68–97.

Coffee, N. (2009) "Statius' Theseus: Martial or Merciful?," *CPh* 104: 221–8.

Coleman, K. ed. (1988) *Statius Silvae IV*, Oxford: Clarendon.

——(2003) "Introduction," in D. R. Shackleton Bailey, ed., *Statius. Vol. 2: Thebaid, Books 1–7*, Cambridge, MA: Harvard University Press.

——ed. (2006) *M. Valerii Martialis: Liber Spectaculorum*, Oxford: Oxford University Press.

Conte, G. B. (1968) "La guerra civile nella rievocazione del popolo: Lucano 2.67–233," *Maia* 20: 224–53.

——(1985) *Memoria dei poeti e Sistema letterario. Catullo, Virgilio, Ovidio, Lucano*, 2nd ed., Torino, Italy: Einaudi.

Courtney, E. ed. (1980) *A Commentary on the Satires of Juvenal*, London: The Athlone Press.

——ed. (1990) *P. Papini Stati Silvae*, Oxford: Clarendon.

——ed. (1993) *The Fragmentary Latin Poets*, Oxford: Oxford University Press.

Criado, C. (2015) "The Constitutional Status of Euripidean and Statian Theseus: Some Aspects of the Criticism of Absolute Power in the *Thebaid*," in W. J. Dominik, C. E. Newlands, and K. Gervais, eds., *Brill's Companion to Statius*, Leiden, The Netherlands/Boston: Brill: 291–306.

Dabrowa, E. (2000) "Legio III Gallica," in Y. Le Bohec, ed., *Les légions de Rome sous le Haut-Empire*, Lyon, France: Diffusion De Boccard: 309–315.

Dacos–Giuliano–Pannuti (1973): N. Dacos, A. Giuliano, and U. Pannuti, *Il Tesoro di Lorenzo il Magnifico I: Le gemme*, Florence, Italy: Sansoni.

D'Alessio, G. B. ed. (2007) *Callimaco. Inni, Epigrammi, Ecale, Aitia, Giambi e altri frammenti*, 4th ed., Milan: BUR.

Daltrop–Hausmann–Wegner (1966): G. Daltrop, U. Hausmann, and M. Wegner, *Die Flavier: Vespasian, Titus, Domitian, Nerva, Julia Titi, Domitilla, Domitia*, in M. Wegner, ed., *Das römische Herrscherbild*, vol. II.1, Berlin: Gebr. Mann.

Davis, P. J. (1994) "The Fabric of History in Statius' *Thebaid*," in C. Deroux, ed., *Studies in Latin Literature and Roman History*, vol. 7, Brussels: Latomus: 464–83.

Degl'Innocenti Pierini, R. (1990) *Tra Ovidio e Seneca*, Bologne: Patron.

——(2007) "*Pallidus Nero* (Stat. *silv.* 2,7,118 s.): il 'personaggio' Nerone negli scrittori dell'età flavia," in A. Bonadeo and E. Romano, eds., *Dialogando con il passato: Permanenze e innovazioni nella cultura latina di età flavia*, Florence: Le Monnier: 136–59.

Delarue, F. (2000) *Stace, poète épique: originalité et cohérence*, Leuven, Belgium/Paris: Peeters.

——(2006) "La cité vue de l'Olympe: La théologie civile dans la *Thébaïde* de Stace," in P. Galand-Hallyn and C. Lévy, eds., *Vivre pour soi, vivre dans la cité: De l'antiquité à la Renaissance*, Paris: Presses de l'université Paris-Sorbonne: 107–20.

Delvigo, M. L. (2001) "Litus ama: Linguaggio e potere nella regata virgiliana," *MD* 47: 9–33.

Depew, M. (2004) "Gender, Power, and Poetics in Callimachus' Book of Hymns," in M. A. Harder, R. F. Regtuit, and G. C. Wakker, eds., *Callimachus II*, Leuven, Belgium/Paris/Dudley, MA: Peeters.

Dewar, M. ed. (1991) *Statius. Thebaid IX*, Oxford: Clarendon.

——(1994) "Laying It On With a Trowel: The Proem to Lucan and Related Texts," *CQ* 44: 199–211.

Diggle, J. ed. (1970) *Euripides: Phaethon*, Cambridge: Cambridge University Press.

Dominik, W. J. (1994) *The Mythic Voice of Statius. Power and Politics in the Thebaid*, Leiden, The Netherlands/New York/Cologne: Brill.

——(1996) "Statius' *Thebaid* in the Twentieth Century," in R. Faber and B. Seidensticker, eds., *Worte, Bilder, Töne: Studien zur Antike und Antikerezeption*, Würzburg, Germany: Königshausen und Neumann: 129–42.

Dorion, L.-A. (2003) "Une allusion à la Cyropédie au livre III des Lois (694c)," in S. Scolnicov and L. Brisson, eds., *Plato's Laws: From Theory Into Practice*, Sankt Augustin, Germany: Academia: 281–5.

Duret, L. (1988) "Néron-Phaéton, ou la témérité sublime," *REL* 66: 139–55.

Fantham, E. ed. (1992a) *Lucan: De Bello Civili 2*, Cambridge: Cambridge University Press.

——(1992b) "Lucan's Medusa-Excursus: Its Design and Purpose," *MD* 29: 95–119.

——(1995) "The Ambiguity of Virtus in Lucan's Civil War and Statius' *Thebaid*," *Arachnion* 3 (http://www.cisi.unito.it/arachne/arachne.html).

——(1997) "'Envy and Fear the Begetter of Hate': Statius' *Thebaid* and the Genesis of Hatred," in S. Morton Braund and C. Gill, eds., *The Passions in Roman Thought and Literature*, Cambridge: Cambridge University Press: 185–212.

Fantuzzi–Hunter (2002): M. Fantuzzi and R. Hunter, *Muse e modelli. La poesia ellenistica da Alessandro Magno ad Augusto*, Bari, Italy: Laterza.

Fears, J. R. (1981) "The Cult of Jupiter and Roman Imperial Ideology," *ANRW* II.17.1: 3–141.

Fedeli, P. (1989) "Il *Panegirico* di Plinio nella critica moderna," *ANRW* II.33.1: 387–514.

Feeney, D. C. ed. (1982) *A Commentary on Silius Italicus Book 1*, PhD dissertation, Oxford University.

——(1986) "Following After Hercules, in Virgil and Apollonius," *PVS* 18: 47–85.

——(1991) *The Gods in Epic: Poets and Critics of the Classical Tradition*, Oxford: Clarendon.

——(2007) *Caesar's Calendar: Ancient Time and the Beginnings of History*, Berkeley: University of California Press.

Fernandelli, M. (1996) "Stat. Theb. 4.116–144 e l'imitatio Vergiliana," *Sileno* 22: 81–97.

Ferri, R. ed. (2003) *Octavia, a Play Attributed to Seneca*, Cambridge: Cambridge University Press.

Finglass, P. J. ed. (2007) *Sophocles: Electra*, Cambridge: Cambridge University Press.

Fitch, J. G. ed. (1987) *Seneca's Hercules Furens. A Critical Text With Introduction and Commentary*, Ithaca, NY/London: Cornell University Press.

—— ed. (2002) *Seneca. Hercules, Trojan Women, Phoenician Women, Medea, Phaedra*, Cambridge, MA: Harvard University Press.

——ed. (2004) *Seneca. Oedipus, Agamemnon, Thyestes, Hercules on Oeta, Octavia*, Cambridge, MA: Harvard University Press.

Flower, H. I. (2005) *The Art of Forgetting: Disgrace and Oblivion in Roman Political Culture*, Chapel Hill: University of North Carolina Press.

Fontenrose, J. E. (1939) "Apollo and Sol in the Latin Poets of the First Century BC," *TAPhA* 70: 439–55.

——(1940) "Apollo and the Sun-God in Ovid," *AJPh* 61: 429–44.

Fowler, D. (2000) *Roman Constructions. Readings in Postmodern Latin*, Oxford: Oxford University Press.

Franchet d'Espèrey, S. (1999) *Conflit, violence et non-violence dans la Thébaïde de Stace*, Paris: Les Belles Lettres.

Galinsky, G. K. (1972) *The Herakles Theme: The Adaptations of the Hero in Literature From Homer to the Twentieth Century*, Oxford: Blackwell.

——(1996) *Augustan Culture: An Interpretive Introduction*, Princeton, NJ: Princeton University Press.

Gallia, A. B. (2012) *Remembering the Roman Republic: Culture, Politics and History Under the Principate*, Cambridge/New York: Cambridge University Press.

Ganiban, R. T. (2007) *Statius and Virgil. The Thebaid and the Reinterpretation of the Aeneid*, Cambridge: Cambridge University Press.

Gasparri, C. ed. (2009) *Le sculture Farnese. 2. I ritratti*, Naples: Electa Napoli.

Georgacopoulou, S. A. (1996a) "Indices intertextuels et intergénériques: La présentation des coursiers d'Amphiaraüs et d'Admète au livre 6 de la Thébaïde de Stace (*Theb.* 6, 326–339)," *Mnemosyne* 49: 445–52.

——(1996b) "Ranger/Déranger: Catalogues et listes des personnages dans la Thébaïde de Stace," in F. Delarue, S. Georgacopolou, P. Larens, and A. M. Taisne, eds., *Epicedion: Hommage à P. Papinius Statius*, Poitiers, France: La Licorne 93–129.

——(2005) *Aux frontières du récit épique: L'emploi de l'apostrophe du narrateur dans la Thébaïde de Stace*, Brussels: Editions Latomus.

George, E. (1974) *Aeneid VIII and the Aitia of Callimachus*, Leiden, The Netherlands: Brill.

Geyssen, J. W. (1996) *Imperial Panegyric in Statius: A Literary Commentary on Silvae 1.1*, New York/Washington, DC/Baltimore, MD/Bern/Frankfurt am Main/Berlin, Vienna/Paris: Lang.

Ginsberg, L. D. (2013) "Wars More Than Civil: Memories of Caesar and Pompey in the Octavia," *AJPh* 134: 637–74.

Giuliano, A. (1987) *Museo Nazionale Romano, 1. Le sculture, 9. Magazzini. I ritratti, 1*, Rome: De Luca.

———(1989) *I cammei della collezione medicea nel Museo Archeologico di Firenze*, Rome: De Luca.

Gowing, A. M. (2005) *Empire and Memory. The Representation of the Roman Republic in Imperial Culture*, Cambridge: Cambridge University Press.

Gransden, K. W. ed. (1976) *Virgil: Aeneid Book VIII*, Cambridge: Cambridge University Press.

Green, S. J. ed. (2004a) *Ovid, Fasti 1. A Commentary*, Leiden, The Netherlands: Brill.

———(2004b) "Playing With Marble: The Monuments of the Caesars in Ovid's *Fasti*," *CQ* 54: 224–39.

Grenier, J.-C. (2009) "L'obelisco di Domiziano a piazza Navona," in F. Coarelli, ed., *Diuus Vespasianus, il bimillenario dei Flavi*, Rome: Electa 234–9.

Grewing, F. ed. (1997) *Martial, Buch VI (Ein Kommentar)*, Göttingen, Germany: Vandenhoeck & Ruprecht.

Griffin, M. T. (1976) *Seneca: A Philosopher in Politics*, Oxford: Clarendon.

———(1984) *Nero: The End of a Dynasty*, London: Batsford.

———(2000) "The Flavians," in A. K. Bowman, P. Garnsey, and D. Rathbone, eds., *The Cambridge Ancient History*, 2nd ed., vol. XI, Cambridge: Cambridge University Press: 1–83.

Gurval, R. A. (1995) *Actium and Augustus: The Politics and Emotions of Civil War*, Ann Arbor: University of Michigan Press.

Haaland, G. (2005) "Josephus and the Philosophers of Rome: Does *Contra Apionem* Mirror Domitian's Crushing of the 'Stoic Opposition'?," in J. Sievers and G. Lembi, eds., *Josephus and Jewish History in Flavian Rome and Beyond*, Leiden, The Netherlands/Boston: Brill: 297–316.

Habinek, T. N. (2000) "Seneca's Renown: 'Gloria, Claritudo,' and the Replication of the Roman Elite," *CA* 19: 264–303.

Hannestad, N. (1986) *Roman Art and Imperial Policy*, Aarhus, Denmark: Aarhus University Press.

Harder, A. ed. (1985) *Euripides' Kresphontes and Archelaos. Introduction Text and Commentary*, Leiden, The Netherlands: Brill.

———ed. (2012) *Callimachus: Aetia*, Oxford/New York: Oxford University Press.

Hardie, A. (1983) *Statius and the Silvae: Poets, Patrons, and Epideixis in the Graeco-Roman World*, Liverpool, UK: Francis Cairns.

———(2003) "Poetry and Politics at the Games of Domitian," in A. J. Boyle and W. J. Dominik, eds., *Flavian Rome. Culture, Image, Text*, Leiden, The Netherlands/Boston: Brill: 125–47.

Hardie, Ph. (1986) *Virgil's Aeneid: Cosmos and Imperium*, Oxford: Clarendon.

———(1987) "Ships and Ship-Names in the Aeneid," in M. Whitby, Ph. Hardie, and M. Whitby, eds., *Homo Viator: Classical Essays for John Bramble*, Bristol, UK: Bristol Classical Press: 163–71.

———(1990) "Ovid's Theban History: The First 'Anti-Aeneid'?," *CQ* 49: 224–35.

——— (1993) *The Epic Successors of Virgil: A Study in the Dynamics of a Tradition*, Cambridge: Cambridge University Press.

———(1997) "Virgil and Tragedy," in Ch. Martindale, ed., *The Cambridge Companion to Virgil*, Cambridge: Cambridge University Press: 312–26.

——— (1998) *Virgil*, Greece and Rome New Surveys in the Classics 28, Oxford: Oxford University Press.

——(2002) "Another Look at Virgil's Ganymede," in T. P. Wiseman, ed., *Classics in Progress: Essays on Ancient Greece and Rome*, Oxford/New York: Oxford University Press: 333–61.

Harrison, S. J. ed. (1991) *Virgil, Aeneid 10*, Oxford: Clarendon.

——(1992) "The Arms of Capaneus: Statius, Thebaid 4.165–77," *CQ* 42: 247–52.

——(1997) "The Survival and Supremacy of Rome: The Unity of the Shield of Aeneas," *JRS* 87: 70–6.

——(2006) "The Epic and Monuments: Interactions Between Virgil's *Aeneid* and the Augustan Building Programme," in M. J. Clarke, B. G. F. Currie, and R. O. A. M. Lyne, eds., *Epic Interactions Perspectives on Homer, Virgil, and the Epic Tradition Presented to Jasper Griffin by Former Pupils*, Oxford: Oxford University Press: 159–83.

Haselberger, L. ed. (2014) *The Horologium of Augustus: Debate and Context, JRA* Supplement 99, Portsmouth, RI: Journal of Roman Archaeology.

Heerink, M. (2014) "Valerius Flaccus, Virgil and the Poetics of Ekphrasis," in M. Heerink and G. Manuwald, eds., *Brill's Companion to Valerius Flaccus*, Leiden, The Netherlands/Boston: Brill.

Heinrich, A. (1999) "Longa Retro Series: Sacrifice and Repetition in Statius' Menoeceus Episode," *Arethusa* 32: 165–95.

Henderson, J. (1991) "Statius' Thebaid / Form premade," *PCPhS* 37: 30–80.

Henriksén, Ch. ed. (2012) *A Commentary on Martial, Epigrams Book 9*, Oxford/New York: Oxford University Press.

Hershkowitz, D. (1995) "Patterns of Madness in Statius' *Thebaid*," *JRS* 85: 52–64.

——(1997) "Parce metu, Cytherea: Failed Intertext Repetition in Statius' Thebaid, or, Don't Stop Me if You've Heard This One Before," *MD* 39: 35–52.

——(1998) *The Madness of Epic: Reading Insanity From Homer to Statius*, Oxford: Oxford University Press.

Heslin, P. J. (2007) "Augustus, Domitian and the So-called Horologium Augusti," *JRS* 97: 1–20.

——(2010) "Virgil's Georgics and the Dating of Propertius' First Book," *JRS* 100: 54–68.

Hill, D. E. (1990) "Statius' *Thebaid*: A Glimmer of Light in a Sea of Darkness," *Ramus* 18: 98–118.

——ed. (1996) *P. Papini Stati Thebaidos Libri XII*, 2nd ed., Leiden, The Netherlands: Brill.

Hind, J. G. F. (1972) "The Death of Agrippina and the Finale of the 'Oedipus' of Seneca," *AUMLA* 38: 204–11.

Hinds, S. (1987) "Generalising About Ovid," *Ramus* 16: 4–31.

Hollis A. S. (1994) "Statius' Young Parthian King (*Thebaid* 8.286–93)," *G&R* 41: 205–12.

Horsfall, N. ed. (2000) *Virgil, Aeneid 7. A Commentary*, Leiden, The Netherlands/Boston/Cologne: Brill.

——ed. (2008) *Virgil, Aeneid 2. A Commentary*, Leiden, The Netherlands/Boston: Brill.

——ed. (2013) *Virgil, Aeneid 6. A Commentary*, Berlin/Boston: De Gruyter.

Housman, A. E. (1910) "Carm. Bucol. Einsidl. II 34," *CQ* 4: 47–48.

Hutchinson, G. ed. (2006) *Propertius. Elegies Book IV*, Cambridge: Cambridge University Press.

Huttner, U. (1997) *Die politische Rolle der Heraklesgestalt im griechischen Herrschertum*, Stuttgart, Germany: Steiner.

Janko, R. ed. (1994) *The Iliad: A Commentary. Volume IV: Books 13–16*, Cambridge: Cambridge University Press.

Jones, B. W. (1973) "Domitian's Attitude to the Senate," *AJPh* 94: 70–90.

——(1983) "C. Vettulenus Civica Cerialis and the False Nero of a.d. 88," *Athenaeum* 61: 516–21.

——(1992) *The Emperor Domitian*, London/New York: Routledge.

Joseph, T. (2012) *Tacitus the Epic Successor: Virgil, Lucan, and the Narrative of Civil War in the Histories*, Leiden, The Netherlands/Boston: Brill.

Kay, N. M. ed. (1985) *Martial Book XI: A Commentary*, London: Duckworth.

Keith, A. (2002) "Ovidian Personae in Statius' *Thebaid*," *Arethusa* 35: 381–402.

——(2013) "Medusa, Python, and Poine in Argive Religious Ritual," in A. Augoustakis, ed., *Ritual and Religion in Flavian Epic*, Oxford/New York: Oxford University Press: 303–17.

Kellum, B. (1985) "Sculptural Programs and Propaganda in Augustan Rome: The Temple of Apollo on the Palatine," in R. Winkes, ed., *The Age of Augustus: Interdisciplinary Conference Held at Brown University, April 30–May 2, 1982*, Leuven, Belgium: Institut Supérieur d'Archéologie et d'Histoire de l'Art/Providence, RI: Center for Old World Archaeology and Art, Brown University: 169–76.

Keuls, E. (1974) *The Water Carriers in Hades*, Amsterdam: Hakkert.

Kienast, D. (1999) *Augustus: Prinzeps und Monarch*, 3rd ed., Darmstadt, Germany: Wissenschaftliche Buchgesellschaft.

Klinnert, T. C. (1970) *Capaneus-Hippomedon: Interpretationen zur Heldendarstellung in der Thebais des P. Papinius Statius*, dissertation, Heidelberg.

Kytzler, B. (1955) *Statius Studien. Beitrage zum Verstandnis der Thebais*, dissertation, Berlin.

Labate, M. (2010) *Passato remoto: Età mitiche e identità augustea in Ovidio*, Pisa/Rome: Fabrizio Serra.

La Penna, A. (2005) *L'impossibile giustificazione della storia. Un'interpretazione di Virgilio*, Rome/Bari, Italy: Laterza.

Lapidge, M. (1979) "Lucan's Imagery of Cosmic Dissolution," *Hermes* 107: 344–70.

La Rocca, E. (2014) "Augustus' Solar Meridian and the Augustan Urban Program in the Northern Campus Martius: Attempt at a Holistic View," in L. Haselberger, ed., *The Horologium of Augustus: Debate and Context*, *JRA* Supplement 99, Portsmouth, RI: Journal of Roman Archaeology: 121–65.

Latte, K. (1960) *Romische Religionsgeschichte*, Munich: Beck.

Laubscher, H.P. (1997) "Der schlangenwürgende Herakles. Seine Bedeutung in der Herrscherikonologie," *JDAI* 112: 159–66.

Lega, C. (1989–1990) "Il Colosso di Nerone," *BCAR* 93: 339–378.

Legras, L. (1905) *Étude sur la Thébaïde de Stace*, Paris: Société nouvelle de librairie et d'édition.

Leigh, M. (1993) "Hopelessly Devoted to You: Traces of the Decii in Virgil's *Aeneid*," *PVS* 21: 89–110.

——(1997) *Lucan: Spectacle and Engagement*, Oxford: Clarendon.

——(2006) "The Sublimity of Statius' Capaneus," in M. J. Clarke, B. G. F. Currie, and R. O. A. M. Lyne, eds., *Epic Interactions: Perspectives on Homer, Virgil, and the Epic Tradition Presented to Jasper Griffin by Former Pupils*, Oxford: Oxford University Press: 217–41.

Levene, D. (1993) *Religion in Livy*, Leiden, The Netherlands: Brill.

Levick, B. (1982) "Domitian and the Provinces," *Latomus* 41: 50–73.

——(1999) *Vespasian*, London: Routledge.

Lewis, C. S. (1998) *Medieval and Renaissance Literature*, Cambridge: Cambridge University Press.

Lorenz, S. (2002) *Erotik und Panegyrik: Martials epigrammatische Kaiser*, Tübingen, Germany: Narr.

Lovatt, H. (1999) "Competing Endings: Re-Reading the End of the *Thebaid* Through Lucan," *Ramus* 28: 126–51.

———(2002) "Statius' Ekphrastic Games: *Thebaid* 6.531–47," *Ramus* 31: 73–90.

———(2005) *Statius and Epic Games: Sport, Politics, and Poetics in the Thebaid*, Cambridge: Cambridge University Press.

MacMullen, R. (1966) *Enemies of the Roman Order: Treason, Unrest, and Alienation in the Empire*, Cambridge, MA: Harvard University Press.

Malamud, M. (1995) "Happy Birthday Dead Lucan: (P)raising the Dead in Silvae 2.7," in A. J. Boyle, ed., *Roman Literature and Ideology: Ramus Essays for J. P. Sullivan*, Bendigo, Australia: Aureal Publications: 169–98.

Marks, R. (2005a) *From Republic to Empire. Scipio Africanus in the Punica of Silius Italicus*, Frankfurt am Main: Lang.

———(2005b) "Per uulnera regnum: Self-destruction, Self-sacrifice and Deuotio in Punica 4–10," *Ramus* 34: 127–51.

Martin, B. (1996) "Calpurnius Siculus' 'New' Aurea Aetas," *Acta Classica* 39: 17–38.

Massimilla, G. ed. (1996) *Callimaco, Aitia. Libri primo e secondo*, Pisa: Giardini.

Mastronarde, D. J. ed. (1994) *Euripides: Phoenissae*, Cambridge: Cambridge University Press.

Matern, P. (2002) *Helios und Sol. Kulte und Ikonographie des griechisches und römisches Sonnengottes*, Istanbul: Ege Yayinlari.

McGuire, D. T. (1997) *Acts of Silence: Civil War, Tyranny and Suicide in the Flavian Epics*, Hildesheim, Germany/Zurich/New York: Olms-Weidmann.

McNelis, C. (2007) *Statius' Thebaid and the Poetics of Civil War*, Cambridge: Cambridge University Press.

Micozzi, L. (1999) "Aspetti dell'influenza di Lucano nella *Tebaide*," in P. Esposito and L. Nicastri, eds., *Interpretare Lucano. Miscellanea di Studi*, Naples: Università degli Studi di Salerno: 343–87.

———(2004) "Memoria diffusa di luoghi lucanei nella Tebaide di Stazio," in P. Esposito and E. M. Ariemma, eds., *Lucano e la tradizione dell'epica latina. Atti del convegno internazionale di studi Fisciano Salerno, 19–20 Ottobre (2001)*, Naples: Guida 137–51.

Miles, G. B. (1986) "The Cycle of Roman History in Livy's First Pentad," *AJPh* 107: 1–33.

Miller, J. F. (2009) *Apollo, Augustus, and the Poets*, Cambridge/New York: Cambridge University Press.

Mills, S. (1997) *Theseus, Tragedy and the Athenian Empire*, Oxford: Oxford University Press.

Mineo, B. (2006) *Tite-Live et l'histoire de Rome*, Paris: Klincksieck.

Molin, M. (1989) "Le Panégyrique de Trajan: Éloquence d'apparat ou programme politique néo stoïcien?," *Latomus* 48: 785–97.

Momigliano, A. (1935) "Sodales Flaviales Titiales e culto di Giove," *BCAR* 63: 165–71.

Mommsen, Th. (1887–1888) *Römisches Staatsrecht*, 3 vols., Leipzig: Hirzel.

Morford, M. P. O. (1967) *The Poet Lucan: Studies in Rhetorical Epic*, Oxford: Blackwell.

Morgan, M. G. (1992) "The Smell of Victory: Vitellius at Bedriacum (Tac. *Hist.* 2.70)," *CPh* 87: 14–29.

Narducci, E. (1974) "Sconvolgimenti naturali e profezia delle guerre civili: Phars. I 512–695," *Maia* 26: 97–110.

———(1979) *La provvidenza crudele. Lucano e la distruzione dei miti augustei*, Pisa: Giardini.

———(2002) *Lucano. Un'epica contro l'impero*, Rome/Bari, Italy: Laterza.

Nauta, R. (2002) *Poetry for Patrons. Literary Communication in the Age of Domitian*, Leiden, The Netherlands: Brill.

——(2008) "Statius in the *Silvae*," in J. J. L. Smolenaars, H-J. van Dam, and R. R. Nauta, eds., *The Poetry of Statius*, Leiden, The Netherlands: Brill: 143–74.

—— (2010) "*Flauius ultimus, caluus Nero*. Einige Betrachtungen zu Herrscherbild und Panegyrik unter Domitian," in Ch. Reitz and N. Kramer, eds., *Tradition und Erneurung. Mediale Strategien in der Zeit der Flavier*: Berlin/New York: De Gruyter: 239–72.

Newlands, C. E. (2002) *Statius' Silvae and the Poetics of Empire*, Cambridge: Cambridge University Press.

——ed. (2011) *Statius, Silvae. Book II*, Cambridge: Cambridge University Press.

——(2012) *Statius, Poet between Rome and Naples*, London: Bristol Classical Press.

Nisbet, R. G. M. (1978) "Felicitas at Surrentum (Statius, Silvae ii 2)," *JRS* 68: 1–11.

Nisbet–Hubbard (1978): R. G. M. Nisbet and M. Hubbard, eds., *A Commentary on Horace: Odes. Book II*, Oxford: Clarendon.

Nisbet–Rudd (2004): R. G. M. Nisbet and N. Rudd, eds., *A Commentary on Horace: Odes Book III*, Oxford: Oxford University Press.

Ogilvie, R. M. ed. (1965) *A Commentary on Livy Books 1–5*, Oxford: Clarendon.

Paduano, G. (1988) "Sofocle, Seneca e la colpa di Edipo," *RFIC* 94: 298–317.

Pagan, V. E. (2000) "The Mourning After: Statius *Thebaid* 12," *AJPh* 121: 423–52.

Palagia, O. (1986) "Imitation of Hercules in Ruler Portraiture. A Survey from Alexander to Maximinus Dara," *Boreas* 9: 137–51.

Palma B. (1981) "Il piccolo donario pergameno," *Xenia* 1: 45–84.

Parkes, R. (2009) "Hercules and the Centaurs: Reading Statius with Virgil and Ovid," *CPh* 104: 476–94.

——ed. (2012) *Statius, Thebaid 4*, Oxford: Oxford University Press.

Pavan, A. ed. (2009) *La gara delle quadrighe e il gioco della guerra: Saggio di commento a P. Papinii Statii Thebaidos liber VI 238–549*, Alessandria, Italy: Edizioni dell'Orso.

Pease, A. S. ed. (1955–1958) *M. Tulli Ciceronis De Natura Deorum*, 2 vols., Cambridge, MA: Harvard University Press.

Penwill, J. L. (2000) "Quintilian, Statius and the Lost Epic of Domitian," *Ramus* 29: 60–83.

——(2003) "Expelling the Mind: Politics and Philosophy in Flavian Rome," in A. J. Boyle and W. J. Dominik, eds., *Flavian Rome. Culture, Image, Text*, Leiden, The Netherlands/ Boston: Brill: 345–68.

Piętka, R. (2010) "Trina Tempestas" (Carm. Einsidl. II 33)," *HSPh* 105: 177–87.

Pleket, H. W. (1961) "Domitian, the Senate, and the Provinces," *Mnemosyne* 14: 297–315.

Pollmann, K. F. L. ed. (2004) *Statius, Thebaid 12: Introduction, Text, and Commentary*, Paderborn: Schöningh.

Poulsen, B. (1991) "The Dioscuri and Ruler Ideology," *SO* 66: 119–46.

Putnam, M. C. J. (1998) *Virgil's Epic Designs: Ekphrasis in the Aeneid*, New Haven, CT/ London: Yale University Press.

Rawson, E. (1974) "Religion and Politics in the Late Second Century B.C. at Rome," *Phoenix* 28: 193–212.

Rebeggiani, S. ed. (2005) *Saggio di Commento a Stazio Thebais V 17–295; il Racconto di Ipsipile*, MA dissertation, Pisa.

———(2017) "Buried Treasures, Hidden Verses (Re)Appropriating the Gauls of Pergamon in Flavian Rome," in M. Loar, C. MacDonald, and D. Padilla Peralta, eds., *Empire of Plunder: The Dynamics of Roman Appropriation*, Cambridge: Cambridge University Press: 69–81.

———*forthcoming* (1): "The Seven Against Rome: Lutatius Catulus and the Temple of Fortuna Huiusce Diei."

———*forthcoming* (2): "Theban myth in Virgil's *Aeneid*: a preliminary exploration."

Reed, J. (1998) "The Death of Osiris in *Aeneid* 12.258," *AJPh* 119: 399–418.

Ripoll, F. (1998) *La morale héroïque dans les épopées latines d'époque flavienne: Tradition et innovation*, Leuven, Belgium: Peeters.

———(2000) "Variations épiques sur un motif d'ecphrasis: l'enlèvement de Ganymède," *REA* 102: 479–500.

Roche, P. ed. (2009) *Lucan: De Bello Civili Book 1*, Oxford: Oxford University Press.

———(2015) "Lucan's *De Bello Civili* in the *Thebaid*," in W. J. Dominik, C. E. Newlands, and K. Gervais, eds., *Brill's Companion to Statius*, Leiden, The Netherlands/Boston: Brill: 393–407.

Rogers, R. S. (1960) "A Group of Domitianic Treason-Trials," *CPh* 55: 19–23.

Rosati, G. (2006) "Luxury and Love: The Encomium as Aestheticisation of Power in Flavian Poetry," in R. R. Nauta, H.-J. van Dam, and J. J. L. Smolenaars, eds., *Flavian Poetry*, Leiden, The Netherlands/Boston: Brill: 41–58.

———(2008) "Statius, Domitian and Acknowledging Paternity: Rituals of Succession in the *Thebaid*," in J. J. L. Smolenaars, H.-J. van Dam, and R. R. Nauta, eds., *The Poetry of Statius*, Leiden, The Netherlands/Boston: Brill: 175–94.

Rosenbloom, D. (1993) "Shouting "Fire" in a Crowded Theater: Phrynichos's *Capture of Miletus* and the Politics of Fear in Early Attic Tragedy," *Philologus* 137: 159–96.

Rühl, M. (2006) *Literatur gewordener Augenblick. Die Silven des Statius im Kontext literarischer und sozialer Bedingungen von Dichtung*, Berlin/New York: De Gruyter.

Sablayrolles, R. (1994) "Domitien, 'Auguste ridicule,'" *Pallas* 40: 113–44.

Samuel, A. E. (1972) *Greek and Roman Chronology: Calendars and Years in Classical Antiquity*, Munich: Beck.

Sauron, G. (1981) "Aspects du Néo–Atticisme à la fin du Ier siècle avant J. C.: formes et symboles," *CEFR* 55: 285–319.

Sauter, F. (1934) *Der Römische Kaiserkult bei Martial und Statius*, Stuttgart/Berlin: Kohlhammer.

Schetter, W. (1960) *Untersuchungen zur epischen Kunst des Statius*, Wiesbaden, Germany: Harrassowitz.

Schiesaro, A. (2003) *The Passions in Play: Thyestes and the Dynamics of Senecan Drama*, Cambridge: Cambridge University Press.

Schmitzer, U. (1990) *Zeitgeschichte in Ovids Metamorphosen*, Stuttgart: Teubner.

Schubert, C. (1998) *Studien zum Nerobild in der lateinischen Dichtung der Antike*, Stuttgart: Teubner.

Schubert, W. (1984) *Jupiter in den Epen der Flavierzeit*, Frankfurt am Main/Bern: Lang.

Schütz, M. (1990) "Zur Sonnenuhr des Augustus auf dem Marsfeld," *Gymnasium* 97: 432–57.

Scott, K. (1930a) "Drusus, Nicknamed 'Castor,'" *CPh* 25: 155–61.

———(1930b) "The Dioscuri and the Imperial Cult," *CPh* 25: 379–80.

———(1936) *The Imperial Cult Under the Flavians*, Stuttgart/Berlin: Kohlhammer.

Scott, R. T. (1968) *Religion and Philosophy in the Histories of Tacitus*, Rome: The American Academy.

Shackleton Bailey, D. R. (1982) "Notes on Riese's Anthologia Latina (Vol. 2)," *CPh* 77: 113–32.

——ed. (2003) *Statius. Vol. 1: Silvae; Vol. 2: Thebaid, Books 1–7; Vol. 3: Thebaid, Books 8–12, Achilleid*, Cambridge, MA: Harvard University Press.

Sherwin-White, A. N. ed. (1966) *The Letters of Pliny. A Historical and Social Commentary*, Oxford: Clarendon.

Simon, E. (1986) *Augustus. Kunst und Leben in Rom um die Zeitwende*, Munich: Hirmer.

Skutsch, O. (1953) "The Fall of the Capitol," *JRS* 43: 77–8.

——(1978) "The Fall of the Capitol Again: Tacitus Ann. II.23," *JRS* 68: 93–4.

——ed. (1985) *The Annals of Q. Ennius*, Oxford: Oxford University Press.

Smith, R. R. R. (2000) "Nero and the Sun-god: Divine Accessories and Political Symbols in Roman Imperial Images," *JRA* 13: 532–542 [review of Bergmann (1998)].

Smolenaars, J. J. L. ed. (1994) *Thebaid VII. A Commentary*, Leiden, The Netherlands/New York/Cologne: Brill.

Snell, B. (1928) *Aischylos und das Handeln im Drama*, Leipzig: Dieterich.

Southern, P. (1997) *Domitian: Tragic Tyrant*, London/New York: Routledge.

Spannangel, M. (1999) *Exemplaria Principis. Untersuchungen zu Entstehung und Ausstattung des Augustusforums*, Heidelberg: Archäologie und Geschichte.

Spawforth, A. J. S. (2012) *Greece and the Augustan Cultural Revolution*, Cambridge: Cambridge University Press.

Stafford, E. (2000) *Worshipping Virtues: Personification and the Divine in Ancient Greece*, Swansea, UK: Duckworth and the Classical Press of Wales.

Stockton, D. (1970) *Cicero: A Political Biography*, Oxford: Oxford University Press.

Stewart, A. (2000) "*Pergamo ara marmorea magna*: On the Date, Reconstruction, and Functions of the Great Altar of Pergamon," in N. T. de Grummond and B. Ridgway, eds., *From Pergamon to Sperlonga: Sculpture and Context*, Berkeley: University of California Press: 32–57.

——(2004) *Attalos, Athens, and the Akropolis. The Pergamene 'Little Barbarians' and Their Roman and Renaissance Legacy. With an Essay by Manolis Korres*, Cambridge: Cambridge University Press.

Stover, T. (2012) *Epic and Empire in Vespasianic Rome*, Oxford: Oxford University Press.

Syme, R. (1930) "The Imperial Finances under Domitian, Nerva and Trajan," *JRS* 20: 55–70.

——(1958) *Tacitus*, 2 vols., Oxford: Clarendon.

——(1980) *Some Arval Brethren*, Oxford: Oxford University Press.

——(1988) *Roman Papers*, Vol. 4, Oxford: Clarendon.

——(1991) *Roman Papers*, Vol. 7, Oxford: Clarendon.

Syndikus, H. P. (1972–1973) *Die Lyrik des Horaz. Eine Interpretation der Oden*, 2 vols., Darmstadt, Germany: Wissenschaftliche Buchgesellschaft.

Taisne, A.-M. (1991) "Une scène de nécromancie à Thèbes chez Stace (Th. 4.406–645) d'après Sénèque le dramaturge (Oed. 530–659)," in R. Chevallier and R. Poignault, eds., *Présence de Sénèque*, Paris: Touzot: 257–72.

——(1994) *L'esthetique de Stace. La peinture des correspondances*, Paris: Les Belles Lettres.

Tandoi, V. (1979) "I due frammenti di Turno poeta satirico," in *Studi di poesia latina in onore di Antonio Traglia*, II, Rome: Edizioni di Storia e Letteratura: 801–831.

Tarn, W. W. (1933) "Two Notes on Ptolemaic History," *JHS* 53: 57–68.

Taylor, P. R. (1994) "Valerius' Flavian *Argonautica*," *CQ* 44: 212–35.

Thomas, R. F. ed. (2011) *Horace: Odes Book IV and Carmen Saeculare*, Cambridge/New York: Cambridge University Press.

Thompson–Bruère (1970): L. Thompson and R. T. Bruère, "The Virgilian Background of Lucan's Fourth Book," *CPh* 65: 152–72.

Tuplin, C. (1989) "The False Neros of the First Century," in C. Deroux, ed., *Studies in Latin Literature and History* 5, Brussels: Latomus: 364–404.

Van Dam, H.-J. ed. (1984) *P. Papinius Statius, Silvae Book 2: A Commentary*, Leiden, The Netherlands: Brill.

Varner, R. (2004) *Mutilation and Transformation: Damnatio Memoriae and Roman Imperial Portraiture*, Leiden, The Netherlands: Brill.

Vasaly, A. (1993) *Representations: Images of the World in Ciceronian Oratory*, Berkeley: University of California Press.

Venini, P. ed. (1970) *Thebaidos Liber Undecimus. Introduzione, Testo Critico, Commento e Traduzione*, Florence: La Nuova Italia.

——(1971) *Studi Staziani*, Pavia, Italy: Tipografia del Libro.

Verdière, R. ed. (1954) *T. Calpurnii Siculi De laude Pisonis et Bucolica et M. Annaei Lucani De laude Caesaris. Einsiedlensia quae dicuntur carmina*, Brussels: Latomus.

Vermeule, C. C. (1981) *Greek and Roman Sculpture in America*, Berkeley: University of California Press.

Versnel, H. S. (1981) "Self-Sacrifice, Compensation and the Anonymous Gods," in O. Reverdin and B. Grange, eds., *Le sacrifice dans l'Antiquité*, Entretiens sur l'Antiquité classique, vol. 27, Geneva: Fondation Hardt: 135–85.

Vessey, D. W. T. (1971) "Noxia Tela: Some Innovations in Statius, Thebaid 7 and 11," *CPh* 66: 87–92.

——(1973) *Statius and the Thebaid*, Cambridge: Cambridge University Press.

Vinchesi, M. A. (1976) "La fortuna di Lucano dai contemporanei all'età degli Antonini," *Cultura e Scuola*: 39–64.

——ed. (2014) *Calpurni Siculi, Eclogae*, Florence: Le Monnier.

Waters, K. H. (1964) "The Character of Domitian," *Phoenix* 18: 49–77.

——(1969) "Traianus Domitiani continuator," *AJPh* 90: 385–405.

Weinreich, O. (1928) *Studien zu Martial*, Stuttgart: Kohlhammer.

Weir, R. (1999) "Nero and the Herakles Frieze at Delphi," *BCH* 123: 397–404.

Wenning, R. (1978) *Die Galateranatheme Attalos I: eine Untersuchung zum Bestand und zur Nachwirkung pergamenischer Skulptur (PergForsch 4)*, Berlin: De Gruyter.

Whitby, M. ed. (1998) *The Propaganda of Power: The Role of Panegyric in Late Antiquity*, Leiden, The Netherlands/Boston/Cologne: Brill.

Williams, R. D. ed. (1972) *Thebaidos liber decimus*, Leiden, The Netherlands: Brill.

Williams, G. (1978) *Change and Decline: Roman Literature in the Early Empire*, Berkeley: University of California Press.

Williams, J. H. C. (2001) *Beyond the Rubicon: Romans and Gauls in Republican Italy*, Oxford: Oxford University Press.

von Wilamowitz-Moellendorff, U. (1959) *Der Glaube der Hellenen*, 3rd ed., repr., Darmstadt, Germany: Wissenschaftliche Buchgesellschaft.

Wirszubski, C. (1968) *Libertas as a Political Idea at Rome During the Late Republic and Early Principate*, Cambridge: Cambridge University Press.

Bibliography

Wiseman, T. P. (1982) "Calpurnius Siculus and the Claudian Civil War," *JRS* 72: 57–67.

Wuilleumier, P. (1927) "Cirque et astrologie," *MEFR* 44: 184–209.

Zanker, P. (1968) *Forum Augustum*, Tübingen, Germany: Wasmuth.

——(1983) "Der Apollotempel auf dem Palatin. Ausstattung und politische Sinnbezüge nach der Schlacht von Actium," *ARID*, Suppl. 10 (Rome): 21–40.

—— (1988) *The Power of Images in the Age of Augustus*, Ann Arbor: University of Michigan Press [English translation of *Augustus und die Macht der Bilder*, Munich: Beck 1987].

Zanker–Ewald (2008): P. Zanker and B. C. Ewald, *Vivere con i miti. L'iconografia dei sarcofagi romani*, Torino: Bollati Boringhieri [Italian translation of *Mit Mythen leben. Die Bilderwelt der römischen Sarkophage*, Munich: Hirmer 2004].

Zeitlin, F. (1986) "Thebes: Theater of Self and Society in Athenian Drama," in J. P. Euben, ed., *Greek Tragedy and Political Theory*, Berkeley: University of California Press: 101–41.

Zissos, A. ed. (2008) *Valerius Flaccus' Argonautica, Book 1: A Commentary*, Oxford/New York: Oxford University Press.

INDEX LOCORUM

Aeschines
1.190   225

Aeschylus
Septem contra Thebas
1–2   263
1–3   112
170   36
375–652   36
422–4   254
463–4   36
711   178
727–30   178
876–7   178
902–8   178

Ammianus Marcellinus
18.4.5   60

Ampelius
20.7   203, 253

Apollodorus
1.6.1–2   132

Apollonius Rhodius
1.331–62 114
4.522–36 218
4.1547–50 218

Appian
Bella Ciuilia
2.36   185
2.76   130
2.150   242
Gallica
Fr. 1.1   240
Fr. 2–9   240
Italica
Fr. 8.2   240

Aurelius Victor
De Caesaribus
11.2   9

Bucolica Einsidlensia
1.37   62
2.32–4   159
2.38   62

Callimachus
Aetia
fr. 22–23c   217
fr. 24–25d   217
fr. 25e–31b   206, 217
fr. 31a   217
fr. 31–31b   218
fr. 54–60j   214, 217
fr. 54.1–6   218
fr. 65–66   217
fr. 66.1   218
fr. 76b–77d   217
fr. 86–89a   214
Hymnus in Apollinem
97–104   219
Hymnus in Delum
165–87   219
171–6   240
171–87   242
Iambi
16   117
fr. 228   117

Calpurnius Siculus
Eclogae
1   43
1.33–8   160
1.43–4   158
1.46–51   44, 156
1.50   157
1.54–62   157
1.55   158
1.57   158, 194
1.62   165
1.69–73   158
1.151   159
4   43
4.137–40   45
4.159   62
7.83–4   62

Cassius Dio
12.2–3   52
13.3   52
14.2   52
44.24.3   129
55.1.5   118
55.27.3–4   118
57.14.9   118

61.2.1   61, 96
61.13   73
61.19–20   61, 97, 107
62.10.2   63, 130
62.16.2   102
62.18.1   266
63.6.2   61
63.9.4–5   63, 72, 130, 264
63.10.2   72, 264
63.18.1   60
63.20.1–21.1   62
63.20.1–21.2   97
63.20.5   63, 130
63.22.6   63, 72, 130
63.28.5   24, 73
64.1.3   184
64.8.3   57
64.9.3   39
64.13   203
65.10.1   57
66.3.4   19, 50
66.19.3   39
66.22–3   204
66.24   204
67.2.3   60
67.3   205
67.3.3   52
67.3.3–4   52
67.4.5   52
67.4.7   9
67.7.1–3   46
67.12.1   60
67.13   52, 53
67.13.2   52
67.13.3–4   9
68.1   54

Cato
Origines
fr. 31   129

Censorinus
22.16   96

Cicero
Brutus
112   113
De Diuinatione
1.17–22.6   199

1.88   117

De Finibus Bonorum et Malorum

1.23   236

De Lege Agraria

2.95   129

De Natura Deorum

2.14   199

2.27.68   111

De Officiis

3.82   33

3.112   236

De Prouinciis Consularibus

34   243

De Senectute

59.1   113

Epistulae ad Atticum

1.19.2   242

7.11.1   33

9.11a.2   257

Epistulae ad Quintum fratrem

1.1.23   113

In Catilinam

3.19–22   242

4.12–3   242

In Pisonem

6   243

91   225

In Verrem

5.113   225

Philippicae

5.37   242

7.3   242

7.8   257

13.37   242

14.20   257

Pro Fonteio

46   242

Tusculanae Disputationes

4.49.10   236

Conon

FGrH 26 F 1.19   216

Cornelius Severus

fr. 13.1–2   133

Culex

26–7   163

363   203

Curtius Rufus

3.3.13   236

Dio Chrysostomus

45.1   9

Diodorus Siculus

5.39   129

14.113–7   240

Dionysius of Halicarnassus

13.6ff.   240

Donatus

Vita Vergili

32   6

Ennius

Annales

79–83 Skutsch   106

227 Skutsch   249

Epicedion Drusi

283   118

359–60   107

409–10   118

Epitome de Caesaribus

11.6   9

Euripides

Archelaos

TrGFr

228–64   217, 218

Hercules Furens

178–80   132

1193–4   132

Phaëthon

168–70 Diggle   108

Phoenissae

80   178

506   33

524–5   33

601   178

638–89   78

1128–33   254

Supplices

14–5   178

153–4   178

399–462   87

Eutropius

1.20   240

7.2   52

7.2–3   52

7.23   9

7.23.2   52

Festus

430L   248

Florus

1.7.13–9   240

2.16 (4.6) 5   133

Gellius

4.9.5   242

5.17.2   242

Hercules Oetaeus

82–4   63, 130

Herodotus

1.46–52   117

8.137   217, 218

Homer
Iliad

5.35–41   111

5.853–4   140

5.815–24   111

20.247   128

Horace
Carmina

1.35   199

2.12.5–6   128

2.12.6–7   132

3.3.10–3   117

3.6.1–8   199

3.6.12   236

3.30.8–9   241

4.2.45–8   95, 99

4.5.5–8   95, 99

Epodi

7.13–20   34, 177

7.17–20   199

John of Antioch

fr. 104M   39

Josephus
Bellum Judaicum

4.601   115

4.645–55   237

4.647–9   245

4.649   252

7.244–51   120

Juvenal

4.9–10   205

4.37–8   56

8.198–230   232

8.211–2   233

8.215–21   73

8.228   72

8.236–68   233

9.22   212

Livy

5.32   243

5.32–55   240

5.36   243

5.40.1   241

5.41   201, 253

5.41.8   256

5.45.4   241

5.49.7   258

5.50.1   244

5.50.1–8   244

5.50.4   248

5.51.7–8   243

5.52.11   248

5.54.5   241

7.6   203, 251

8.9.10   256

22.57.2–6   199

24.42.8   236

Lucan
Bellum Ciuile

1.4   153

1.12   159

1.33–8   154

1.45–52   100, 159

1.49   100

1.46–52   26

1.50   103

1.60–2	154, 159
1.72–80	169
1.80	173
1.92–3	177, 182
1.93–5	34, 177
1.93–7	179
1.96–7	180
1.129–31	183
1.152–4	179
1.188	179
1.248–57	185
1.324	185
1.324–35	192
1.449	179
1.469–86	186
1.549–52	34
1.552–83	199
1.557	186
1.562	186
1.572–7	202
1.673–94	184, 186, 189
1.669–72	26, 153
2.1–2	199
2.64–233	192
2.67–233	177, 185
2.70	2
2.166–8	133
2.169	192
2.207–9	192
2.221–2	159
2.248–57	177
2.306–18	201
2.477–525	155
2.601–7	182
4.188	185
4.549–51	35
4.593–660	139
4.629–32	140
4.649–53	140
4.702–14	134
5.27–8	249
5.366	185
5.668	185
6.395	35
6.657–8	187
6.667–94	187
6.695	225
6.695–718	187
6.777–99	188

6.787	192
6.804–5	165
6.811	188
7.305	133
7.391–6	35
7.552–6	189
7.569–71	209
7.599–616	155
7.638–41	26, 154
7.771–6	188
7.786–94	192
7.789–99	184
7.794–9	190
7.847–54	184, 189
7.851–68	177
9.193–4	185
10.14–9	47
10.20–1	47
10.42	47

Lucilius
11.409	236

Macrobius
Saturnalia
1.14.13–5	96
1.16.23	242

Martial
1.6	89
1.8	52
1.14	89
1.22	89
1.48	89
1.51	89
1.60	89
1.104	89
2.1	58
2.60	60
2.91.2	238
4.1.5	90
4.8.12	239
5.1.7–8	238
5.2.6–8	90
5.5.7–8	239
5.6	239
5.6.18–9	62
5.19.1–2	46
5.25.9–19	62

5.65	131	*Octauia*	
6.2	60	23–4	278
6.3	45	89	60
6.4	60	227–32	75
6.5	105, 263	235–7	74, 231
6.7	60	235–44	75
6.10	239	236	76
6.22	60	240	76
6.45	60	240–1	60
7.21	277	249	59
7.22	277	368–76	73
7.23	277	437–61	74
7.34.4	58	439–71	75
7.56	239	439–592	162
7.60.1–2	238	449	60
7.99	239	471	75
8.14	239	477–81	162
8.21	99	488	257
8.24	239	503–13	161, 194
8.38	65	508	162
8.49	247	510–4	133
8.82	239	831	102
9.3.7–9	248		
9.3.9	204	Orosius	
9.20.9–10	238	7.10	9
9.28	239	7.10.2	52
9.34.5	62		
9.39	239	Ovid	
9.64.1–2	131	*Ars Amatoria*	
9.65.2	131	1.74	220
9.7	60	*Epistulae Ex Ponto*	
9.86	239	1.1.32	257
9.86.4	206	1.2.121–6	172
9.91	239	2.2.81–4	118
9.101.1–2	131	*Fasti*	
9.101.11–6	131	1.705–8	118
9.101.12–3	116	*Ibis*	
9.101.13–4	131	575–6	206
9.101.14	132, 163, 247	*Metamorphoses*	
10.50	62	1.60	168
10.53	62	1.168–252	170
10.54.1–4	62	1.199–205	171
10.72.3	9	1.253–8	171
11.1.16	62	2.126–40	108
11.5.9–12	87, 166	2.185–7	108
11.9	59	2.195–8	108
11.33	56	2.329–31	111, 113
14.1	239	2.340–66	109

6.146–312	195
6.148–310	228
9.1–88	139
9.33–4	140
9.35–6	140
9.37–8	140
9.39–41	140
9.46–9	140
9.53–6	140
9.54–6	140
9.56	140
9.60–1	140
12.189ff.	128
12.324–5	266
13.681–99	34
15.429	35

Tristia

2.167–8	118
3.1.62	220
5.5.135–6	34

Pausanias

1.17.1	86
1.34.1–5	117
1.43.7	216
1.43.7–8	216, 218
2.16	218
2.17.6	130

Philostratus
Nero

5	63, 130
10	73

Vita Apollonii

4.38	73
5.7	72, 130
6.42	60
7.24	90

Pindar
Nemean Odes

1.67–8	132

Plato
Leges

694c–95b	113

Res Publica

566d	101

Pliny the Elder
Naturalis Historia

2.92	111
14.68	59
16.637	221
22.96	57
30.14–7	74
34.45	57
34.60	36
34.79	213
34.84	245
35.51	57
36.71–2	96
36.71–3	98
37.50	57

Pliny the Younger
Epistulae

1.5	55
1.5.2	52, 53
3.11	52, 53, 55
3.16	55
3.18.2–3	11
4.11	205
4.22.7	63
4.24	55
5.5	65
6.16	204
6.20.15	204
6.29.1	50
7.14	55
7.19	55
7.19.5	52
7.19.6	52
7.27.14	55
7.33	55
7.33.7	53
9.13	19, 55
9.13.2–3	50
9.13.8	51
9.13.16	50

Panegyricus

4.1	11
5.5–6	115
7–8	274
7.6	115
8.2	115
8.5–6	115

42.1	60
46.1–2	60
53.3–4	56
54	10
54.1	239
90.5	55
95.3–5	55

Plutarch
Camillus

15–30	240
30.3.4	244

Galba

9.3	57
16–7	56

Marius

27.9	242
38.2	2

Otho

3.1–2	57
9.4	185

Quaestiones Romanae

50	204
277C–D	248

Romulus

25.5	248

Polybius

1.6.2–4	240
2.18.1–4	240
2.20.6–7	242
2.22.4–5	240

Propertius

1.7.1–5	33
1.7.1–6	33
2.31.3–4	220
2.31.14	195
2.34.37–46	33
4.6.35–6	200
4.6.47–50	128
4.10.41–4	236, 237
4.10.44	236

Quadrigarius

10b Peter	236

Quintilian
Institutio Oratoria

3.7.4	102, 239
10.1.91–2	239
10.1.94	59

Satyros
FGrH 3c 631 217

Schol. Iuv. *Sat.*

1.20	59

Schol. Stat. *Theb.*

9.647	113

Seneca the Elder
Suasoriae

6.17	133

Seneca the Younger
Apocolocyntosis

1.1	44
4.1.7–11	45
4.1.20–32	62, 97
4.3–19	43
4.20–2	43
4.23–4	43
4.24	158
4.25–32	43
10.4	158
12.2	44, 158
12.3.19–20	158
14.1	158

De Clementia

1.1.1	172, 272
1.1.1–5	11
1.1.2	135
1.1.3–4	44, 270
1.1.4	158
1.1.7	101
1.3.3–4	270
1.4.2–3	172
1.5.5	89, 268
1.5.7	134, 270
1.6.1	44
1.7.1	135
1.7.1–3	270

1.9.1	44, 46, 157, 162	154–79	79
1.9.1–11	270	171–5	79
1.9.2–12	51	171–9	77
1.10.1–4	270	178	79
1.10.3	134	237	78
1.11.1–2	157, 162	238	79
1.11.1–3	44	314–28	78
1.11.3	47	321–2	34
1.11.4	47	325–7	81
1.11.4–1.13.5	44, 270	359–64	78
1.17.4	46	518–9	82
1.21.3	47	530–658	77
1.25.1	47, 134	558	80
1.25.1–1.26.4	44	572	80
1.25.3	47	634	82
2.3.1	44	638–40	80
2.3.1–2.7.5	44, 270	640–1	83
Dialogi		642–6	78
11.6.5	46	659–708	82
11.13.1	43	669–708	75
11.16.6	46	702	75
11.16.6	43	730–50	78
11.17.3	101	948–51	79, 81
Hercules Furens		949	78
58	134	965	78
63–74	145	977	78
84–5	132	1005–6	82
250	257	1061	82
271–2	149	1032–9	82
332	178	1038–9	73, 82
431	149	*Phoenissae*	
735–47	134	54	178
828	134	354–5	35
920–4	149	*Naturales Quaestiones*	
936–7	149	7.17.2	111
955–70	145	7.21.3–4	111
955–91	134	7.29.3	111
963–73	144	*Thyestes*	
1138–44	148	1–121	31
Oedipus		23–67	264
19	81	67–73	264
25	81	193–5	264
36	76	201–4	264
1–109	77		
110–25	77	Servius	
114–6	77	*ad Aen.*	
117–9	77	2.135	2

2.557	I
5.121	106
7.304	126
ad Ecl.	
4.10	95

Silius Italicus

1.624–6	249
3.571–629	86
3.607–10	132
3.609–10	238, 252
3.618–21	239
15.425–32	207
17.651–4	248

Solinus

1.45–7	96

Sophocles
Electra

836–41	117

Statius
Achilleid

1.14–8	239

Siluae

1 *praef.* 5–9	72
1 *praef.* 18	164
1.1	12, 23, 89, 99, 112, 148, 151, 250
1.1.15	151
1.1.15–6	46
1.1.25	151
1.1.25–7	47, 151, 270
1.1.26	47
1.1.27–8	87, 166
1.1.33	99
1.1.37–9	211
1.1.37–40	90
1.1.52–5	48, 109
1.1.55	99
1.1.66–83	232
1.1.69–70	251
1.1.71	99
1.1.74–83	109, 249, 273
1.1.77	99
1.1.78–9	251
1.1.78–81	163
1.1.79	238, 240
1.1.80	163
1.1.84–7	110

1.1.85–91	47, 270
1.1.99–107	164
1.1.103–4	99
1.1.136	205
1.4.38–49	23, 48, 165
1.4.40	29, 172, 272
1.4.41	165
1.4.43	165
1.6	12
1.6.81–4	8
1.6.84	9
2. *praef.* 23–6	66, 277
2.1	65
2.1.189–207	65
2.2	66
2.2.95–6	66, 277
2.2.133	277
2.2.137	66, 277
2.3	65
2.3.77	65
2.4	65
2.5	89, 268
2.7	58, 66, 67, 70, 85, 103, 114, 176, 192, 277
2.7.58	277, 278
2.7.58–61	66
2.7.60–1	102, 277, 278
2.7.61–2	58, 102
2.7.68	70
2.7.71	103
2.7.100	66
2.7.100–1	277, 278
2.7.100–4	70
2.7.108–9	278
2.7.111–5	70
2.7.111–9	114
2.7.116–9	70, 165
2.7.117–9	277, 278
2.7.118–9	58, 74
3 *praef.* 4–8	277
3.1	66
3.1.35	149
3.1.91ff.	277
3.4.73–7	60
4.1.1–4	46, 98
4.1.10	165
4.1.13–5	46
4.1.28–33	46
4.1.40–3	265

4.2.35–7	265	1.80–1	224
4.2.38–43	45	1.80–7	264
4.2.46–51	123	1.86–7	28
4.2.47–8	118	1.126–30	181
4.2.47–51	265	1.127–30	115
4.2.50–1	131	1.130	272
4.2.55–6	247	1.131–8	182, 186
4.3	58, 60, 103, 104	1.133	169, 273
4.3.1–3	58	1.144–51	178
4.3.1–19	104	1.150–1	28
4.3.7–15	58	1.155–64	28, 180
4.3.127–32	46	1.158–96	29
4.3.134–8	104	1.168	181
4.3.154–9	265	1.168–73	272
4.3.155	131	1.171–2	29
4.4.76	165	1.171–3	172
4.6.50–4	150	1.173–96	185
4.6.55	151	1.180–5	177, 223
4.6.55–8	150	1.193	170
4.6.59–93	150	1.193–6	169, 273
4.6.106–9	150	1.197–302	4, 224
4.8	66	1.205–8	170
4.8.20–1	277	1.207	170
4.8.45–62	277	1.214–7	174
5.1.14–5	62	1.214–47	126, 171
5.2.31–4	58	1.219–23	171
5.2.33	142	1.224–6	224
5.2.102	60	1.225–6	208
5.3.178	205	1.235	79, 83
5.3.195	202	1.236–8	79
5.3.195–8	163, 240	1.250–82	136
5.3.196	240	1.292–311	266
5.3.196–204	239	1.312–4	83
5.3.207–8	204	1.324–6	264
Thebaid		1.364–556	205
1.16–21	20	1.383–4	137
1.17–22	167, 238	1.384–5	137
1.17–31	273	1.390–2	183
1.21–2	138, 240	1.390–7	136
1.22	132	1.457–60	127
1.22–31	132, 167, 258	1.469–89	186
1.27–31	104	1.482–90	136
1.41	153	1.483–7	136, 137
1.46–8	78	1.488–90	141
1.56–87	4, 5	1.522–83	186
1.56–130	181	1.542	223
1.68	83	1.543–51	207
1.68–92	4	1.533–6	222
1.74–80	4	1.554	209

1.557–60	215	3.80	228
1.557–668	151	3.82	70
1.557–672	206	3.93–5	70
1.562–71	214	3.96	70
1.567–8	228	3.99–104	69
1.570	222	3.101	69
1.601	225	3.101–2	71
1.605–16	151	3.102	194, 274
1.606–8	216	3.108–10	70
1.638–61	151	3.108–11	69
1.644	216, 226	3.133–68	30, 195
1.648–50	226	3.140–6	193
1.661–2	226	3.154–6	195
1.667–8	215	3.179–217	192
1.668	222	3.180–3	193
1.673–95	186	3.191–2	193
1.688–92	83	3.195	193
1.696–720	121	3.206–8	193
1.708	111	3.216	194, 274
1.709–15	228	3.336–44	142
1.716–20	121	3.441	208
1.717–20	99, 227	3.460–5	208
1.720	24	3.604–7	127
2.1–133	266	4.69–73	182
2.65–70	264	4.87	83, 142
2.94–124	79	4.92	83
2.105–8	112, 263	4.106–9	140
2.116–9	264	4.132–5	223
2.184–5	264	4.139–44	125, 126, 267
2.214–23	222	4.147–52	136
2.220	229	4.156–7	136
2.221	209	4.165–77	142
2.221–3	208	4.169–70	143
2.222	223, 224	4.214–5	110, 117
2.278	208	4.214–6	125
2.323–32	83, 182	4.234–6	117
2.353–5	4	4.267–8	143
2.410–51	4, 82	4.369–73	186
2.442–5	186	4.374	186
2.469–77	141	4.374–7	186
2.482–3.98	68	4.375	186
2.487	194	4.375–6	79
2.527–743	139	4.377–405	186
2.559–64	126	4.397–404	182
2.563–4	139	4.406–645	177, 187
2.613–9	127	4.434–42	177, 189
2.613–28	136	4.443–72	187
3.59–77	68	4.473–87	187
3.71–7	193	4.488–93	187

4.500–18	187		6.301–13	110
4.519	80		6.301–15	110
4.520	80		6.301–19	125
4.553–78	188		6.311–3	126
4.592–8	193		6.313	126
4.592–602	188		6.316–25	108
4.614	81		6.318–9	108
4.626–32	80		6.326–9	117, 125
4.633–44	80		6.326–31	110
4.652–63	265		6.332–4	125
4.721	226		6.346	127, 136
4.726	225		6.346–50	125
4.742	226		6.385–8	111
4.747	226		6.389–530	106
5.56–122	266		6.424–31	125
5.57–69	266		6.431–3	126
5.64–6	263		6.436–8	125
5.85–142	266		6.437–8	125
5.116–8	226		6.443–4	126
5.117–9	223		6.450–3	108
5.125	143		6.491–506	126
5.183–5	266		6.491–512	108
5.202–3	266		6.495–8	209
5.257	266		6.498–501	108
5.261–4	266		6.504–12	2
5.265–86	265		6.513–7	109
5.452–7	226		6.518–30	126
5.463	225, 226		6.531–9	106, 124
5.499–540	225		6.534	125
5.499–709	29		6.536–7	126
5.505–33	226		6.722–825	144
5.531–3	226		6.740–6	144
5.543–4	143		6.753–5	144, 228
5.583–7	226		6.824–910	139
5.566–70	143, 226		6.830–9	140
5.579–87	226		6.836–9	136, 140
5.583–7	143		6.838–9	140
5.609	225		6.844–5	140
5.644	226		6.847–9	140
5.668	143		6.850–1	140
5.733–52	263		6.854–9	140
5.750–2	212		6.861–2	140
6.64–6	225		6.862–6	140
6.218–9	143		6.872–5	140
6.270–1	125, 137		6.876–80	140
6.271–3	136		6.878–80	140
6.286–7	208, 209		6.878–84	140
6.287–8	226		6.887–93	140
6.296–350	106		6.888–903	140

6.890–3	140	8.279–82	116
6.893–6	140	8.283–5	114
7.48–52	265	8.286–93	112
7.151–226	265, 266	8.329–38	125
7.199–209	174	8.456–9	141
7.203	126	8.456–520	136
7.215–8	30	8.497–516	141
7.218–21	32	8.500–18	135
7.238–9	189	8.532–5	141
7.254–8	268	8.607–54	30
7.304–7	126	8.688	228
7.354–8	81	8.742	264
7.355	81	8.745–50	141, 144
7.417	209	8.751–64	142
7.470–538	267	8.753	142
7.528–63	4, 5	9.8–20	142
7.538–63	142	9.46–81	4
7.539–63	267	9.220–2	127, 267
7.564–607	267	9.481–5	127, 268
7.692–5	111	9.504–39	127
7.700–1	111	9.510–9	136
7.703–4	111	9.637–69	111
7.711	228	9.640	268
7.723–35	268	9.647–9	111, 113
7.752–3	111	9.657–9	113
7.757	268	9.679–82	228
7.758–9	268	9.728–31	228
7.772–7	30	9.745	228
7.776	114	9.758	229
7.779–88	111	9.841–4	268
7.791–3	117	9.862–6	140
7.819–20	111	9.875–6	228
8.24–5	225	10.49–83	136
8.25–8	136	10.156–218	266
8.34–42	145	10.202–6	111, 114
8.42–4	145	10.249	136, 140
8.65–74	145	10.259–61	140
8.75–9	145	10.531–8	236
8.90–1	268	10.598–603	81
8.101	268	10.610–5	255
8.141	142	10.632–3	261
8.195–205	113	10.636–7	147
8.212–4	112, 263	10.646–9	147
8.240–54	5	10.664–5	147
8.267–70	112, 263	10.665	258
8.271–85	272	10.670–1	256
8.275–82	114, 274	10.671	260
8.277–82	115	10.672–3	260

10.680–1	260	11.482–96	5
10.683–5	257	11.547–5	111
10.756–9	255	11.574–9	7, 189
10.780–1	258, 260	11.580–82	81
10.781–2	147	11.605–7	81
10.783–90	257	11.605–26	6
10.811	147	11.611	82
10.827–31	7	11.614–5	82
10.832–6	146	11.634–41	82
10.834	146	11.652–4	227
10.845–6	147	11.673–707	82
10.848–52	146	11.684	86
10.845–5	225	11.707	82
10.848–52	254	12.60–104	5
10.890–1	135, 136	12.64–7	148, 258
10.899–901	136	12.93–4	86, 87
10.909–10	254	12.105–348	30
10.913–7	146	12.165–6	88, 89, 127, 275
10.915–7	254	12.184	82
11.5–11	146	12.291–311	136
11.7–8	254	12.413–5	109
11.12–7	228	12.512–3	89
11.21–6	259	12.540–98	89
11.45–8	135	12.546–59	223
11.46–8	136	12.553–4	127
11.97–101	7	12.555–8	88
11.119–35	4	12.582	149
11.122–35	174	12.583–4	149
11.125–35	266	12.601–5	182, 187
11.127–9	264	12.606–10	210, 211, 275
11.136–54	4, 5	12.642–4	88, 173
11.150–4	210	12.642–7	210, 227
11.193–204	4	12.646	225
11.196–204	5	12.650–5	173, 273, 275
11.223–5	136	12.665–71	122, 125
11.226–7	81	12.665–76	143
11.234–8	127	12.666–71	227
11.251–6	182	12.667–92	89
11.264	274	12.672–4	174
11.273–5	225	12.680	82
11.298–308	82	12.715–20	190
11.318–20	82	12.719–20	191
11.329–53	4	12.730–6	174
11.342	82	12.736–40	89
11.382–9	4	12.771	173
11.382–404	5	12.782–5	149
11.387–92	4	12.782–8	88
11.403–4	266	12.782–96	16

12.786–8	265
12.791–3	16
12.795	17
12.797–809	16, 29, 85
12.810–19	7, 16
12.811–2	20
12.814	17

Strabo

3.175	225
9.1.22	117
9.2.10–1	117

Suetonius

Augustus

31.2	96
73	9
94.4–6	95
95.1	95

Caligula

| 11.1 | 101 |

Domitianus

1.2	232, 237
1.3	19, 50
2.2	239
3.2	52
4.4	102
4.4.1	63
5.2	238
6.1	90
7.1	60, 62
8.3	60, 205
8.4	205
8.3–5	60
8.5	204
10	71
10.1	19, 52
10.2	51
10.3	52, 53, 65
10.4	52
10.5	52
13.1	116
13.1–2	9
13.3	10
15.3	90
18.1	56
23.1	54

Galba

| 10.1 | 56 |

Iulius

| 30.4 | 184 |

Nero

6	62
6.1	61, 96
7	59
10	43
12.3	63
21	63, 102
21.2	195
21.3	72, 130
24	102, 130
25.1–2	62, 97
28.1	60
31	61
31.3	59
33.1	158
34.4	74
36	111
38.1	102
38.2	266
39.2	73
44.1	131
46.3	24, 72, 73, 130
48.3–49.4	38
51	56
53	63, 97, 102, 130
54	60
57.1	38
57.2	39, 120

Otho

| 7 | 57 |
| 10.2 | 57 |

Tiberius

| 20.1 | 118 |

Titus

2.1	57
7.1	57, 99
8.3	204
8.3–4	204

Vespasianus

5.7	187
8.5	204, 246
12.1	8, 63, 131

Vitellius

| 8.1 | 26, 183 |

9.1	184
10	57
11	245
15.3	237
18.1	184

Tacitus
Agricola

2.1	52, 65
3.1	166
3.2	19, 52
41	90
44.5	52
45.1	52
45.1–2	52, 54

Annales

11.11	62
13.4	157
13.4–5	43, 44
13.6	101
13.11	44
14.8	73
14.14	102
14.14–15	61, 97, 107
14.22	60, 74
14.22.1	111
15.38	102
15.39	266
15.41	244
15.42	59
15.44	107
15.74	107, 195
16.2–4	195
16.3	73
16.4	63, 102
16.26.4–5	50

Historiae

1.1.1	272
1.2	120
1.2–3	203
1.3	202
1.4	38
1.11	244
1.16	172
1.16.1	116, 272
1.41	203
1.50	184
1.53–4	244

1.57	244
1.78	57
2.8–9	39
2.20	244
2.38	184, 185
2.39–45	184
2.55	203
2.70	184
2.71	57
2.77	274
2.91	245
3.24	93
3.25–34	184
3.63–74	237
3.71	238
3.72	203, 245
3.74	238
3.85	203
4.53	204, 205, 246
4.54	254
4.86	239

Tertullian
De Spectaculis

5	248
8	94

Theocritus

15.97	217
17.16–27	217
22	117
24.78	217
24.104ff.	217

Thucydides

2.99.3	217, 218

Tibullus

2.5.24	179

Turnus

fr. 1	59

Valerius Flaccus

1.12–4	239
1.71	172
1.563–5	247
1.730–851	263

1.761	172		7.45–53	183
1.796	225		7.170–8	223
2.78–431	267		7.304	126
2.112	236		7.310–571	31
2.408–17	207		7.317	37, 183
5.1–72	263		7.323–562	181
5.65–70	114		7.335	33
5.407–454	262		7.371–2	221
5.429–32	101, 262		7.409–12	221
			7.456–7	260

Valerius Maximus

5.5.3.26–8	118		7.526	33
5.6.2	203, 251		7.655–69	143
			7.670–4	221
			7.670–7	127, 129

Varro
De Lingua Latina

5.148	203, 251		7.783–8	33
			7.789–92	221
			7.794	221
			8.185–305	133

Virgil
Aeneid

			8.196–7	133
1.28	212		8.198	215
1.50–123	168		8.219–32	216
1.55	170		8.228–32	133
1.55–7	169		8.293–302	121
1.124–56	168		8.362–8	133, 222
1.227–96	265		8.671–728	37
1.257–96	85		9.446–9	241
1.289–96	156		9.722–7	236
1.293–6	157		10.194–7	128
1.728–30	207		10.207–8	128
2.254–9	221		10.317–22	133
2.554–8	1		10.518–20	143
2.589–621	265		10.777–82	133
3.551	133		11.243–5	221
4.576–7	260		11.715–7	129
5.114–285	106		12.458	254
5.121–2	128		12.468–72	111
5.250–5	207		12.548–9	223
5.250–7	212		12.632–49	111
5.362–460	144		12.700	173
5.362–484	139		12.715–24	186
5.410–4	133		12.843–952	31, 275
6.63–71	200		12.845	261
6.89–90	221		12.859–60	261
6.243	143		12.946–7	133

Eclogues

6.392–3	133		4	95

Georgics

6.791–805	46			
6.801–3	133		1.24–42	155
6.830–1	183		1.464–88	199

1.466–8	114
1.476–7	79
1.489–97	177, 184, 188
1.498–501	201
1.501–2	199
1.511–4	106
2.168	129
2.455–7	124
2.496	168
2.506	179
4.543–4	143

Zonaras

7.23	240
11.15	39
11.18	39

GENERAL INDEX

Adrastus 4, 83, 107–10, 125, 136, 182–4, 188, 197–8, 205–9, 212, 215, 222–4, 226–9
Aeschylus 223
  Septem contra Thebas 33, 35–6, 112, 178, 235, 254
Agrippina (mother of Nero) 56, 73, 165
Agylleus 136, 139–40
Aletes 5, 14, 177, 192–4, 196, 274
Alexander the Great 44, 47, 110, 134–5, 150, 217–18, 270
Allecto 31, 33, 181, 260–1
Amphiaraus 30, 94, 106, 110–19, 124–6, 128, 145, 208, 212, 221, 228, 263, 268, 272, 274
Annaeans 20, 25, 41, 65–8, 277–8
anonymous Theban 29, 169, 171–2, 176–7, 185, 272
Antaeus 134, 139–40
Antonius Primus, M. 57, 93, 121, 184, 232, 237–8
Antonius Saturninus, L. 50–2, 163
Antony 8, 37, 120, 128, 130, 133, 152, 195, 200, 220–1, 242
Apollo 3, 24, 30, 43, 61–2, 69–70, 73, 94–7, 99, 102, 105–6, 108, 110–11, 113–14, 117, 119, 121–2, 126, 132, 151, 186, 195–6, 199–200, 205–7, 209–12, 214–15, 218–20, 222, 224–8, 230–2, 245

apotheosis 86, 95–6, 101, 124, 132, 141, 147, 155, 159, 167, 212–13, 216, 219, 229, 232, 258, 260, 263
Argentaria Polla 6, 19, 65–6, 70, 277–9
Argentarius, M. 65
Argia 5, 12, 30, 84, 109, 183
Argos 3–4, 30, 68, 83, 130, 136–8, 141, 142, 144, 198, 205, 206, 208, 214–15, 224, 225, 226, 227, 228, 231, 232, 234, 259
  and Alexandria 216–19
  and Rome 219–24
Arion 106, 108–10, 117, 125–6
Arria 19, 50, 52, 55
Atedius Melior 65
atonement 197–8, 200, 215, 219, 229–30, 244–6
Augustus/Octavian 6, 9, 10, 13, 22, 23, 30, 37, 43, 44, 51, 61, 62, 63, 85, 93–4, 95–6, 97, 98, 99, 101, 102, 107, 121, 128, 130, 133, 152, 154, 155–6, 158–9, 161–2, 167–8, 170–1, 175, 176, 184, 195–6, 200, 201, 211, 219, 220, 222–3, 224, 250, 257, 273
Avidius Quietus, T. 50

Bacchus 30, 123, 136, 186, 209, 226, 265, 267
barbarians 35–7, 128, 253
  See also Gauls, Senones
battlefield, tour of 184, 190–1, 192

315

bestiality 134–5, 138–42, 146, 267–8, 271
Blaesus, *see* Junius Blaesus
boar 126, 136, 141–4
Brennus 237, 240, 242, 245, 254
Britannicus, Tiberius Claudius Caesar 57, 59, 264
Bucolica Einsidlensia 43–4, 158–60, 162, 194

Cacus 130–1, 133, 138, 149, 151, 206, 214–16,
    220–1, 231–2, 254
Caesar, C. Julius 2, 26–8, 32–4, 44, 47, 59, 76,
    80, 96, 98, 110, 114, 118, 120, 130, 133–4, 147,
    151, 153, 155, 163, 165–6, 177, 180–8, 190–2,
    243, 270
Caligula 101–3, 105, 147, 158
Callimachus 149, 197–8, 206, 214–22, 226, 229,
    231, 233, 242, 246–7
Calpurnius Siculus 22–3, 28, 43–5, 50, 61, 97,
    156–61, 164–5, 194
Camillus, M. Furius 241–9, 254, 257–8
Capaneus 5, 81, 127, 138, 142–7, 148, 152, 226, 228,
    254, 258–60, 267, 271
    and Hercules 142–7
    aristeia 7, 144–7, 254
Capitol 241–3, 248–9
    battle 7, 27, 131–2, 138, 163, 167, 203–4, 237–40,
    244–7, 250, 251–6, 258, 266–7, 273
Castor 109–10, 117–18, 125
    horse, *see* Cyllarus
    See also Dioscuri
Catiline 106, 128–9, 188, 242
Cato 52, 70, 87, 134, 165–6, 201
Celtomachy 235, 240, 242, 246–7, 254
Centauromachy 124, 125–9, 266
Centaurs 124, 125–9, 139, 143, 145, 266–8
chariot racing 57, 61–2, 94–5, 106
    as a metaphor for government/power 101,
    106, 112
    as a metaphor for the course of life 107, 111
    Nero's interest in 97, 130, 136–7
    in the *Thebaid* 94, 105, 106–10, 111–12, 119,
    124–6, 128
Chromis (son of Hercules) 106, 125
    for a different Chromis *see* 126–7
Cicero 11, 32, 33, 233, 242–3, 257
Circus 61, 94–5, 97, 107, 111, 195
civil war 13, 26, 32–4, 35, 37, 43, 74, 76–81, 85, 95,
    99, 106, 122, 128, 129, 130, 133, 150, 176–7,
    178–80, 183, 188, 197–8, 199, 210, 211–12, 220,
    222–4, 225, 226, 227, 228, 230, 231, 233, 261, 266

and cosmic upheaval 99, 167–71, 173, 273, 275
and imperial power 153–76
and religion 198–202
and tyranny 157–9, 161–2, 191–6, 272
of 69 CE 15, 27, 31, 74, 83, 90, 93, 129, 131,
    151–2, 163, 176, 178, 184–6, 188, 191, 231–2,
    234–5, 246, 248, 253, 266, 273
of Pompey and Caesar 2, 27, 34
Claudius (emperor) 22, 41, 43–4, 49–51, 57, 158
Clementia (goddess) 16, 87–88, 89, 223
clementia 16–18, 20, 22, 40, 42, 43–4, 49–52,
    54–5, 67, 68, 70, 84–92, 150–2, 158, 162,
    165, 174, 180, 194, 196, 207, 227, 270–2,
    274, 276–7
Cleopatra 195–6
Colossus of Nero 57, 61, 97, 99
commoners 29, 171–2, 272–3
compassion 4, 6, 15, 86, 88, 149
concordia 115–16, 116–19, 274
continuity between Domitian and Nero 23–4,
    49, 61–5, 93, 97–9
Coroebus 34, 151, 188, 197–8, 205–7, 208–11,
    212–13, 214–16, 222–4, 257–8, 266
    and Flavian Rome 229–33
    and Hercules 151, 216
    and Ptolemaic ideology 216–19
    and the *Thebaid*'s plot 224–9
corona ciuica 250–2, 258
cosmic upheaval and civil war 99, 167–71, 173,
    273, 275
Cremona I (first battle of Cremona/Bedriacum)
    57, 184, 187, 203
Cremona II (second battle of Cremona/
    Bedriacum) 93, 120, 184, 191
Creon 5, 14, 16, 18, 29, 32, 74, 75, 82, 84, 86, 89,
    127, 149–50, 173, 187, 189–91, 211, 227, 232,
    259, 261, 271, 275
Crotopus 206, 209, 214, 216, 217–18, 222, 230, 231
Curio, C. Scribonius 133–4, 141
Curtius, M. 110, 163, 203, 231–2, 251–3, 256, 258
    Lacus Curtius 203, 251
Cyllarus 109–10, 117, 125

Danaus 198, 207, 217–18
death
    of the king 112–14
    premature 107, 112, 117, 141, 212, 263, 268
Decius Mus 202, 203, 255–6
De Clementia, see Seneca

deuotio 27, 201–3, 231–2, 241, 244, 252–3, 255–8, 260
Diana 30, 110, 113, 228
didactic function of panegyric 11–12, 55
didactic perspective in the *Thebaid* 40–1, 67, 88, 269, 279
Dioscuri 116–19
   See also Castor, Pollux
Dis 31, 145–6
Domitia Longina (wife of Domitian) 19, 50
Domitian *passim*
   and the army 120–2
   and the East 119–22
   and the elite 18–21, 39–40, 49–55
   and Hercules 131–2
   and Jupiter 164, 167, 174–5
   as a second Nero 21, 22–4, 40, 54, 56, 66, 103–4, 269–70
   damnatio memoriae 54–5
   demonization of 19, 40–1
   dominus et deus 9–10
   equestrian statue (Equus Domitiani) 46–7, 109–10
   legislation 59–60
   panegyric of 12, 13, 14, 17, 19, 23, 41–2, 51, 85, 89–90, 115–16, 163–5, 166–7, 232, 238–9, 248–9, 252–3, 256, 265, 266–7, 269
   religious policy 204–5
Domitius Corbulo 19, 50, 120

ekphrasis 221, 249
   of Adrastus' cup 198, 207–13, 223, 229
   of Hercules' crater 124–9, 148, 266
Ennius 106, 249
Epaphroditus (freedman of Nero) 38
Erichto 187, 193
Eteocles 4, 5, 28–9, 32, 35–6, 68–70, 79–80, 79–83, 115, 127, 169, 178–9, 182, 185, 187–8, 193–4, 196, 266
   and Domitian 68–72
   and Nero 6, 22, 195
   and Oedipus (similarity) 80, 82–3
Eteocles and Polynices *passim*
   and Romulus and Remus 34, 178–80
   as archetype of civil war 178–81
   as bulls 169, 182, 186
Euripides
   Archelaos 217–18
   Phaethon 108

Phoenissae 32–3, 36, 78, 82, 178, 254, 259
Supplices 17, 86–7

Fabius Rusticus 57, 66
false Neros 38–9, 120
Fannia 50, 52, 55
Fannius, C. 65
fire of Rome
   of 390 BCE 241, 244
   of 64 CE 66, 97, 102–3, 204, 244, 266, 277–8
   of 80 CE 97, 204, 230, 239, 248
   burning of the Capitol in 69 CE 7, 204, 237–9, 252, 267
Flavia Julia 45
Flavius Sabinus (Vespasian's brother) 237–8
freedom of speech 51, 88, 273–4
   See also libertas
Furies 4, 5, 28, 31, 32, 74, 165, 210, 211, 212, 260, 266, 267
   See also Tisiphone, Allecto

Galba 56–7, 131, 172, 203
games
   Augustus' quinquennial games 63
   Capitoline Games, Capitolia, Ludi Capitolini, Agon Capitolinus 59, 63, 64, 102, 204, 238–9, 248
   Funeral games for Opheltes 2, 124–6, 136, 137–8
   Neronia 63, 102, 195
   Nero's participation in games 2, 61, 62–3, 97, 130, 138
Ganymede 198, 207–8, 208, 212–13, 229
Gauls 27, 199, 233, 235–7, 240–4, 244–9, 250, 254, 256
   See also Senones
Giants 36, 132, 140, 143–4, 146, 219, 247, 254, 258
   See also Gigantomachy
Gigantomachy 132, 143–4, 146, 160, 163, 167, 235, 240, 246–7, 253–4, 258
gods
   absence of 16–17, 31–2, 90, 229
   pessimistic view of 30–1, 230–1
   role with regards to political crises and civil war 198–202, 202–5, 230
   see also religion
Golden Age 22, 43, 45, 49, 85, 94, 154, 159, 175, 276
Golden Day (of Nero) 61, 62, 97, 119

Golden House (Domus Aurea) 57, 61, 97

Gratilla (wife of Junius Arulenus Rusticus) 52

Hadrian 232–3
Haemon 74, 136, 141, 260
Helvidius Priscus, C. 49–50, 52–3, 65
Helvidius the Younger 50–2, 53–5, 71
Hercules 114, 217, 219, 231–2, 265, 268–9, 271, 277
    Adsertor 130–1
    and Augustus 128, 130, 133
    and Capaneus 142–7
    and Coroebus 151, 216, 232
    and Domitian 23, 63–4, 123–4, 129,
        131–2, 151–2
    and Menoeceus 147–8, 258
    and Nero 25, 62–3, 72–3, 130–1
    and Polynices 135–8
    and Theseus 148–50
    and Tydeus 138–42
    and Vespasian 8, 97, 129
    and Vindex 130–1
    crater 106, 124–8, 266
    fighting Giants 132, 247, 258
    horse, see Arion
    in Callimachus 217, 219
    in Lucan 133–4
    in Seneca's Hercules Furens 42, 134–5
    in Silius' Punica 131–2
    in the Aeneid 121, 133, 214–16, 220–1, 222
Herennius Pollio, M. Annius 50
Herennius Senecio 52–3, 55, 65, 71
Hippomedon 125, 127, 139, 223, 267–8
historiography 39, 57, 71, 185
Horace 76, 99, 128, 176, 199
hubris 142–3, 146, 152
humanitas 17, 88, 271
Hypsipyle 29, 106, 223, 225–6, 265–7

Ide 30, 193, 195–6
incest 24, 73, 78–9, 82–3
Io 217–18, 221

Jocasta 73, 81–3, 267
Josephus 57, 115, 120, 237–8, 244–5, 252
Julia (daughter of Titus), see Flavia Julia
Julius Menecrates 66, 277
Julius Vindex 130–1, 138, 147, 265
Junius Arulenus Rusticus 50, 52–4, 55, 65
Junius Blaesus 65

Junius Mauricus 50, 52
Juno 33, 37, 121, 126, 135, 136, 137, 145, 168, 181, 183, 212, 275
Jupiter 4, 12, 18, 29, 30–2, 79, 81, 90, 102, 104, 111, 117, 126, 127, 131, 132, 143, 155, 159, 160, 163–4, 167–8, 170–1, 173–5, 204, 208, 212, 213, 224, 225–6, 237–9, 245, 247, 251–2, 254, 258, 259–60, 261, 265, 266, 273, 275
Juvenal 56, 60, 213, 232–3

Laius 4, 77–9, 80–2, 264, 266
Legio III Gallica 93, 120
Lex Iulia 60
Lex Scantinia 60
libertas 19–20, 22, 40, 42–4, 49, 51–2, 54–5, 67, 68–71, 88, 91, 116, 160, 161, 165–6, 194, 196, 270, 273–4, 276–7
Ligures 128–9
Linus 151, 198, 206, 207, 208, 214, 215, 217, 218, 225, 263
lion 63, 130, 136–7, 141
    leo mansuetus (tamed lion) 89, 268, 271
    Nemean lion 125, 136, 143, 219, 221
Livy 199, 240–1, 243, 253, 256
Lucan 6, 19–20, 65–6, 70, 165–6, 175
    as intellectual model for Statius 26, 92, 277
    Bellum Ciuile 13–14, 15, 34–5, 43, 46, 62, 66, 76, 97, 99, 100–1, 133–4, 199, 201–2, 209, 211, 273
    reception of Lucan in the Thebaid 25–6, 27–8, 29, 62, 68, 99, 102–3, 103–4, 138–9, 140–1, 171, 173, 176–91, 209, 273
    view of imperial power 153–5, 159–61
Lucusta 59

madness 15, 28, 37, 83, 134–5, 152, 156, 179, 180, 181, 189, 212, 260, 264, 275–6
Maeon 5, 6, 12, 14, 22, 41, 68–72, 88, 89, 91, 139, 193, 194, 274
magnus annus 240–4
Manto 77, 80, 147, 177, 187, 268
Marius, C. 2, 159, 177, 185, 188, 192, 233, 242
Mars 16, 123, 126, 174, 211, 261, 265, 275
    fields of 35, 177, 189
Martial 9, 10, 23, 45, 52, 58, 60, 62, 65, 89, 90, 118, 131, 132, 138, 159, 166, 204, 206, 238, 239, 247, 248, 250, 277
martyrology 21, 65, 272
martyrs of Nero 22, 50–5, 65–8, 71, 91, 262
masses, see commoners

Medusa 207–12, 275
Melanippus 141–2, 144
Menoeceus 5, 12, 74, 81, 151, 152, 229, 254–61
    and Aeneas 260
    and Hercules 147–8
    and Turnus 260
Minerva 90, 139, 141, 148, 209, 210, 211
misericordia, see compassion
Mithras 24, 61–2, 97, 99, 120–2, 227
Molorchus 149–50, 214, 220, 222
month, renaming of 10, 98–9
Mucianus, Gaius Licinius 50, 93

necromancy 77–80, 177, 187, 189
Nero 11–12, 204, 230, 232–3, 262, 264
    and Apollo/Sol 61–2, 96–7, 120–1
    and Caesar 191–2
    and Domitian 21–4, 49, 56–65, 97–100,
        104–5, 119, 150, 152, 166–7, 167–8, 175–6
    and Eteocles 70–1
    and Hercules 130–1, 138, 152
    and Oedipus 24–5, 75, 83–4
    and Orestes 72–3
    and Phaethon 101–3, 105, 119
    and Polynices 111, 116, 137–8
    and the theatre 24, 72–4
    death of 38
    demonization of (vulgate on Nero the
        monster) 21, 40, 57–60, 66, 73–6
    false Neros 38–9, 120
    Flavian views of 21–2, 41, 57–60, 74–6, 161–2,
        165, 271–2
    impiety of 31, 74, 75–6
    in the *Thebaid* 22, 24–5, 68–72, 75, 83–4, 111,
        116, 137–8, 147, 150, 191–7
    martyrs of Nero, *see* martyrs
    memory of 41, 56–60
    panegyric of 22, 39–40, 43–44, 156–61
    praise of Nero (in Lucan) 14, 26, 100–1, 154,
        159–61, 175
Nerva 41, 54, 55, 110, 166
Nigidius Figulus 154
Niobe 34, 193, 195–6, 228
Nonius Calpurnius Asprenas, L. 38
Novius Vindex 150–1

obelisk 94, 195
    Augustus' obelisks 95–6, 98
    Domitian's obelisk 10, 62, 64, 98

Octauia 20, 25, 57, 66–7, 73–6, 80, 83, 89, 91,
    161–2, 194, 196, 257, 264, 278
Octavian, *see* Augustus
Oedipus, see Seneca
Oedipus 24, 25, 35, 73–4, 75, 264
    in Seneca's *Oedipus* 42, 75–8, 83
    in the *Thebaid* 3–4, 5–6, 28, 78–84, 143, 181,
        224, 264, 266
omina (portents) 76, 77, 79–80, 186, 199, 245
Opheltes 29, 124, 137, 143, 208, 212, 225, 263
Osiris 99, 119, 121
Otho 26, 27, 56–7, 60, 74, 83, 183–7, 188, 203
Ovid
    Fasti 118
    Metamorphoses 33–4, 35, 108, 139–40, 168,
        170–1, 177, 195, 197, 211, 273

Pacorus 120
Panegyricus, see Pliny the Younger
Papinius (Statius' father) 239–40
Parthenopaeus 143, 228, 268
Parthia 39, 61, 62, 64, 97, 99, 113, 120–1
passions 15, 134–5, 139, 142, 147, 152, 267, 270, 271
Pausanias 215–16
Pergamon 236, 240, 245, 247, 254
Perseus 198, 207–13, 221, 229
pessimism 17, 28–32, 86, 175, 198, 231, 260, 261, 276
Phaethon
    and Nero 101–3, 105
    and Polynices 107–9
    and the emperor 101–3
    in Lucan 100–1
    in the *Thebaid* 103–5, 107–9, 111, 119, 171
Pharsalus 35, 155, 177–8, 182, 184–5, 188,
    189–91, 211
Philippi 120, 157, 177–8, 184–5, 188, 189, 191, 211
Phorbas 80–1
pietas 6, 12, 44, 63, 81, 106, 118, 151, 152, 206, 216,
    230, 232, 260
Pliny the Elder 57, 60, 96, 97, 102, 213
Pliny the Younger 11, 19, 50, 51, 52, 55, 56, 63, 91,
    115, 204, 274, 276
    Panegyricus 11, 55, 270, 274
Plutarch 185, 188
Poine 151, 209, 214, 225, 230
Polla, *see* Argentaria Polla
Pollius Felix 66, 277, 279
Pollux 110, 117, 118, 123, 144
    See also Dioscuri

Polynices 2, 4, 5, 6, 28, 93–4, 106–9, 111–12, 115–16, 119, 125–6, 152, 169, 182, 205, 209–10, 212, 267
  and Hercules 117, 135–8
  and Nero 111, 116, 137–8
  and Oedipus (similarity) 83
  and Phaethon 107–9
Pompey 1–2, 27–8, 32–3, 34, 48, 76, 130, 133, 134, 153, 165–6, 177, 180, 181, 182, 183–4, 185, 187, 188, 191, 192
Poppaea Sabina 56–7, 72–3
Propertius 33, 128, 200, 236, 254
proscriptions 133, 158–9, 162, 192–5
Psamathe 206, 209, 218, 225, 226

recusatio 9, 115, 128, 274
religion 30–1
  and civil war in Rome 197–205
  eastern 62, 99, 120
  in the Flavian period 60, 203–6, 230–1
  See also gods
Republic 26, 27, 51, 87, 154–5, 158, 161, 166, 173, 185, 192, 273
Romulus and Remus 33–4, 106, 176–7, 179–80, 199
  new Romulus 241, 243, 246, 248, 249
Rutilius Gallicus 48, 165

sack of Rome of 390 BCE 6, 233, 237, 240–4
  appropriations of 242–3
  in Flavian culture 244–9
Salvidienus Orfitus, Ser. Cornelius (Scipio) 50
Sarapis 98–9
Saturninus, *see* Antonius Saturninus, L.
self-sacrifice 81, 148, 152, 201, 202–3, 233, 252–3, 256–7
  See also deuotio
Seneca 7, 15, 44, 65–8, 101, 161–2, 175, 195, 233, 277–8
  Apocolocyntosis 22, 23, 45, 46, 62, 97, 99
  as intellectual model for Statius 26, 92, 277
  De Clementia 11–12, 18–19, 22, 23, 25, 42, 44, 46–8, 51, 74, 88, 89, 90, 91, 134, 135, 146–7, 151–2, 161–2, 165, 172, 175, 267, 270, 271, 272, 276, 278
  Hercules Furens 134–5, 138, 142, 144–7, 150, 271
  Oedipus 25, 35, 73, 74–6, 76–84, 89, 188
  Phoenissae 35, 264

reception of Senecan tragedy in the *Thebaid* 3, 7, 25, 31, 76–84, 144–7, 264
  Thyestes 31, 264
Senones Gauls 27, 240, 245, 249
Silius Italicus 12, 14, 86, 132, 173, 205, 207, 248–9, 252, 255
similes 82, 89, 106, 112–13, 127, 139, 140, 142, 168, 173–4, 209, 254, 258, 268, 271, 275
  bull similes 169, 182, 186–7
Sol/Helios 61–2, 94–7, 98, 99, 100, 102, 107, 110, 111, 120–1, 164
solar imagery 61–2, 64, 93–4, 95–100, 101, 104–5, 110–11, 119–22
Spartoi 33–5, 74, 78, 176–8, 189, 191, 193, 223, 255
Sporus 57, 60
Statilia Messalina 57
Stoicism 12–13, 15, 52–3, 134–5, 169, 267, 271
stoic opposition 53–5, 66, 142, 169, 267, 271
storm imagery 168–9, 170–1, 173, 275
succession 62, 94, 98, 100–1, 104–5, 110, 112–13, 114–16, 263, 268, 274, 276
Suetonius 9, 19–20, 27, 51–2, 56, 71, 73, 101, 102, 120, 131, 184, 187, 195, 204
Sulla 150, 158–9, 162, 177, 185, 192–5
Sulpicius Maximus 102, 239
sundial, Augustus' 10, 96, 97, 98
Sun god, *see* Sol/Helios
survival of the city/Rome 235, 241, 251, 254–60

Tacitus 52, 54, 73, 102, 120, 166, 172, 175, 184, 185–6, 188, 195, 202–3, 204, 231, 237, 238, 244–5, 272
Temple
  of Divus Iulius 47
  of Janus 156, 159
  of Jupiter Capitolinus 204, 211, 245, 249
  of Palatine Apollo 61, 95, 97, 195, 200, 220, 224
  of Peace (Templum Pacis) 213, 245
Terentius Maximus 38–9
Thebes and Rome 13, 32–7, 253–9
Theocritus 217
Theseus 29, 32, 84–92, 127, 134, 146, 182, 187, 189–91, 207, 223, 225, 260–1, 265, 268–9, 271, 273, 275–6
  and Coroebus 225–30
  and Domitian 89–91
  and Hercules 127–8, 148–50
  and Jupiter 173–5

and Mithras 121–2, 227

and Perseus 210–12

scholarly views of 12, 14–18

Thiodamas 112, 114–19, 125, 263, 274

Thoas 106

Thrasea Paetus 50, 52, 53, 65, 69, 71

Tiphys 112, 263

Tiresias 77, 79, 80, 81, 177, 187, 254

Tiridates 61, 97, 120

Tisiphone 4, 31, 108, 187, 224, 267

Titus 49, 51, 57, 61, 62, 63, 64, 94, 97, 99, 115–19, 132, 204, 230, 231, 232, 256, 263

torquis 236–7, 254

Trajan 11, 41, 49, 54, 55, 63, 87, 91, 98

Turnus (satirist) 59

Turnus (character of the *Aeneid*) 16, 33, 85, 89, 133, 149, 150, 182, 186, 212, 221, 222, 260, 161, 275

Tydeus 4, 68, 126–7, 136, 143, 144, 146–7, 148, 150, 152, 188, 192–3, 194, 205, 267, 271

and Hercules 138–42

tyranny/tyrant 5, 6, 9, 13, 14–15, 21, 22, 24, 25, 40–2, 49, 54, 57, 60, 66, 68, 70–1, 74–5, 77, 89–90, 102, 135, 158, 185, 191–6, 262, 270, 271

Valerius Patruinus, P. 39

Venus 265–6

Vespasian 8, 10, 12, 27, 49, 51, 53, 57–8, 61, 62–3, 64, 65, 84, 97, 98, 102, 104, 116, 118, 120, 122, 129, 131, 132, 184, 204, 213, 232, 245–6, 247, 248, 263

Vestal Virgins 60, 199, 205

Virgil 7, 13, 175

Aeneid 1–2, 6, 16, 27–8, 31, 33, 35, 37, 106, 121, 127–9, 133, 135, 139, 144, 149–50, 151, 156–7, 159, 168–9, 181–3, 186–7, 198, 206, 212, 214–16, 220–3, 232, 233, 235, 254, 261, 265–6, 276

Eclogues 45, 95, 156, 158

Georgics 76, 106, 114, 155, 167, 177–8, 188, 201, 273

Vitellius 26, 27, 36, 37, 56, 57, 60, 65, 74, 83, 93, 131, 132, 163, 183–4, 187, 191, 203, 232, 234, 235, 237, 238, 244, 245, 246, 250, 253, 266

Vologaeses 113, 120